Microsoft Intune Cookbook

Over 75 recipes for configuring, managing, and automating
your identities, apps, and endpoint devices

Andrew Taylor

BIRMINGHAM—MUMBAI

Microsoft Intune Cookbook

Copyright © 2023 Packt Publishing

Group Product Manager: Pavan Ramchandani

Publishing Product Manager: Prachi Rana

Book Project Manager: Ashwini Gowda

Senior Editor: Mohd Hammad

Technical Editor: Yash Bhanushali

Copy Editor: Safis Editing

Proofreader: Safis Editing

Indexer: Manju Arasan

Production Designer: Vijay Kamble

DevRel Marketing Coordinator: MaryLou De Mello

First published: December 2023

Production reference: 1221223

Published by Packt Publishing Ltd.

Grosvenor House

11 St Paul's Square

Birmingham

B3 1RB, UK

ISBN 978-1-80512-654-6

www.packtpub.com

To my wonderful daughters, Lili and Poppy – the world is at your feet; you can do anything you want to do! This book is dedicated to you both with all of my love.

Contributors

About the author

Andrew Taylor has been working in the IT industry for over 20 years across a variety of roles and industries, always with a passion for end-user computing and automation. Now working as an EUC architect, primarily using Microsoft technologies (Intune, Windows 365, PowerShell, and Graph), he develops, creates, and deploys new technologies and environments to a variety of customers. He is also a keen blogger and shares many scripts with the community.

Living in the north-east of England with his wife and two children, Andrew is a two-time Microsoft MVP and holds many Microsoft certifications (13 at the time of writing). Outside of work and family time, he is a film fan and can often be found at the local cinema.

A special thanks to my wife, Julia, and my two daughters, Lili and Poppy, for their support and unending patience, and for putting up with me typing away at all hours of the night.
Thanks also to everyone in the Intune community for showing an interest in my work.

About the reviewers

Niels Kok is a highly experienced cloud engineer with over 13 years of expertise in Microsoft Cloud products. He possesses a deep understanding of the intricacies of the Microsoft Cloud ecosystem and has a proven track record of success in delivering complex cloud solutions. Niels is an expert in scripting, with a strong background in PowerShell, Bicep, and YAML.

His expertise in these technologies enables him to write efficient, scalable, and easily maintainable scripts that automate cloud infrastructure deployments. Niels is a valuable asset to any organization seeking to leverage the power of the Microsoft Cloud to achieve their business goals.

Andrew Jones is a Microsoft MVP for Enterprise Mobility and has over 27 years' experience in IT. After initially developing intranet web services for BT, he progressed his career, working across various technical teams and technologies and leading large infrastructure IT projects. For the last eight years, he has worked as a technical architect in a customer-facing consultant role, leading M365 Modern Desktop services within a Microsoft Cloud practice. During COVID, he launched himself into the technical online communities and co-founded his YouTube channel *Cloud Management.Community*. He also publishes Microsoft-focused blogs on his own site at Move2modern.co.uk and dedicates his time to creating a collaborative community for cloud professionals.

Jannik Reinhard is a 25-year-old senior solution architect who works in the internal IT department of the largest chemical company in the world. He is the technical lead of **artificial intelligence for IT operations (AIOps)** and specializes in modern device management. Jannik is a proud enterprise mobility Microsoft MVP, a contributor to the largest LinkedIn community, and owner of the largest Twitter Intune community.

In his free time, Jannik invests a lot of time in learning and trying out new things related to IT, which is not only his profession but also his hobby.

He loves to blog on jannikreinhard.com and speak at events, sharing his knowledge with others and creating innovative solutions.

Nicklas Ahlberg is a trusted security advisor employed at Onevinn AB, a leading corporate entity specializing in providing cutting-edge security solutions. His primary objective revolves around assisting organizations in seamlessly navigating the complex terrain of Intune, ensuring they obtain an optimal and highly secure user experience.

At the core of his methodology lies a strong emphasis on automation, as he firmly believes it to be a cornerstone in achieving operational excellence. Nicklas actively showcases the power of automation through his dedicated blog, located at `https://rockenroll.tech`.

Table of Contents

4

Setting Up Enrollment and Updates for Windows   103

5

Android Device Management   145

6

iOS Device Management   183

7

macOS Device Management   221

8

Setting Up Your Compliance Policies   269

9

Monitoring Your New Environment   317

10

Looking at Reporting 369

11

Packaging Your Windows Applications 405

12

13

14

Preface

Microsoft Intune is a market-leading **Mobile Device Management (MDM)** tool for securely managing your Apple iOS, macOS, Android, and Windows devices anywhere in the world.

With the rapid move to hybrid working and more employees now wanting flexibility, traditional device management tools such as Active Directory are limited for staff working outside of the office, without implementing complicated Always On VPN.

As Microsoft Intune is fully cloud-based, devices can be managed comprehensively from any location. This can be further improved by implementing Windows Autopilot for machine provisioning, and devices can be shipped directly to end users with no input required from the IT department.

Configuring your new environment to work reliably can be a daunting task with multiple options to configure settings, and this is where *Microsoft Intune Cookbook* can help, running through every stage, from purchasing your licenses to enrolling your devices in a working environment.

On top of this, automation is a key part of working with IT systems; automating a repeatable task reduces the risk of user error as well as significantly improving productivity. As well as demonstrating how to configure your environment in the web portal, this book will also show you how to leverage Microsoft PowerShell and Microsoft Graph to automate your daily tasks. For this purpose, several recipes have an *Automating it* section included.

Included at the following URL are links to some excellent community resources, which are worth reading and following as you embark on your Intune journey:

```
https://github.com/PacktPublishing/Microsoft-Intune-Cookbook/blob/
main/blogs-links-communities.md
```

Note that during the writing of this book, Microsoft renamed *Azure Active Directory* to *Microsoft Entra ID*, so there may be occasions where the old Azure Active Directory naming is used, especially in screenshots where the portals had not been updated.

Who this book is for

This book is ideal for anyone either starting out on their Intune journey or existing Intune users who want to learn Microsoft Graph for automation.

This could be system administrators, end-user computer administrators, cloud administrators, or even support staff looking to take the next step up the ladder.

As it is a hands-on cookbook, while it touches on architectural considerations, the primary demographic is technical staff who are implementing a solution.

While the book does not cover the basics of PowerShell scripting, you should be able to follow the scripts with a limited knowledge of PowerShell commands.

What this book covers

Chapter 1, Getting Started with Microsoft Intune, is an introduction to Intune. It takes a look at licensing requirements and setting up the first tenant. It then moves onto Entra ID, covering MDM and **Mobile Application Management** (**MAM**) enrollment scopes, the creation of both static and dynamic groups, and then assigning roles and looking at device settings.

Chapter 2, Configuring Your New Tenant for Windows Devices, looks at the policy options available for Windows devices and how to use them to comprehensively manage your Windows fleet.

Chapter 3, Securing Your Windows Devices with Security Policies, covers all the important security policies available for Windows devices and how to best configure them for your environment.

Chapter 4, Setting Up Enrollment and Updates for Windows, looks at Windows Update and autopatch, configuring Windows Hello for Business, before finally looking at the enrollment of devices using Autopilot and the **Enrollment Status Page** (**ESP**).

Chapter 5, Android Device Management, covers the management of your Android devices using Google Play. It runs through the full end-to-end process of configuring your managed Google Play account, connecting it to Intune, and using it to deploy applications. After configuring the connections, the chapter will run through configuring your enrollment profiles for different use cases and then move on to the policies themselves, including looking at **Original Equipment Manufacturer** (**OEM**) specific policies. Finally, it will cover the use of app protection policies for **Bring your Own Device** (**BYOD**) scenarios.

Chapter 6, Apple iOS Device Management, looks at the management of both iOS and macOS devices from Apple, with devices managed by Apple Business Manager and Apple Volume Purchase Program for applications. After running through configuring Apple Business Manager, the chapter then demonstrates how to connect it to Intune, add the required certificates, and set up enrollment profile tokens. Once the basic environment is configured, it moves on to configuring policies and deploying (and protecting) applications from the app store for iOS.

Chapter 7, macOS Device Management, continues the Apple journey with macOS devices. It covers configuring your first policy and then deploying scripts and applications to your devices, before finally looking at keeping your macOS up to date.

Chapter 8, Setting Up Your Compliance Policies, explores the very important, but often overlooked, area of compliance. When tied to Conditional access, it is the best way to secure your environment against risky/infected machines. The chapter covers configuring compliance policies for all currently supported operating systems and the various settings available for each. For Windows devices, it also dives into the more complex but powerful custom compliance policies. Finally, it demonstrates how to link your compliance policies to a Conditional access policy.

Chapter 9, Monitoring Your New Environment, runs through the monitoring options available within Intune. It looks at monitoring your applications (both installed and detected) and your critical app protection policies and then moves on to the devices. In device monitoring, you can learn how to review the success of your configuration profiles, device compliance, and device enrollment successes and failures. The chapter will then look at checking your device update status and, finally, review any admin tasks within the portal itself, including device actions and audit logs for policy/app changes.

Chapter 10, Looking at Reporting, covers all of the available reports within Intune initially, including security and Endpoint analytics. It then moves beyond Intune, covering connecting PowerBI to the Intune Data Warehouse and deploying Windows Update for Business Reports within an Azure Log Analytics Workspace. Finally, it will cover how to export your diagnostics events to Azure for further alerting or management.

Chapter 11, Packaging Your Windows Applications, examines application packaging and deployment, which can be a blocker to many. The chapter runs through deploying all Windows applications, starting with your straightforward Microsoft Store apps and then covering packaging in the MSIX or Win32 format, using the official Microsoft tools. It also covers application dependencies and supersedence for Win32 applications.

Chapter 12, PowerShell Scripting across Intune, looks at all of the available scripts inside Intune, starting with the basic device scripts. It will then move on to the very useful proactive remediations before looking at how they can be used when deploying apps – in particular, during detection and requirement checking.

Chapter 13, Tenant Administration, runs through the options within the **Tenant Administrative** menu within Intune, including your day-to-day admin tasks (monitoring connectors, troubleshooting, and version checking). It also covers the more set-once options such as terms and conditions, setting roles, and customizing. Finally, it covers using filters to manage assignments, sending organizational messages, and looking at multi-admin approval.

Chapter 14, Looking at Intune Suite, looks at the additional licensed features currently included in the Intune Suite. We will look at Remote Help, Microsoft Tunnel for Android/iOS, device anomalies, and Endpoint Privilege Management.

To get the most out of this book

For the sections on automation, you will need a machine capable of running PowerShell; version 5 or version 7 will work fine. While you can simply download and run the scripts, using an editor will aid in following the steps.

Software/hardware covered in the book	Operating system requirements
PowerShell 5 or 7	Windows or macOS
A web browser	Any operating system

If you are using the digital version of this book, we advise you to type the code yourself or access the code via the GitHub repository (link available in the next section). Doing so will help you avoid any potential errors related to the copying and pasting of code.

Download the example code files

You can download the example code files for this book from GitHub at `https://github.com/PacktPublishing/Microsoft-Intune-Cookbook`. If there's an update to the code, it will be updated in the existing GitHub repository.

We also have other code bundles from our rich catalog of books and videos available at `https://github.com/PacktPublishing/`. Check them out!

Conventions used

There are a number of text conventions used throughout this book.

`Code in text`: Indicates code words in text, database table names, folder names, filenames, file extensions, pathnames, dummy URLs, user input, and Twitter handles. Here is an example: "For these devices, remove them using `Remove-MgDevice`."

A block of code is set as follows:

```
$Headers = @{
    "Authorization" = "Bearer " + $resourceToken
    "Content-type" = "application/json"
    "X-Requested-With" = "XMLHttpRequest"
    "x-ms-client-request-id" = [guid]::NewGuid()
    "x-ms-correlation-id" = [guid]::NewGuid()
}
```

Any command-line input or output is written as follows:

```
((Invoke-MgGraphRequest -Method GET -Uri "https://graph.microsoft.com/
beta/deviceManagement/configurationSettings?&`$filter=categoryId eq
'4a5e4714-00ac-4793-b0cc-5049041b0ed7'" -OutputType PSObject).value
 | select-object name, description, '@odata.type', rootDefinitionId,
options, @{Name="Platform"; Expression={ $_.applicability | Select-
Object platform}},@{Name="technologies"; Expression={ $_.applicability
 | Select-Object technologies}},valuedefinition, id) | out-gridview
```

Bold: Indicates a new term, an important word, or words that you see on screen. For example, words in menus or dialog boxes appear in the text like this. Here is an example: "Now that we have our licensing in place, we need to create a **tenant**"

> **Tips or important notes**
> Appear like this.

Sections

In this book, you will find several headings that appear frequently (*Getting ready, How to do it..., Automating it, There's more...*, and *See also*).

To give clear instructions on how to complete a recipe, use these sections as follows.

Getting ready

This section tells you what to expect in the recipe and describes how to set up any software or any preliminary settings required for the recipe.

How to do it...

This section contains the steps required to follow the recipe.

Automating it

This section shows you how to leverage Microsoft PowerShell and Microsoft Graph to automate your daily tasks.

There's more...

This section consists of additional information about the recipe in order to make you more knowledgeable about it.

See also

This section provides helpful links to other useful information for the recipe.

Get in touch

Feedback from our readers is always welcome.

General feedback: If you have questions about any aspect of this book, email us at customercare@packtpub.com and mention the book title in the subject of your message.

Errata: Although we have taken every care to ensure the accuracy of our content, mistakes do happen. If you have found a mistake in this book, we would be grateful if you would report this to us. Please visit www.packtpub.com/support/errata and fill in the form.

Piracy: If you come across any illegal copies of our works in any form on the internet, we would be grateful if you would provide us with the location address or website name. Please contact us at copyright@packt.com with a link to the material.

If you are interested in becoming an author: If there is a topic that you have expertise in and you are interested in either writing or contributing to a book, please visit authors.packtpub.com.

Share Your Thoughts

Once you've read *Microsoft Intune Cookbook*, we'd love to hear your thoughts! Scan the QR code below to go straight to the Amazon review page for this book and share your feedback.

https://packt.link/r/1805126547

Your review is important to us and the tech community and will help us make sure we're delivering excellent quality content.

Download a free PDF copy of this book

Thanks for purchasing this book!

Do you like to read on the go but are unable to carry your print books everywhere?

Is your eBook purchase not compatible with the device of your choice?

Don't worry, now with every Packt book you get a DRM-free PDF version of that book at no cost.

Read anywhere, any place, on any device. Search, copy, and paste code from your favorite technical books directly into your application.

The perks don't stop there, you can get exclusive access to discounts, newsletters, and great free content in your inbox daily

Follow these simple steps to get the benefits:

1. Scan the QR code or visit the link below

https://packt.link/free-ebook/9781805126546

2. Submit your proof of purchase
3. That's it! We'll send your free PDF and other benefits to your email directly

1

Getting Started with Microsoft Intune

Microsoft Intune is the leader in the Gartner Magic Quadrant for **unified endpoint management** (**UEM**) and is an excellent tool for managing your end user devices, especially in the modern hybrid workforce. This book is your comprehensive guide to getting you started with using and configuring Microsoft Intune with only a basic understanding of end user compute management and PowerShell (for automation and scripting).

Intune is a cloud management software service that can fully manage your entire end user computing estate wherever you are. This includes Windows, iOS, iPadOS, macOS, Android, and Linux for both corporate and personally owned devices, as well as cloud computing with Windows 365 and Azure Virtual Desktop.

You can secure corporate data on any device, and Intune follows the zero-trust security model. As well as compliance and policy management, Intune will also handle your application deployment across devices.

Before digging into the finer points of using the platform, first, we need to look at the prerequisites and have a general look at **Entra ID** (previously **Azure AD**; you may find references to both in documentation and blog posts). While Microsoft Intune is part of the Microsoft 365 suite, it relies on Entra ID for groups, users, conditional access policies, and more, so an understanding of how these work will make your life significantly easier. In this chapter, we will look at how we can leverage Microsoft Entra to set the foundations for a successful Intune deployment.

This chapter will include the following recipes:

- Creating a tenant
- Creating a user
- Assigning Entra ID roles
- Configuring Entra ID Device settings

- Configuring Entra ID ESR

- Creating Entra ID static groups

- Creating Entra ID dynamic groups

- Configuring Entra ID MDM/MAM scopes

Technical requirements

For this chapter, you will need a modern web browser and a **PowerShell code editor** such as **Visual Studio Code** (**VS Code**) or the PowerShell ISE.

All of the scripts referenced in this chapter can be found here: `https://github.com/PacktPublishing/Microsoft-Intune-Cookbook/tree/main/Chapter1`.

Chapter materials

Microsoft licensing can be tricky at the best of times, so we will start there.

To use Intune, you will need an Intune license, which comes in three flavors:

- **Intune Plan 1**: This includes your standard Intune functionality, including reporting and **Endpoint analytics**.

- **Intune Plan 2**: This adds **Microsoft Tunnel** for iOS and Android application-level VPNs and support for specialty devices (such as VR headsets and large conference screens).

- **Intune Suite**: This includes everything in Plans 1 and 2 plus **Remote Help**, **Endpoint Privilege Management**, and **Advanced Endpoint Analytics** (all of which will be covered in greater depth in *Chapter 14*). These can all be purchased individually on Plan 1, but it can work out to be more cost-effective to purchase the suite.

You can purchase your Intune licensing on a standalone plan or as part of the following Microsoft SKUs:

- Microsoft 365 E3

- Microsoft 365 E5

- Microsoft 365 F1

- Microsoft 365 F3

- Microsoft 365 A3 (Education Only)

- Microsoft 365 A5 (Education Only)

- Microsoft Business Premium

- Enterprise Mobility + Security E3

- Enterprise Mobility + Security E5

If you are purchasing Intune on a standalone plan, you will also need to purchase an **Entra ID license** as well as a **Defender for Endpoint license** (if required).

These licenses are all per-user; however, Intune device-based licensing is available for some niche use cases, such as multi-user kiosk machines or manufacturing facilities with non-user-assigned devices.

On top of the Intune licensing, there are some additional Windows-only features that require a Windows Enterprise license over the standard Professional one.

This license is included in the M365 E3/E5/F3/F5/A3/A5 SKUs or can be added as an additional license.

Adding Windows Enterprise adds the following features:

- Defender for Endpoint Plan 2

- AppLocker

- Credential Guard

- Windows Autopatch

- Windows Virtualization Rights

- Remediations

A very useful site for referencing licensing SKUs and what each contains is `https://m365maps.com/`.

Creating a tenant

Now that we have our licensing in place, we need to create a **tenant**. This recipe will run you through the steps to create your new Microsoft 365/Intune/Azure tenant.

A tenant can be used across the full Microsoft platform, so it will apply to Microsoft 365, Azure, and Intune. If you have Active Directory set up currently, you can synchronize your users/groups/devices into Entra ID to give your users a hybrid identity (you need to ensure they do not have a `.local` suffix for this to succeed).

You can synchronize multiple Active Directory forests into a single Entra tenant, but you cannot synchronize one on-premises AD domain/forest into multiple Entra tenants.

A tenant can be configured with a custom domain name rather than the *.onmicrosoft.com* one, which is automatically configured when you create your new tenant. Within a tenant, you can have multiple Azure subscriptions but only one Intune configuration. There is also no built-in functionality to copy or migrate devices and settings between tenants using Intune.

Getting ready

If you would rather follow this book using a demo tenant, head over to the **Microsoft 365 Developer Program**, where you will be able to grab a free developer tenant with licenses to cover most aspects we will be covering here: `https://developer.microsoft.com/en-us/microsoft-365/dev-program`.

> **Important note**
>
> The licenses do not include Windows Enterprise, so you will not be able to test the chapters on Autopatch and Remediations.

How to do it...

To create your live tenant, first, you need to obtain your licenses. These can be purchased from any VAR or directly from Microsoft. If you are using a developer tenant, *Steps 1* and *2* can be skipped:

1. For this book, we are going to grab a Microsoft 365 Business Premium trial license (Microsoft 365 E3 and E5 require an annual purchase); the screen will look as follows:

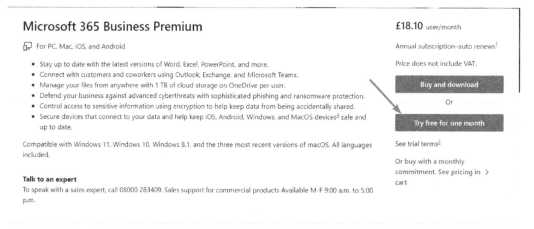

Microsoft 365 Business Premium

£18.10 user/month

Annual subscription–auto renews[1]

🖵 For PC, Mac, iOS, and Android

- Stay up to date with the latest versions of Word, Excel, PowerPoint, and more.
- Connect with customers and coworkers using Outlook, Exchange, and Microsoft Teams.
- Manage your files from anywhere with 1 TB of cloud storage on OneDrive per user.
- Defend your business against advanced cyberthreats with sophisticated phishing and ransomware protection.
- Control access to sensitive information using encryption to help keep data from being accidentally shared.
- Secure devices that connect to your data and help keep iOS, Android, Windows, and MacOS devices[3] safe and up to date.

Price does not include VAT.

Buy and download

Or

Try free for one month

See trial terms[2]

Or buy with a monthly commitment. See pricing in cart >

Compatible with Windows 11, Windows 10, Windows 8.1, and the three most recent versions of macOS. All languages included.

Talk to an expert
To speak with a sales expert, call 08000 283409. Sales support for commercial products Available M-F 9:00 a.m. to 5:00 p.m.

Figure 1.1 – Microsoft licensing page

After clicking the **Try free for 1 month** button, enter an email address to use for the tenancy. If it does not exist, it will create it for you, so long as it is on a Microsoft domain (`outlook.com`, for example).

You will also be required to verify your identity, so make sure you enter a valid telephone number.

2. Once completed, you will be taken to the **Microsoft 365 admin center**, where you can double-check your licenses in the **Licenses** menu under **Billing**.

That is all we need to do within the **Microsoft 365 admin center**. Now, we must navigate to `https://entra.microsoft.com` and log in with the same account that was licensed when we set up the tenant.

Before moving on to the next recipe, from here on, we are going to include the PowerShell and JSON code (where possible) to complete the steps both in the GUI and from a command line.

Microsoft Graph is the technology that is used underneath most Microsoft products to handle all of the commands that are sent via the web interface. Fortunately, it includes a powerful API that we can use to automate these using PowerShell.

To use the command-line scripts, you will need to install the **Microsoft Graph PowerShell** module and connect to Graph (we are going to set up a connection with full access so that you can reuse the connection at all stages). For this, use your preferred code editor (VS Code is a good choice and is platform agnostic) or use the built-in PowerShell ISE on a Windows device:

1. First, load up the PowerShell console and install, then import, the module:

    ```
    Install-Module -Name Microsoft.Graph.Authentication -Scope
    CurrentUser -Repository PSGallery -Force
    ```

2. Now, import the newly installed module:

    ```
    import-module microsoft.graph.authentication
    ```

3. Finally, we need to connect:

    ```
    Connect-MgGraph -Scopes RoleAssignmentSchedule.
    ReadWrite.Directory, Domain.Read.All, Domain.
    ReadWrite.All, Directory.Read.All, Policy.ReadWrite.
    ConditionalAccess, DeviceManagementApps.ReadWrite.
    All, DeviceManagementConfiguration.ReadWrite.All,
    DeviceManagementManagedDevices.ReadWrite.All, openid,
    profile, email, offline_access, Policy.ReadWrite.
    PermissionGrant,RoleManagement.ReadWrite.Directory, Policy.
    ReadWrite.DeviceConfiguration, DeviceLocalCredential.Read.
    All, DeviceManagementManagedDevices.PrivilegedOperations.All,
    DeviceManagementServiceConfig.ReadWrite.All, Policy.Read.All,
    DeviceManagementRBAC.ReadWrite.All
    ```

    After pressing *Enter*, you will be prompted to log in with your new credentials and then approve the permissions for your tenant by checking the **Consent on behalf of your organization** box and then clicking **Accept**.

We now have a working tenant and a Microsoft Graph connection that we can use in the following recipes and chapters.

Creating a user

Now that our tenant has been set up, we can create our first user. This recipe will run through how to create your first user and then look at what is happening in the **Graph API** underneath.

Getting ready

Navigate to the **Microsoft Entra portal** at `https://entra.microsoft.com/#home`.

Here, you will find an overview of your tenant, including your tenant ID, which you will find yourself needing when setting up policies such as OneDrive within Intune. You cannot display it within Intune directly, so you will have to navigate back to Entra ID to find it.

Within Entra ID, click on **Users**, then **All users**; you will see the user you set up when enrolling the tenant. This user will have Global Administrator access across the whole tenant, so we will create a new user to test role assignment, license assignment, and group membership.

How to do it...

Follow these steps to create an additional non-admin user in your tenant. The new user screen runs across a few pages, so we will concentrate on cropped screenshots of the appropriate areas:

1. Click on + **New user** and then **Create new user**.

2. Fill in the basic details. You will be prompted to change your password on your first login, but if you are auto-generating, click the eye icon to show the password so that you can use it to log in later:

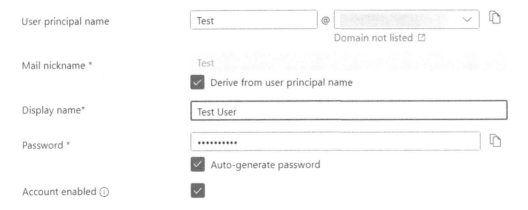

Figure 1.2 – Entra user details

3. Leave **Groups** and **Roles** empty for now; we will run through those in the *Creating Entra ID groups* recipe.

4. Add a **Usage location** value on this screen; it will not let you assign a license without one set:

Settings

Usage location
| United Kingdom | ⌄ |

Figure 1.3 – Entra user license details

5. Optionally, you can fill in **Job Info**, but this is not a requirement at this stage.

6. Finally, click **Create**.

With that, you have created your first account in your new tenant.

Automating it

Now, we can learn how to automate user creation.

You will need the PowerShell ISE or VS Code running for this, as we will be setting variables to send to Microsoft Graph.

Follow these steps in a new PowerShell script to create your user with Microsoft Graph:

1. First, create the variables to populate – in this case, this is everything we set in the GUI. Setting these as variables instead of hardcoding them within the JSON gives us the option to run within a loop and change the variables each time in the future:

```
$displayname = "User One"
$givenname = "User"
$surname = "One"
$usageLocation = "GB"
$mailNickname = "user1"
$password = "PASSWORD HERE"
$domainname = "DOMAIN HERE"
```

2. Now, populate the JSON with these variables:

```
$json = @"
{
    "accountEnabled": true,
    "displayName": "$displayname",
    "givenName": "$givenname",
    "mailNickname": "$mailNickname",
```

```
    "passwordProfile": {
        "forceChangePasswordNextSignIn": true,
        "password": "$password"
    },
    "surname": "$surname",
    "usageLocation": "$usageLocation",
    "userPrincipalName": "$mailnickname@$domainname"
}
"@
```

As you can see, the JSON is a fairly straightforward array. Watch the names of the items as they are case sensitive; as an example, `accountEnabled` will fail if it is listed as `AccountEnabled` or `accountenabled`. The error will be a standard malformed request, so it is always a good idea to start here with any troubleshooting.

You can also see that `passwordProfile` is a nested array as it has further child items.

3. Next, tell it where to send the request. There are two versions of the Graph API – V1.0 and Beta. The Beta API receives the latest features ahead of the general release. In this case, either will work, but when creating groups, some aspects, such as being able to assign roles to them, require the beta version.

4. Next, we must point to the **Users** section of the Graph API:

    ```
    $uri = "https://graph.microsoft.com/beta/users"
    ```

5. Finally, send the request to Microsoft Graph. There are different types of requests you can use; we will run through them quickly so that you understand the difference:

    *   GET: This simply retrieves values from Graph to manipulate, export, and more

    *   POST: This sends new values to Graph that do not currently exist (a new user, new policy, and so on)

    *   PATCH: This updates an existing record

    *   PUT: This is similar to PATCH but needs a full URL, including the ID being created

    *   DELETE: This deletes whatever you are pointing it at

    This is a new account we are creating, and a PUT request is more complex than a POST request, so we will stick with POST:

    ```
    Invoke-MgGraphRequest -Method POST -Uri $uri -Body $json
    -ContentType "application/json"
    ```

    This command sends a POST request to the URL we specified earlier (in this case, `users`) to pass the JSON we wrote. The content type tells it to look for JSON.

Now that we have our user, we can assign a role to it.

Assigning Entra ID roles

Before we proceed further, we need to understand what roles are within Entra ID. A role gives a user specific permissions to items within Entra ID/Microsoft 365/Intune. There are numerous built-in roles, and you can also create a custom role with specific permissions applied.

It is always worth working from the principle of the least required permissions. It is better to give an admin multiple roles with strict permissions rather than going for a global administrator with keys to the kingdom.

A list of the built-in roles can be found here: `https://learn.microsoft.com/en-us/ azure/active-directory/roles/permissions-reference`.

As this is an Intune book, the two main roles we are interested in initially are **Intune Administrator** and **Entra Joined Device Local Administrator**. As its name suggests, Intune Administrator gives full access to everything within Intune.

Entra Joined Device Local Administrator gives users full administrative access over *all* Entra joined devices. While this is useful for support teams, if licensed, it is worth considering using **privileged identity management** (**PIM**), which you can use for role access for a limited amount of time with full reporting.

You can find out more about PIM here: `https://learn.microsoft.com/en-us/azure/ active-directory/privileged-identity-management/pim-configure`

Intune also has specific **role-based access control** (**RBAC**) to restrict access within the Intune portal itself. We will cover this further in *Chapter 13*.

There are two ways to assign roles, so we will use one for each.

How to do it...

Follow these steps to assign a built-in role to your newly created user:

1. Navigate to **Entra admin center** within your new tenant by going to `https://entra. microsoft.com`.

2. Within Entra, click on **Show more**, then expand the **Roles & admins** dropdown and click on **Roles & admins**.

3. You will be presented with this menu:

Figure 1.4 – Entra ID – Roles and administrators

4. You will now see this screen:

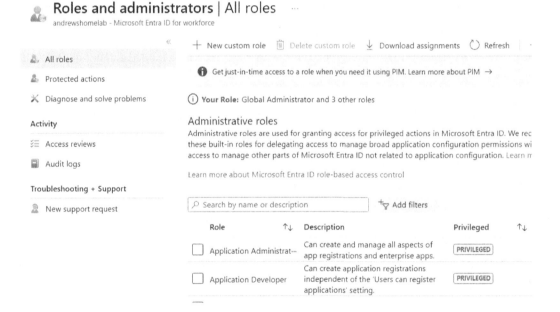

Figure 1.5 – Entra ID – Roles and administrators | All roles

For this, we will use the in-built roles, but if you need something more granular, you can create a custom role based on the exact permissions you require.

5. Select **Intune Administrator**.

6. On the screen that appears, click + **Add Assignments** and find your new user:

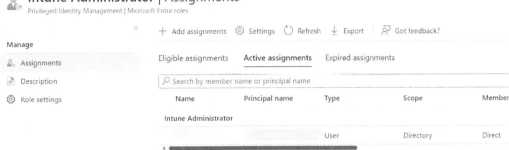

Figure 1.6 – Assigned Intune Administrator role

7. The other way we can do this is within the **Users** blade; navigate back to **Entra ID** and click on **Users**, then the user you created.

8. Within the user details, click on **Assigned roles**.

9. Then, click + **Add assignments**.

10. This time, select **Microsoft Entra Joined Device Local Administrator** and click **Add**.

Following these steps has granted your user administrative rights on your cloud-joined devices.

Automating it

By automating the assignment of roles, we can add to our previous user creation to create an automated onboarding function for user management across job roles.

Adding roles via PowerShell is slightly more complex as we need to find the role ID to be able to assign it.

Create a new PowerShell script and follow these steps:

1. For this, we will need to install and import an additional module:

```
Install-Module Microsoft.Graph.DeviceManagement.Enrolment -Scope
CurrentUser -Repository PSGallery -Force
Import-Module Microsoft.Graph.DeviceManagement.Enrolment
```

2. Set the variables, the role name, and the user we are assigning it to (at the time of writing, the role is still called Azure AD Joined Device Local Administrator, but it may change to Entra Joined Device Local Administrator in the future to match the UI):

```
$rolename = "Azure AD Joined Device Local Administrator"
$user = "test@test.onmicrosoft.com"
```

3. We need to get the ID from the **User Profile Name (UPN)**. We are querying the Users API to the user's UPN, passing the output as `PSObject`, and then retrieving the ID from it. This can be done with two commands, one for grabbing the user details and the second for grabbing the ID from the first variable, but wrapping the query in brackets does the same job and runs quicker:

    ```
    $userid = (Invoke-MgGraphRequest -Uri "https://graph.microsoft.
    com/beta/users/$user" -Method Get -OutputType PSObject).id
    ```

    Note that we are passing `OutputType` and using a `GET` request with this first command. Setting `OutputType` allows us to use the output within PowerShell.

4. The next stage is to find the details for the role we are looking for. We can do this by grabbing all the roles and then using `where-object` to grab the role we are looking for, after which we can pass the output to a PowerShell object. We grab the roles from `roleDefinitions` within the whole directory in Graph, in the `roleManagement` subsection of the API:

    ```
    $uri = "https://graph.microsoft.com/beta/roleManagement/
    directory/roleDefinitions"
    $roletoassign = (((Invoke-MgGraphRequest -Uri $uri -Method Get
    -OutputType PSObject).value) | where-object DisplayName -eq
    $rolename).id
    ```

5. Now that we have the role ID and the user ID, we just need to put them together and assign the role. As we are using a PowerShell module instead of JSON, we must pass parameters instead of raw JSON. Here, we are setting `ScopeID` to `"/"` to cover the entire directory:

    ```
    $params = @{
        "@odata.type" = "#microsoft.graph.unifiedRoleAssignment"
        RoleDefinitionId = "$roletoassign"
        PrincipalId = "$userid"
        DirectoryScopeId = "/"
    }
    New-MgRoleManagementDirectoryRoleAssignment -BodyParameter
    $params
    ```

By completing these steps, we have created our script to automate role assignment in Microsoft Entra using the Graph API.

Configuring Entra ID Device settings

The first settings we need to look at are the **Device settings**. This is where we can configure what users can and cannot do with their devices. This includes setting who can enroll devices into Intune and Entra ID, as well as the security around it.

How to do it...

While the vast majority of our device settings will be configured within Intune, there are a few within Entra ID that are worth setting up before we move into the Intune configuration.

Following these steps will configure your Entra environment for device enrollment:

1. First, within Entra ID, expand **Devices**, click **Overview**, and then click **Device Settings**.

2. We need to ensure **Users may join devices to Microsoft Entra** is set to either **All** or **Selected** as we need our machines to be Entra ID joined. We can restrict device types later within Intune, so it is best just to leave this one set to **All**.

   Regarding **Multi-factor authentication**, leave this set to **No** and use **Conditional Access** as recommended. This will give you much more granular control and reporting.

   The maximum number of devices is something to note here. It is also a setting within Intune, so there are two places where you can check if users have issues enrolling devices. The Entra ID setting here is for all registered devices, so it will include any personally enrolled devices that are not Intune joined. It is also worth noting that this will include any previous devices as Entra ID does not automatically clean stale devices (although this can be scripted; see the following *Automating it* section).

   Unless you have a large number of devices per user, leave this set to 50 devices per user.

   You can ignore the blue text link, as we configured that with the Entra ID roles earlier.

   The final setting here (**Restrict non-admin users from recovering the BitLocker key(s) for their owned devices (preview)**) lets your end users retrieve their own BitLocker keys (after authenticating). This is a personal preference; changing it to **Yes** would result in additional support calls in the event of a power cut or other events that could trigger BitLocker. For this example, we are leaving it set to **No**.

3. Once you have configured the settings, click **Save**.

This recipe has allowed our tenant to accept Intune device enrollment.

Automating it

Again, we can use PowerShell to automate this configuration to make it more easily repeatable:

1. Set some variables and change them so that they match your environment:

```
$devicequota = 50
##Set to 0 to block Entra ID Registration
$azureadregister = 1
##Set to 0 to block Entra ID Join
$azureadjoin = 1
##Set to 1 to require MFA
```

```
$mfa = 0
##Set to False to block BitLocker
$bitlocker = "true"
```

While this is displaced on one screen in the GUI, these are two separate policies, so we need to create the JSON for the non-BitLocker settings. This JSON will include some nested arrays, as each section of the page is an array in itself.

2. These settings are all configured with defaults from the initial tenant configuration, so if you need to check the raw JSON values, run a GET request against this URL: `https://graph.microsoft.com/beta/policies/authorizationPolicy/authorizationPolicy`.

3. We are simply manipulating the retrieved values to receive our new values. You can copy and paste this script block as we set our values in *Step 1*:

```
$jsonsettings = @"
{
"@odata.context":"https://graph.microsoft.com/
beta/$metadata#policies/deviceRegistrationPolicy/$entity",
"multiFactorAuthConfiguration":"$mfa",
"id":"deviceRegistrationPolicy",
"displayName":"Device Registration Policy",
"description":"Tenant-wide policy that manages intial
provisioning controls using quota restrictions, additional
authentication and authorization checks",
"userDeviceQuota":$devicequota,
"azureADRegistration":{
"appliesTo":"$azureadregister","allowedUsers":null,
"allowedGroups":null,"isAdminConfigurable":false
},
"azureADJoin":{
"appliesTo":"$azureadjoin","allowedUsers":[],"allowedGroups":[],
"isAdminConfigurable":true
}
}
"@
```

4. Then, we manipulate the BitLocker settings:

```
$jsonbitlocker = @"
{"defaultUserRolePermissions":
{"allowedToReadBitlockerKeysForOwnedDevice":$bitlocker}}
"@
```

5. Now, set the URLs for each setting we are changing:

```
$registrationuri = "https://graph.microsoft.com/beta/policies/
deviceRegistrationPolicy"
$bitlockeruri = "https://graph.microsoft.com/beta/policies/
authorizationPolicy/authorizationPolicy"
```

6. For `deviceRegistrationPolicy`, we need to send a PUT request:

```
Invoke-MgGraphRequest -Method PUT -Uri $registrationuri -Body
$jsonsettings -ContentType "application/json"
```

7. For the BitLocker policy, we must send a PATCH request as we are amending existing settings:

```
Invoke-MgGraphRequest -Method PATCH -Uri $bitlockeruri -Body
$jsonbitlocker -ContentType "application/json"
```

These steps have configured our tenant to allow enrollment and let users view their BitLocker keys.

As we mentioned earlier, clearing out stale devices requires a script, so we will run through that quickly as well:

1. For this, we need a different module:

```
Install-Module -Name Microsoft.Graph.Identity.
DirectoryManagement -Repository PSGallery -Force -Scope
CurrentUser
import-module Microsoft.Graph.Identity.DirectoryManagement
```

2. Set the necessary variables:

```
$daystodisable = 90
$daystoremove = 120
```

Now, we will disable anything over 90 days (or whatever the variable is set to). It is always best to do something slightly less drastic initially.

3. After setting the date we are looking for, loop through the devices and find any that have not been seen in that time, then disable them.

4. We are using the `Get-MgDevice` module here to retrieve all devices from Entra ID. This is the same as running a GET request against this URL: `https://graph.microsoft.com/beta/devices`.

We are adding `-All` to get everything and not restrict with pagination and then filtering on devices that have not logged on in the last 90 days.

For each of the devices we find, we are calling the `Update-MgDevice` command, which is the same as running a `POST/PATCH` request against the same URL. However, rather than having to retrieve, manipulate, and then upload the JSON, this module takes inline parameters to do the hard work for us:

```
$dt = (Get-Date).AddDays(-$daystodisable)
$Devices = Get-MgDevice -All | Where-Object {$_.
ApproximateLastLogonTimeStamp -le $dt}
foreach ($Device in $Devices) {
    $deviceid = $Device.Id
    Update-MgDevice -DeviceId $deviceid -AccountEnabled $false
}
```

5. Then, do the same retrieval, but look for anything older than our delete date, which is also disabled (this will stop us from deleting something we had to re-enable previously but still has not been seen for whatever reason). For these devices, remove them using `Remove-MgDevice`. This is the same as running a `DELETE` command against the `Devices/DeviceID` section of Graph:

```
$dt = (Get-Date).AddDays(-$daystoremove)
$Devices = Get-MgDevice -All | Where-Object {($_.
ApproximateLastLogonTimeStamp -le $dt) -and ($_.AccountEnabled
-eq $false)}
foreach ($Device in $Devices) {
    $deviceid = $Device.Id
    Remove-MgDevice -DeviceId $deviceid
}
```

This script has configured your tenant to allow enrollment and configured key device settings.

Configuring Entra ID ESR

Now, we will look at **Enterprise State Roaming** (**ESR**), which automatically backs up some device user preferences into Azure for a more seamless experience when moving between Windows devices.

How to do it...

The other device setting within Entra ID is ESR. This is similar to the older **User Experience Virtualization** (**UE-V**), which can be found in the **Microsoft Desktop Optimization Pack** (**MDOP**).

It backs up certain user settings within Intune and Edge and backs them up to Azure Storage (outside the subscription and without cost).

The following Windows settings are currently backed up:

- **Keyboard**: Turn on toggle keys (off by default)
- **Date, time, and region**: Country/region
- **Date, time, and region**: Region format (locale)
- **Language**: Language profile
- **Keyboard**: List of keyboards
- **Mouse**: Primary mouse button
- **Passwords**: Web credentials
- **Pen**: Pen handedness
- **Touchpad**: Scrolling direction
- **Wi-Fi**: Wi-Fi profiles (only WPA)

The following settings are backed up on Edge:

- Favorites
- Passwords
- Addresses and more (form-fill)
- Collections
- Settings
- Extensions
- Open tabs (available in Microsoft Edge version 88 or later)
- History (available in Microsoft Edge version 88 or later)

To enable ESR, follow these steps:

1. Navigate to **Entra ID | Devices | Overview | Device settings** and click on **Enterprise State Roaming**.
2. Change the **Users may sync settings and app data across devices** setting to **All** or **Selected**. As there is no cost regarding this, it is recommended to set it to **All**.
3. Then, click **Save**.

You have now enabled ESR across your tenant.

Automating it

This one is slightly more complicated as it does not work with the Graph API; instead, you have to access the more hidden Azure **Identity and Access Management (IAM)** API:

1. Set the necessary variables:

    ```
    ##Set to 2 to disable or 0 to enable
    $esrstatus = 0
    $tenantid = "Your-Tenant-ID"
    ```

2. Create the JSON. If we had set it to a select user group, it would be populated within the `syncSelectedUsers` array. As we are doing an all-or-nothing, we will simply leave the array blank:

    ```
    $json = @"
    {
        "isAdminConfigurable": true,
        "isRoamingSettingChanged": true,
        "syncSelectedUsers": [],
        "syncSetting": $esrstatus
    }
    "@
    ```

3. Set the URL (note the non-Graph setup of it):

    ```
    $url = "https://main.iam.ad.ext.azure.com/api/
    RoamingSettings?ESRV2=true"
    ```

4. Now, create the access token and headers.

5. When you run this section, you will be presented with a hyperlink and some code that you must enter to authenticate. Click the link, enter the code, and then accept the numerous prompts.

6. Here, we are using `Invoke-Restmethod` to send a POST request to the `oauth2` Microsoft login URL for the tenant and requesting a token for the Entra ID IAM client ID.

    As this one requires user interaction, we will add a `while` loop to wait until the request has been requested and approved within the web browser. If no activity is detected, the script will stop with an error code:

    ```
    ##Create Access Token
    $clientid = "1950a258-227b-4e31-a9cf-717495945fc2"
    $response = Invoke-RestMethod -Method POST -UseBasicParsing
    -Uri "https://login.microsoftonline.com/$tenantId/oauth2/
    ```

```
devicecode" -ContentType "application/x-www-form-urlencoded"
-Body "resource=https%3A%2F%2Fmain.iam.ad.ext.azure.com&client_
id=$clientId"
Write-Output $response.message
$waited = 0
while($true){
    try{
        $authResponse = Invoke-RestMethod -uri "https://login.
microsoftonline.com/$tenantId/oauth2/token" -ContentType
"application/x-www-form-urlencoded" -Method POST -Body "grant_
type=device_code&resource=https%3A%2F%2Fmain.iam.ad.ext.
azure.com&code=$($response.device_code)&client_id=$clientId"
-ErrorAction Stop
        $refreshToken = $authResponse.refresh_token
        break
    }catch{
        if($waited -gt 300){
            Write-Verbose "No valid login detected within 5
minutes"
            Throw
        }
        #try again
        Start-Sleep -s 5
        $waited += 5
    }
}
$response = (Invoke-RestMethod "https://login.windows.
net/$tenantId/oauth2/token" -Method POST -Body
"resource=74658136-14ec-4630-ad9b-26e160ff0fc6&grant_
type=refresh_token&refresh_token=$refreshToken&client_
id=$clientId&scope=openid" -ErrorAction Stop)
    $resourceToken = $response.access_token
```

7. The previous command has given us our access token, which we can then add to the header to
    call our webrequest. The authorization section always needs to start with "Bearer" and
    then the access token (in this case, $resourceToken):

```
$Headers = @{
    "Authorization" = "Bearer " + $resourceToken
    "Content-type"  = "application/json"
    "X-Requested-With" = "XMLHttpRequest"
    "x-ms-client-request-id" = [guid]::NewGuid()
    "x-ms-correlation-id" = [guid]::NewGuid()
}
```

8. Finally, send the request to enable or disable ESR:

```
Invoke-RestMethod -Uri $url -Headers $Headers -Method PUT -Body
$json -ErrorAction Stop
```

This script has automated enabling ESR using the IAM API.

Creating Entra ID static groups

Now that our new user has been configured, we need a way to assign our policies to them and any machines they may use. For this, we need to configure Entra ID groups, which come in two flavors – static and dynamic.

If you are familiar with traditional Active Directory groups, these are very similar, except they include dynamic groups, where a group is populated automatically based on a particular query or filter that has been configured.

Getting ready

First, load the Entra portal, expand **Groups**, and click on **All Groups** (you can also access groups within the Intune portal, which loads the same window).

How to do it...

A **static group** is pretty straightforward to use – you manually add either users or devices to it:

1. Click on **New Group** and enter the necessary details. Set **Group type** to **Security** and enter **Group name** and **Group description** values. If you want to be able to assign roles directly to the group instead of at the user level (for example, you want a group of Intune administrators), change the setting to **Yes**. Set **Membership type** to **Assigned**. Optionally, add any members and an owner to manage the group. Then, click **Create**.

2. Once your group has been created, click on it to look at some of the other actions you can take against it. You can also get an overview of the group membership, as well as the group ID:

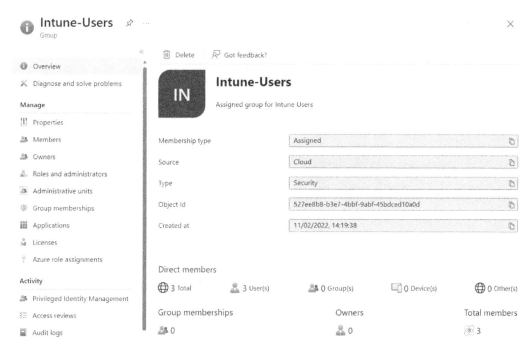

Figure 1.7– Entra ID group menu

Members and **Owners** are pretty self-explanatory. **Administrative units** is a useful feature if you want to delegate within your environment. Say, for example, you want your service desk to be able to perform tasks on a particular group of users – you can create an administrative unit and assign users and groups to it. You can then configure a custom Azure role with specific access *only* to that administrative unit. **Group memberships** is for nested groups. Clicking the **Licenses** option allows you to assign a license at a group level rather than directly to the users. If you selected **Yes** earlier, you can also assign Azure roles to the group in the **Azure role assignments** menu.

With that, you have created a static Microsoft Entra group.

Automating it

Creating this PowerShell script will automate your Entra group creation process, which will be useful when you need to bulk-create groups during your tenant management.

This is a fairly easy one to automate:

1. As usual, we need to start with the variables:

    ```
    $groupname = "TestGroup123"
    $groupdescription = "TestGroupDescription"
    ```

2. Convert the group name into lowercase and remove any special characters so that we can use it as the mail nickname:

    ```
    $groupnickname = ($groupname -replace '[^a-zA-Z0-9]', '').
    ToLower()
    ```

3. Set the URL. Here, we are using the **Groups** subsection of Graph:

    ```
    $uri = "https://graph.microsoft.com/beta/groups/"
    ```

4. Populate the JSON. We do not need mail for this group as it is for Entra ID and Intune membership only and it is a security group, so we need to pass this through:

    ```
    $json = @"
    {
        "description": "$groupdescription",
        "displayName": "$groupname",
        "mailEnabled": false,
        "mailNickname": "$groupnickname",
        "securityEnabled": true
    }
    "@
    ```

5. Send the command to create the group:

    ```
    Invoke-MgGraphRequest -Uri $uri -Method Post -Body $json
    -ContentType "application/json"
    ```

    This can also be completed by using the `New-mgGroup` module and passing variables through if required.

You now have a script to create your static Entra groups automatically.

Creating Entra ID dynamic groups

In this recipe, we will configure Entra ID dynamic groups, where we can configure a group to automatically populate based on specified criteria. This example will cover both user and device-based queries.

Getting ready

First, load the Entra portal, expand **Groups,** and click on **All groups** (you can also access groups within the Intune portal, which loads the same window).

How to do it...

Dynamic groups are automated; you set a membership rule (the user is a member of a particular location, device prefix, and so on), and then Entra ID reviews the rules on a schedule and adds/removes members accordingly. It is worth noting that there can be a delay while Entra queries the membership rules to populate the group membership.

For this example, we will create one Office user group and one Autopilot device dynamic group that we can use later on.

The user group will collect any users with an Office Business license (not the Enterprise ones), while the device group will collect all of your **Autopilot devices**; we will cover this in more detail in *Chapter 4.*

Creating a dynamic Office user group

Follow these steps to create a dynamic group containing only licensed Office users:

1. Starting with the user group, click **New Group** and enter the basic details:

    A. **Group type**: **Security**.

    B. Enter **Group name** and **Group description** details.

    C. Change the membership type to **Dynamic User**.

2. You will notice that we have to create a dynamic query. So, click **Add dynamic query**. This will take you to the **Configure Rules** interface and is where you can view the properties available and set them accordingly. If you already know the query, you can add it directly into the **Rule syntax** window.

    To detect Office users, we are going to check the user assigned plans:

    A. For **Property**, select **assignedPlans**.

    B. Set **Operator** to **Any**.

      C.   The **Value** needs to be `(assignedPlan.servicePlanId -eq "43de0ff5-c92c-492b-9116-175376d08c38" -and assignedPlan.capabilityStatus -eq "Enabled"))`.

      D.   It should look like this in the syntax (sometimes, you may need to edit it to add the final closing brackets):

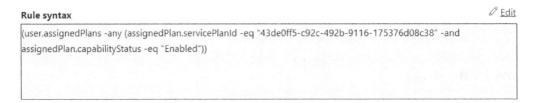

Figure 1.8 – Entra ID – new dynamic rule result

3.   Now, click the **Validate Rules** button.

4.   Add a user who has an Office license assigned and click **Select**.

5.   Then, click **Validate**. Here, you can see I have only assigned the license to one of my two users:

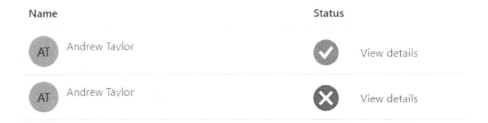

Figure 1.9 – User validation results

With that, we have created a dynamic user group for users with an Office license.

To find the `servicePlanId` value for individual products, you can use a downloadable CSV from the Microsoft site. You can use this to create any other dynamic groups: `https://learn.microsoft.com/en-us/azure/active-directory/enterprise-users/licensing-service-plan-reference`.

Creating a dynamic Autopilot device group

When we create our Autopilot profile later, in *Chapter 4*, we will configure it to automatically pick up all users/devices. However, in a pilot or **Proof of Concept (PoC)**, we may only want to target those devices enrolled in Autopilot. For this, we can query the device's ZTID, which is added when we import it (covered in *Chapter 4*).

Follow this process to create our dynamic grou:.

1. Create a **New Group** value in Entra ID, but this time, pick **Dynamic Device** as the membership type. Set **Group type** to **Security**. Then, add the **Group name** and **Group description** values. Finally, click **Add dynamic query**.

2. This one is slightly more straightforward. Set **Property** to **devicePhysicalIds**, **Operator** to **Any**, and **Value** to (_ -startsWith " [ZTDid]:

Property	Operator	Value
devicePhysicalIds	Any	(_ -startsWith "[ZTDid]

Figure 1.10 – Dynamic rule creator

3. It should look like this (sometimes, you may need to edit it to add the final closing brackets). Click **OK** on this screen:

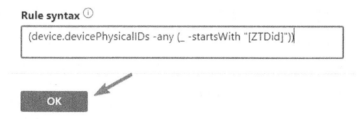

Rule syntax ⓘ

(device.devicePhysicalIDs -any (_ -startsWith "[ZTDid]"))

OK

Figure 1.11– Dynamic device query

We do not need to validate this one as we do not have a device enrolled yet anyway.

4. Now, click **Save**, then **Create** on the following screen.

With that, we have created our dynamic Autopilot devices group so that it is ready to enroll devices in *Chapter 4*.

Automating it

This script will demonstrate how we can use Graph and PowerShell to create both of our dynamic groups, demonstrating the different queries.

Dynamic Office user group

This is similar to a static group, except we must add an extra line for the dynamic rule:

1. Set the necessary variables:

    ```
    $groupname = "TestGroup123"
    $groupdescription = "TestGroupDescription"
    $membershiprule = '(user.assignedPlans -any (assignedPlan.
    servicePlanId -eq \"43de0ff5-c92c-492b-9116-175376d08c38\" -and
    assignedPlan.capabilityStatus -eq \"Enabled\"))'
    $groupnickname = ($groupname -replace '[^a-zA-Z0-9]', '').
    ToLower()
    ```

> **Important note**
>
> We have single quotes around the rule because we are using double quotes in the rule and also escaping the double quotes.

2. Now, give it a URL:

    ```
    $url = "https://graph.microsoft.com/beta/groups"
    Populate the JSON
    $json = @"
    {
        "description": "$groupdescription",
        "displayName": "$groupname",
        "groupTypes": [
            "DynamicMembership"
        ],
        "mailEnabled": false,
        "mailNickname": "$groupnickname",
        "membershipRule": "$membershiprule",
        "membershipRuleProcessingState": "On",
        "securityEnabled": true
    }
    "@
    ```

    Finally, submit our Graph request:

    ```
    Invoke-MgGraphRequest -Uri $url -Method Post -Body $json
    -ContentType "application/json"
    ```

This script will create a dynamic group for users who have an active Office license based on the SKU and license properties.

Dynamic Autopilot device group

This is the same as the user group but with a different rule. The Graph backend does not differentiate between user and device groups.

We can now create a PowerShell script to create a dynamic group:

1. Set the necessary variables:

    ```
    $groupname = "TestGroup123"
    $groupdescription = "TestGroupDescription"
    ```

2. Set the mail nickname:

    ```
    $groupnickname = ($groupname -replace '[^a-zA-Z0-9]', '').
    ToLower()
    ```

3. Set the membership rule:

    ```
    $membershiprule = '(device.devicePhysicalIDs -any (_ -startsWith
    "[ZTDid]"))'
    ```

4. Set the URL:

    ```
    $url = "https://graph.microsoft.com/beta/groups"
    ```

5. Populate the JSON:

    ```
    $json = @"
    {
        "description": "$groupdescription",
        "displayName": "$groupname",
        "groupTypes": [
            "DynamicMembership"
        ],
        "mailEnabled": false,
        "mailNickname": "$groupnickname",
        "membershipRule": $membershiprule,
        "membershipRuleProcessingState": "On",
        "securityEnabled": true
    }
    "@
    ```

6.   Finally, submit our Graph request:

```
Invoke-MgGraphRequest -Uri $url -Method Post -Body $json
-ContentType "application/json"
```

We now have a script for creating our dynamic Autopilot group.

Configuring Entra ID MDM/MAM scopes

The last thing we must do before we move on to Intune is allow our users to enroll devices into **Mobile Device Management (MDM)** and, if required, **Mobile Application Management (MAM)**.

MDM is for enrolling your corporate-owned devices into Intune, while MAM is for your **bring-your-own devices (BYODs)**. MAM uses **Windows Information Protection (WIP)**, which is only supported on Android and iOS, but we can block personal Windows devices within Intune so that we can still set this to everyone and let Intune handle the rest.

How to do it...

Follow these steps to configure your Entra ID MDM and MAM scopes:

1.   Within Microsoft Entra ID, expand **Settings** and click on **Mobility**.

2.   Within the **Mobility** portal, click **Microsoft Intune**:

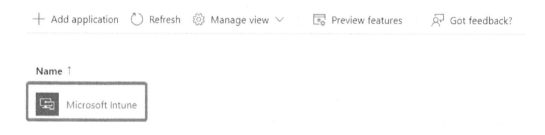

Figure 1.12 – The Mobility (MDM and MAM) screen

3.   For this environment, set them both to **All**. Note you can restrict by groups – for example, only allowing users with an Intune license based on a dynamic group, or block users from enrolling completely. Leave the default URLs as is and then click **Save**.

With that, we have configured our Microsoft Entra environment for device enrollment.

Automating it

This is a tricky one to automate. Not only does it use the IAM API that we used for ESR, but the MDM application ID is also tenant-specific.

Let us build a PowerShell script to automate these settings:

1. First, in your browser window, look in the address bar and grab the ID:

    https://**entra.microsoft.com**/#view/Microsoft_AAD_IAM/MdmConfiguration.ReactView/appName/Microsoft%20Intune/appId/0000000a-0000-0000-c000-000000000000

    Figure 1.13 – Address bar object ID

2. Set the necessary variables, including this ID. A setting of 2 means enabled for all, while 0 means disabled:

    ```
    $MDMstatus = 2
    $MAMstatus = 2
    $policyid = "Policy ID grabbed from browser"
    ```

3. Populate the JSON. As with the Entra ID device settings, we are manipulating the default values so that we can retrieve the current JSON with a GET request. In this case, we are only changing two settings; everything else remains the same:

    ```
    $json = @"
    {
        "appCategory": "Mdm",
        "appData": {
            "complianceUrl": "https://portal.manage.microsoft.
    com/?portalAction=Compliance",
            "enrollmentUrl": "https://enrollment.manage.microsoft.
    com/enrollmentserver/discovery.svc",
            "mamComplianceUrl": "",
            "mamEnrollmentUrl": "https://wip.mam.manage.microsoft.
    com/Enroll",
            "mamTermsOfUseUrl": "",
            "termsOfUseUrl": "https://portal.manage.microsoft.com/
    TermsofUse.aspx"
        },
        "appDisplayName": "Microsoft Intune",
        "appId": "0000000a-0000-0000-c000-000000000000",
        "isOnPrem": false,
        "logoUrl": null,
        "mamAppliesTo": $MAMstatus,
        "mamAppliesToGroups": [],
        "mdmAppliesTo": $MDMstatus,
    ```

```
        "mdmAppliesToGroups": [],
        "objectId": "$policyid",
        "originalAppData": {
            "complianceUrl": "https://portal.manage.microsoft.
com/?portalAction=Compliance",
            "enrollmentUrl": "https://enrollment.manage.microsoft.
com/enrollmentserver/discovery.svc",
            "mamComplianceUrl": "",
            "mamEnrollmentUrl": "https://wip.mam.manage.microsoft.
com/Enroll",
            "mamTermsOfUseUrl": "",
            "termsOfUseUrl": "https://portal.manage.microsoft.com/
TermsofUse.aspx"
        }
    }
}
"@
```

4. Set the URL:

```
$url = "https://main.iam.ad.ext.azure.com/api/MdmApplications
/$policyid?mdmAppliesToChanged=true&mamAppliesToChanged=true"
```

5. Authenticate against the IAM API:

```
##Create Access Token
$clientid = "1950a258-227b-4e31-a9cf-717495945fc2"
$response = Invoke-RestMethod -Method POST -UseBasicParsing
-Uri "https://login.microsoftonline.com/$tenantId/oauth2/
devicecode" -ContentType "application/x-www-form-urlencoded"
-Body "resource=https%3A%2F%2Fmain.iam.ad.ext.azure.com&client_
id=$clientId"
Write-Output $response.message
$waited = 0
while($true){
    try{
        $authResponse = Invoke-RestMethod -uri "https://login.
microsoftonline.com/$tenantId/oauth2/token" -ContentType
"application/x-www-form-urlencoded" -Method POST -Body "grant_
type=device_code&resource=https%3A%2F%2Fmain.iam.ad.ext.
azure.com&code=$($response.device_code)&client_id=$clientId"
-ErrorAction Stop
        $refreshToken = $authResponse.refresh_token
        break
    }catch{
        if($waited -gt 300){
            Write-Verbose "No valid login detected within 5
minutes"
            Throw
```

```
        }
        #try again
        Start-Sleep -s 5
        $waited += 5
    }
}

$response = (Invoke-RestMethod "https://login.windows.
net/$tenantId/oauth2/token" -Method POST -Body
"resource=74658136-14ec-4630-ad9b-26e160ff0fc6&grant_
type=refresh_token&refresh_token=$refreshToken&client_
id=$clientId&scope=openid" -ErrorAction Stop)
    $resourceToken = $response.access_token
```

6. Create the headers:

```
$Headers = @{
    "Authorization" = "Bearer " + $resourceToken
    "Content-type"  = "application/json"
    "X-Requested-With" = "XMLHttpRequest"
    "x-ms-client-request-id" = [guid]::NewGuid()
    "x-ms-correlation-id" = [guid]::NewGuid()
}
```

7. Configure the policy:

```
Invoke-RestMethod -Uri $url -Headers $Headers -Method PUT -Body
$json -ErrorAction Stop
```

We now have a script to amend the MDM and MAM enrollment scopes.

2

Configuring Your New Tenant for Windows Devices

Now that your tenant is built and we have some **Entra ID** groups and roles configured, we can start populating the Intune environment.

To do so, we use policies that are equivalent to **Group Policies** in a traditional Active Directory configuration. These are used to configure your devices with the settings chosen within the Intune portal. This chapter looks at the different policy options for Windows devices to configure any non-security settings.

There are a variety of ways to configure policies, which we will cover in this chapter. This chapter will include the following recipes:

- Configuring a Settings catalog policy
- Configuring a Custom policy
- Importing and ingesting an ADMX policy
- Group policy analytics

Technical requirements

For this chapter, you will need a modern web browser and a PowerShell code editor such as **Visual Studio Code** or **PowerShell ISE**.

All of the scripts referenced can be found here:

https://github.com/PacktPublishing/Microsoft-Intune-Cookbook/tree/main/Chapter2

Before following the following recipes, you may first need to re-authenticate to Microsoft Graph, as covered in *Chapter 1*.

Chapter materials

Before moving on to configuring our policies, there are a couple of things to keep in mind.

Firstly, some settings can be configured in multiple places, especially when looking at security policies, so it is always worth keeping in mind what you are configuring and where to avoid making conflicting policies. Even if a setting has the same value in two different policies, it will be marked as a conflict within the GUI.

The other thing is the concept of **tattooing**. Some settings when applied can leave the setting configured on a device when switched to **Not Configured** within Intune. If there is a setting with the **Enabled** or **Not Configured** options, changing it to **Not Configured** does not send a signal to undo the configuration on the device; it simply tells Intune not to do anything with that particular setting and leave it to whatever happens to be set on the device already. Normally, this will just be the default Windows settings, but if it is a policy you have previously applied, it will remain at that value.

Remember, all settings configured in Intune are ultimately just registry or file-level changes, so there is no *best* way of deploying a policy, but (as we will see in the next chapter) applying policies within the Endpoint security blade adds a few extra options on top of using a standard policy, or a baseline.

This chapter covers the most-used options when setting a new policy, but there are multiple different options available:

- **Settings catalog**: This is also known as the **Unified Settings catalog**. This contains over 25,000 settings in an easy-to-use interface and is the current direction of travel for most policies within Intune. We will cover this in the following chapter.

- **Administrative templates**: This is the legacy approach for your traditional **Administrative Template XML-Based (ADMX)**-based policies. These have been transitioned into the Settings catalog, which is recommended for new policies.

- **Custom**: This is for policies not currently natively supported but backed by a **Configuration Service Provider (CSP)**, and they can be created directly. This is also covered in the following chapter.

- **Delivery optimization**: This is a way to configure devices to check machines in the local network/VPN for any files previously retrieved from Microsoft, saving bandwidth across the WAN. You can read more here: `https://learn.microsoft.com/en-gb/mem/intune/configuration/delivery-optimization-windows`.

- **Device firmware configuration interface (DFCI)**: For devices that support DFCI, you can use these policies to configure **Basic Input/Output System (BIOS)** settings on your **Autopilot devices**. You can read more here: `https://learn.microsoft.com/en-gb/mem/intune/configuration/device-firmware-configuration-interface-windows`.

- **Device restrictions**: These are legacy restriction policies from when Intune was first introduced. It is worth using Settings catalog for these.

- **Device restrictions (Windows 10 Team)**: These are restrictions for Teams devices only.

- **Domain join**: Best avoided where possible. This is for when Autopilot is used with **hybrid Entra Join**.

- **Edition upgrade and mode switch**: This can be used to switch the Windows Edition or move in or out of **S mode** (a security-streamlined Windows version).

- **Email**: Fairly self-explanatory, this sets an email server and configuration for the mail client on a machine.

- **Endpoint protection**: Another legacy policy where you can configure some basic security settings. It is recommended to use the Endpoint security blade covered in *Chapter 3*.

- **Identity protection**: Similar to the Endpoint protection, these have also been migrated to the Security blade.

- **Imported Administrative templates**: Covered in this chapter, this is used to import third-party ADMX policies.

- **Kiosk**: This allows you to configure devices to run in single or multi-app kiosk mode, where devices auto-login with a local account and are restricted to running only the allowed application(s).

- **Microsoft Defender for Endpoint**: Another legacy security policy. Again, use the Security blade to set this.

- **Network boundary**: When using **Windows Defender Application Guard**, you can configure certain sites to be blocked by setting a network boundary. You can find out more here: `https://learn.microsoft.com/en-gb/mem/intune/protect/endpoint-protection-windows-10`.

- **Public Key Cryptography Standards (PKCS) certificate**: Configure a **Public Key Pair Certificate** for certificate-based authentication.

- **PKCS imported certificate**: Use an imported PKCS for **Secure/Multipurpose Internet Mail Extensions (S/MIME)** email encryption.

- **Simple Certificate Enrollment Protocol (SCEP) certificate**: Use a SCEP for certificate-based authentication.

- **Secure assessment**: This is for educational customers to create a restricted device for exam-type scenarios.

- **Shared multi-user device**: Specific settings when dealing with shared multi-user devices such as profile management. You can read more here: `https://learn.microsoft.com/en-us/windows/configuration/set-up-shared-or-guest-pc?tabs=intune#shared-pc-mode-concepts`.

- **Trusted certificate**: Used to import your trusted root certificate from a certificate authority.

- **VPN**: Create a VPN profile for your devices.

- **Wi-Fi**: Fairly self-explanatory – create a profile for your wireless network settings. Supports both basic and enterprise networks.

- **Windows Health Monitoring**: This configures what data is sent to Microsoft from your devices. When dealing with **Autopatch** (which we will cover in *Chapter 4*), it is a requirement.

- **Wired network**: Similar to Wi-Fi, but for wired networks.

When it comes to automating, creating some of these policies can be quite complicated so it is worth familiarizing yourself with **Graph Explorer** (`https://cmd.ms/ge`) and also the *F12* developer tools in your browser. When creating your policies in the GUI, you can use these to see what is happening at the network level, including the URLs and payload. The **Graph Xray extension** for Chrome and Edge will also display the exact PowerShell commands you can use to recreate whatever is configured in the GUI (`https://graphxray.merill.net`).

A useful tip when navigating some of these policies is to use the `out-gridview` functionality in PowerShell. If you grab all of the settings for a particular policy type, this gives you a useful GUI with filtering options and search functionality, rather than having to scroll through the command-line output.

Configuring a Settings catalog policy

We will start with Settings catalog (or Unified Settings catalog) policies, which will be your primary policy type moving forward. Many of the *older* policies are being migrated to Settings catalog, and due to the nature of the Graph underneath these new policy types, this allows for significantly more available settings (there are well over 25,000 at the time of writing).

Settings catalog is also cross-platform and can be used for Windows, macOS, and iOS policies at present, with more being migrated daily. You will find the vast majority of your traditional on-premises **Group Policy Objects (GPOs)** here as well. If there is a setting you cannot find, there are other deployment methods, which will be covered in the following recipes.

As a Settings catalog policy can contain many thousands of policy settings, it can become more difficult to troubleshoot and slow to load and edit within a browser. Similar to when dealing with on-premises GPO, less is more; create multiple policies with fewer settings in each so that you can have a policy for each particular task (OneDrive, Office, Edge, etc.). It is also worth noting that Intune policies do not run during login and halt logins; they run while a user is logged in, so adding more policies does not impact login speed. Intune will also queue the policy deployment, based on the current activity of tasks on your tenant, and automatically deploy to Windows devices. The speed with which the policy settings are deployed, received, and configured may depend on the state of the device (is it off or on?), the network connectivity of the device, and when it was last checked into Intune for an update.

How to do it...

Now, let us move on to creating our very first policy. For this one, we will configure some OneDrive settings to make life for your users easier:

1. Within the Intune portal, navigate to **Devices**, then select **Windows**, click on **Configuration profiles**, and finally, click **Create profile**.

2. Select **Windows 10 and later**, then **Settings catalog**, and click **Create**.

3. Give your policy a meaningful name and description. Remember that while you will know what the policy is doing now, in the future you may not remember as easily, or someone else may be managing your tenant so giving policies a sensible name and description makes future changes so much easier.

    Once you have added your name and description, click **Next**.

4. Now, we need to add some settings, so click the blue text that says **+ Add settings**.

    At this point, note that you can select a category or perform a search. A category can contain many settings (within sub-categories), so it is often quicker to perform a search. When searching, the UI will display all of the categories containing policies with your search term, which you can then click through to find the correct policy.

5. In our case, **OneDrive** has its own category, so we can simply scroll down and select it by clicking on it.

6. Once you have clicked on the category, you will see all of the available settings available for selection. You can select all of them here, or just select individual settings. For this policy, we will configure **Files On-Demand**, **single sign-on (SSO)**, and **Known Folder Move (KFM)**. Tick the boxes labeled as follows:

    - **Silently move Windows known folder to OneDrive**

    - **Silently sign in users to the OneDrive sync app with their Windows credentials**

- **Use OneDrive Files On-Demand**

  > ☑ Silently move Windows known folders to OneDrive   ⓘ

  > ☐ Silently move Windows known folders to OneDrive   ⓘ

  ☑ Silently sign in users to the OneDrive sync app with their Windows credentials   ⓘ

  > ☐ Specify SharePoint Server URL and organization name   ⓘ

  > ☐ Specify the OneDrive location in a hybrid environment   ⓘ

  > ☐ Sync Admin Reports   ⓘ

  ☑ Use OneDrive Files On-Demand   ⓘ

Figure 2.1 – OneDrive settings selection

7. You will then see the settings in the left-hand panel with their default values (in this case, all are set as **Disabled**).

    If you decide that you do not want to set a particular policy, click on the - button to the right. You can also remove an entire category by clicking the blue **Remove category** text.

8. Now, we want to enable all of these policies, which is simply a case of clicking on the slider. For the first two settings, it is a simple on/off switch, but note that for KFM, more settings will appear underneath:

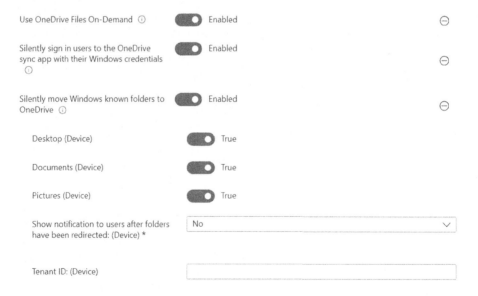

Figure 2.2 – OneDrive settings enabled

Enter your **tenant ID** here (if you do not have it to hand, load the Entra portal and navigate to **Entra Active Directory**), and optionally select whether you want your users to receive a toast notification when complete.

9. After entering your details, click **Next**.

10. We can ignore the **Scope tags** for now, as this is a simple environment. They are a way to differentiate policies and settings, used with split permissions in an estate with multiple levels of administrators. They will be covered in *Chapter 13*, so click **Next**.

11. Now, we need to assign the policy. As these are user settings, we will assign the policy to the group we created earlier containing your users. Alternatively, you could click the **All Users** option if you want it to be deployed to everyone. You will also see the ability to **Filter** here, which will also be covered in *Chapter 13*.

12. After selecting your group, click **Select**.

13. Once your assignments are configured, click **Next**.

14. You will now see a final screen to confirm everything you are creating in your new policy, as well as the policy details and the assignment. Once you are happy with them, click **Create**.

Here, we have learned how to configure our first Settings catalog policy to learn how the policies work and configure our OneDrive settings.

Automating it

Due to the nature of the Settings catalog and the use of categories, creating our policy via PowerShell is a little more tricky than some of the more straightforward policies, such as **Device restrictions** or **Compliance**. Here, we will configure our OneDrive policy using PowerShell and Graph:

1. Before showing you how to create this particular policy, we first need to understand exactly how the JSON is assembled.

    We need to find the category ID containing the policy we wish to configure. We can either search for it or simply list all the categories.

    Listing the categories involves running a GET command against one of these URLs. We are working now in the deviceManagement section of Graph, which is where most Intune settings reside. Within there, we will then work in configurationCategories for the Settings catalog. We can then filter further on the platform for the different operating systems. Security settings also use microsoftSense technology instead of the default mdm, helping to differentiate between the operating systems we are configuring:

    - Windows:

    ```
    https://graph.microsoft.com/beta/deviceManagement/
    configurationCategories?=&$filter=(platforms has 'windows10')
    and (technologies has 'mdm')
    ```

- iOS:

```
https://graph.microsoft.com/beta/deviceManagement/
configurationCategories?=&$filter=(platforms has
'iOS') and (technologies has 'mdm' or technologies has
'appleRemoteManagement')
```

- Windows Security:

```
https://graph.microsoft.com/beta/deviceManagement/
configurationCategories?templateCategory=True&$filter=(platforms
has 'windows10') and (technologies has 'microsoftSense')
```

- macOS:

```
https://graph.microsoft.com/beta/deviceManagement/
configurationCategories?=&$filter=(platforms has
'macOS') and (technologies has 'mdm' or technologies has
'appleRemoteManagement')
```

> **Important note**
>
> If using PowerShell, you will need to escape the $ before filter with a backtick `` ` ``.

2. If you want to search and find the category, add this to the end of the GET URL:

    ```
    &$search="SEARCH TERM HERE"
    ```

    In your results, you need to grab the category ID.

3. Now that we have the ID, we can list the policies within it. This is another GET command, as we are requesting information from Graph:

    ```
    https://graph.microsoft.com/beta/deviceManagement/
    configurationSettings?&`$filter=categoryId eq 'CATEGORY ID'
    ```

    Grab the root definition ID for the policy; you will need that later when configuring the final JSON.

4. For a simple enable/disable policy, you then need to look in the `options` array within the policy and grab the itemID for the value you want.

    For those with a further child setting, you need to look at the `options` array and investigate the `dependedOnBy` array, which will show you which sub-settings are activated when you enable the policy.

    In the case of OneDrive KFM, this gives the following:

    ```
    device_vendor_msft_policy_config_onedrivengscv2.
    updates~policy~onedrivengsc_kfmoptinnowizard_kfmoptinnowizard_
    textbox
    True
    device_vendor_msft_policy_config_onedrivengscv2.
    ```

```
updates~policy~onedrivengsc_kfmoptinnowizard_kfmoptinnowizard_
dropdown
True
device_vendor_msft_policy_config_onedrivengscv2.
updates~policy~onedrivengsc_kfmoptinnowizard_kfmoptinnowizard_
desktop_checkbox
True
device_vendor_msft_policy_config_onedrivengscv2.
updates~policy~onedrivengsc_kfmoptinnowizard_kfmoptinnowizard_
documents_checkbox
True
device_vendor_msft_policy_config_onedrivengscv2.
updates~policy~onedrivengsc_kfmoptinnowizard_kfmoptinnowizard_
pictures_checkbox
True
```

This aligns with the fact there are two different Policy checkboxes for KFM within the Settings catalog. One is to enable it and supply the tenant ID, and the other is to specify which folders to redirect.

Now that we know what a Settings catalog policy comprises, let us have a look at the policy for OneDrive, as created in the GUI earlier.

5. First, as usual, we set our variables:

    ```
    $policyname = "Onedrive Configuration"
    $policydescription = "Configures OneDrive"
    $tenantid = "TENANT ID HERE"
    $groupid = "AAD GROUP ID HERE"
    ```

6. Then, we need the URL to create the policy:

    ```
    $url = "https://graph.microsoft.com/beta/deviceManagement/
    configurationPolicies"
    ```

    Now, set the JSON with the policy details that we found using the methods in the previous steps. You can find the JSON here: https://github.com/PacktPublishing/Microsoft-Intune-Cookbook/blob/main/Chapter2/onedrive-settings-catalog.ps1.

7. When creating the policy, we want the output in a variable so that we can then find the policy ID to assign it:

    ```
    $policy = Invoke-MgGraphRequest -Method POST -Uri $url -Body
    $json -ContentType "application/json" -OutputType PSObject
    ```

    Note that we use -OutputType here to return the policy as a PowerShell object; otherwise, it would return raw JSON, which would involve more steps to grab the ID.

8. Find the policy ID from our created policy:

    ```
    $policyid = $policy.id
    ```

9. Set the URL for assignment to include the policy ID:

```
$assignurl = "https://graph.microsoft.com/beta/deviceManagement/
configurationPolicies('$policyid')/assign"
```

10. Create the JSON with the Entra ID Group ID. This is a nested array and uses the `@odata.type` of `"#microsoft.graph.groupAssignmentTarget"`, which tells it to include that group:

```
$assignjson = @"
{
    "assignments": [
        {
            "target": {
                "@odata.type": "#microsoft.graph.
groupAssignmentTarget",
                "groupId": "$groupid"
            }
        }
    ]
}
"@
```

11. Finally, assign our new policy:

```
$assign = Invoke-MgGraphRequest -Method POST -Uri $assignurl
-Body $assignjson -ContentType "application/json"
```

We have now created our OneDrive settings catalog policy using PowerShell and Graph.

There's more...

When working with Settings catalog and retrieving data, pagination is used to limit the results to more manageable amounts, which, when looking in a GUI, would display a link to show the next 25 results.

When working in Graph, obviously there is no way to click a link, but it displays as `@odata.nextLink`.

Therefore, when retrieving data, you need to be aware of pagination and work around it. The way to do this is to run your initial GET request, then look for the link, and run another GET request against that, continuing in this method until you have all of the results added to your array.

Here is some example code you can use:

```
$uri = "URL HERE"
$response = (Invoke-MgGraphRequest -uri $uri -Method Get -OutputType
PSObject)
$allsettings = $response.value
```

```
$allsettingsNextLink = $response."@odata.nextLink"
while ($null -ne $allsettingsNextLink) {
$allsettingsResponse = (Invoke-MGGraphRequest -Uri
$allsettingsNextLink -Method Get -outputType PSObject)
$allsettingsNextLink = $allsettingsResponse."@odata.nextLink"
$allsettings += $allsettingsResponse.value
}
$allsettings
```

This keeps looping through until the nextLink value is empty, at which point it has reached the end and returns the data.

Configuring a custom policy

While the Settings catalog (and other options in the following recipes) will capture 99% of your needs in a standard environment, there may be times when you need to set CSP settings directly on machines and there is no template available.

For this recipe, we are going to use the policy that skips the **User Settings** section within the **Enrollment Status Page** (**ESP**) (there will be more on that in *Chapter 4*), which can be useful if you are happy that all of the key apps are targeted at the device setup and you do not want users to wait for the user-targeted apps to finish installing.

A custom **Open Mobile Alliance Uniform Resource Identifier** (**OMA-URI**) policy allows you to directly set the CSP settings, but you have to be careful that what you enter matches exactly what is expected, as these policies are very exact and will fail if a setting is incorrect.

Getting ready

As mentioned, for this example, we will skip the user status page, details of which can be found at the bottom of the page in the following link:

`https://learn.microsoft.com/en-us/troubleshoot/mem/intune/device-enrollment/understand-troubleshoot-esp`

The exact settings are specified, which is what you would expect when configuring a policy such as this.

How to do it...

Following these instructions will configure your custom policy:

1. First, in the Intune portal, navigate to **Devices**, then click **Windows**, and finally, select **Configuration profiles**. Then, click **Create profile**.
2. This time, you need to select **Windows 10 and later** | **Templates** | **Custom**, and then click **Create**.

3. Give your policy a name and description; remember to make it clear what the policy is doing, and future you will thank you when you need to find a specific policy. Then, click **next**.

4. On the next screen, we want to add a setting. Some policies can have multiple **Open Mobile Alliance Uniform Resource Identifier** (**OMA-URI**)settings, but this one is a more simple one with a single setting. Click the **Add** button.

   Add a name and description for the individual setting.

5. For the **OMA-URI** value, you need to enter the following: `./Vendor/MSFT/DMClient/ Provider/MS DM Server/FirstSyncStatus/SkipUserStatusPage`.

   Note the dot at the front, which is important. We can see it is a vendor policy, and in this case, the vendor is Microsoft (MSFT).

   You have multiple settings available for the value, so again, check the documents carefully. In our case, it is a Boolean (`True` or `False`), and we need to set it to `True`.

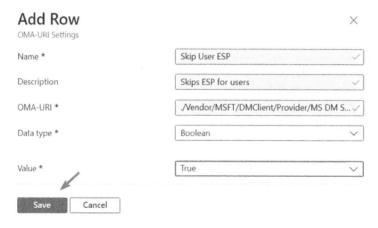

Figure 2.3 – OMA-URI settings values

Click **Save**, and as this is the only policy being configured here, we can click **Next**. Some custom policies may have multiple rows, which you would populate here before continuing.

Figure 2.4 – OMA-URI settings configured

6. This is a user-targeting policy, so we will assign it to the Intune-users group we created in *Chapter 1* (or all users if required).

   We do not need any filters on this, as it should be applicable to all devices for the selected users. Therefore, click **Next**.

7. We will cover applicability rules in *Chapter 14*, but at a basic level, we could restrict this policy to only certain OS versions, which is not required for this policy, as we want it to apply to all devices without restrictions, so again, click **Next**.

8. Give everything a final sense check on the **Review + create** page, and then click **Create**.

This step configures a custom policy to skip the **Account Setup** screen during the **Out of Box Experience (OOBE)**.

Automating it

Fortunately, these policies are easier to automate than the previous Settings catalog policies. We will use PowerShell and Graph to automate this policy creation:

1. As usual, we will start with our variables. For this particular policy, we will need to set the OMA-URI, the value type (Boolean, string, or integer), and the value itself. To make things easier, the script takes the type in plain text and then converts it to what the JSON needs:

   ```
   $groupid = "00000000-0000-0000-0000-000000000000"
   $name = "Skip User ESP"
   $description = "Skips Enrollment Status Page Users section"
   $omauri = "./Vendor/MSFT/DMClient/Provider/MS DM Server/
   FirstSyncStatus/SkipUserStatusPage"
   $omavalue = "true"
   ##Value Type can be string, integer or Boolean
   $valuetype = "boolean"
   ```

2. Next, specify the URL. Custom policies use the `deviceConfigurations` subcategory within the `deviceManagement` area of Graph:

   ```
   $url = "https://graph.microsoft.com/beta/deviceManagement/
   deviceConfigurations"
   ```

3. We will let PowerShell do the clever bits with the value type, using a simple `Switch` command. This takes the value we have sent and converts it to the value that the JSON needs:

   ```
   ##Switch on the valuetype
   switch ($valuetype) {
       "boolean" {
           $policytype = "#microsoft.graph.omaSettingBoolean"
       }
   ```

```
    "string" {
        $policytype = "#microsoft.graph.omaSettingString"
    }
    "integer" {
        $policytype = "#microsoft.graph.omaSettingInteger"
    }
}
```

4. Now that we have all of the data we need, we can create the JSON. As this is a new policy, there is no ID. If we were manipulating a current policy, we would need to pass through the ID here.

    omaSettings are in an array of their own, as signified by the *square brackets [ ]*:

```
$json = @"
{
    "@odata.type": "#microsoft.graph.
windows10CustomConfiguration",
    "description": "$description",
    "deviceManagementApplicabilityRuleOsVersion": null,
    "displayName": "$name",
    "id": "00000000-0000-0000-0000-000000000000",
    "omaSettings": [
        {
            "@odata.type": "$policytype",
            "description": "$description",
            "displayName": "$name",
            "omaUri": "$omauri",
            "value": "$omavalue"
        }
    ],
    "roleScopeTagIds": [
        "0"
    ]
}
"@
```

5. As we are assigning the policy again, we will run the request to output to a variable. We are creating a new policy, so we use the POST command:

```
$policy = Invoke-MgGraphRequest -Method POST -Uri $url -Body
$json -ContentType "application/json" -OutputType PSObject
```

    To assign it, use the same method as the previous policy but with a slightly different URL. Obtain the policy ID to populate the URL:

```
$policyid = $policy.id
```

6. Create the URL:

```
$assignurl = "https://graph.microsoft.com/beta/deviceManagement/
deviceConfigurations/$policyid/assign"
```

7. Create the JSON:

```
$assignjson = @"
{
    "assignments": [
        {
            "target": {
                "@odata.type": "#microsoft.graph.
groupAssignmentTarget",
                "groupId": "$groupid"
            }
        }
    ]
}
"@
```

8. Finally, assign the policy:

```
Invoke-MgGraphRequest -Method POST -Uri $assignurl -Body
$assignjson -ContentType "application/json"
```

We have created a new script here to disable account setup during OOBE

Importing and ingesting an ADMX policy

A relatively new (and welcome) addition is the ability to ingest ADMX policies directly within the console. This is useful for your third-party products, which do not have policies configured within the Settings catalog and are easier to configure than custom OMA-URI policies.

Getting ready

For this example, we will use the Mozilla Firefox policy templates. The templates can be downloaded from this location: https://github.com/mozilla/policy-templates/releases.

The process is the same for any ADMX-based **Architecture Description Markup Language (ADML)**, so feel free to use others if needed.

After downloading and extracting your templates, you will need firefox.admx and the matching ADML for your preferred language.

How to do it...

Follow this recipe to ingest and configure a policy for Mozilla Firefox:

1. Inside the Intune portal, navigate to **Devices | Windows | Configuration profiles**.

    At the top, next to where it says **Profiles**, you will see an **Import ADMX** text link. Click it.

2. Now, we need to click the **+ Import** button and select the ADMX and ADML files, downloaded in the *Getting ready* section.

    Before we can import the Firefox files, we need to import the Mozilla base files, as they are a prerequisite for Firefox admin templates. Click on the folder icons, and navigate to `mozilla.admx` and `mozilla.adml` from within the files downloaded in the *Getting ready* section. Then, click **Next**:

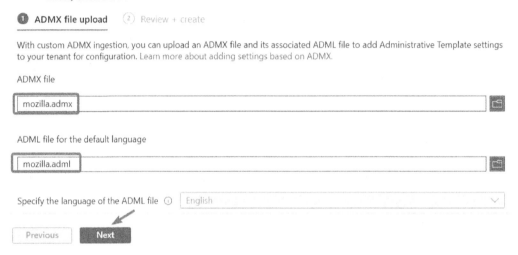

Figure 2.5 – Importing Mozilla policies

3. On the **Review + create** screen, check that the filenames are correct and click **Create**.

4. After clicking **Create** on the previous screen, we are taken to the following page, where we wait for the upload to complete:

Figure 2.6 – The Mozilla ADMX upload in progress

After the upload has completed, we will see this screen:

Template Name	Version	Status
mozilla.admx	4.8	✓ Available

Figure 2.7 – The Mozilla ADMX upload complete

5. Now, we can upload the Firefox-specific policies, following the same process as before. Click the folders, select the `firefox.admx` and `firefox.adml` files, and then click **Next**.

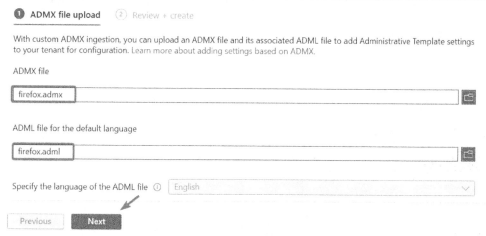

Figure 2.8 – Importing the Firefox module

6. On the **Review + create** screen, confirm the filenames are correct, and click **Create**.

7. Again, wait for the notification that the upload has completed.

Once complete, you will see this screen:

Template Name	Version	Status
firefox.admx	4.10	✓ Available
mozilla.admx	4.8	✓ Available

Figure 2.9 – Firefox and Mozilla ADMX complete

8. Now that we have our policies available, we need to create a policy to use them. Click on the **Profiles** text/button, and then click **Create profile**.

9. This time, we want to select **Windows 10 and later | Templates | Imported Administrative templates (Preview)**. Now, click **Create**.

> **Important note**
>
> At the time of writing, this is in preview, and therefore, the steps may change during general availability.

10. Give the new profile a name and description, and then click **Next**.

11. On the next screen, you will see the available policies for both the user and the device. I am going to keep it simple and force a start page at the device level, as this is likely to be the most used setting. For your environment, select whichever policies apply. Select **URL for Home page**:

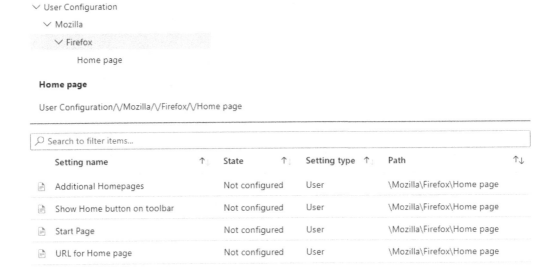

Figure 2.10 – Profile Setting Options

12. In the flyout, set the policy to **Enabled**, enter your home page URL, and then click **OK**.

13. After you have configured your settings, press **Next**.

14. We do not need to target this policy at a device level, so press **Next** again to skip the scope tags.

15. At this point, you can assign to either users or devices, depending on what you have configured. For this example, we will assign to **Intune Users**. Then, click **Next**.

16. Check throughout that everything looks correct and then click **Create**.

These steps have ingested a third-party set of administrative templates for Mozilla Firefox and used them to configure a start page for the browser.

Automating it

Now, we can create a PowerShell script to automate this using Graph.

Ingestion

Ingesting the policy files is reasonably straightforward; we need to grab the files, convert them to `Base64`, and then upload them to Intune:

1. First, create your variables with the file paths and ADML language:

   ```
   $admxpath = "PATH TO ADMX FILE"
   $admlpath = "PATH TO ADML FILE"
   $language = "en-US"
   ```

2. Set the URL, this time using the `groupPolicyUploadedDefinitionFiles` subcategory:

   ```
   $url = "https://graph.microsoft.com/beta/deviceManagement/
   groupPolicyUploadedDefinitionFiles"
   ```

3. Grab the filenames from the paths. We will use this by splitting the path into objects and then using the `-leaf` command to grab the final value. We will need these when populating the JSON later:

   ```
   $admxfile = Split-Path -Path $admxpath -Leaf
   $admlfile = Split-Path -Path $admlpath -Leaf
   ```

4. Convert the files to `base64` and store them in the variables, using the .NET functionality built into PowerShell. We will grab the file, read it, and then convert it to Base64:

   ```
   $admxcontent = [System.Convert]::ToBase64String([System.
   IO.File]::ReadAllBytes($admxpath))
   $admlcontent = [System.Convert]::ToBase64String([System.
   IO.File]::ReadAllBytes($admlpath))
   ```

5. Create the JSON:

   ```
   $json = @"
   {
       "content": "$admxcontent",
       "defaultLanguageCode": "",
       "fileName": "$admxfile",
       "groupPolicyUploadedLanguageFiles": [
           {
               "content": "$admlcontent",
               "fileName": "$admlfile",
               "languageCode": "$language"
           }
   ```

```
        ]
      }
    "@
```

6. Run our newly created import JSON:

```
invoke-mggraphrequest -Method POST -Uri $url -Body $json
-ContentType "application/json"
```

This has ingested our templates into Intune, which we can now use to create a policy.

Policy creation

For imported policies, we need to create an empty policy first and then run a second POST command to add the values to it.

Similar to the Settings catalog, we first need to do some exploring to find the details to populate the JSON:

1. First, we need to get the policy definition ID by running a GET command against this URL:

```
https://graph.microsoft.com/beta/deviceManagement/
groupPolicyDefinitions
```

    If you want to narrow it down, you can append a search to the end of the URL:

```
?$search="SEARCH TERM"
```

2. Make a note of the ID (not groupPolicyCategoryId), as we will need this to populate the JSON. Watch for the class type field here as well, which differentiates between your user and machine policies.

3. In the JSON, we also need to add the presentation details (the ID and value), so with your ID from the previous step, add it to this URL to find the presentations:

```
https://graph.microsoft.com/beta/deviceManagement/
groupPolicyDefinitions/POLICYID/presentations
```

    Here, you need the ID and the selected value. Keep an eye on the @odata.type value as well; if it is a textbox, it is safe to assume we are passing a string, but for a checkbox, it will be a Boolean value, as a checkbox can only be true or false. These will have to match in the JSON we are passing to Graph, as you will see in our example.

    Now that you know how to find the details we need, we can test with the policy we created earlier in the GUI.

4. Set your variables:

```
$name = "Mozilla Firefox"
$description = "ADMX templates to configure Mozilla Firefox"
$groupid = "0000000000000000"
```

5. Set the policy creation URL using the `groupPolicyConfigurations` subcategory:

```
$url = "https://graph.microsoft.com/beta/deviceManagement/
groupPolicyConfigurations"
```

6. Create the JSON for the policy:

```
$json = @"
{
    "description": "$description",
    "displayName": "$name",
    "roleScopeTagIds": [
        "0"
    ]
}
"@
```

7. Create the (empty) policy, and grab the details to use to both populate and assign it:

```
$policy = Invoke-MgGraphRequest -Method POST -Uri $url -Body
$json -ContentType "application/json" -OutputType PSObject
```

8. Now, find the policy ID:

```
$policyid = $policy.id
```

9. Create the URL to update the policy content:

```
$updateuri = "https://graph.microsoft.com/beta/deviceManagement/
groupPolicyConfigurations('$policyid')/updateDefinitionValues"
```

10. Add the JSON with the values we found earlier:

```
$updatejson = @"
{
    "added": [
        {
            "definition@odata.bind": "https://graph.microsoft.
com/beta/deviceManagement/groupPolicyDefinitions(<POLICYID>)",
            "enabled": true,
            "presentationValues": [
                {
                    "@odata.type": "#microsoft.graph.
groupPolicyPresentationValueText",
                    "presentation@odata.
bind": "https://graph.microsoft.com/beta/
deviceManagement/groupPolicyDefinitions('POLICYID')/
presentations('PRESENTATIONID>)",
                    "value": "homepage"
```

```
                }
            ]
        },
        {
            "definition@odata.bind": "https://graph.microsoft.
com/beta/deviceManagement/groupPolicyDefinitions(<POLICYID')",
            "enabled": true,
            "presentationValues": [
                {
                    "@odata.type": "#microsoft.graph.
groupPolicyPresentationValueText",
                    "presentation@odata.
bind": "https://graph.microsoft.com/beta/
deviceManagement/groupPolicyDefinitions(<POLICYID>)/
presentations(<PRESENTATIONID>)",
                    "value": "https://www.packtpub.com/"
                },
                {
                    "@odata.type": "#microsoft.graph.
groupPolicyPresentationValueBoolean",
                    "presentation@odata.
bind": "https://graph.microsoft.com/beta/
deviceManagement/groupPolicyDefinitions(<POLICYID')/
presentations('PRESENTATIONID')",
                    "value": true
                }
            ]
        }
    ],
    "deletedIds": [],
    "updated": []
}
"@
```

11. Run the update script we have created to add the values:

```
Invoke-MgGraphRequest -Method POST -Uri $updateuri -Body
$updatejson -ContentType "application/json"
```

Now that we have a complete policy, we finally need to assign it.

12. Populate the URL:

```
$assignurl = "https://graph.microsoft.com/beta/deviceManagement/
groupPolicyConfigurations('$policyid')/assign"
```

13. Create the JSON:

```
$assignjson = @"
{
    "assignments": [
        {
            "id": "",
            "target": {
                "@odata.type": "#microsoft.graph.
groupAssignmentTarget",
                "groupId": "$groupid"
            }
        }
    ]
}
"@
```

14. Run the JSON:

```
invoke-mggraphrequest -Method POST -Uri $assignurl -Body
$assignjson -ContentType "application/json"
```

These steps have created a PowerShell script to automate the ingestion of third-party administrative templates and the creation of a policy using them.

Group policy analytics

While it is generally recommended to create your new policies from scratch to reduce the amount of *technical debt* when migrating to Intune, you may have certain group policies configured in your on-premises Active Directory that you feel are good enough to be migrated directly to Intune. For this, we can use Group Policy analytics, which will ingest your policies, tell you which can be migrated, and also, if selected, migrate them for you.

Getting ready

The first thing we need is an XML export of the group policy we wish to inspect for compatibility with Intune. If you do not have a domain controller available, there is an example within GitHub here: `https://github.com/PacktPublishing/Microsoft-Intune-Cookbook/blob/main/Chapter2/gpreport.xml`:

1. Within **Active Directory**, navigate to **Group Policy Objects**:

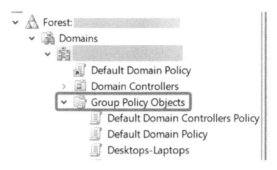

Figure 2.11 – Group Policy Objects

2. Right-click on the Group Policy in question and click **Back Up…**.

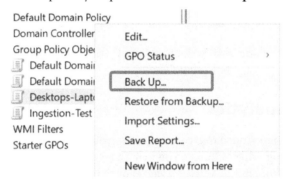

Figure 2.12 – Backing up GPO

3. Select a location and click **Back Up**:

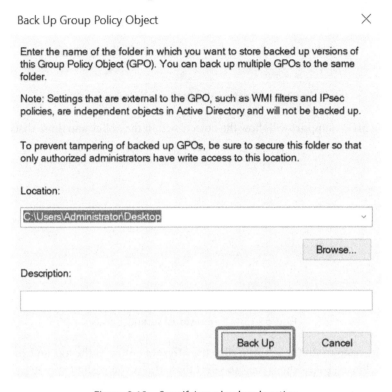

Figure 2.13 – Specifying a backup location

4. Within the export location, we will need the gpreport.xml file.

How to do it...

We will now ingest the XML file into Intune to check for compatibility:

1. Within the Intune console, click **Devices** and then **Group Policy analytics**.
2. Click the **Import** button.
3. Select the GPReport file, and click **Next**.
4. Click **Next** on the **Scope tags** page.
5. Now, click **Create**.

6. Once complete, you can see the status of the GPO:

Migrate ↑↓	Group policy name ↑	Active directory t... ↑↓	MDM support ↑↓
☐	Desktops-Laptops	Desktops-Laptops	⚠ 71%

Figure 2.14 – Checking the status of the imported GPO

Clicking **MDM support** will show the objects within the policy and those that are supported:

Setting name ↑	Group policy sett... ↑	MDM support ↑	Value ↑	Scope ↑	Min OS version ↑
Choose drive encrypti...	Windows Components...	✅ Yes	7	Device	15063
Choose drive encrypti...	Windows Components...	✅ Yes	7	Device	15063
Choose drive encrypti...	Windows Components...	✅ Yes	4	Device	15063
Choose drive encrypti...	Windows Components...	⚠ No	AES 256-bit	Device	0
Choose drive encrypti...	Windows Components...	⚠ No	AES 256-bit	Device	0
Do not keep history of...	Start Menu and Taskbar	✅ Yes	Enabled	Device	17755
Turn off File History	Windows Components...	✅ Yes	Enabled	Device	18362

Figure 2.15 – The individual settings status

If you are happy with the settings, click the **Migrate** button at the top, and you will be taken to the following page, where you can select the settings you wish to migrate, and click **Next**:

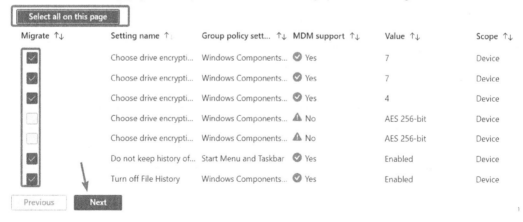

Figure 2.16 – Selecting settings to migrate

7. You will then be taken to the following screen, where you can change any settings as required in the textbox, and click **Next**:

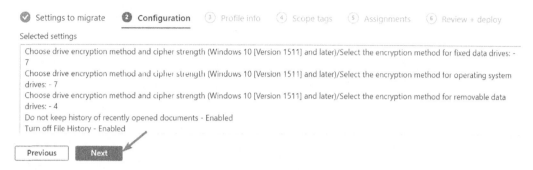

Figure 2.17 – Reviewing the settings configuration

8. Provide a name and description for the policy you will be creating, and click **Next**.

9. After clicking **Next**, assign the newly created policies as required, and click **Next**.

10. Finally, you will see a list of everything configured. Confirm that everything looks OK, and click **Deploy**.

We have now ingested an XML export of our on-premises Group Policies and used the migration functionality to create new Intune policies on the back of it.

Automating it

As the policy creation is largely dependent on the settings you require, we will only automate the ingestion of the XML here. Therefore, we will create a PowerShell script using Microsoft Graph to ingest this file automatically and then review it in the GUI:

1. First, we need to set the URL and also the path to the XML:

    ```
    $url = "https://graph.microsoft.com/beta/deviceManagement/
    groupPolicyMigrationReports/createMigrationReport"
    $filepath = ""
    ```

2. Inside the JSON, we need to pass both the file content in the Base64 format as well as the name of the GPO itself. We could manually enter that, but why not let PowerShell extract it from the XML for us by using Get-Content and specifying XML:

    ```
    $xml = [xml](Get-Content -Path "$filepath")
    $policyname = $xml.gpo.name
    ```

3. Then, grab the Base64 contents:

```
$bytes = [System.IO.File]::ReadAllBytes($filepath)
$base64 = [System.Convert]::ToBase64String($bytes)
```

4. Populate the content and name into the JSON:

```
$json = @"
{
    "groupPolicyObjectFile": {
        "content": "$base64",
        "ouDistinguishedName": "$policyname",
        "roleScopeTagIds": [
        ]
    }
}
"@
```

Finally, send the POST request to ingest the Base64 contents of the XML file:

```
Invoke-MgGraphRequest -Method POST -Uri $url -Body $json
-ContentType "application/json"
```

Using this script, we have ingested an on-premises Group Policy into Intune to then review in the GUI.

3

Securing Your Windows Devices with Security Policies

Chapter 2 showed you the basics of each of the core policy types, as well as what happens behind the scenes. This chapter will take that knowledge and extend it into the **Endpoint Security** blade within Microsoft Intune. You will find out how to secure your devices with the various policies and settings available.

We will configure the four policies that are most critical in a new environment: Antivirus, BitLocker, Firewall, and **Advanced surface reduction** (**ASR**). These, combined with your baseline, will give you an excellent security footprint to build upon.

You can configure a lot of these security settings within standard policies as well as within Endpoint Security, but using the dedicated **Endpoint security** blade gives you a couple of advantages:

- On the policy overview, you can see the status of your policies and devices, as well as running remedial actions where required
- With Intune's **role-based access control** (**RBAC** – covered later) roles, you can configure a separate role with restricted access to this area only so that you can provide your security team with access to review and act upon incidents, but without giving them access to everything else

This chapter will include the following recipes:

- Setting up a security baseline
- Configuring an antivirus policy
- Configuring Windows Security Experience
- Configuring your BitLocker policy
- Configuring Windows Firewall
- Deploying ASR rules

- Enrolling in Defender for Endpoint

- Deploying Windows **Local Admin Password Solution (LAPS)**

Technical requirements

For this chapter, you will need a modern web browser and a PowerShell code editor such as Visual **Studio Code (VS Code)** or PowerShell ISE.

All of the scripts that are referenced in this chapter can be found here: `https://github.com/ PacktPublishing/Microsoft-Intune-Cookbook/tree/main/Chapter3`.

Chapter materials

Before we start configuring our policies, we should look at best practices to ensure our Windows devices are as secure as possible. For this, there are resources available that can offer guidance.

An example of this is the NCSC Windows guidance, available at `https://www.ncsc.gov.uk/ collection/device-security-guidance/platform-guides/windows`.

You can also download a CSV file including all recommended settings or pre-configure **Group Policy Objects (GPOs)** that you can import directly into Intune (as covered in *Chapter 2*). These files are available here: `https://github.com/ukncsc/Device-Security-Guidance-Configuration-Packs/tree/main/Microsoft/Windows`.

You can find best practice recommendations from CIS regarding their Intune baselines at `https:// www.cisecurity.org/benchmark/intune`.

The CIS downloads also include GPOs that you can import into Intune directly.

> **Tip**
> While simply enabling every setting would provide you with a quick, secure environment, this is not necessarily the best approach, as you need to ensure you are not causing issues for your own applications or user experience. It is best to review all settings and enable those required for your environment after careful testing.

Setting up a security baseline

Security baselines are a *quick start* group of settings selected by Microsoft to quickly secure your tenant. They are available for Windows, Edge, Windows 365, and Microsoft Defender for Endpoint.

While they do not have the granularity of using the more bespoke *Settings catalog*-backed policies (covered in this chapter), they are a quick, easy, and useful way to get you up and running.

Should you decide to move to the more dedicated policies, make sure you change the associated setting in your baseline to **Not configured**; otherwise, you will find yourself with policy conflicts. There is an example JSON extract in this book's GitHub repository that you can import (using the script found at `https://andrewstaylor.com/2022/12/07/intune-backing-up-and-restoring-your-environment-new-and-improved/`) into your environment and amend accordingly to get you started.

Microsoft also updates the baseline policies on a regular cadence to ensure you are always receiving the latest versions. When an update is released, your current policies will continue working but will change to read-only mode within the Intune console. To make any changes, you will need to update them to their latest versions; this will be covered in this recipe.

Configuring any of the baselines follows the same process, so for this recipe, we will configure the Microsoft Edge baseline as that is least likely to conflict with any other policy settings.

How to do it...

To set up a security baseline, please perform the following steps:

1. Navigate to the Intune console and click **Endpoint security**, then **Security baselines**.

2. Click **Security Baseline for Microsoft Edge** and then **Create profile**.

3. When adding **Name** and **Description** values, you will see the current version of the baseline that is available. Then, click **Next**.

4. On the next screen, you will see all of the available settings. Change these to suit your requirements. Pay attention to the **Control which extensions cannot be installed** setting as, by default, this is set to **Block all extensions**. Once you have set these, click **Next**.

5. Click **Next** on the **Scope tags** page; we will cover scope tags later in *Chapter 13*.

6. While there is no right or wrong answer, assigning security policies at the device level is a good option, as they will be needed across users. So, we are going to assign this one to the **Autopilot Devices** group.

7. Click **Next**, and if you are happy that everything looks correct, click **Create**.

We have now configured our Edge baseline in the GUI and can look at doing so via automation.

Automating it

Now, let us use Graph and PowerShell to complete the same tasks.

Security baselines run from templates within Graph, so the first thing we need to do is find the template ID:

1. First, we need to run a GET command against this URL. We can do this in Graph Explorer or using the *F12* browser development tools: `https://graph.microsoft.com/beta/deviceManagement/templates/`.

2. Find the Microsoft Edge baseline and make a note of the ID.

3. If you are deploying the defaults without any configuration changes, this is a simple one, but first, let's look at how we can change settings at the Graph level.

    If we look at the default policy JSON, we will see that we have an empty `settingsDelta` array:

    ```
    {
        "description": "Edge Baseline",
        "displayName": "Edge Baseline",
        "roleScopeTagIds": [
            "0"
        ],
        "settingsDelta": [
        ]
    }
    ```

    This is where we add any settings outside of the defaults, but we need to find the settings now! To do this, we need to go through Graph again.

4. Using the same ID as before, run a GET command against this URL: `https://graph.microsoft.com/beta/deviceManagement/templates/{TEMPLATE-ID}/categories/`.

5. You should be presented with another ID. Add that to the aforementioned URL and run the GET command again for the following URL: `https://graph.microsoft.com/beta/deviceManagement/templates/TEMPLATE-ID/categories/CATEGORY-ID/recommendedSettings`.

6. Here, you can find the details for each of the settings, including the recommended setting value in the **valueJSON** field. If, for example, you want to allow extensions to be installed, your `settingsDelta` would look like this:

    ```
        "settingsDelta": [
            {
                "@odata.type": "#microsoft.graph.
    deviceManagementStringSettingInstance",
                "definitionId": "admx--microsoftedge_
    ExtensionInstallBlocklist",
                "id": "aa6e4219-055b-47ae-96da-d72718d6a82d",
                "value": "disabled"
            }
        ]
    ```

Since the demo contains stock settings, creating this policy is a bit more simple. Let us take a look:

1. First, we need to add the group ID:

    ```
    $groupid = "00000000000000000000"
    ```

2. Then, we must set the URL (including the template ID we found earlier if it is different):

    ```
    $uri = "https://graph.microsoft.com/beta/deviceManagement/
    templates/a8d6fa0e-1e66-455b-bb51-8ce0dde1559e/createInstance"
    ```

    You will notice that the URL ends in createInstance, so it is creating a copy of the default template.

3. The JSON is extremely straightforward for this one:

    ```
    $json = @"
    {
        "description": "Edge Baseline",
        "displayName": "Edge Baseline",
        "roleScopeTagIds": [
            "0"
        ],
        "settingsDelta": [
        ]
    }
    "@
    ```

4. Now, create the policy and output it in a variable so that we can grab the policy ID for assignment:

    ```
    $policy = Invoke-MgGraphRequest -Method POST -Uri $uri -Body
    $json -ContentType "application/json" -OutputType PSObject
    ```

5. Find the policy ID:

    ```
    $policyid = $policy.id
    ```

6. Set the URL for policy assignment (security policies are listed under the intents category):

    ```
    $assignuri = "https://graph.microsoft.com/beta/deviceManagement/
    intents/$policyid/assign"
    ```

7. Now, create the assignment JSON:

    ```
    $assignjson = @"
    {
        "assignments": [
            {
                "target": {
    ```

```
                    "@odata.type": "#microsoft.graph.
          groupAssignmentTarget",
                    "groupId": "$groupid"
                }
            }
        ]
    }
    "@
```

8. Finally, assign it:

```
Invoke-MgGraphRequest -Method POST -Uri $assignuri -Body
$assignjson -ContentType "application/json"
```

If you want to deploy defaults across all baselines, there is an additional PowerShell script in this book's GitHub repository that you can use.

There's more…

As mentioned earlier, Microsoft releases updates for its security baselines, which you need to implement to be able to make any changes to existing deployed policies.

The best thing to do is to duplicate your current policy so that you can test the changes before deploying to production. Let us take a look at how to do this:

1. Click on the baseline and click the three dots to the right of the policy. Then, click **Duplicate**.

2. Next, place a tick into the checkbox to the left of your new duplicate policy and click the **Change Version** button.

3. Here, you can select the version to update to and how you want to handle the changes. Usually, you would select the first option (**Accept baseline changes but keep my existing setting customizations**) to keep any changes you have made to the defaults.

4. Then, it is simply a case of clicking **Submit** and testing.

Once you are happy that everything is working as it should, follow the same procedure for your original policies. It is worth keeping the duplicate one to use next time there is an update.

Now that our baselines have been configured, we can start exploring the **Endpoint Security** blade and configure some other policies. There are numerous policy options here, from your standard BitLocker and Firewall to Account Protection and enumerating additional administrative accounts.

Configuring an antivirus policy

This recipe will run through how to configure your antivirus policy and also configure the UI on your end user devices to restrict what the user can and cannot see.

How to do it...

We will start with the antivirus policy:

1. Navigate to **Endpoint security** in Intune, click **Antivirus**, and then click **Create Policy**.

> **Important note**
> You may have noticed the **Reusable settings** tab at the top. This is currently only for firewall rules, so you can ignore it for now. We will cover it in the *Configuring Windows Firewall* recipe.

2. For the policy type, select **Microsoft Defender Antivirus** in the **Profile** dropdown. We will cover Security Experience in the *Configuring Windows Security Experience* recipe.

3. Set the policy's **Name** and **Description**.

4. Configure the settings as per your environment. If there are any you are not sure about, the lowercase **i** in a circle next to each field will give you further details. Once your settings have been configured, click **Next**.

5. Click **Next** on the **Scope tags** page.

6. Once you have configured your settings, assign the policy to your **Autopilot Devices** group.

7. Review your settings (click the arrow next to **Defender** to expand them) and click **Create**.

Your policy has now been created.

Automating it

Now, we can move on to deploying the policy with PowerShell and Graph.

This policy is running from the **Unified Settings catalog**, but as well as **Mobile Device Management (MDM)**, it has Microsoft Sense (used by Microsoft Security and Defender for Endpoint) as the second technology. So, we can use the security policies URL to list what is available with this tag, or we can just do a search and check the tag in the results:

```
https://graph.microsoft.com/beta/deviceManagement/
configurationCategories?templateCategory=True&`$filter=(platforms
has 'windows10') and (technologies has 'mdm' or technologies has
'microsoftSense')
```

Since we have already learned how Settings catalog works, this is the code for the policy created earlier:

1. First, set the group:

    ```
    $groupid = "00000000000000000000000000"
    ```

2. Set the URL. Note that it is in `configurationPolicies`, so it is using Settings catalog underneath:

```
$policyurl = "https://graph.microsoft.com/beta/deviceManagement/
configurationPolicies"
```

3. Set the JSON (we are just including one setting here to save space, but the example file includes the whole code):

```
$policyjson = @"
{
    "description": "Default Anti-Virus Policy",
    "name": "Anti-Virus Policy",
    "platforms": "windows10",
    "roleScopeTagIds": [
        "0"
    ],
    "settings": [
        {
            "@odata.type": "#microsoft.graph.
deviceManagementConfigurationSetting",
            "settingInstance": {
                "@odata.type": "#microsoft.graph.
deviceManagementConfigurationChoiceSettingInstance",
                "choiceSettingValue": {
                    "@odata.type": "#microsoft.graph.
deviceManagementConfigurationChoiceSettingValue",
                    "children": [],
                    "settingValueTemplateReference": {
                        "settingValueTemplateId": "1de23cd5-
23f3-4600-88d7-570e8ebbbf39"
                    },
                    "value": "device_vendor_msft_defender_
configuration_securityintelligenceupdateschannel_5"
                },
                "settingDefinitionId": "device_vendor_msft_
defender_configuration_securityintelligenceupdateschannel",
                "settingInstanceTemplateReference": {
                    "settingInstanceTemplateId": "368be8ef-11aa-
4c0d-919f-d6ed16bc6950"
                }
            }
        }
    ],
    "technologies": "mdm,microsoftSense",
```

```
        "templateReference": {
            "templateId": "804339ad-1553-4478-a742-138fb5807418_1"
        }
    }
"@
```

4. Create the policy and pass it to a variable, then grab the ID:

```
$policy = Invoke-MgGraphRequest -Method POST -Uri $policyurl
-Body $policyjson -ContentType "application/json" -OutputType
PSObject
$policyid = $policy.id
```

5. Populate the URL for assignment:

```
$assignurl = "https://graph.microsoft.com/beta/deviceManagement/
configurationPolicies/$policyid/assign"
```

6. Create the JSON:

```
$assignjson = @"
{
    "assignments": [
        {
            "target": {
                "@odata.type": "#microsoft.graph.
groupAssignmentTarget",
                "groupId": "$groupid"
            }
        }
    ]
}
"@
```

7. Assign it:

```
Invoke-MgGraphRequest -Method POST -Uri $assignurl -Body
$assignjson -ContentType "application/json"
```

With that, we have configured our antivirus policy using automation tools.

Configuring Windows Security Experience

This one is not quite as critical, but it is worth configuring so that users do not get bombarded with notifications.

How to do it...

We will now configure the **Windows Security Experience** policy to amend the end user experience when looking at the security settings within Windows:

1. Navigate back to the **Antivirus** menu in **Endpoint security** and create a new policy, this time selecting **Windows Security Experience**.

2. Set the policy's **Name** and **Description** and click **Next**.

3. Most of these are personal preferences, but right at the bottom, make sure you enable **Tamper Protection**. Since this is a corporate machine, disable **Family UI**. After that, make any changes that apply to your environment.

4. Click **Next**.

5. Assign the policy to **Autopilot Devices**.

6. Then, review and click **Create**.

We have now configured Windows Security Experience for our devices.

Automating it

Let us replicate how we configured our Security Experience policy, but this time using Graph and PowerShell.

This is another one based on Settings catalog. Again, we have cut down the policies that are listed here with just Tamper Protection, but the rest are in the example script:

1. First, set the group ID and policy URL, as well as the name and description:

    ```
    $groupid = "00000000000000000000000000"
    $policyurl = "https://graph.microsoft.com/beta/deviceManagement/
    configurationPolicies"
    $name = "Windows Security Experience"
    $description = "UI Settings"
    ```

2. Now, populate the JSON:

    ```
    $policyjson = @"
    {
        "description": "$description",
        "name": "$name",
        "platforms": "windows10",
        "roleScopeTagIds": [
            "0"
        ],
    ```

```
    "settings": [
        {
            "@odata.type": "#microsoft.graph.
deviceManagementConfigurationSetting",
            "settingInstance": {
                "@odata.type": "#microsoft.graph.
deviceManagementConfigurationChoiceSettingInstance",
                "choiceSettingValue": {
                    "@odata.type": "#microsoft.graph.
deviceManagementConfigurationChoiceSettingValue",
                    "children": [],
                    "settingValueTemplateReference": {
                        "settingValueTemplateId": "fc365da9-
2c1b-4f79-aa4b-dedca69e728f"
                    },
                    "value": "vendor_msft_defender_
configuration_tamperprotection_options_0"
                },
                "settingDefinitionId": "vendor_msft_defender_
configuration_tamperprotection_options",
                "settingInstanceTemplateReference": {
                    "settingInstanceTemplateId": "5655cab2-7e6b-
4c49-9ce2-3865da05f7e6"
                }
            }
        },
    "technologies": "mdm,microsoftSense",
    "templateReference": {
        "templateId": "d948ff9b-99cb-4ee0-8012-1fbc09685377_1"
    }
}
"@
```

Again, you can see that the technologies include Microsoft Sense.

3. Now, create the policy and grab the ID:

```
$policy = Invoke-MgGraphRequest -Method POST -Uri $policyurl
-Body $policyjson -ContentType "application/json" -OutputType
PSObject
$policyid = $policy.id
```

4. Finally, populate the assignment URL with the ID and the assignment JSON with our group ID. Then, send a POST request to assign our policy:

```
$assignurl = "https://graph.microsoft.com/beta/deviceManagement/
configurationPolicies/$policyid/assign"
$assignjson = @"
{
    "assignments": [
        {
            "target": {
                "@odata.type": "#microsoft.graph.
groupAssignmentTarget",
                "groupId": "$groupid"
            }
        }
    ]
}
"@
Invoke-MgGraphRequest -Method POST -Uri $assignurl -Body
$assignjson -ContentType "application/json"
```

We have now configured a Windows Security Experience policy using PowerShell and Graph

Configuring your BitLocker policy

Another important thing to consider is **BitLocker** drive encryption. While antivirus and firewall protect the machine when in use, this protects the data if your machine is lost or stolen. You should always use the strongest encryption possible and make it a requirement for **device compliance** and **conditional access** (more on those in *Chapter 8*).

There are specific settings for this policy to enable silent encryption during Autopilot, so you need to make sure these are set correctly.

How to do it...

The following steps will show you how to configure your **BitLocker drive encryption** policy:

1. Within **Endpoint security**, click on **Disk encryption** and create a policy.

    Set the policy's **Name** and **Description** and click **Next**.

2. Set the **Base Settings** values as per the following screenshot:

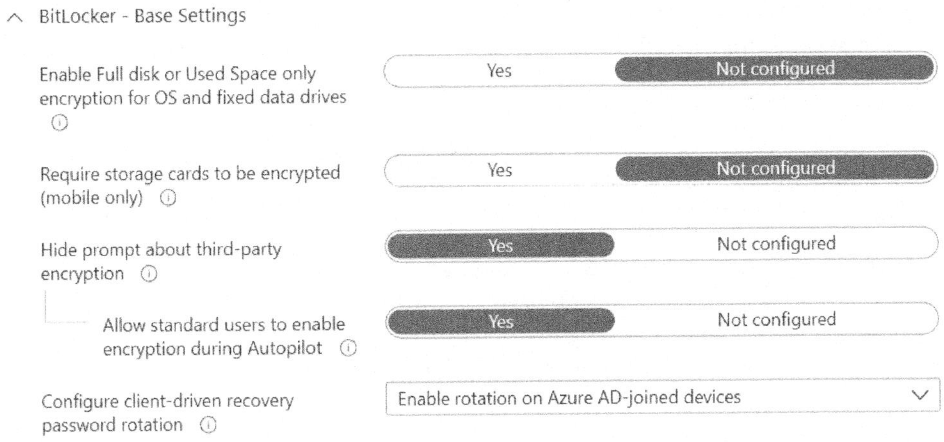

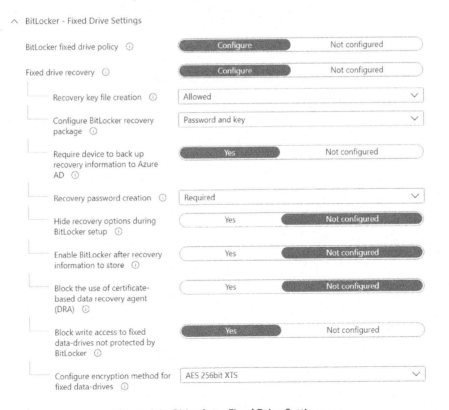

Figure 3.1 – BitLocker – Base Settings

3. Set the **Fixed Drive Settings** values as per the following screenshot:

Figure 3.2– BitLocker – Fixed Drive Settings

4. For **OS Drive Settings**, the only required setting is to set the encryption method, but you may want to set **Startup authentication required** to **Yes**, especially if you're looking for CIS compliance:

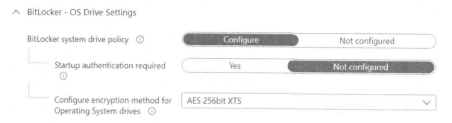

Figure 3.3 – BitLocker – OS Drive Settings

5. **Removeable Drive Settings** are for your USB sticks. If you are blocking completely, this is less important, but it is worth setting it anyway just to be on the safe side. Here, we are using CBC encryption instead of XTS for these:

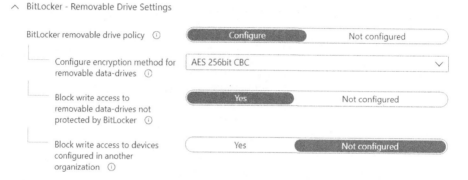

Figure 3.4 – BitLocker – Removable Drive Settings

Click **Next**.

6. Now, assign it to **Autopilot Devices** and click **Next**.

7. Review the settings and click **Create**.

With that, we have successfully created our BitLocker policy in the UI.

Automating it

Now, we can learn how to create the same policy using Graph.

This policy is more like a security baseline, where we are creating an instance with the JSON configured. The thing to note here is that a policy can have multiple settings stored in a single array. While with the baseline, each setting had its own value, these can have `valuejson` configured with comma-separated array values. The speech marks are also escaped with a \ character.

For example, the removable drive policy settings would be as follows:

```
        {
                "@odata.type": "#microsoft.graph.
deviceManagementComplexSettingInstance",
                "definitionId": "deviceConfiguration--windows10EndpointPro
tectionConfiguration_bitLockerRemovableDrivePolicy",
                "id": "ed70ea1b-7f30-4a78-995e-8b4282d5d11b",
                "valueJson": "{\"encryptionMethod\":\"aesCbc256\",
\"requireEncryptionForWriteAccess\":true,
\"blockCrossOrganizationWriteAccess\":false}"
        }
```

On the other hand, a policy for allowing standard user encryption involves using a simple yes/no value (note that this is just an example; the full script is available on GitHub):

```
        {
                "@odata.type": "#microsoft.graph.
deviceManagementBooleanSettingInstance",
                "definitionId": "deviceConfiguration--windows10EndpointPro
tectionConfiguration_bitLockerDisableWarningForOtherDiskEncryption",
                "id": "f4e6b4ea-579a-45e0-9aa0-5705ca646b0c",
                "value": true
        }
```

As with our previous Settings catalog policies, the settings themselves can be found by looping through the categories using a `GET` command and then checking the recommended settings for each category: `https://graph.microsoft.com/beta/deviceManagement/templates/d1174162-1dd2-4976-affc-6667049ab0ae/categories/CATEGORY-ID/recommendedSettings`.

This is another long policy, so grab the PowerShell script from this book's GitHub repository and amend or deploy it as required. It follows the same basic principles as before: sets the intents URL, populates the JSON, and creates and assigns the policy.

Configuring Windows Firewall

When we look at Windows Firewall, we will be introduced to the **Reusable settings** option. An environment will often have multiple firewall policies for different user and device groups to allow a piece of software to run or to further restrict a selection of devices. The idea behind Reusable Settings is that you can configure your specific firewall rules and then apply those across policies without needing to manually add them each time.

To give you an idea, this rule would block all Google domains:

Auto Resolve ⓘ	Keyword ⓘ	Configure settings
True	*.google.com	+ Edit instance

Figure 3.5 – Windows Firewall – Reusable Settings

In this recipe, we will stick with a basic firewall to block incoming traffic and allow outbound traffic as our first line of defense.

How to do it...

Now that we have looked at reusable settings, follow these steps to configure the standard Microsoft Defender firewall policy:

1. In the portal, navigate to **Endpoint security**, then **Firewall**. Choose **Create Policy**.

   We want **Windows 10, Windows 11 and Windows Server** and a **Windows Firewall** policy.

2. Set the policy's **Name** and **Description**.

3. On the next screen, there are a *lot* of available options. If you have a dedicated networking or security team, it is always worth working with them on something like this to ensure you have the best security available but with your applications and services still able to function.

> **Important note**
>
> Each setting has a lowercase **i** enclosed in a circle. You can click on it to gain thorough information about each setting. Use these if you are not sure exactly what a setting does – the last thing you want to do is enable everything and find that your machines stop working properly.

   As mentioned previously, we are keeping this one simple by enabling the firewall on all profiles, blocking inbound traffic, and allowing outbound traffic.

4. Once you have configured your settings, click **Next**.

5. On the **Scope tags** page, click **Next**.

> **Important note**
>
> We are using device assignment, but there may be cases where you need to assign a firewall policy to users if you have a particular application that needs custom rules. That way, you can be confident the firewall exception will apply only to machines when those users are logged in. It gives a seamless experience for users, saves time administering groups when machines are replaced, and adds a layer of security for users who do not need the exception.

6. Once assigned, check everything looks correct and click **Create.**

With that, you have configured your firewall policies using the UI.

Automating it

Now, we can look at how to deploy our firewall policy using PowerShell.

You can find the firewall templates within the templates we used previously for BitLocker, as well as the baselines (run a GET command against the following URL to see them: `https://graph. microsoft.com/beta/deviceManagement/templates/c53e5a9f-2eec-4175- 98a1-2b3d38084b91/categories/fae9ad7a-772f-4cae-a60b-14a10fa827f7/ recommendedSettings`).

The settings we have configured in the preceding section are based on the **Unified Settings catalog** under the **4a5e4714-00ac-4793-b0cc-5049041b0ed7** category ID.

If you run the following command, you will be able to see all of the available policy options for the firewall:

```
((Invoke-MgGraphRequest -Method GET -Uri "https://graph.microsoft.com/
beta/deviceManagement/configurationSettings?&`$filter=categoryId eq
'4a5e4714-00ac-4793-b0cc-5049041b0ed7'" -OutputType PSObject).value
| select-object name, description, '@odata.type', rootDefinitionId,
options, @{Name="Platform"; Expression={ $_.applicability | Select-
Object platform}},@{Name="technologies"; Expression={ $_.applicability
| Select-Object technologies}},valuedefinition, id) | out-gridview
```

You will notice that I have tweaked the output to make it more accessible by selecting the fields to display and also output to gridview to give us a UI.

When viewing the output, the policy names are the same across the different profiles. So, pay attention to `rootDefinitionID` as that will differentiate between them:

name	description	@odata.type	rootDefinitionId
DefaultInboundAction	This value is the action that the Hyper-V Firewall does...	#microsoft.graph.device...	vendor_msft_firewall_mdmstore_hypervvmsettings_{vmcreatorid}
DefaultInboundAction	This value is the action that the firewall does by defaul...	#microsoft.graph.device...	vendor_msft_firewall_mdmstore_domainprofile_enablefirewall
DefaultInboundAction	Specifies how to filter inbound traffic. The acceptable...	#microsoft.graph.device...	vendor_msft_firewall_mdmstore_publicprofile_enablefirewall
DefaultInboundAction	This value is the action that the Hyper-V Firewall does...	#microsoft.graph.device...	vendor_msft_firewall_mdmstore_hypervvmsettings_{vmcreatorid)
DefaultInboundAction	Specifies how to filter inbound traffic. The acceptable...	#microsoft.graph.device...	vendor_msft_firewall_mdmstore_privateprofile_enablefirewall
DefaultInboundAction	This value is the action that the Hyper-V Firewall does...	#microsoft.graph.device...	vendor_msft_firewall_mdmstore_hypervvmsettings_{vmcreatorid)

Figure 3.6 – Policy definition IDs

The `Options` field is an additional array that contains the values you can set for each policy. In the case of `InboundActions`, they are *block* (0) and *allow* (1):

```
vendor_msft_firewall_mdmstore_domainprofile_defaultinboundaction_0
vendor_msft_firewall_mdmstore_domainprofile_defaultinboundaction_1
```

Now that you know the theory behind it, let us look at our policy in action. The full code is available in this book's GitHub repository; we will just include one setting to see how it works:

1. First, as usual, set the group ID and URL:

   ```
   $groupid = "00000000000000000000"
   $uri = "https://graph.microsoft.com/beta/deviceManagement/
   configurationPolicies"
   ```

   You will see that the URL is a standard configuration policy (Settings catalog) rather than an intent or a template.

2. Set the JSON. Note that it has populated default values for the settings we did not change when configuring originally. This is expected behavior:

   ```
   $json = @"
   {
       "description": "Baseline Firewall Settings",
       "name": "Windows Firewall Settings",
       "platforms": "windows10",
       "roleScopeTagIds": [
           "0"
       ],
       "settings": [
           {
               "@odata.type": "#microsoft.graph.
   deviceManagementConfigurationSetting",
               "settingInstance": {
                   "@odata.type": "#microsoft.graph.
   deviceManagementConfigurationChoiceSettingInstance",
                   "choiceSettingValue": {
                       "@odata.type": "#microsoft.graph.
   deviceManagementConfigurationChoiceSettingValue",
                       "children": [
                           {
                               "@odata.type": "#microsoft.graph.
   deviceManagementConfigurationChoiceSettingInstance",
                               "choiceSettingValue": {
                                   "@odata.type": "#microsoft.
   graph.deviceManagementConfigurationChoiceSettingValue",
                                   "children": [],
   ```

```
                                    "value": "vendor_msft_firewall_
mdmstore_domainprofile_defaultinboundaction_1"
                                    },
                                    "settingDefinitionId": "vendor_msft_
firewall_mdmstore_domainprofile_defaultinboundaction"
                                    }
                        ],
                        "settingValueTemplateReference": {
                                "settingValueTemplateId": "120c5dbe-
0c88-46f0-b897-2c996d3e5277"
                                },
                        "value": "vendor_msft_firewall_mdmstore_
domainprofile_enablefirewall_true"
                        },
                        "settingDefinitionId": "vendor_msft_firewall_
mdmstore_domainprofile_enablefirewall",
                        "settingInstanceTemplateReference": {
                                "settingInstanceTemplateId": "7714c373-a19a-
4b64-ba6d-2e9db04a7684"
                        }
                }
        }
        ],
        "technologies": "mdm,microsoftSense",
        "templateReference": {
                "templateId": "6078910e-d808-4a9f-a51d-1b8a7bacb7c0_1"
        }
}
"@
```

3. Now, deploy the policy, populate the URL, and assign it:

```
$policy = Invoke-MgGraphRequest -Method POST -Uri $uri -Body
$json -ContentType "application/json" -OutputType PSObject
$policyid = $policy.id
$assignuri = "https://graph.microsoft.com/beta/deviceManagement/
configurationPolicies/$policyid/assign"
$assignjson = @"
{
    "assignments": [
        {
            "target": {
                "@odata.type": "#microsoft.graph.
groupAssignmentTarget",
                "groupId": "$groupid"
        }
```

```
        }
    ]
}
"@
    Invoke-MgGraphRequest -Method POST -Uri $assignuri -Body
    $assignjson -ContentType "application/json"
```

This completes the automation script to configure a firewall policy

Deploying ASR rules

There are some more well-known and documented weak points in a standard machine build that bad actors like to target. Javascript, Office Macros, and Adobe Acrobat Reader are some examples.

Fortunately, there are built-in ASR rules that can be enabled to block these from executing. Additionally, there is the option to enable them in Audit mode if there are concerns about the potential impact on your application.

Getting ready

To configure these, head to the **Endpoint security** blade, click **Attack surface reduction**, and choose to **Create** a new policy. Select **Attack surface reduction** from the list of options.

Once again, you will see that we have reusable settings here; this is where you can specify USB and printer device IDs. These are not relevant to ASR rules; they are for some of the other policies that can be configured in this blade.

How to do it...

These steps will run you through creating your new ASR policy:

1. Set your policy's **Name** and **Description** and then click **Next**.

2. On the **Settings** screen, check each policy and consider if it is going to impact your environment. If you are not sure, or think it might, err on the side of caution and set it to **Audit mode** initially.

    Then, review the reports, and if it is not flagging anything, enable it. Enabled is more secure, but the machines still have to work for the users and apps.

3. We are setting everything to **Block** in this recipe as it is a lab environment, which means we do not have any legacy apps to worry about.

    When changing a setting, you will see **ASR Only Per Rule Exclusions** appear. This can exclude a particular application (type in the application executable) from the policy setting.

    As with other policies, clicking the lowercase **i** enclosed in a circle will tell you exactly what the policy is doing, but again, use **Audit** or **Warn** if in doubt.

4. Once you have configured your policy settings, click **Next**.

5. Again, on the Scope tags page, click **Next**.

6. On the **Assignment** screen, assign to either users or devices, depending on how your user personas look. If, for example, your finance department has an Office add-in, you may want a policy just for them that is slightly more relaxed but not want to have to relax it across the organization.

7. Then, as usual, review and create your policy by clicking **Create**.

We have now configured our ASR rules in the UI to add extra protection to our devices.

Automating it

Now, let us learn how to create this policy using PowerShell.

As these policies are a reasonably new addition, they run entirely from the Settings catalog. If you run a query to list all of the categories in there, you will see one called **Attack surface reduction**. However, do not use this one – it has older settings on an ADMX-backed policy.

The settings we are looking for are in the Defender category with an ID of **e8400c82-34c8-4d6e-bbf9-85220f3205ea**.

As with the firewall, running this command will list the available policies. At this point, you can look through the Options array to see the available values:

```
((Invoke-MgGraphRequest -Method GET -Uri "https://graph.microsoft.com/
beta/deviceManagement/configurationSettings?`$filter=categoryId eq
'e8400c82-34c8-4d6e-bbf9-85220f3205ea'" -OutputType PSObject).value
 | select-object name, description, '@odata.type', rootDefinitionId,
options, @{Name="Platform"; Expression={ $_.applicability | Select-
Object platform}},@{Name="technologies"; Expression={ $_.applicability
 | Select-Object technologies}},valuedefinition, id) | out-gridview
```

As an example, Adobe Reader would give you these options:

```
device_vendor_msft_policy_config_defender_attacksurfacereductionrules_
blockadobereaderfromcreatingchildprocesses_off
```

```
device_vendor_msft_policy_config_defender_attacksurfacereductionrules_
blockadobereaderfromcreatingchildprocesses_block
```

```
device_vendor_msft_policy_config_defender_attacksurfacereductionrules_
blockadobereaderfromcreatingchildprocesses_audit
```

```
device_vendor_msft_policy_config_defender_attacksurfacereductionrules_
blockadobereaderfromcreatingchildprocesses_warn
```

As most ASR rules are similar, once you know the policy name, you can work out the value to use.

The policy we created earlier is available in the repository. So, again, the code here has been condensed, with just one setting included:

1. First, set the group ID and URL:

```
$groupid = "00000000000000000000"
$uri = "https://graph.microsoft.com/beta/deviceManagement/
configurationPolicies"
```

2. Then, configure the JSON (again, there is only one setting here):

```
$json = @"
{
    "description": "Block everything",
    "name": "Attack Surface Reduction",
    "platforms": "windows10",
    "roleScopeTagIds": [
        "0"
    ],
    "settings": [
        {
            "@odata.type": "#microsoft.graph.
deviceManagementConfigurationSetting",
            "settingInstance": {
                "@odata.type": "#microsoft.graph.
deviceManagementConfigurationGroupSettingCollectionInstance",
                "groupSettingCollectionValue": [
                    {
                        "children": [
                            {
                                "@odata.type": "#microsoft.
graph.deviceManagementConfigurationChoiceSettingInstance",
                                "choiceSettingValue": {
                                    "@odata.type": "#microsoft.
graph.deviceManagementConfigurationChoiceSettingValue",
                                    "children": [],
                                    "value": "device_vendor_
msft_policy_config_defender_attacksurfacereductionrules_
blockadobereaderfromcreatingchildprocesses_block"
                                },
                                "settingDefinitionId": "device_
vendor_msft_policy_config_defender_attacksurfacereductionrules_
blockadobereaderfromcreatingchildprocesses"
                            }
                        ]
```

```
                }
            ],
                "settingDefinitionId": "device_vendor_msft_
policy_config_defender_attacksurfacereductionrules",
                "settingInstanceTemplateReference": {
                    "settingInstanceTemplateId": "19600663-e264-
4c02-8f55-f2983216d6d7"
                }
            }
        }
    ],
    "technologies": "mdm,microsoftSense",
    "templateReference": {
        "templateId": "e8c053d6-9f95-42b1-a7f1-ebfd71c67a4b_1"
    }
}
"@
```

3. Finally, create the policy, add the ID to the URL, and assign it to the group you specified earlier:

```
$policy = Invoke-MgGraphRequest -Method POST -Uri $uri -Body
$json -ContentType "application/json" -OutputType PSObject
$policyid = $policy.id
$assignuri = "https://graph.microsoft.com/beta/deviceManagement/
configurationPolicies/$policyid/assign"
$assignjson = @"
{
    "assignments": [
        {
            "target": {
                "@odata.type": "#microsoft.graph.
groupAssignmentTarget",
                "groupId": "$groupid"
            }
        }
    ]
}
"@
Invoke-MgGraphRequest -Method POST -Uri $assignuri -Body
$assignjson -ContentType "application/json"
```

That completes the steps to automate our ASR policy deployment.

There's more...

There are numerous other options for security policies available within the portal. While we won't be running through deploying them all (as they are all pretty similar), this section will briefly outline what they are and where they live within the portal.

- **Microsoft Defender Antivirus exclusions**: Found in **Antivirus | Windows 10, Windows 11 and Windows Server**. This sets your exclusions for files, locations, and more.

- **Defender Update controls**: Found in **Antivirus | Windows 10**. This gives you more control over Defender updates so that you can configure a ring approach to their deployment, similar to Office and Windows (covered in *Chapter 4*).

- **Windows Firewall Rules**: Found in **Firewall | Windows 10, Windows 11 and Windows Server**. This allows you to configure individual firewall rules, similar to how you would in an on-premises scenario (or directly on the device)

- **Endpoint Privilege Management**: This is covered in **Intune Suite**; we will look at it in more detail in *Chapter 14*.

- **Endpoint detection and response**: Found in **Endpoint detection and response | Windows 10, Windows 11 and Windows Server**. This will be covered in the next recipe.

- **Exploit Protection**: Found in **Attack surface reduction | Windows 10 and later**. As well as blocking the ability for users to disable it, you can also upload a custom set of rules in XML format here. To learn more about creating these rules, go to `https://learn.microsoft.com/en-us/microsoft-365/security/defender-endpoint/import-export-exploit-protection-emet-xml?view=o365-worldwide`.

- **Device Control**: Found in **Attack surface reduction | Windows 10 and later**. These give finer controls over the likes of Bluetooth, removable storage, and device installations. Watch for clashes with any security baselines.

- **App and Browser Isolation**: Found in **Attack surface reduction | Windows 10 and later**. Here, you can specify details for any enterprise network settings, as well as restrictions applied to Edge and any isolated Windows environments using Application Guard.

- **Web protection (Microsoft Edge Legacy)**: Found in **Attack surface reduction | Windows 10 and later**. These policies add protection to any machines running the old version of Microsoft Edge (pre-Chromium).

- **Application control**: Found in **Attack surface reduction | Windows 10 and later**. This turns on SmartScreen and configures App Locker for Components, Store Apps, and Smart Locker.

- **Local user group membership**: Found in **Account protection | Windows 10 and later**. This policy allows you to specify specific users or groups to be added to or removed from user groups in the devices themselves. This should be used carefully, especially with the introduction of LAPS.

- **Account Protection**: Found in **Account Protection | Windows 10 and later**. Another place to configure Device Guard and Windows Hello for Business. Again, watch for policy conflicts!

Enrolling in Defender for Endpoint

Microsoft Defender for Endpoint gives you additional controls and monitoring on your devices.

Getting started

While it is managed from within Intune, you first need to onboard your tenant and devices into the service.

> **Important note**
>
> You need a Microsoft Defender for Endpoint P1 or P2 license to complete the following steps (a free trial can be obtained from the Microsoft Admin Center).

To start, we need to navigate to **Security Portal** at `https://security.microsoft.com`.

How to do it...

Now that we are in the portal, follow these settings to enroll your devices:

1. Click **Settings**.
2. Then, click **Endpoints**.
3. Now, scroll to the bottom; there should be a setting marked **Microsoft Intune connection**. Slide that to **On**.
4. Then, click **Save Preferences** and return to the Intune portal.
5. Navigate to **Endpoint security**, then **Endpoint detection and response**, and create a new policy (**Windows 10, Windows 11 and Windows Server**).
6. Set the policy's **Name** and **Description**.
7. As we have enabled Intune Connector within Security Centre, we now have the option to select the **Auto from connector** option from the **Microsoft Defender for Endpoint client configuration package type** dropdown. If it is not there, make sure **Intune Connector** was enabled and saved correctly in the previous steps within **Security Portal**.
8. Set your **sample sharing** and click **Next**.

9. On the **Scope tags** page, click **Next**.

    Defender for Endpoint *only* works at the device level, so either assign to a device group or **All Devices**. This is probably one occasion where **All Devices** is worthwhile.

    Finally, click **Create**.

10. We can now click on the **Microsoft Defender for Endpoint** link in the menu and check that everything is connected.

11. You can also find additional settings here for non-Intune managed and Android/iOS devices. Review them for your needs and enable them as required.

This recipe has enrolled your Intune tenant into Defender for Endpoint and then configured a policy to automatically enroll your devices into Defender for Endpoint.

Deploying Windows LAPS

Although it has been around for years for on-premises directories, this is a very new addition for Entra-managed devices, largely due to the inclusion of the LAPS client within Windows itself rather than needing an additional MSI and AD (Active Directory) schema update.

Before looking at deploying LAPS, it is first worth understanding what it does and why you may want to use it. LAPS is a system that rotates the local admin password on a machine to add an extra layer of security as it ensures no two machines have the same password; this helps prevent lateral traversal attacks.

With the introduction of Autopilot, Intune, and Entra ID, this was removed as the admin account was disabled by default. There are options available for managing these devices (such as the **Cloud Joined Device Local Admin Role** or **Local User Group Membership**), but they both have disadvantages (the role is for all devices and the membership is one policy per device).

Windows LAPS, on the other hand, gives you a password per device that can be retrieved from the Intune or Entra portal and will automatically expire to keep your machines protected.

With the introduction of **Endpoint Privilege Management** as part of Intune Suite (covered in *Chapter 14*), this may replace a lot of the use cases for LAPS, but that is at an additional cost.

When configuring LAPS for the first time, you need to consider if you want to use the built-in admin account and re-enable it (you can also rename it) or create your own account and leave the admin account disabled. The reasons for creating a new account are around security. Firstly, it is a well-known **Security Identifier** (**SID**), so even if you rename it, it can still be targeted. Secondly, the admin account will never lock out due to bad password attempts, so there is always a risk of a brute-force attack; it is extremely unlikely to work with a complex password (to give you an idea, if you set it to 20 characters, uppercase, lowercase, numbers, and special characters, it will take 42 quintillion years to crack... but reset every 30 days!).

In this recipe, you will learn how to deploy with either option so that you are free to decide which works best for you.

Getting started

There are some operating system version-specific requirements for this, so if you are looking to deploy it, make sure you have one of the following:

- Windows 10 20H2 or above with KB5025221 (April 2023 update)
- Windows 11 21H2 or above with KB5025224 (April 2023 update)

This recipe will move between the Entra portal (Entra ID) and the Intune portal (both Configuration Profiles and Endpoint Security).

How to do it...

Follow these steps to configure your policies and deploy Windows LAPS:

1. First, head to **Entra | Devices| Overview | Device Settings**.
2. Toward the bottom, there is the option for **Local administrator settings**. By default, this will be **No** (off), so we need to toggle it to **Yes**.
3. Then, click **Save** at the top.

Now, we need to navigate back to the Intune console and create a policy to either enable the admin or create a new account.

Using the built-in account

If you want to use the built-in account, follow these steps:

1. Navigate to **Devices | Configuration | + Create**.
2. Select **Settings catalog** from the **Profile type** dropdown.
3. Set the policy's **Name** and **Description** and then click **Next**:
4. Now, check the boxes against these settings:

   Local Security Policies Options: **Accounts Enable Administrator Account Status**

   Local Security Policies Options: **Accounts Rename Administrator Account**

5. Enable the account, and if you want, change its name under **Accounts Rename Administrator Account**.
6. Now, assign the policy; this is device level, so choose a device group or **All devices**.
7. Then, create the policy by clicking **Create**.

That completes the steps for configuring LAPS with the built-in admin account.

Creating a new account

If you want to create a new account, the only way currently is to use a custom OMA-URI, as described in *Chapter 2*. We will configure this now:

1. In the console, we want to create a new **Custom profile**.

2. As usual, specify its **Name** and **Description**.

3. On the next page, we need to add two new rows.

   The first one is to create the new user with an **OMA-URI** value of `./Device/Vendor/MSFT/Accounts/Users/lapsadmin/Password`, where `lapsadmin` is your username to be created.

   Data type needs to be a string, and the value is the initial password for the account:

Name *	Create-User
Description	Create lapsadmin and set password
OMA-URI *	./Device/Vendor/MSFT/Accounts/Users/lapsad...
Data type	String
Value *	myincrediblysecretpassword

Figure 3.7– New Account Policy – New User Setting

4. The second row is to add the user to the administrators group on the machines.

   This one uses an **OMA-URI** value of `./Device/Vendor/MSFT/Accounts/Users/lapsadmin/LocalUserGroup`, where, again, `lapsadmin` is the user account.

   Set it to **Integer** with **Value** set to 2:

Figure 3.8– New Account Policy – Admin Group Setting

5. Once you have added these two settings, click **Next**.

6. Now, on the **Assignment** tab, target devices, not users.

7. Click **Next** on the **Applicability Rules** page since we do not need any.

8. Review and click **Create**.

After creating our user or enabling the built-in admin, we can create the LAPS policy itself.

Creating the LAPS policy

Now that our user account has been enabled or created, we need to configure the LAPS policy itself by performing the following steps:

1. For this, navigate to **Endpoint security | Account protection | Create policy**.

2. Select **Windows 10 and later** and **Local admin password solution (Windows LAPS)**.

3. Set the policy's **Name** and **Description**.

4. On the next screen, we have the following fields:

    - **Backup Directory**: We are only using AAD for our devices, so that is what we need here

    - **Password Age Days**: This is worth setting and depends on your security posture

    - **Administrator Account Name**: If you renamed or created a new account, configure this and enter the name of the account

    - **Password Complexity**: Always select the most complex

    - **Password Length**: 20 or more characters makes it pretty much uncrackable

    - **Post Authentication Actions**: You can either reset the password only, force a logoff, or force a reboot, whichever works best for your environment

    - **Post Authentication Reset Delay**: Here, you can specify how many hours after using the password you want it to reset (defaults to 24)

5. Once configured, click **Next**.

6. On the **Scope tags** page, click **Next**.

7. Once configured, assign the policy to your devices and click **Next**.

8. Review the settings and click **Create**.

Once your machines have collected the policy, navigating to them will show the details of the current password and when it is due to rotate.

That completes the LAPS policy configuration.

Accessing and rotating passwords

Now that our devices are using LAPS, we need to be able to view and rotate the passwords. While we have not enrolled any devices into this tenant, we will use a different tenant to demonstrate this here. Follow these steps to retrieve and rotate the passwords:

1. Navigate to **Devices | Windows** and then select one of your devices.

2. Once you are in the device's details, click on **Local admin password**.

    Here, you can click the blue **Show local administrator password** button to view the password for the device.

3. To reset the password, click on the **Overview** option for the device.

4. Now, click the three dots on the far right-hand side of the **Actions** bar and select **Rotate local admin password**.

5. Finally, click **Yes** to rotate.

Now that we have learned how to configure and use LAPS in the UI, we can cover automating it.

Automating it

Fortunately, all of the preceding steps in this recipe can be automated using Graph alone, even the Entra ID part!

As always, the full script can be found in this book's GitHub repository.

Entra ID

Starting with Entra ID, we need to enable the LAPS setting:

1. Set the URL and grab the current settings. This one needs all the settings when amending, so we cannot send a simple command to change one setting – we have to change it in the array and then pass the array back again. Here, we are leaving Intune (the `deviceManagement`

Graph category) and moving into Entra ID *policies*. The relevant settings are within the `deviceRegistrationPolicy` sub-category:

```
$checkuri = "https://graph.microsoft.com/beta/policies/
deviceRegistrationPolicy"
$currentpolicy = Invoke-MgGraphRequest -Method GET -Uri
$checkuri -OutputType PSObject -ContentType "application/json"
```

2. Set the `localAdminPassword.isEnabled` array value from `False` to `True`. To do this, we must grab the entire policy; the value we need is within a nested array. We can dig into that array by using `.`:

    ```
    $currentpolicy.localAdminPassword.isEnabled = $true
    ```

    Setting the value within the nested array will automatically update the master array with the new settings.

3. We converted the output into a PowerShell object to manipulate. So, now, we need to convert it back into JSON:

    ```
    $policytojson = $currentpolicy | ConvertTo-Json
    ```

4. Now, we can re-configure the settings with a PUT command:

    ```
    Invoke-MgGraphRequest -Method PUT -Uri $checkuri -Body
    $policytojson -ContentType "application/json"
    ```

That completes the Entra ID configuration to enable LAPS.

Enabling the local admin and renaming

If you went down this route, as we found earlier, it is a Settings catalog policy under the **Local Policy Security Options** category with an ID of **914a31d0-ae3b-4ae5-bd31-504b9f0b91df**.

Looking through the settings, you can find the setting name and values in the `Options` array. In the case of enabling the account, we have `1` for enable and `0` for disable:

```
device_vendor_msft_policy_config_localpoliciessecurityoptions_
accounts_enableadministratoraccountstatus_1
device_vendor_msft_policy_config_localpoliciessecurityoptions_
accounts_enableadministratoraccountstatus_0
```

For our policy, do the following:

1. Set the account name you wish to use:

    ```
    $accountname = ""
    ```

2. Set the URL:

```
$createurl = "https://graph.microsoft.com/beta/deviceManagement/
configurationPolicies"
```

3. Configure the JSON:

```
$createjson = @"
{
    "description": "Enable and Rename account",
    "name": "Enable Administrator Account",
    "platforms": "windows10",
    "roleScopeTagIds": [
        "0"
    ],
    "settings": [
        {
            "@odata.type": "#microsoft.graph.
deviceManagementConfigurationSetting",
            "settingInstance": {
                "@odata.type": "#microsoft.graph.
deviceManagementConfigurationChoiceSettingInstance",
                "choiceSettingValue": {
                    "@odata.type": "#microsoft.graph.
deviceManagementConfigurationChoiceSettingValue",
                    "children": [],
                    "value": "device_vendor_msft_
policy_config_localpoliciessecurityoptions_accounts_
enableadministratoraccountstatus_1"
                },
                "settingDefinitionId": "device_vendor_
msft_policy_config_localpoliciessecurityoptions_accounts_
enableadministratoraccountstatus"
            }
        },
        {
            "@odata.type": "#microsoft.graph.
deviceManagementConfigurationSetting",
            "settingInstance": {
                "@odata.type": "#microsoft.graph.
deviceManagementConfigurationSimpleSettingInstance",
                "settingDefinitionId": "device_vendor_
msft_policy_config_localpoliciessecurityoptions_accounts_
renameadministratoraccount",
                "simpleSettingValue": {
                    "@odata.type": "#microsoft.graph.
deviceManagementConfigurationStringSettingValue",
```

```
                  "value": "$accountname"
               }
            }
         }
      ],
      "technologies": "mdm"
   }
   "@
```

4. Create the policy:

```
$createpolicy = Invoke-MgGraphRequest -Method POST -Uri
$createurl -Body $createjson -OutputType PSObject -ContentType
"application/json"
```

5. Grab the ID and assign it. In this case, we are using the **All Devices** option, which, rather than using the Group ID, uses "#microsoft.graph.allDevicesAssignmentTarget". For devices, it would be "#microsoft.graph.allUsersAssignmentTarget":

```
$createpolicyid = $createpolicy.id

$createassignurl = "https://graph.microsoft.com/beta/
deviceManagement/configurationPolicies/$createpolicyid/assign"
$createassignjson = @"
{
    "assignments": [
        {
            "target": {
                "@odata.type": "#microsoft.graph.
allDevicesAssignmentTarget"
            }
        }
    ]
}
"@
Invoke-MgGraphRequest -Method POST -Uri $createassignurl -Body
$createassignjson -ContentType "application/json" -OutputType
PSObject
```

This script will enable and rename the local admin account as the first option for using Windows LAPS. Now, we can look at the alternative – creating a new account.

Creating a new account

As this is a custom OMA-URI, the process is a bit more straightforward:

1. First, as we are setting a password, we need a quick function to generate a random, secure one. There are multiple ways to do this; here, we are using built-in commands to generate one:

```
function Get-RandomPassword {
    param (
        [Parameter(Mandatory)]
        [int] $length,
        [int] $amountOfNonAlphanumeric = 1
    )
    Add-Type -AssemblyName 'System.Web'
    return [System.Web.Security.
Membership]::GeneratePassword($length, $amountOfNonAlphanumeric)
}
$password = Get-RandomPassword -Length 20
```

2. Now, set the URL:

```
$customurl = "https://graph.microsoft.com/beta/deviceManagement/
deviceConfigurations"
```

3. Populate the JSON. It is a new policy, so the ID is effectively blank:

```
$customjson = @"
{
    "@odata.type": "#microsoft.graph.
windows10CustomConfiguration",
    "description": "Creates a new user to be used with LAPS",
    "displayName": "Windows-LAPS-User",
    "id": "00000000-0000-0000-0000-000000000000",
    "omaSettings": [
        {
            "@odata.type": "#microsoft.graph.omaSettingString",
            "description": "Create lapsadmin and set password",
            "displayName": "Create-User",
            "omaUri": "./Device/Vendor/MSFT/Accounts/
Users/$accountname/Password",
            "value": "$password"
        },
        {
            "@odata.type": "#microsoft.graph.omaSettingInteger",
            "description": "Add to admins",
            "displayName": "Add-to-group",
```

```
            "omaUri": "./Device/Vendor/MSFT/Accounts/
    Users/$accountname/LocalUserGroup",
                "value": 2
            }
        ],
        "roleScopeTagIds": [
            "0"
        ]
    }
    "@
```

4. Create and assign the policy (again, all devices):

```
$policy = Invoke-MgGraphRequest -Method POST -Uri $customurl
-Body $customjson -OutputType PSObject -ContentType
"application/json"
$policyid = $policy.id
$assignurl = "https://graph.microsoft.com/beta/deviceManagement/
deviceConfigurations/$policyid/assign"
$assignjson = @"
{
    "assignments": [
        {
            "target": {
                "@odata.type": "#microsoft.graph.
allDevicesAssignmentTarget"
            }
        }
    ]
}
"@
Invoke-MgGraphRequest -Method POST -Uri $assignurl -Body
$assignjson -ContentType "application/json" -OutputType PSObject
```

This script will create a new administrator account for use with LAPS. Now, we can create the policy itself.

LAPS policy

Before starting, let us look at how the script works. This runs from a template that can be found by running a GET request at https://graph.microsoft.com/beta/deviceManagement/configurationPolicyTemplates/adc46e5a-f4aa-4ff6-aeff-4f27bc525796_1.

A list of the settings can be found at https://graph.microsoft.com/beta/deviceManagement/configurationPolicyTemplates/adc46e5a-f4aa-4ff6-aeff-4f27bc525796_1/settingTemplates.

As it has several settings, check this book's GitHub repository for the full values. This example will just include one setting:

1. First, we have the policy. We will set its URL:

```
$lapsurl = "https://graph.microsoft.com/beta/deviceManagement/
configurationPolicies"
```

2. Set the JSON:

```
$lapsjson = @"
{
    "description": "Uses lapsadmin created via custom OMA-URI
policy",
    "name": "LAPS Config",
    "platforms": "windows10",
    "roleScopeTagIds": [
        "0"
    ],
    "settings": [
        {
            "@odata.type": "#microsoft.graph.
deviceManagementConfigurationSetting",
            "settingInstance": {
                "@odata.type": "#microsoft.graph.
deviceManagementConfigurationChoiceSettingInstance",
                "choiceSettingValue": {
                    "@odata.type": "#microsoft.graph.
deviceManagementConfigurationChoiceSettingValue",
                    "children": [
                        {
                            "@odata.type": "#microsoft.graph.
deviceManagementConfigurationSimpleSettingInstance",
                            "settingDefinitionId": "device_
vendor_msft_laps_policies_passwordagedays_aad",
                            "simpleSettingValue": {
                                "@odata.type": "#microsoft.
graph.deviceManagementConfigurationIntegerSettingValue",
                                "value": 30
                            }
                        }
                    ],
                    "settingValueTemplateReference": {
                        "settingValueTemplateId": "4d90f03d-
e14c-43c4-86da-681da96a2f92"
                    },
                    "value": "device_vendor_msft_laps_policies_
```

```
backupdirectory_1"
                    },
                "settingDefinitionId": "device_vendor_msft_laps_
policies_backupdirectory",
                "settingInstanceTemplateReference": {
                    "settingInstanceTemplateId": "a3270f64-e493-
499d-8900-90290f61ed8a"
                }
            }
        }
    ],
    "technologies": "mdm",
    "templateReference": {
        "templateId": "adc46e5a-f4aa-4ff6-aeff-4f27bc525796_1"
    }
}
"@
```

3. Create and assign the policy:

```
$lapspolicy = Invoke-MgGraphRequest -Method POST -Uri $lapsurl
-Body $lapsjson -ContentType "application/json" -OutputType
PSObject
$lapspolicyid = $lapspolicy.id
$lapsassignurl = "https://graph.microsoft.com/beta/
deviceManagement/configurationPolicies/$lapspolicyid/assign"
$lapsassignjson = @"
{
    "assignments": [
        {
            "target": {
                "@odata.type": "#microsoft.graph.
allDevicesAssignmentTarget"
            }
        }
    ]
}
"@
Invoke-MgGraphRequest -Method POST -Uri $lapsassignurl -Body
$lapsassignjson -ContentType "application/json"
```

That concludes the creation of the LAPS policy. Now, let us learn how to retrieve and rotate the passwords.

Accessing and rotating passwords

Now that our LAPS policy has been configured, we need to access the passwords for real-world usage:

1. First, we can look at accessing a password. For this, we need the device ID, which we can retrieve from the address bar in the GUI:

https://intune.microsoft.com/#view/Microsoft_Intune_Devices/DeviceSettingsMenuBlade/~/overview/mdmDeviceId/8e0e7e4d-f6cf-4a52-8429-b87848d237fe

Figure 3.9 – Device ID

2. We can add this to the script:

    ```
    $deviceid = "xxxxxxxx-xxxx-xxxx-xxxx-xxxxxxxxxxxx"
    ```

    Or, to avoid using the GUI, we can grab all of our devices:

    ```
    $alldevices = (Invoke-MgGraphRequest -Method GET -Uri "https://
    graph.microsoft.com/beta/deviceManagement/managedDevices"
    -OutputType PSObject).value
    ```

3. Output them into a grid view (with passthrough):

    ```
    $selecteddevice = $alldevices | Out-GridView -PassThru -Title
    "Devices"
    ```

4. Then, select the ID:

    ```
    $deviceid = $selecteddevice.id
    ```

5. Now, we need to add this to the URL. We are using the deviceLocalCredentials category here. The URL must be structured slightly differently as we have both ? and a $ characters, which are reserved in PowerShell. Therefore, we must split the $deviceid variable and add a backtick (`) before $select so that it treats the variable as a raw string:

    ```
    $url = "https://graph.microsoft.com/beta/
    deviceLocalCredentials/" + $deviceid + "?`$select=credentials"
    ```

6. Now, we can grab all the credentials and put them in a variable:

    ```
    $lapspassword = (Invoke-MgGraphRequest -Method GET -Uri $url
    -OutputType PSObject).credentials
    ```

    The account name is straightforward:

    ```
    $accountName = $lapspassword.accountName
    ```

The password is slightly more tricky as it is `Base64` encoded, so we need to wrap that in the `.Net` function to `base64` decode from a string:

```
$password = [System.Text.Encoding]::UTF8.GetString([System.
Convert]::FromBase64String(($lapspassword.passwordBase64)))
```

7. Now, simply output them:

```
write-host "Account Name: $accountName"
write-host "Account Password: $password"
```

Rotating the password is more straightforward:

1. First, using the same device ID as before, add it to the URL:

```
$rotateurl = "https://graph.microsoft.com/beta/deviceManagement/
managedDevices/$deviceid/rotateLocalAdminPassword"
```

This one uses the `managedDevices` category and calls the `rotateLocalAdminPassword` command within it.

2. While it is a `POST` command, it does not need a payload to be attached, so the command is as follows:

```
Invoke-MgGraphRequest -Method POST -Uri $rotateurl -OutputType
PSObject
```

With that, we have configured, deployed, and managed LAPS using PowerShell.

Configuring Application Control

A new feature to Intune is **Application Control**, which extends the **Windows Defender Application Control (WDAC)** functionality but with an easier deployment.

There are two methods of deploying Application Control – via a GUI with boxes to select and using an XML file created for WDAC.

For this example, we will be using the GUI method, but if you would rather have more granular control, you can use the WDAC wizard from Microsoft to assist in creating the file.

You can read more about that here: `https://learn.microsoft.com/en-us/windows/security/threat-protection/windows-defender-application-control/wdac-wizard`.

How to do it...

Before we can create our policy, we need to activate Managed Installer. This allows the Intune Management extension to install applications without restrictions. Follow these steps to configure it in your environment:

1. Click on **Endpoint Security** and then **App Control for Business**.

2. At the top, click the **Managed installer** tab and click **Add**.

3. In the fly-out panel, click **Add**.

4. Press **Yes** to confirm you wish to **Add managed installer**.

5. Now that this has been enabled, we can create our policy. Click **App Control for Business**, then **Create Policy**.

    Things will look familiar now as this uses the standard **Unified Settings catalog** underneath.

6. Specify your policy's **Name** and **Description** and click **Next**.

7. On the next screen, we are going to use the GUI. So, for **Configuration settings format**, select **Use built-in controls**.

    This will change the display in terms of some options (again, this will look similar to Settings catalog):

    - **Enable app control policy to trust Windows components and Store apps**: The only options here are **Enforce** and **Audit**. Setting it to **Audit** will record events, but not block any applications from running.

    - Select additional rules for trusting apps:

        - **Trust apps with good reputation**: This approves applications trusted by Microsoft Intelligent Security Graph.

        - **Trust apps from managed installers**: This uses AppLocker to allow certain installers, such as Configuration Manager. You can read more here: `https://learn.microsoft.com/en-gb/windows/security/threat-protection/windows-defender-application-control/configure-authorized-apps-deployed-with-a-managed-installer`.

    In this example, we will keep everything restricted to Intune only, so leave the two additional rules empty. Once you have configured settings for your environment, click **Next**.

8. We do not need scope tags here, so click **Next**.

   While we wish to assign all security policies at the device level, this is an exception to the rule. If we assign this to all devices, *all* applications will need to be deployed via Intune, even single apps required by IT for troubleshooting or one-off installations. To avoid this, we are going to assign at the user level so that we can add exceptions for IT support staff as required. Populate the groups as required and click **Next**.

9. Finally, review that everything looks correct and click **Create**.

With that, we have configured Application Control in the UI.

Automating it

There are two steps to automating this – enabling the installer and creating the policy.

We will start with the installer. Follow these steps to enable it:

1. To find out if it is already enabled, we can run a GET command against this URL:

   ```
   https://graph.microsoft.com/beta/deviceAppManagement/
   windowsManagementApp/
   ```

2. Check the value of managedInstaller in the response. If it is enabled, you do not have to complete this step.

   If it is not enabled, we simply need to send an empty payload POST request to a URL:

   ```
   $posturl = "https://graph.microsoft.com/beta/
   deviceAppManagement/windowsManagementApp/setAsManagedInstaller"
   Invoke-MgGraphRequest -Method POST -Uri $posturl -Body $body
   -OutputType PSObject
   ```

   Now that this has been enabled, the next step will be similar – we must deploy a Settings catalog policy. The GitHub repository contains a more complex script that configures the JSON for either a GUI or XML setup, but for this example, we will simply replicate what we have created in the web interface:

3. First, we need some variables. We are also including variables for the options we have selected:

   ```
   $url = "https://graph.microsoft.com/beta/deviceManagement/
   configurationPolicies"
   $name = "Application Control"
   $description = "Application Control Policy"
   $groupid = "00000000000"
   $managedinstallers = "false"
   $trustedinstallers = "false"
   $windowsappcontrol = "enable"
   ```

4. Now, we must add that to the JSON (the script is available on GitHub).

There is no mention of the three variables we set as these change the layout of the JSON. Switching the first option to **Audit** changes the settings value to the following:

```
device_vendor_msft_policy_config_applicationcontrol_built_in_
controls_enable_app_control_1
```

If we activate either of the other two settings, new child entries will be added to the JSON – both with the same setting but with slightly different values.

5. For managed installers, use the following code:

```
{
        "@odata.type": "#microsoft.graph.
deviceManagementConfigurationChoiceSettingValue",
        "children": [],
        "value": "device_vendor_msft_policy_config_
applicationcontrol_built_in_controls_trust_apps_1"
}
```

6. For trusted installers, use the following code:

```
{
        "@odata.type": "#microsoft.graph.
deviceManagementConfigurationChoiceSettingValue",
        "children": [],
        "value": "device_vendor_msft_policy_config_
applicationcontrol_built_in_controls_trust_apps_0"
}
```

The GitHub script will automate this for you based on your selections.

With that, we have learned how to automate the process of configuring Application Control.

4

Setting Up Enrollment and Updates for Windows

Now that we have our security and configuration policies in place for our Windows devices, we are almost ready to enroll our first device (we will cover application deployment in *Chapter 11, Packaging Your Windows Applications*, but that is not essential for enrollment).

Before we start enrollment, we have to consider that we are working with devices directly from the manufacturer/distributor that could have been sitting in a warehouse or on a container ship for several months. Therefore, it makes sense to configure our Windows update policies ahead of enrollment so that we can sleep safely at night, knowing that even a newly provisioned device will be kept up to date.

In this chapter, we will look at configuring update rings manually and using **Windows Update for Business** (**WUfB**) as well as **Windows Autopatch**, which you can think of as *Windows Updates as a Service*, where Microsoft does the heavy lifting for you.

Once we have our updates in place, we can look at configuring enrollment profiles and finally enrolling devices.

This chapter will include the following recipes:

- Building your update rings – including feature and quality updates
- Configuring driver updates
- Enrolling and using Autopatch
- Configuring Windows Hello for Business
- Setting up Windows Autopilot Enrollment Profiles
- Configuring an **Enrollment Status Page** (**ESP**)
- Enrolling your Windows device

Technical requirements

For this chapter, you will need a modern web browser and a PowerShell code editor such as **Visual Studio Code** (**VS Code**) or PowerShell ISE.

All of the scripts that are referenced in this chapter can be found here: `https://github.com/ PacktPublishing/Microsoft-Intune-Cookbook`.

Building your update rings – including feature and quality updates

With fully managed machines, the last thing you want is them updating themselves without any control over when they receive updates and which updates to receive, and you especially do not want users opting into insider builds themselves.

If you do not have Windows Enterprise licensing to utilize Autopatch (covered in the next recipe) or would just rather manage the updates yourself, you are going to need to configure some update rings.

Getting ready

Before building the rings, navigate to the Entra ID portal and create some Entra ID (static) groups. We will populate these with devices to assign to each of the rings.

Create four groups:

- 1 for Preview devices.
- 1 for Pilot devices.
- 1 for VIP devices.
- 1 for everything else (broad ring). This could be a dynamic group to save on admin overhead.

Once you have created these groups, navigate to the Intune portal; we will be using the **Update Rings**, **Feature updates**, and **Quality updates** options.

When populating the rings, make sure you add devices to the Preview and Pilot groups. You will often have IT staff in these groups who log into other machines to do repairs and troubleshooting. The last thing you want is for a user to log in and switch a broad ring device on for a pre-release build! You will want some non-IT staff in your non-insider builds as well for some real-world feedback, as you may find that IT staff, especially with administrative rights, simply fix any issues themselves, which will not be an option with standard users.

How to do it...

In this recipe, we are going to create four update rings and a feature update policy. As the update rings are the same but with just different release dates, the screenshots will be combined in places to save repeating content.

Building your update rings

Follow these steps:

1. Navigate to **Devices**, click **Windows**, and select **Update rings for Windows 10 and later**.

2. In the **Update Rings for Windows 10 and later** menu, click **Create profile**.

3. Specify descriptive **Name** and **Description** value. This is especially important here so that you can quickly differentiate them.

4. Now, we need to configure our settings. A lot of these will be dependent on your environment, so we will have a look at what they all are and the recommended settings for each of the rings:

> **UI tip**
> The default options are set to blue and switch to purple upon configuration. If you revert a change, they will remain purple.

- **Microsoft Product updates**: This enables Windows Update. We need this to be enabled.

- **Windows drivers**: This allows Windows Update to search for and install drivers onto the machine. If you would prefer to use vendor-specific apps for this, simply block here.

- **Quality update deferral period**: This allows you to specify the number of days after Patch Tuesday when quality updates will be installed. Check out *Table 4.1* for recommended values.

- **Feature update deferral period**: Set this to 0 so that we can use the feature update policy. Anything other than 0 and Intune will ignore the extra policy.

- **Upgrade Windows 10 devices to the latest Windows 11 release**: Windows 10 is out of support in October 2025, so this is recommended. However, it depends on your upgrade readiness, so set it accordingly.

- **Set feature update uninstall period**: How many days will you allow a rollback after the update has been installed (for your deferred installations, it is the number of days after the deferral period).

- **Enable pre-release builds**: You will need these for your Pilot and Preview rings; check *Table 4.1*. Some details about the different channels can be found in *Figure 4.1*:

Pre-Release Channels

Channel	Dev Channel	Beta Channel	Release Preview Channel
Suggested Users	Very technical users, a few key members of IT team, ideally on test machines.	Early adopters, usually IT staff, but on non-test machines for more real-world testing	Key power-users
Group Type	Device based	Device based	Device
Description	This is the very latest Windows builds at the very early stages of the development lifecycle and should be used for testing.	These builds are more than likely going to become full releases, but may have some issues.	Access releases a few weeks early to fully test the user experience and applications. Best for key users across the estate.
Concerns	More likely to crash. Regular updates which may require restarts. Some features may appear and then be removed.	Updates are validated. More stable than dev channel.	Fully supported builds, no concerns over a standard release
Update Ring	Pilot (or earlier)	Pilot	Preview

Figure 4.1 – Pre-release channels

- **Automatic update behavior**: Here, you can set when updates are downloaded and installed, including active hours. If you select **Reset to default**, the machine will detect the active hours and install accordingly. Set this as appropriate for your environment (for example, 7:00 A.M. to 7:00 P.M. for your standard office workers).

- **Restart Checks**: Checks whether battery life is over 40%, a user is at the machine, it is not in presentation mode, a full-screen app, mid-phone call, mid-game, and so on.

- **Option to pause Windows updates**: You can pause centrally. This happens at the user level.

- **Option to check for Windows updates**: Allows or stops users from checking for updates.
- **Use deadline settings**: This forces updates to be installed, provides a grace period, and allows auto-updates. It is usually best to turn this on so that you can force a reboot on end user devices so that they cannot constantly postpone and leave the devices at risk.

As mentioned earlier, here are some recommended settings:

	Pilot Ring	**Preview Ring**	**Broad Ring**	**VIP Ring**
Service Channel	Beta	Release preview	Retail	Retail
Quality Deferral	0	7 days	10 days	30 days
Feature Deferral	0	0	0	0

Table 4.1 – Windows Update recommended settings

5. Once you have configured your settings, click **Next**.

6. Now, we need to assign the policy. For our Pilot, Preview, and VIP policies, it is a straightforward process – simply assign them to the groups we created earlier.

7. Once you have added your assignments, click **Next**.

We need the broad ring to collect *everything* not in any of the other rings so that we can ensure all of the devices are being updated. So, we will create an included assignment under **Autopilot Devices** but exclude the other rings:

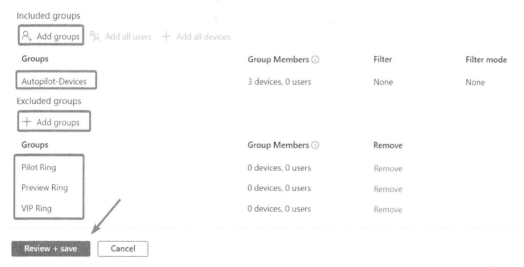

Figure 4.2 – Broad update ring assignment

As mentioned earlier, ensure that your Preview/Pilot groups contain devices!

8. Review your settings and click **Create**.

    VIP ring is for your mission-critical devices (and often executive users) and is where you want full control over when they install and reboot.

    Often, it is best to disable forced reboot and set a maintenance window where someone can be present at the machine to ensure everything installs and reboots OK. All deferrals are set to maximum as well to give the maximum time to test updates first.

Now that we have created our Windows update rings, we need to configure feature update rings that match.

Building feature updates

Now that we have the update rings in place, we need to look after the feature updates as we set all deferrals to 0 days; otherwise, the machines are all going to upgrade to Windows 11 or any new semi-annual release on the following Patch Tuesday:

1. Within the Intune portal, click **Devices | Windows | Feature Updates for Windows 10 and later**, then **Create profile**.

    Generally, you want your devices to be on a fixed version across the estate, but should you have specific requirements, you can create multiple profiles here and include/exclude them accordingly.

    For this example, we will set devices to the current latest Windows 11 22H2 version. This policy will bring all devices to Windows 11 22H2 and fix them there until we update the policy. When 23H2 is released, the devices will remain on 22H2 unless this policy is updated accordingly:

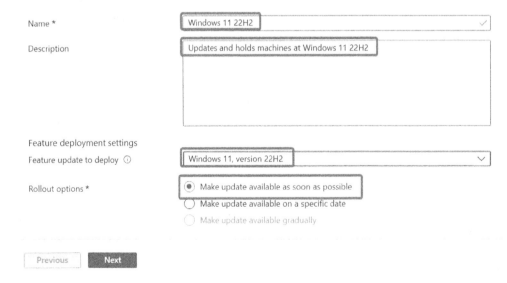

Figure 4.3 – Feature update settings

Note that the feature update list only includes operating system versions that are in their support date, so if you are running anything pre-Windows 10 21H1, your machines are going to upgrade to whatever you set here.

You can also specify the rollout options to gradually deploy for larger estates. You can also create multiple policies with specific dates and use your assignment groups to target should you want more control.

2. Once you have configured these settings, click **Next**.

3. To align everything, assign the policies to **Autopilot Devices** to capture everything in the estate. Then, click **Next**.

4. Now, review your policy and click **Create**.

Now that we have configured our update settings in the UI, we can look at how to automate it.

Automating it

In this section, we will cover how to automate our update rings and feature updates for quicker, more reliable deployments.

Building update rings

There is a lot of repetition when creating all of these policies. So, for this example, we will use the broad ring as that is the most complex to assign.

A PowerShell script is included in this book's GitHub repository that will deploy and assign all four of the update rings; you can amend the JSON based on the knowledge you will have picked up configuring this one. Run these scripts in a PowerShell editor of your choice; remember to connect to Microsoft Graph first:

1. As usual, start with our variables – in this case, group IDs:

```
$pilotgroupid = "xxxxxxxx-xxxx-xxxx-xxxx-xxxxxxxxxxxx"
$previewgroupid = "xxxxxxxx-xxxx-xxxx-xxxx-xxxxxxxxxxxx"
$broadgroupid = "xxxxxxxx-xxxx-xxxx-xxxx-xxxxxxxxxxxx"
$vipgroupid = "xxxxxxxx-xxxx-xxxx-xxxx-xxxxxxxxxxxx"
```

2. Now, set the URL to create the policy:

```
$url = "https://graph.microsoft.com/beta/deviceManagement/
deviceConfigurations"
```

3. Set the JSON:

```
$broadjson = @"
{
```

```
    "@odata.type": "#microsoft.graph.
windowsUpdateForBusinessConfiguration",
    "allowWindows11Upgrade": true,
    "automaticUpdateMode": "autoInstallAtMaintenanceTime",
    "autoRestartNotificationDismissal": "notConfigured",
    "businessReadyUpdatesOnly": "userDefined",
    "deadlineForFeatureUpdatesInDays": 5,
    "deadlineForQualityUpdatesInDays": 5,
    "deadlineGracePeriodInDays": 3,
    "description": "",
    "displayName": "Windows Updates - Broad Ring",
    "driversExcluded": false,
    "engagedRestartDeadlineInDays": null,
    "engagedRestartSnoozeScheduleForFeatureUpdatesInDays": null,
    "engagedRestartSnoozeScheduleInDays": null,
    "engagedRestartTransitionScheduleForFeatureUpdatesInDays":
null,
    "engagedRestartTransitionScheduleInDays": null,
    "featureUpdatesDeferralPeriodInDays": 0,
    "featureUpdatesPaused": false,
    "featureUpdatesRollbackWindowInDays": 10,
    "id": "",
    "installationSchedule": {
        "@odata.type": "#microsoft.graph.
windowsUpdateActiveHoursInstall",
        "activeHoursEnd": "17:00:00.0000000",
        "activeHoursStart": "08:00:00.0000000"
    },
    "microsoftUpdateServiceAllowed": true,
    "postponeRebootUntilAfterDeadline": false,
    "qualityUpdatesDeferralPeriodInDays": 10,
    "qualityUpdatesPaused": false,
    "roleScopeTagIds": [],
    "scheduleImminentRestartWarningInMinutes": null,
    "scheduleRestartWarningInHours": null,
    "skipChecksBeforeRestart": false,
    "updateNotificationLevel": "restartWarningsOnly",
    "updateWeeks": null,
    "userPauseAccess": "enabled",
    "userWindowsUpdateScanAccess": "enabled"
}
"@
```

Here, you can see that `"allowWindows11Upgrade"` is set to `true`, so we are not blocking that one.

The preceding code also sets active hours, deadlines, notifications, and all of the other settings we configured in the GUI. Fortunately, these are all fairly well named, so you can work out what is being set and how to change it as needed.

The only thing to watch here are some of the double negatives. If you look at `driversExclude`, setting that to `false` will allow driver updates because we are saying no to a block. If we set `allowWindows11Upgrade` to `true`, this will allow them:

1. Now, create the policy and grab the ID:

    ```
    $broadpolicy = Invoke-MgGraphRequest -Uri $url -Method Post
    -Body $broadjson -ContentType "application/json" -OutputType
    PSObject
    $broadpolicyid = $broadpolicy.id
    ```

2. Populate the ID with the assignment URL:

    ```
    $broadassignurl = "https://graph.microsoft.com/beta/
    deviceManagement/deviceConfigurations/$broadpolicyid/assign"
    ```

3. Then, set the JSON:

    ```
    $broadjsonassign = @"
    {
        "assignments": [
            {
                "target": {
                    "@odata.type": "#microsoft.graph.
    groupAssignmentTarget",
                    "groupId": "$broadgroupid"
                }
            },
            {
                "target": {
                    "@odata.type": "#microsoft.graph.
    exclusionGroupAssignmentTarget",
                    "groupId": "$pilotgroupid"
                }
            },
            {
                "target": {
                    "@odata.type": "#microsoft.graph.
    exclusionGroupAssignmentTarget",
                    "groupId": "$previewgroupid"
                }
            },
            {
    ```

```
            "target": {
                "@odata.type": "#microsoft.graph.
exclusionGroupAssignmentTarget",
                "groupId": "$vipgroupid"
            }
        }
    ]
}
"@
```

As you can see, we are using both included and excluded groups here. They are differentiated by @odata.type:

```
#microsoft.graph.groupAssignmentTarget - INCLUDED
#microsoft.graph.exclusionGroupAssignmentTarget - EXCLUDED
```

4. Finally, assign the policy:

```
Invoke-MgGraphRequest -Method POST -Uri $broadassignurl -Body
$broadjsonassign -ContentType "application/json"
```

Now that we have automated the update rings, we can look at feature updates.

Building feature updates

While this policy is smaller in terms of code, the update to deploy would normally be taken from the drop-down list in the GUI. So, to avoid having to use that, we are going to grab the options directly from Graph:

1. We still need our fixed variables first:

```
$groupid = "00000000-0000-0000-0000-000000000000"
$description = "Fixes machines on Windows 11 22H2"
$displayname = "Windows 11 22H2"
```

2. To find the available versions, we need to run a GET request against this URL: https://graph.microsoft.com/beta/deviceManagement/windowsUpdateCatalogItems/microsoft.graph.windowsFeatureUpdateCatalogItem.

    Then, we can output it in grid view format (you may need to use out-consolegridview on PowerShell Core for non-Windows operating systems) with passthrough enabled so that selections will be sent to our JSON:

```
$allupdatesurl = "https://graph.microsoft.com/beta/
deviceManagement/windowsUpdateCatalogItems/microsoft.graph.
windowsFeatureUpdateCatalogItem"
$availablefeatures = (Invoke-MgGraphRequest -Uri $allupdatesurl
-Method GET -OutputType PSObject).value
```

```
$latest = $availablefeatures | Out-GridView -PassThru
$selected = $latest.version
```

3. Set the URL:

```
$createurl = "https://graph.microsoft.com/beta/deviceManagement/
windowsFeatureUpdateProfiles"
```

4. Create the JSON:

```
$createjson = @"
{
    "description": "$description",
    "displayName": "$displayname",
    "featureUpdateVersion": "$selected",
    "roleScopeTagIds": [],
    "rolloutSettings": {
        "offerEndDateTimeInUTC": null,
        "offerIntervalInDays": null,
        "offerStartDateTimeInUTC": null
    }
}
"@
```

5. Create the policy, grab the ID, and assign it:

```
$policy = Invoke-MgGraphRequest -Method POST -Uri $createurl
-Body $createjson -ContentType "application/json" -OutputType
PSObject
$policyid = $policy.id
$assignurl = "https://graph.microsoft.com/beta/deviceManagement/
windowsFeatureUpdateProfiles/$policyid/assign"
$assignjson = @"
{
    "assignments": [
        {
            "target": {
                "@odata.type": "#microsoft.graph.
groupAssignmentTarget",
                "groupId": "$groupid"
            }
        }
    ]
}
"@
Invoke-MgGraphRequest -Method POST -Uri $assignurl -Body
$assignjson -ContentType "application/json" -OutputType PSObject
```

This script will create a feature update policy using PowerShell and Graph.

There's more…

There might be occasions when you need to expedite quality updates on machines that are considerably out of date.

For this, you can use the **Quality updates** option within Intune.

Normally, your update rings will tackle quality updates without any issues. If you need to rapidly deploy expedited updates, this is configured in the same way as the feature updates we configured earlier.

There are plenty of warnings here, which is why this is for only critical situations.

You can set the minimum update level and then specify when to force an update. The maximum is 2 days, so you can see how urgent these updates are. Users will *not* be allowed to postpone this reboot – you have been warned!

Configuring driver updates

You can also use Intune to gain finer control over driver updates on your devices so that you can include automatic deployments or manual approval before deploying. This will allow you to test drivers for any issues before a full-scale deployment.

Intune will automatically check your estate and populate the drivers as appropriate. If you have chosen not to share telemetry with Microsoft, you will need to do so for driver updates to present themselves.

How to do it…

Follow these steps:

1. First, select **Devices** and then **Windows 10 and later updates**.
2. Now, click **Driver updates for Windows 10 and later** and create a new profile.
3. Specify your profile's **Name** and **Description** and click **Next**.

   Here, you must set if you want updates to be manually approved or automatically updated. Note that you cannot change this setting after configuring it; you will need to delete the profile and create a new one.

4. In this case, we are going to manually manage drivers for greater control. Once selected, click **Next**.

   If you select **Automatic**, you will be given a second prompt to set the number of days before drivers are approved.

5.   We are not setting scope tags in this example, so click **Next**.

Assignments are very much device-based policies, so it is best to assign to **Device groups** until filters are available.

In this case, we are going to assign to Autopilot devices.

6.   Confirm that everything looks correct and click **Create**.

With that, we have created a driver update policy in the UI. Now, we can look at our automation process.

Automating it

This is one of the easiest policies to automate as it only has one real setting whose options are *manual* and *automatic*.

It sends a POST request to deviceManagement/windowsdDriverUpdateProfiles. Follow these steps:

1.   As usual, we will start with the basics:

```
$name = "Driver Updates"
$description = "Driver Update Management"
$groupid = "000000-0000-0000-0000-000000000000"
```

2.   Now, configure the approval type:

```
$driversetting = "manual"
```

3.   Set the URL:

```
$url = "https://graph.microsoft.com/beta/deviceManagement/
windowsDriverUpdateProfiles"
```

4.   Populate the JSON:

```
$json = @"
{
    "approvalType": "$driversetting",
    "description": "$description",
    "displayName": "$name",
    "roleScopeTagIds": [
        "0"
    ]
}
"@
```

As mentioned earlier, if you select **Automatic**, you also need to set the number of days before approval:

```
"approvalType": "automatic",
"deploymentDeferralInDays": 3,
```

5. Create the profile and grab the ID:

```
$driverpolicy = Invoke-MgGraphRequest -Method POST -uri $url
-body $json -ContentType "application/json" -OutputType PSObject
$policyid = $driverpolicy.id
```

6. Populate the URL and JSON and assign them:

```
$assignurl = "https://graph.microsoft.com/beta/deviceManagement/
windowsDriverUpdateProfiles/$policyid/assign"
$assignjson = @"
{
    "assignments": [
        {
            "target": {
                "@odata.type": "#microsoft.graph.
groupAssignmentTarget",
                "groupId": "$groupid"
            }
        }
    ]
}
"@
Invoke-MgGraphRequest -Method POST -uri $assignurl -body
$assignjson -ContentType "application/json" -OutputType PSObject
```

With that, you have automated your first driver deployment policy.

There's more...

After a day or two, Intune will retrieve your device details and will show you any outstanding driver updates to review:

Name ↑	Assigned	Approval method	Drivers to review
	✔ Yes	Manual	✔ 0 to review
	✔ Yes	Automatic	✔ 0 to review

Figure 4.4 – Driver approval

Clicking the blue text link under **Drivers to review** will take you to the drivers, where you can approve or pause the updates. When approving, you can select the date for Windows Update to download and install the drivers:

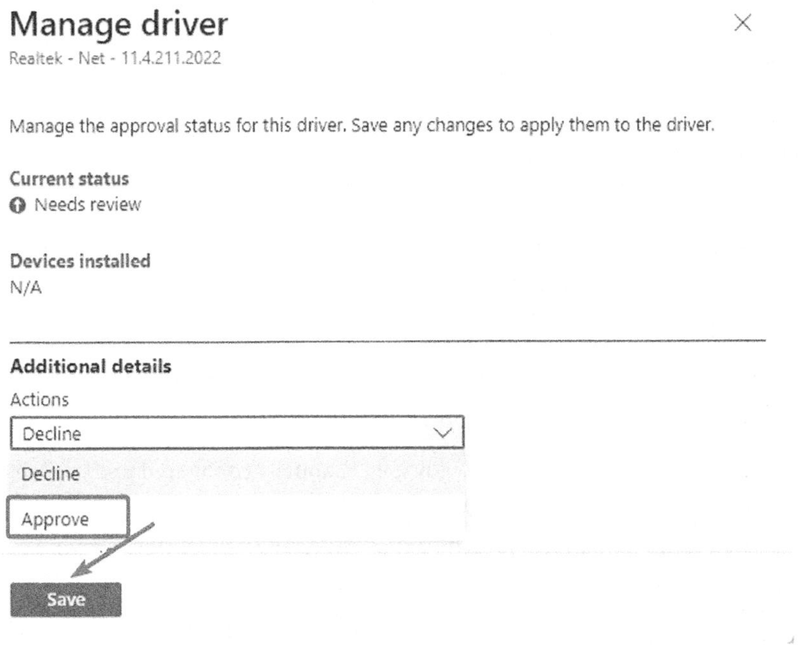

Manage driver ✕

Realtek - Net - 11.4.211.2022

Manage the approval status for this driver. Save any changes to apply them to the driver.

Current status
ⓘ Needs review

Devices installed
N/A

Additional details

Actions

| Decline ∨ |

Decline

Approve

Save

Figure 4.5 – Approving the driver

You can find out more here: `https://learn.microsoft.com/en-us/mem/intune/protect/windows-driver-updates-overview`.

Enrolling and using Autopatch

If you have Windows Enterprise Licensing (Microsoft 365 E3, E5, or Windows E3), instead of manually configuring and populating your Windows update rings, you can use Windows Autopatch from Microsoft. This is a semi-managed service that automates updates for Windows, Microsoft Office, Microsoft Teams, Edge, Drivers, SQL ODBC, and .NET. When using Autopatch, Microsoft can also centrally pause updates so that if it notices a particular update is causing issues, it can block it before it is installed on your devices and then automatically resume it when the issue has been resolved.

As well as the *click-and-forget* option, you can also use Autopatch groups for more granular control over your updates. This will be covered in the *There's more...* section of this recipe.

Getting ready

Before we deploy any configuration, you need to onboard your tenant into the service. For this, you will need two administrative contacts and a user account with global admin access across the tenant.

How to do it...

Follow these steps to enroll your tenant and configure your policies for Windows Autopatch. While we do not have any devices in the tenant at present, we will run through how to enroll your devices as you add them:

1. Navigate to **Tenant admin** and then click on **Tenant Enrollment** under **Windows Autopatch**.

2. Before onboarding, you will need to accept the terms so that the service can do some pre-enrollment checks. Check the box and click **Agree**.

    It will now go and check if your environment is ready for Autopatch and report back accordingly.

3. Click **View Details** to check for errors and advisories.

    The main one here will be if you already have manually configured update rings assigned – it will not let you proceed until they are unassigned or removed.

    Under **Co-Management**, there will be a warning about tenants, but unless you are using Configuration Manager, it can be safely ignored.

    There are also buttons here that you can use to find out what each check is doing and also to re-run checks after making changes.

4. Press the **X** button in the top right to return to the previous screen.

5. Now, click **Enroll**.

6. Microsoft will need to add an app registration to your tenant, so you need to approve that. Check the box and click **Agree**.

7. Enter the details for your first contact and click **Next** (note that the telephone number needs to be in +XX XXXXXXXXXX format with a space between the country code and the rest of the number).

8. Enter the second set of admin details and click **Complete**.

    Autopatch will now configure your tenant.

9. When it has completed, click **Continue**.

    You will now be taken to the Autopatch screen, where you can view your devices and see what update ring(s) they are in. We do not have any devices yet, as the textbox mentions, so we have to add devices to an Entra ID group.

10. To add our devices, navigate to **Groups** in the Intune menu (or you can switch to Entra and access the groups there). Clicking the blue **Windows Autopatch Device Registration** link will take you there directly.

11. Now, find and click **Windows Autopatch Device Registration**:

	Name ↑↓	Object Id
☐	**WA** Windows Autopatch Device Registration	576c690f-acbc-4a47-ae17-9debb8887284

Figure 4.6 – Autopatch Entra ID device registration group

12. Now, click on **Members**.

Fortunately, Entra ID and Autopatch both support group nesting, so we can add our **Autopilot Devices** group here so that all current and future devices will automatically be added.

13. Click **Add members**.

14. Click on **Autopilot Devices** and then click **Select**.

We have not enrolled any devices yet, so we will switch to a pre-configured tenant to show further functionality here.

After adding devices, you will see this screen (accessible via **Devices | Windows Autopatch | Devices**):

Figure 4.7 – Autopatch devices overview

From this screen, you can see the status of devices as well as which deployment rings they are included in.

15. To move or de-register a device, check the box next to it and click the **Device actions** button.

16. On the fly-out screen, you can choose a deployment ring and then click **Save**.

17. Clicking **Not Ready** will show you the devices that are not working with Autopatch.

18. If you click on the device's name, which will be in blue text, you will receive an explanation as to why the device is not ready:

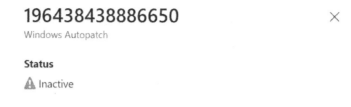

196438438886650

Windows Autopatch

Status

⚠ Inactive

The device has not synchronized with Intune for the past 28 days.

Figure 4.8 – The device's reason for not being ready

19. Clicking the **X** button will close the details window.

20. Now, clicking **Not Registered** will show any devices not enrolled in Autopatch.

21. Again, clicking the device's name will further expand the reasons.

22. To find out what each deployment ring is configured for, navigate to **Devices** and then look at the Autopatch policies in **Update rings for Windows 10 and Later**.

23. The **Feature updates for Windows 10 and Later** page will also appear if the version that is being released is in active support.

24. Finally, navigate to **Devices** and then **Release management** (under **Windows Autopatch**).

25. Clicking **Windows quality updates** or **Windows feature updates** will display the deployment rings and current status.

26. Clicking **Pause** will stop the deployment of your quality or feature update. Simply fill in the form presented and click **OK**.

27. Back on the **Release management** screen, click **Release announcements** to view the details of all of the updates being deployed. A blue hyperlink will appear next to each so that you can find out more.

28. **Release settings** allows you to further customize the configuration, including allowing expedited updates and Microsoft 365 application updates:

Expedited quality updates

Windows Autopatch will
continuously evaluate threat and
vulnerability information of each
new revision of Windows Quality
Update. If determined to be critical
to security, Windows Quality
Updates deployment will be
expedited. You must be a Global
Administrator to make changes to
the setting.

 Allow

Microsoft 365 apps updates

When set to **Allow**, Windows
Autopatch will manage Microsoft
365 apps automatically. To
manage them yourself, select the
switch to turn it off. You must be
an Intune Administrator to make
changes to the setting. Learn more
about Microsoft 365 apps updates.
⤴

 Allow

Windows driver updates

Windows Autopatch will manage
Windows drivers automatically. To
manage them yourself, set the
switch to self-managed. It could
take up to 24 hours for these
changes to go into effect. You
must be an Intune Administrator
to make changes to the setting.
Any previous driver approvals will
be reverted if this setting is
changed. Learn more about driver
updates ⤴.

 Automatic

Figure 4.9 – Autopatch release settings

29. The **Customize** button allows you to change the settings of the deployment rings so that you can change the deployment cadence and notification settings.

30. Change any settings as required (you can set the cadence, deferral period, deadline, and grace period) and click **Save**.

31. Alternatively, change the notification settings (use the default, only restart, or no notifications) and click **Save**.

Following this recipe, we have successfully enrolled our tenant and devices into Windows Autopatch.

Automating it

Windows Autopatch does not use the Microsoft Graph API and runs from the **Microsoft Managed Desktop (MMD)** API instead. While there is a limited API for MMD, it does not include any Autopatch settings. At the time of writing, there is no publicly available API for the Autopatch service.

There's more...

While for most, using Autopatch is an excellent way of letting Microsoft deal with the entire Windows Update service, including patch window (in preview at the time of writing), in larger organizations, you may want more granular control over quality and feature updates (especially when you are planning larger operating system upgrades). For this, you can use Autopatch Groups, which allows you to configure additional update rings and populate them with custom Entra ID groups.

You could use this to deploy by department or building or use hardware-specific details such as make or manufacturer. As these are standard Entra ID groups, you can also use dynamic device queries to automate this for you.

To configure this, navigate to **Devices | Release management** and click **Autopatch groups**.

You can create up to 49 groups on top of the default one, so even larger organizations can use this for a phased rollout.

When adding groups, you can have a minimum of two or a maximum of 15.

To add groups, carry out the following steps:

1. Click **Create**.
2. Set **Name** and **Description** values and click **Next: Deployment rings**.

    On the next screen, you can use **static** or **dynamic** groups, but these differ from the Entra ID groups of the same name.

    For a dynamic group, you can point Autopatch to a single group; it automatically splits the devices between the rings. In this example, we will use static groups as we want as much control as possible.

3. We have created four Entra ID groups – **Test Devices**, **Ring 1**, **Ring 2**, and **Remainder**.
4. On the **Add Autopatch group** screen, click **Add deployment ring** twice to add additional rings.
5. For each ring, click **Add group to ring** and select the groups we created earlier.
6. Once you have added your groups, click **Next: Windows update settings**.
7. Here, you can click the three dots to configure the relevant settings, as covered earlier in this recipe. Once you have done so, click **Next: Review + create**.
8. Confirm that the settings are correct and click **Create**.

That completes our recipe on Windows Autopatch. Now, we can look at Windows Hello for Business.

Configuring Windows Hello for Business

Windows Hello for Business (**WHfB**) provides **multi-factor authentication** (**MFA**) on Windows devices via either PIN, biometrics (face, fingerprint), or a FIDO2 security key.

This can be configured either at a tenant level (via the **Device** Enrollment menu) or at a more granular level using Settings catalog. In this recipe, we will cover both methods, starting with the tenant level, as that needs to be left set to **Not Configured** for Settings catalog to work.

The recommended approach is to use Settings catalog.

How to do it...

We will start this recipe by covering how to enable WHfB in the GUI.

Configuring at the tenant level

Follow these steps:

1. Navigate to **Devices**, then **Enrollment**, and click on the **Windows** tab. Then, click on **Windows Hello for Business**.

    This will load a fly-out window where we can configure the **Configure Windows Hello for Business** and **Use security keys for sign-in** settings.

2. Change **Configure Windows Hello for Business** from **Not configured** to **Enabled**. This will load up further options to be configured.

3. TPM is required for Windows 11 anyway, so it makes sense to require it here as well.

4. The other settings are environment-specific; the options for **Lowercase**, **Uppercase**, and **Special characters** are **Not allowed**, **Allowed**, and **Required**.

5. Here, you can also set a PIN expiry time and how many previous PINs are remembered before they can be re-used. This is a matter of weighing up a secure PIN setup, but it is not too complicated as this results in users either forgetting or, worse still, writing it down.

    One important thing to keep in mind is that this PIN is *only* set on the device. The same PIN will not work on any other devices unless the same PIN was configured while setting up WHfB. This PIN will also not work on any Microsoft 365 apps. If you are using SSO, it will access the machine, which will then send the password to Microsoft 365 apps, but the PIN itself is device-level only. Most environment attacks are remote and not at the device itself.

    If a user gets the PIN wrong more than once, they will be prompted to reboot to attempt another PIN login.

6. The next option is to allow biometric authentication – that is, face and fingerprint. You will still need to set a PIN for recovery when using these options.

7. Anti-spoofing requires specific cameras and adds an extra layer of security when using facial recognition. It is worth enabling when it becomes available.

8. Finally, allow phone sign-in using a supported application on a mobile device (such as Microsoft Authenticator) to act as an authentication method for Windows.

9. The other available setting is **Use security keys for sign-on**, which allows FIDO 2 authentication keys for device login.

10. Once you have configured your settings, click **Save**.

This recipe covered how to enable WHfB at the tenant level, but you may have scenarios where you only want specific user groups to use WHfB. We will look at this next.

Configuring at the group level

As you saw on the previous fly-out, these settings are automatically applied to all users with no way of excluding users. If this does not work for your environment, you can switch the global configuration to **Not configured** (which is the default if it was not previously configured) and use a Settings catalog policy instead:

1. For this, navigate to **Devices**, then **Windows**, then **Configuration profiles**, and click +**Create** and select +**New policy.**

2. Select **Windows 10 and Later**, then **Settings catalog**, and click **Create**.

3. Specify **Name** and **Description** values and click **Next**.

4. Click **Add settings** and find **Windows Hello for Business** toward the bottom of the categories.

   There is a mix of user and device settings in this category, so do not select all settings. Instead, select any settings that apply to your environment. In this case, we are selecting the same settings that we did at a tenant level, plus adding a few features only available here (enhanced anti-spoofing for facial features).

   You could also combine the two, use the tenant-level settings for most, and add to it with a Settings catalog policy; just watch out for conflicts.

5. Once you have configured your settings, click **Next**:

6. On the **Scope tags** page, click **Next**.

7. Assign as required for your environment. Remember that you can duplicate Settings catalog policies to quickly create near-identical policies if needed. Then, click **Next**.

8. Review and click **Create**.

Now that we know how to manually configure this, we can look at how to automate this from the command line.

Automating it

This section will cover how we can configure WHfB using automation.

Configuring at the tenant level

The JSON for this one is very straightforward, but the catch here is that the URL requires the policy ID of the existing WHfB configuration:

1. To do that, we need to run a GET request against the following URL:

    ```
    https://graph.microsoft.com/beta/deviceManagement/
    deviceEnrollmentConfigurations
    ```

2. This will return all of the enrollment and restriction policies, so we need to filter further on our results using where-object and look for the following @odata.type:

    ```
    #microsoft.graph.
    deviceEnrollmentWindowsHelloForBusinessConfiguration
    ```

    Let us wrap all of this so that we only retrieve the ID:

    ```
    $policyid = ((Invoke-MgGraphRequest -Method GET -uri
    "https://graph.microsoft.com/beta/deviceManagement/
    deviceEnrollmentConfigurations" -OutputType PSObject).
    value | where-object '@odata.type' -eq "#microsoft.graph.
    deviceEnrollmentWindowsHelloForBusinessConfiguration").id
    ```

3. Now that we have the ID, we can populate the URL:

    ```
    $url = "https://graph.microsoft.com/beta/deviceManagement/
    deviceEnrollmentConfigurations/$policyid"
    ```

4. Now, we can configure the JSON, which, fortunately, is straightforward and understandable:

    ```
    $json = @"
    {
        "@odata.type": "#microsoft.graph.
    deviceEnrollmentWindowsHelloForBusinessConfiguration",
        "enhancedBiometricsState": "enabled",
        "pinLowercaseCharactersUsage": "allowed",
        "pinPreviousBlockCount": 3,
        "pinSpecialCharactersUsage": "allowed",
        "pinUppercaseCharactersUsage": "allowed",
        "securityDeviceRequired": true,
        "securityKeyForSignIn": "enabled",
        "state": "enabled"
    }
    "@
    ```

5. Finally, deploy it. As it is an existing policy, it is a PATCH request:

```
Invoke-MgGraphRequest -Method PATCH -Uri $url -Body $json
-ContentType "application/json" -OutputType PSObject
```

Now that we have configured WHfB at the tenant level, we can look at the granular approach.

Configuring at the group level

Here, we will use the Settings catalog, which we ran through in *Chapter 2, Configuring Your New Tenant for Windows Devices*. Following on from what we learned there, we need to look at the settings within Category ID:

```
e7ae2b99-0479-475f-af5c-96457121fcd0
```

Some of the values will be true or false, such as Allow Biometrics:

```
device_vendor_msft_passportforwork_biometrics_usebiometrics_true
```

Others will have a 1/0 (Enabled/Disabled) value, such as Use Security Key for Sign-In:

```
device_vendor_msft_passportforwork_securitykey_
usesecuritykeyforsignin_1
```

Those that require a numeric value simply have this set:

```
"value": 3
```

The full script is available in this book's GitHub repository, so we will only configure one setting here:

1. Set the URL as usual:

```
$settingsurl = "https://graph.microsoft.com/beta/
deviceManagement/configurationPolicies"
```

2. Configure the JSON:

```
$json = @"
{
    "description": "",
    "name": "Windows Hello for Business",
    "platforms": "windows10",
    "roleScopeTagIds": [
        "0"
    ],
    "settings": [
        {
            "@odata.type": "#microsoft.graph.
deviceManagementConfigurationSetting",
```

```
                    "settingInstance": {
                        "@odata.type": "#microsoft.graph.
    deviceManagementConfigurationChoiceSettingInstance",
                        "choiceSettingValue": {
                            "@odata.type": "#microsoft.graph.
    deviceManagementConfigurationChoiceSettingValue",
                            "children": [],
                            "value": "device_vendor_msft_
    passportforwork_biometrics_usebiometrics_true"
                        },
                        "settingDefinitionId": "device_vendor_msft_
    passportforwork_biometrics_usebiometrics"
                    }
                }
        ],
        "technologies": "mdm"
    }
    "@
```

Run it and output to a variable as we will need the ID for assignment:

```
$policy = Invoke-MgGraphRequest -Uri $settingsurl -Method Post
-Body $json -ContentType "application/json" -OutputType PSObject
$policyid = $policy.id
```

3. Set the group ID and assign it accordingly:

```
$groupid = "xxxxxxxx-xxxx-xxxx-xxxx-xxxxxxxxxxxx"
$assignurl = "https://graph.microsoft.com/beta/deviceManagement/
configurationPolicies/$policyid/assign"
$assignjson = @"
{
    "assignments": [
        {
            "target": {
                "@odata.type": "#microsoft.graph.
groupAssignmentTarget",
                "groupId": "$groupid"
            }
        }
    ]
}
"@
Invoke-MgGraphRequest -Uri $assignurl -Method Post -Body
$assignjson -ContentType "application/json" -OutputType PSObject
```

That covers setting up WHfB at the group level.

Setting up Windows Autopilot Enrollment Profiles

Now that we have our policies in place to manage devices, we can start configuring the policies so that we can enroll and provision them. The first of these is the Windows Autopilot Enrollment Profile, which tells the device what to do when it hits the Autopilot service during the **Out of Box Experience (OOBE)**.

You can have multiple profiles assigned to different Entra ID groups, usually using the Group Tag functionality, which we will cover in *Chapter 14*. By using group tags when adding devices to Autopilot, you can then add devices to Dynamic Entra ID groups and assign them to the appropriate Autopilot profile. Here are a couple of examples of why you would want multiple profiles:

- **Kiosk devices (using self-deploying mode)**: These profiles self-deploy and require no user input during provisioning. This means they can be configured to automatically sign in using a local device account. You can then configure policies to force them to run in a single application mode, often a web browser.

- **International organizations**: You specify the operating system language during Autopilot provisioning, so you could use group tags to assign a different profile based on the language required.

How to do it...

For this example, we will set up a standard user-driven deployment. Follow these steps to configure and amend as appropriate for your environment:

1. Navigate to **Devices**, then **Enrollment**. Select **Windows** and then click on **Deployment profiles**.

2. Click **Create profile** and select **Windows PC**.

3. Specify the profile's **Name** and **Description**. You also have the **Convert all targeted devices to Autopilot** option. If you target this profile at an Entra ID group containing devices not enrolled or provisioned via Autopilot, it will automatically enroll them into the service, and any future device resets will automatically go through Autopilot during OOBE.

4. In our case, we are only targeting Autopilot devices, but there is no harm in setting it to **Yes** anyway. Then, click **Next**.

    On the next screen, we can set the basic settings during OOBE, including the language and what the users can see when they are setting up their devices.

5. In this case, your **Deployment mode** needs to be user-driven, which is where the user logs in during OOBE and configures accordingly. Self-driven is for kiosk-type devices where there is no fixed user.

6. For **Join to Microsoft Entra ID as**, leave it set to **Microsoft Entra joined**. Hybrid join is possible but does not work well with Autopilot and should be avoided where possible. As we are configuring a whole new tenant and environment, try to avoid bringing technical debt with you.

7. The best practice is to always keep **User account type** set to **Standard**. There are ways around providing administrative rights as required, including using the Entra ID role, which we covered in *Chapter 1*, Windows LAPS, as covered in *Chapter 3*, or Endpoint Privilege Management, as will be covered in *Chapter 14*.

    Allow pre-provisioned deployment (previously called **White Glove**). This is where an IT admin can, during OOBE, press the Windows key five times and pre-configure all of the device-targeted policies and applications, leaving the user just needing to complete the user enrollment steps. This can be useful where you have quite a heavy deployment or users on low bandwidth connections, but it is also worth looking at how quickly your environment changes. If you have applications with regular updates, you may find users receiving devices with out-of-date applications if the device has been pre-provisioned too far in advance.

    We are also configuring a device naming template of the serial number of the device (or **%SERIAL%**). With Intune, the device name is a lot less important than it used to be, so this is not hugely important.

8. When you have configured the settings as required for your environment, click **Next**.

9. Now, we want to assign this to our Autopilot devices group. This group is set to add devices as soon as they are enrolled into the Autopilot service and, therefore, picks them up quicker. Add the group and click **Next**.

10. Finally, review your settings and click **Create**.

This section has covered configuring our first deployment profile. Now, we can look at automating it using PowerShell and Graph.

Automating it

Now that we know how to configure our profile in the GUI, we can learn how to automate it:

1. As usual, first, we need to set our group ID:

    ```
    $groupid = "xxxxxxxx-xxxx-xxxx-xxxx-xxxxxxxxxxxx"
    ```

2. Now, we need to set the URL. This time, we will be adding to `windowsDeviceAutopilotProfiles`:

    ```
    $autopiloturl = "https://graph.microsoft.com/beta/
    deviceManagement/windowsAutopilotDeploymentProfiles"
    ```

3. When looking at the JSON, note that there is a nested array covering the OOBE settings. Amend the settings as required. For the description, \ adds a line break. Watch for any special characters – they will cause the deployment to fail:

    ```
    $json = @"
    {
    ```

```
    "@odata.type": "#microsoft.graph.
azureADWindowsAutopilotDeploymentProfile",
    "description": "User Driven\nNon Administrators\nSerial
Device Name",
    "deviceNameTemplate": "%SERIAL%",
    "deviceType": "windowsPc",
    "displayName": "Autopilot Profile",
    "enableWhiteGlove": true,
    "extractHardwareHash": true,
    "hybridAzureADJoinSkipConnectivityCheck": false,
    "language": "en-GB",
    "outOfBoxExperienceSettings": {
        "deviceUsageType": "singleUser",
        "hideEscapeLink": true,
        "hideEULA": true,
        "hidePrivacySettings": true,
        "skipKeyboardSelectionPage": true,
        "userType": "standard"
    },
    "roleScopeTagIds": []
}
"@
```

4. Now, we need to deploy the profile and grab the ID to populate the assignment URL:

```
$policy = Invoke-MgGraphRequest -Method POST -Uri $autopiloturl
-Body $json -ContentType "application/json" -OutputType PSObject
$policyid = $policy.id
$assignurl = "https://graph.microsoft.com/beta/deviceManagement/
windowsAutopilotDeploymentProfiles/$policyid/assignments"
```

5. The assignment JSON is the same as it is for any other policy:

```
$assignjson = @"
{
    "target": {
        "@odata.type": "#microsoft.graph.groupAssignmentTarget",
        "groupId": "$groupid"
    }
}
"@
Invoke-MgGraphRequest -Method POST -Uri $assignurl -Body
$assignjson -ContentType "application/json" -OutputType PSObject
```

That covers your deployment profile. The next recipe covers your Enrollment Status Page or ESP.

Configuring an ESP

The final step before we can deploy a Windows device using Autopilot is to configure our ESP. This is the screen that users see after entering their credentials during OOBE and displays the progress of their device configuration and onboarding. It also has the potential to be where you will experience most of your issues, so be sure to check out the *There's more...* section for some troubleshooting tips.

How to do it...

Follow these instructions:

1. First, navigate to **Devices**, then click on **Enrollment**. Select **Windows** and then **Enrollment Status Page**.

    You can have multiple pages configured that are queried according to their priority (and then also queried for group membership).

    As the ESP is used to block a device until a particular subset of applications has been installed, you may find yourself needing more than one, should different departments/regions/groups have key applications that must be installed before they can log in and use the machines.

    Note that you cannot delete the **Default** page here, and while you can edit it, we will instead create a new one.

    As we have not deployed any applications into this environment yet (this will be covered in *Chapter 11*), we have added the **Microsoft To-Do** store application to demonstrate configuring an ESP.

2. Click the **Create** button.

3. Provide **Name** and **Description** values and click **Next**.

4. Now, we need to tell Intune to display an ESP. So, change the **Show app and profile configuration progress** setting to **Yes**.

    This will open up the other available settings:

    *   **Show an error when installation takes longer than the specified number of minutes**: When configuring this setting, you need to look at the applications being deployed and also configure the slowest broadband connection your users could be using. If you set this too high and misconfigure an application or script, the ESP will remain on-screen until the timeout is reached, even if nothing is going to happen until the error is fixed. This is not a great user experience. Similarly, if you set the value too low and have a particularly large or complex application, you could find the ESP timing out when the configuration is completed as planned. Usually, 60-120 minutes is adequate.

- **Show custom message when time limit or error occurs**: If you have a support desk or a particular number for users to call when configuring a new device, enter that here, along with some instructions for them. Should Autopilot fail or time out, this is the message that will be displayed.

- **Turn on log collection and diagnostics page for end users**: This is useful when troubleshooting. Should a machine fail, the users will be presented with a button to retrieve the logs from the device itself. It will not be visible before then.

- **Only show page to devices provisioned by out-of-box experience (OOBE)**: It is suggested that you set this to **No**. If you set this to **Yes**, after provisioning a machine, any future account logins that are not done by the primary user will see the ESP when logging in for the first time. Your IT staff will not thank you for disabling this when they are logging into a machine to troubleshoot something.

- **Block device use until all apps and profiles are installed**: This enables or disables the next three settings. If you set it to **No**, you will not be able to block until applications are installed.

- **Allow users to reset device if installation occurs**: You have three options if Autopilot fails – reset the device, allow the users to continue using it, or do nothing at all. This is the first option; it will display a **Reset** button to attempt provisioning again.

- **Allow users to use a device if installation error occurs**: This is the second option. Setting it to **Yes** will display a **Continue** button on failure, which will send the users to their desktop. Setting both to **No** is the third option.

- **Block device use until required apps are installed if they are assigned to the user/device**: If you set this to **All**, users will not be able to log in until every application is deployed as required to all users/all devices or any groups the user/device are members of completes installation. Setting this to **Selected** allows you to pick from your deployed applications. As mentioned previously, we are selecting **Microsoft To Do** for this example.

- There is also the **Only fail selected blocking apps in technician phase** option. This is used with pre-provisioning and forces your selected apps when a user enrolls a device. However, during pre-provisioning, it installs all required applications instead.

5. Once you have configured your settings, click **Next**.

   If you are only ever going to need one ESP, it can be deployed to all users or all devices. For this example, we will deploy to our Intune users group so that there are more options in the future should you want to add multiple ESP configurations for different user groups, for example.

6. Once you have selected your deployment group, click **Next**.

7. On the **Scope tags** page, click **Next**.

8. Finally, review that everything looks correct and click **Create**.

Now that we have created our ESP in the GUI, we can look at how we can automate it.

Automating it

The JSON for an ESP is a friendly one with simple true/false statements and a numerical input for the timeout. The only tricky part is the application blocking, which is a nested array. This uses the application ID, which can be grabbed from the URL or directly from Graph by performing a GET request on this URL: `https://graph.microsoft.com/beta/deviceAppManagement/mobileApps`.

Alternatively, you can install the `Install-Script -Name GetIntuneApps` script, which will list all applications and their details.

After installing it, simply run `GetIntuneApps.ps1` in a PowerShell window.

Now that we have the application ID, we can continue with the PowerShell script:

1. As usual, set our assignment group:

    ```
    $groupid = "xxxxxxxx-xxxx-xxxx-xxxx-xxxxxxxxxxxx"
    ```

2. Set the URL for the ESP itself:

    ```
    $espuri = " https://graph.microsoft.com/beta/deviceManagement/
    deviceEnrollmentConfigurations"
    ```

3. Add our JSON:

    ```
    $espjson = @"
    {
        "@odata.type": "#microsoft.graph.
    windows10EnrollmentCompletionPageConfiguration",
        "allowDeviceResetOnInstallFailure": true,
        "allowDeviceUseOnInstallFailure": false,
        "allowLogCollectionOnInstallFailure": true,
        "allowNonBlockingAppInstallation": true,
        "blockDeviceSetupRetryByUser": false,
        "customErrorMessage": "Please call IT support on xxx",
        "description": "120 minute time-out\nContinue on Error\
    nForce installation of Microsoft To Do",
        "disableUserStatusTrackingAfterFirstUser": true,
        "displayName": "Standard Enrollment",
        "id": "28aa4055-b08d-41bb-b030-8c1adef7fbed",
        "installProgressTimeoutInMinutes": 120,
        "installQualityUpdates": true,
        "roleScopeTagIds": [
            "0"
        ],
        "selectedMobileAppIds": [
    ```

```
            "2d7531e9-a16c-43a3-b65b-7f3c550b8a4c"
        ],
        "showInstallationProgress": true,
        "trackInstallProgressForAutopilotOnly": true
    }
"@
```

4. Create the policy and output it to a variable for the assignment ID. You may notice that for this one, the ID also includes _Windows10EnrollmentCompletionPageConfiguration. This is perfectly normal behavior:

```
$esp = Invoke-MgGraphRequest -Method POST -Uri $espuri -Body
$espjson -OutputType PSObject -ContentType "application/json"
$policyid = $esp.id
```

5. Set the URL and assign the policy:

```
$assignurl = "https://graph.microsoft.com/beta/deviceManagement/
deviceEnrollmentConfigurations/$policyid/assign"
$assignjson = @"
{
    "enrollmentConfigurationAssignments": [
        {
            "target": {
                "@odata.type": "#microsoft.graph.
groupAssignmentTarget",
                "groupId": "48efa53f-466b-41ea-b734-
a0aa72a73f89"
            }
        }
    ]
}
"@
Invoke-MgGraphRequest -Method POST -Uri $assignurl -Body
$assignjson -OutputType PSObject -ContentType "application/json"
```

This completes this recipe for configuring our ESP.

There's more...

While you can obtain and send logs after a device has failed, when testing your deployments, it is sometimes useful to see what is happening in the background:

1. The first step here is to press *Shift + F10*, which will load up an elevated Command Prompt. This is running in the full Windows environment, not the PE environment, which you may be used to from the SCCM/MDT days.

From this Command Prompt, you can access the usual Task Manager, File Explorer, Registry, and more to establish what is happening.

2. In **Task Manager**, select **Details**.

3. Right-click on **Name** at the top and choose **Select columns**.

4. Select **Command line** and click **OK**.

This will show you the exact command, which is especially useful with your application deployments.

Some useful troubleshooting tips can be found here: `https://learn.microsoft.com/en-us/troubleshoot/mem/intune/device-enrollment/understand-troubleshoot-esp`.

You can also deploy this script to launch some useful tools during ESP: `https://andrewstaylor.com/2022/08/16/autopilot-troubleshooting-tools-during-esp/`.

The Intune Debug Toolkit is also extremely useful for troubleshooting issues during device enrollment and can be found here: `https://msendpointmgr.com/intune-debug-toolkit/`

Enrolling a Windows device

We now have everything in place and can enroll our first Windows device into Intune using Autopilot. This recipe will run through the different options for adding the hardware hash into Autopilot and then provisioning a new machine.

Getting ready

For this recipe, you will need a Windows machine capable of running Windows 11. This can include a **virtual machine** (**VM**) that we will be using, but it has to haveTrusted Platform Module (**TPM**) enabled to pass the prerequisites for Windows 11. The machine will be wiped during the process, so please ensure there is no data on it.

To add devices, you will also need the `get-windowsautopilotinfo` PowerShell script: `https://www.powershellgallery.com/packages/Get-WindowsAutoPilotInfo`.

Once you have a machine ready, follow the steps to build it.

How to do it...

The first thing we need to do is add the device to the Autopilot service. We have a few options available for this.

Requesting from your hardware vendor

You can speak to your hardware supplier and ask them to add your devices to your tenant (you will need to provide them with the appropriate permissions).

JSON injection within the operating system

Another option is to inject the JSON directly into an ISO with which to build devices (known as offline enrollment). To do this, follow these steps:

1. Install and import the `WindowsAutopilotIntune` module:

    ```
    Install-Module WindowsAutopilotIntune
    import-module WindowsAutopilotIntune
    ```

2. Then, run the following command to output the JSON (watch for the encoding – it is important):

    ```
    Get-AutopilotProfile ConvertTo-AutopilotConfigurationJSON |
    Set-Content -Encoding Ascii "c:\temp\AutopilotConfigurationFile.
    json"
    ```

3. Then, you need to add this JSON file to your build image in `c:\windows\provisioning\autopilot\path`.

    You can also use a tool such as OSD Cloud to do this for you: `https://www.osdcloud.com/`.

    If you go down the offline route, you will also need to amend the dynamic rule on your Autopilot devices to the following:

    ```
    (device.devicePhysicalIDs -any (_ -contains "[ZTDid]")) -or
    (device.enrollmentProfileName -eq "PROFILENAME")
    ```

    Here, `PROFILENAME` is from your JSON export.

This covers using JSON injection to provision your devices. Now, we can look at further options.

CSV import

For existing devices, you can grab the hardware hash from the machines, export it to a CSV file, and then import that into Autopilot:

1. On your devices, run this command:

    ```
    Get-WindowsAutoPilotInfo.ps1 -OutputFile c:\mydevice.csv
    ```

2. Once you have your CSV, navigate to **Devices**, then **Enrollment**. Select **Windows** and then click on **Devices**.

3. Click on **Import**.

4. Select your CSV and click **Import**.

This covers exporting a CSV from your device and importing it directly into the console as a further provisioning option.

Online enrollment

The other option is to skip the CSV output and import directly on the device. This can be on a current machine or during OOBEL

1. Launch an elevated Command Prompt (*Shift + F10* during OOBE).

2. Set the script's execution:

    ```
    Set-ExecutionPolicy Unrestricted
    ```

3. Install the script:

    ```
    Install-script get-windowsautopilotinfo
    ```

4. Run the script with the -online parameter:

    ```
    get-windowsautopilotinfo.ps1 -online
    ```

    It will install some additional modules before prompting for credentials. Enter them into the standard Microsoft Online sign-in screen and click **Next**.

5. Consent to the permissions (you will need appropriate permissions within Azure/Entra to configure application registrations) and click **Accept**.

    The script will now grab and import your device details:

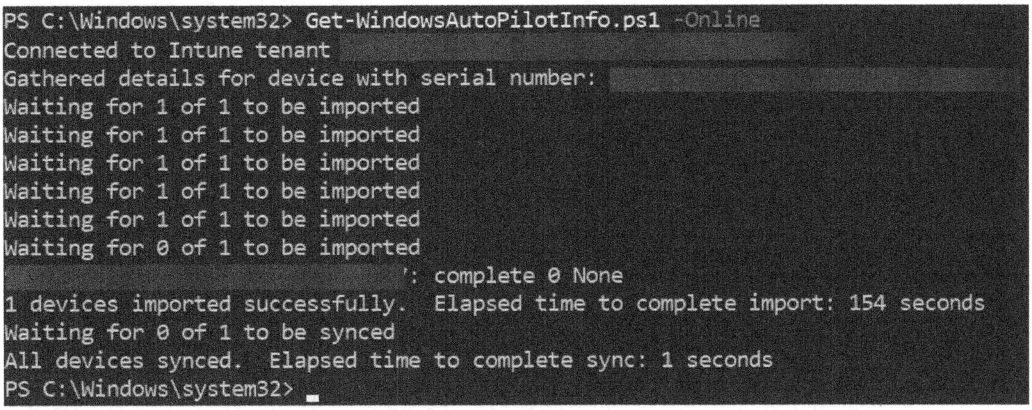

```
PS C:\Windows\system32> Get-WindowsAutoPilotInfo.ps1 -Online
Connected to Intune tenant
Gathered details for device with serial number:
Waiting for 1 of 1 to be imported
Waiting for 1 of 1 to be imported
Waiting for 1 of 1 to be imported
Waiting for 1 of 1 to be imported
Waiting for 1 of 1 to be imported
Waiting for 0 of 1 to be imported
                              ': complete 0 None
1 devices imported successfully.  Elapsed time to complete import: 154 seconds
Waiting for 0 of 1 to be synced
All devices synced.  Elapsed time to complete sync: 1 seconds
PS C:\Windows\system32>
```

Figure 4.10 – Enrollment complete

After enrolling our devices into the tenant, let us learn how to build the Windows operating system and configure it.

Building the device

This recipe will run through how we can build the devices we have enrolled into Autopilot using our configured ESP and settings:

1. In the portal, you should see your device under **Devices** | **Enroll Devices** | **Devices** with the profile set to **Assigned**.

    We can now continue with the build.

2. If you ran the previous command during OOBE, within the PowerShell window, type the following:

    ```
    C:\windows\system32\sysprep\sysprep.exe
    ```

    Keep the default values and click **OK**:

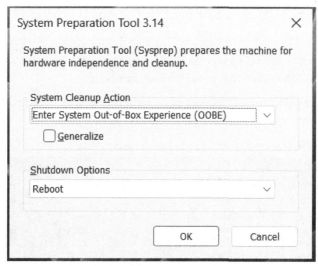

Figure 4.11 – System preparation

    If you enrolled with another method, you need to rebuild the device from a Windows ISO.

3. Your machine should detect that Autopilot has been enrolled and take you to a Microsoft 365 login screen. Enter your user details and click **Next**. Enter your password and click **Sign in**.

    You may briefly see a screen that says **Please wait while we set up your device.**

At this point, the ESP we configured earlier will run:

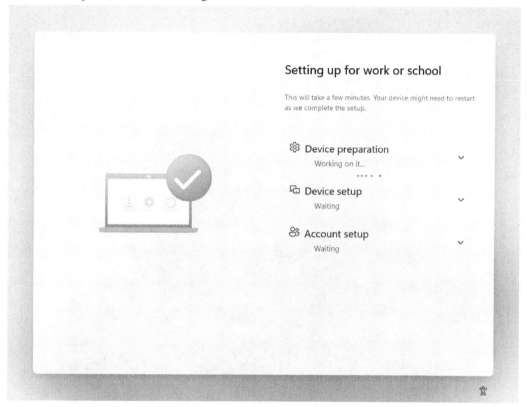

Figure 4.12 – ESP screen

4. Once completed, as we have previously configured Windows Hello, you will be prompted to configure it. Click **OK**.

    After completion, you will be sent to the desktop, where you will see that your previous OneDrive policy has worked and that the app has automatically signed in:

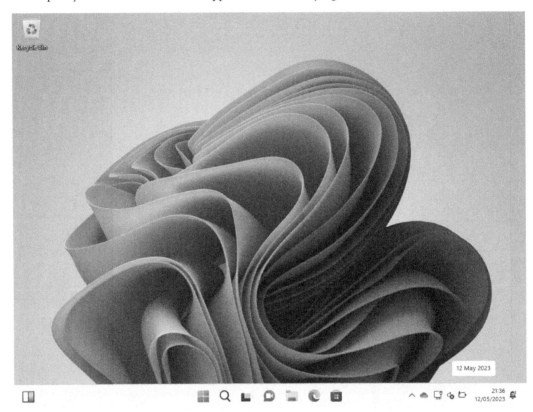

Figure 4.13 – Windows 11 start screen

Congratulations – you have configured and enrolled your first Windows device into Intune and Autopilot!

There's more...

As mentioned earlier, a device can also be pre-provisioned, which pre-installs any device-targeted apps as well as applies any policies at the device level. This can be useful for quicker deployments where some larger apps are required, or for users on lower bandwidth connections.

It is worth remembering that if you pre-provision a device and an application is updated, it will update itself when the user logs in, so keep an eye on how long devices are left before being deployed.

> **Important note**
> This requires TPM attestation, so it cannot be tested on a virtual machine.

Follow these steps to pre-provision a device:

1. To pre-provision a machine, after adding it to Autopilot, on the login screen, press the Windows key five times; this will take you to the following screen. Click **Pre-provision with Windows Autopilot** and then **Next**:

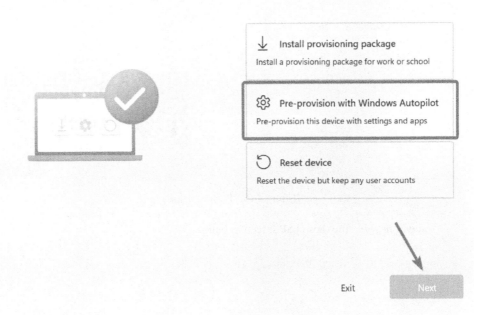

Figure 4.14 – The pre-provision menu

The device will check for updates.

2. When you are presented with the following screen, click **Next**:

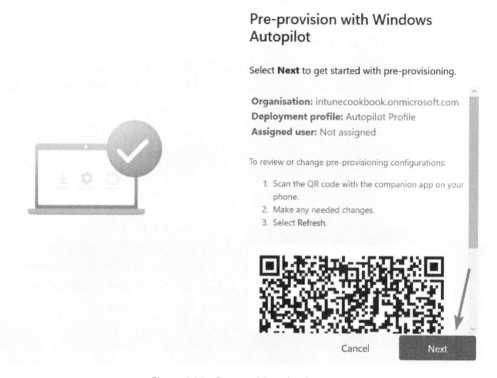

Pre-provision with Windows Autopilot

Select **Next** to get started with pre-provisioning.

Organisation: intunecookbook.onmicrosoft.com
Deployment profile: Autopilot Profile
Assigned user: Not assigned

To review or change pre-provisioning configurations:

1. Scan the QR code with the companion app on your phone.
2. Make any needed changes.
3. Select Refresh.

Cancel   Next

Figure 4.15 – Pre-provision check

You will now see the same ESP screen as before.

3. Once you have done this, click **Reseal**:

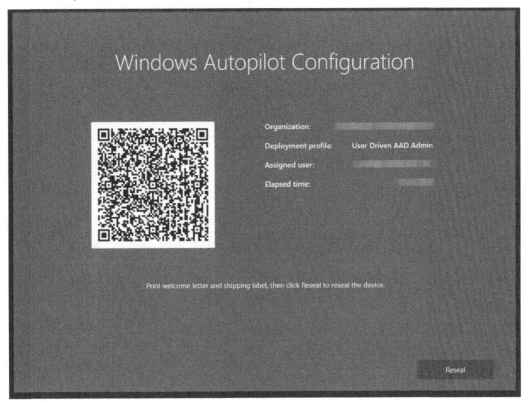

Figure 4.16 – Reseal

With that, we have enrolled our first device into Autopilot and also learned how to use pre-provisioning to pre-configure devices for our users.

5
Android Device Management

After the excitement of enrolling and provisioning our first Windows device, we can now look at the other supported operating systems. This chapter looks at Android device management, configuring policies to manage enterprise-owned and managed devices, and then app protection policies to protect your user-owned **Bring Your own Device (BYOD)**.

It will also run through the process of configuring Intune to work with a managed Google Play account and deploying applications from the Play Store.

Finally, we will enroll both a managed device and a BYOD.

This chapter includes the following recipes:

- Setting up a managed Google Play account
- Configuring enrollment profiles
- Adding a Google Play application
- Configuring a device restrictions policy
- Configuring an OEM policy
- Configuring a Wi-Fi policy
- Adding an app protection policy
- Enrolling an Android device – managed
- Enrolling an Android device – BYOD

Chapter materials

As with *Chapter 2*, this chapter will not cover all available policy types, so we will run through them all now to get a better understanding of what is available for Android devices. All profiles are available for creation for either corporate-owned (fully managed, dedicated, or work profile) or personally owned (work profile) devices. These profile types will be explained in the first recipe. We will also be concentrating on Android Enterprise devices; **Android Device Administrator** is now legacy and should not be used. **Android Open Source Project (AOSP)** is improving, but it is still less popular and has fewer options available.

The available profile types are as follows:

- **OEM Config**: We will cover this later in this chapter. It is for configuring manufacturer-specific OEM settings (where applicable).

- **Derived credential**: This is used for certificate authentication within apps. You can read more here: `https://learn.microsoft.com/en-gb/mem/intune/protect/derived-credentials`.

- **Device restrictions**: This is the primary configuration for Android devices; we will cover this shortly.

- **PKCS certificate**: This configures a public key pair certificate for authentication.

- **PKCS imported certificate**: This sets up an imported PKCS for S/MIME email authentication.

- **SCEP certificate**: This is used for certificate-based device authentication.

- **Trusted certificate**: This imports a trusted root certificate from an on-premises certificate authority server.

- **VPN**: This configures a VPN connection for your Android devices.

- **Wi-Fi**: This configures Wi-Fi profiles, both basic and enterprise-supported, and can be used with certification profiles where applicable.

As with our Windows security policies, there are suggested policy settings and other guidance from government agencies. Using these as a baseline will assist you in securing the devices, especially if it is required for external auditing.

The following guidance is available:

- CIS: `https://www.cisecurity.org/benchmark/google_android`

- NCSC: `https://www.ncsc.gov.uk/collection/device-security-guidance/platform-guides/android`

- NCSC also includes baseline configurations on GitHub: `https://github.com/ukncsc/Device-Security-Guidance-Configuration-Packs/tree/main/Google/Android`

Technical requirements

For this chapter, you will need a modern web browser and a PowerShell code editor such as **Visual Studio Code (VS Code)** or PowerShell ISE.

All of the scripts that are referenced in this chapter can be found here: `https://github.com/PacktPublishing/Microsoft-Intune-Cookbook`.

For enrolling devices, you will need a factory-reset Android device.

> **Tip**
>
> If your device is already enabled for another MDM, you will need to remove any previous management that has been configured and then wipe the device before enrolling into Intune.

Setting up a managed Google Play account

Before we configure any Android policies or settings, we need to attach Intune to a managed Google Play account. We will then use this for enrolling devices as well as deploying applications.

You do not need an existing Google account for this, as we can set it up during the process (ideally an Android Enterprise account). It is also worth using a shared/generic account rather than one linked to a particular member of staff.

Follow this recipe to link Intune and a managed Google Play account.

How to do it...

Follow these steps:

1. First, we need to navigate to **Devices** from the Intune menu.

2. Then, click **Enrollment**; in the old portal, click **Enroll Devices**.

3. Now, click **Android**.

4. Click **Managed Google Play**.

5. Check the box to agree to the permissions and click the **Launch Google to connect now** button.

6. In the pop-up window, click either of the **Sign In** buttons.

7. Now, click **Create Account** (not **Sign in**).

8. Select **For work or my business**.

    Here, you can create a new `gmail.com` account, or set it to use one linked to your custom domain (remember, do not use a personal account). If you choose to use a custom email, you will need to confirm you own the account.

9. In this case, we will use a Gmail account purely for ease. Once you have entered the necessary information, click **Next**.

10. For security, you will need to verify with a telephone number; enter one and click **Next**. This does not necessarily have to be a mobile.

11. Enter the verification code you received and click **Next**.

12. Enter your recovery information and click **Next**.

13. On the **Get more from your number** screen, click **Skip**.

14. The next few options are for advertising preferences. As this account will only be used for Intune management, Express will be fine, but you can configure it more granularly if required here. Select the desired option and click **Next**.

15. Accept the terms by clicking **I Agree**.

16. We do not want to set up a business profile here, so click **Not Now**.

17. Click **Get Started**.

18. Enter your company details and click **Next**.

19. Complete the form with the required contact details (optional), check the box to agree to the terms, and click **Confirm**.

20. Finally, click **Complete Registration**.

    The window will now close and return you to Intune, where you can confirm that the connection has been established:

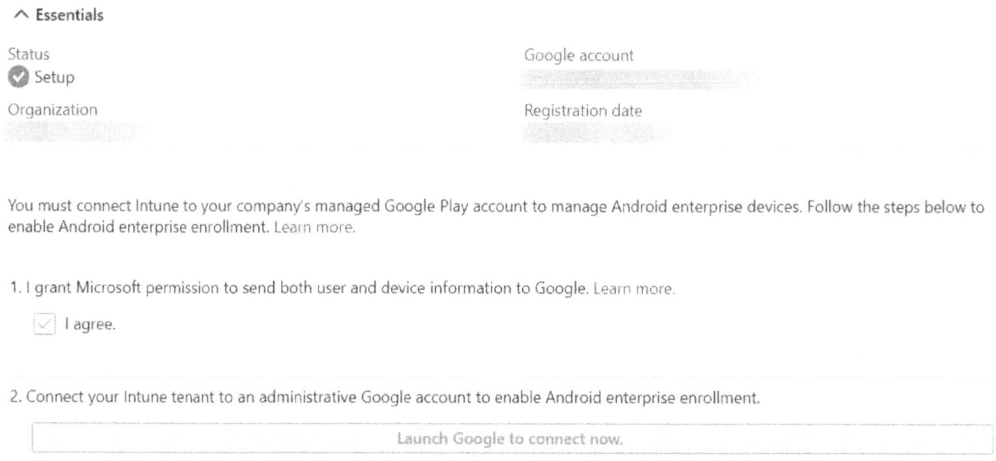

∧ Essentials

Status
✓ Setup

Google account

Organization

Registration date

You must connect Intune to your company's managed Google Play account to manage Android enterprise devices. Follow the steps below to enable Android enterprise enrollment. Learn more.

1. I grant Microsoft permission to send both user and device information to Google. Learn more.

   ☑ I agree.

2. Connect your Intune tenant to an administrative Google account to enable Android enterprise enrollment.

   Launch Google to connect now.

Figure 5.1 – Google Play – connection established

With that, you have successfully connected your tenant to Google Play. We can now use this to enroll our devices and deploy applications.

Configuring enrollment profiles

Now that our Google Play account has been linked, we can configure a profile to allow devices to be enrolled. This will provide us with a QR code and text code we can use when setting up a new device.

Before we run through the process of creating a profile, we need to understand all of the options available on the Android device enrollment screen:

- **Zero-touch enrollment**: This is a way of bulk enrolling devices into your profile without needing to configure any steps during device configuration and enrollment (similar to Apple iOS and Apple Business Manager **Automated Device Enrollment** (**ADE**), which will be covered in the next chapter). It requires specific devices that have to be enrolled into the service by the distributor or service provider. Samsung Knox is a popular example that is free to configure and use, as well as Android Zero Touch for non-Samsung devices.

- **Personally-owned devices with work profile**: This button just loads an information page where nothing can be configured. When a user enrolls a personal device via the Company Portal, it will add the applications to a separate profile on the device to secure the data within them. It is enabled by default.

- **Corporate-owned dedicated devices**: This is for Kiosk-style devices without a specific user assigned.

- **Corporate-owned, fully managed user devices**: These are the most common profiles for your standard users who have a corporate phone assigned to them that is fully managed. This is the profile we will be configuring in this recipe.

- **Corporate-owned devices with work profile**: This is for a corporate-owned device, but where the device is also for personal use, and the applications reside in a work profile to protect the data contained.

- **AOSP Corporate-owned, user-associated devices**: This is similar to fully managed user devices, but this is for devices running AOSP (which is Android) but without the Google Play services. Your hardware supplier will inform you if you have these devices. Often, they are for specific use cases, such as those manufactured by Zebra.

- **AOSP Corporate-owned userless devices**: This is for Kiosk devices not running Google Play services.

- **Android Administrator Personal and corporate-owned devices with device administrator privileges**: This is a legacy method and should not be used for new devices.

How to do it...

Now that we know what everything does, we will configure a profile for corporate-owned, fully managed user devices in this recipe:

1. First, click on **Corporate owned, fully managed user devices**.

2. Click **Create profile**.

   Creating a profile is extremely straightforward. Apart from a name and description, there are no settings to configure, and no assignment is required.

3. Enter your **Name** and, optionally, a **Description** value and click **Next**.

4. There is not much to review here, but it is always best to check for errors. Once you have done that, click **Create**.

5. Now, you will see your profile in the list. It is worth noting that the tokens are valid for 90 days, after which you will need to create a new one (of course, you can use the automation steps to automate this for you in something such as an Azure Runbook). Click on the newly created profile.

6. Now, click **Token**.

    Here, you will find your QR code and token, which you can provide to users to enroll their devices. You can also revoke a token should you need to and also export it in JSON format.

Automating it

As these tokens expire, automation can be a useful way to keep on top of device enrollments, especially in a larger organization with multiple devices. This code could be used with an Entra ID application registration process or configured to run every 90 days (or you could go one step further and check the expiry date before running), after which you can export the code to Teams, email, or anywhere else.

When creating the JSON here, the available fields are for all of the token types, so not all are applicable. In this case, you cannot set Wi-Fi networks on this enrollment type; that is for dedicated devices:

1. First, as usual, we need our name and description:

    ```
    $name = "Android Enrollment Profile"
    $description = "Corporate Owned, Fully Managed"
    ```

2. Then, we need the URL we are sending the request to, which in this case is androidDeviceOwnerEnrollmentProfiles:

    ```
    $url = "https://graph.microsoft.com/beta/deviceManagement/
    androidDeviceOwnerEnrollmentProfiles"
    ```

3. We do not want to hard-code an expiry date here; otherwise, we will need to edit it every time the script runs. So, we will let PowerShell do the work for us. We are taking the current date, adding 90 days, and then converting it into the format Graph is looking for (yyyy-MM-ddTHH:mm:ss.fffZ, where fff is milliseconds):

    ```
    $tokenExpirationDateTime = (Get-Date).AddDays(90).
    ToUniversalTime().ToString("yyyy-MM-ddTHH:mm:ss.fffZ")
    ```

4. Now, drop these values into the JSON:

    ```
    $json = @"
    {
        "configureWifi": false,
    ```

```
    "description": "$description",
    "displayName": "$name",
    "enrollmentMode": "corporateOwnedFullyManaged",
    "roleScopeTagIds": [],
    "tokenExpirationDateTime": "$tokenexpirationdatetime",
    "wifiHidden": false,
    "wifiPassword": "",
    "wifiSecurityType": "none",
    "wifiSsid": ""
}
"@
```

Make sure you do not use the $profile variable at any point here, that is reserved for PowerShell and will cause you errors.

Now, create the profile, grab the ID and populate it into the URL so we can grab the token details:

```
$androidprofile = Invoke-MgGraphRequest -Uri $url -Method Post
-body $json
$profileid = $androidprofile.id
$tokenurl = "https://graph.microsoft.com/beta/deviceManagement/
androidDeviceOwnerEnrollmentProfiles/$profileid"
```

5. We need to run a GET command against our URL to retrieve the policy details. This one is not inside the `value` property, so we just need the full response:

```
$androidtokendetails = Invoke-MgGraphRequest -Uri $tokenurl
-Method Get
```

6. The token QR code is stored within an array called `qrcodeimage` and contains the image type under `type` and the image itself, stored in Base64 format under `value`. Therefore, we must grab the value of that array:

```
$qrbase64 = ($androidtokendetails.qrcodeimage).value
```

7. We need the image to be stored somewhere:

```
$Image = "c:\temp\AndroidQR.png"
```

8. The next step is to use the `[convert]::FromBase64String` .NET command to read and decode the value and convert it into raw bytes:

```
[byte[]]$Bytes = [convert]::FromBase64String($qrbase64)
```

9. Finally, we must export the raw bytes as the image:

```
[System.IO.File]::WriteAllBytes($Image, $Bytes)
```

It is also worth grabbing the token code in case there is a situation where the code cannot be scanned (talking a user through enrollment over the phone, for example).

10. This is stored as plain text in the `tokenvalue` field, so we simply need to retrieve that and output it to a text file. It could also be used in an email:

```
$androidtoken2 = ($androidtokendetails.tokenvalue)
$androidtoken2 | out-file "c:\temp\token.txt"
```

In this recipe, we learned how to configure a managed Google Play account and retrieve an enrollment token, both in the GUI and using PowerShell.

Adding a Google Play application

Before we look at our configuration policies, it is best to cover application deployment as we will need applications in the tenant for both device restrictions and OEM policies.

This recipe is going to concentrate on managed Google Play applications as they are the preferred choice for application deployment in an enterprise environment. It is worth covering the other application options so that we are aware of what is available:

- **Android Store app**: This adds applications that are effectively shortcuts to the Play Store. Users will need a Google account, and you will need your restrictions to leave the store open, which means users can install anything they want.

- **Managed Google Play app**: This adds a managed application that does not require a Google Play account. The store can be restricted to only approved applications.

- **Web link**: Deploys a web link to devices onto the home screen.

- **Built-in app**: These are pre-approved and curated applications that can be deployed without using the Play Store. They are also the apps that are pre-configured for App Protection (covered later in this chapter).

- **Line-of-business app**: This was the way of deploying custom APK links to Android device administrator devices. When using Enterprise, it is best to add to the private Google Play Store. An important note is that the app package's name needs to be unique – not just in your environment but across Google Play. You can read more here: `https://learn.microsoft.com/en-us/mem/intune/apps/apps-add-android-for-work`.

- **Android Enterprise system app**: This is for deploying built-in applications, usually from the manufacturer. You need to add the exact application name (for example, *com.microsoft.word*).

Now that we understand all of the different application types, we can continue and add our first managed Google Play app.

How to do it...

Follow these steps:

1. First, click on **Apps**.

> **Important note**
>
> Upon connecting to the managed Google Play Store, the applications required to enroll a device are automatically added to Intune. These are Intune Company Portal, Managed Home Screen, Microsoft Authenticator, and Microsoft Intune.

2. Then, click **Android**.
3. Click **Add** at the top.
4. Select **Managed Google Play app** from the dropdown and click **Select**.
5. This will load the Play Store within the Intune portal.
6. Search for the application you want to deploy. We will use **Microsoft Outlook**, as that is common to most environments. Click on the application in the search results.
7. Click **Approve**.
8. Check that you are happy with the permissions that are required and click **Approve**.
9. You will now be asked what the default behavior is if those permissions change. Select what suits your environment (keep it approved when the app requests new permissions or revoke approval when the app requests new permissions) and click **Done**.
10. The app will be approved. However, you can still unapprove it or change the preferences you set before:

Microsoft Outlook

Microsoft Corporation   ★ ★ ★ ★ ✦ 9,124,022 ≗

 ✓ ⟨ APPROVED ⟩

▣ PEGI 3

Contains Ads · Offers in-app purchases

⬇ This app offers managed configuration

ⓘ This app is only available in certain countries

Select

Figure 5.2 – Outlook options post-approval

11. Finally, we need to click the **Sync** button at the top to add the application to Intune.

12. After a couple of minutes, the application will appear in Intune. However, note that it has not been assigned, so we need to click **Microsoft Outlook**.

13. Click **Properties**.

14. Click **Edit** next to **Assignments**.

   Here, we have a few options:

   - **Required**: This will automatically install the application on any managed and enrolled devices. It can be targeted to user or device groups (or the **All Users/All Devices** virtual group).

   - **Available for enrolled devices**: This displays the application in the Company Portal for enrolled devices. As it is an available application, it can only be targeted at the user level.

   - **Available with or without enrollment**: This displays the applications in the Company Portal, even if the device itself is not enrolled in Intune (a BYOD using MAM, for example). This can only be targeted at the user level, and the users must have an Intune license.

   - **Uninstall**: This removes the application without prompting. It can be targeted at either the user or device level.

15. As we are demonstrating both corporate and BYOD in this chapter, we will deploy with and without enrollment to our Intune user's Entra ID group. Clicking **Included** or **Default** under **Update Priority** lets you set if the assignment is included or excluded, as well as increase or decrease the priority for updates. Once everything has been configured, click **Review + Save**.

16. If you are happy that everything is correct on the review screen, click **Save**.

Automating it

While you can automate adding the other application types, due to most of the work happening within the Google Play Store, adding a managed Google Play application is currently a manual process. We can, however, automate how the applications are assigned after adding them.

We can do this by finding the application ID and then assigning it:

1. First, set the name we are looking for. We will let PowerShell and Graph do the hard work for us:

   ```
   $appname = "Microsoft Authenticator"
   ```

2. Now, we can run a GET request against all of the mobile apps in the tenant. We only want managed Google Play deployed applications using the @odata.type variable as #microsoft. graph.androidManagedStoreApp. Once we have the Play apps, we can find just those that match the name. Finally, we just want the ID (nested within Value):

   ```
   $appid = ((Invoke-MgGraphRequest -Uri "https://graph.
   microsoft.com/beta/deviceAppManagement/mobileApps" -Method
   ```

```
Get -ContentType "application/json" -OutputType PSObject).
value | Where-Object {$_.'@odata.type' -eq '#microsoft.graph.
androidManagedStoreApp'} | Where-Object {$_.displayName -eq
$appname}).id
```

3. Populate the URL with $appid:

```
$url = "https://graph.microsoft.com/beta/deviceAppManagement/
mobileApps/$appid/assign"
```

4. Add our variables for GroupID and the assignment type (this can be Required, Available, Uninstall, or AvailableWithoutEnrollment):

```
$groupid = "00000000-0000-0000-0000-000000000000"
$assignmenttype = "Available"
```

5. Now, we need the JSON. We have set this to be available for Intune-Users with or without enrollment:

```
$json = @"
{
    "mobileAppAssignments": [
        {
            "@odata.type": "#microsoft.graph.
mobileAppAssignment",
            "intent": "$assignmenttype",
            "settings": {
                "@odata.type": "#microsoft.graph.
androidManagedStoreAppAssignmentSettings",
                "androidManagedStoreAppTrackIds": [],
                "autoUpdateMode": "default"
            },
            "target": {
                "@odata.type": "#microsoft.graph.
groupAssignmentTarget",
                "groupId": "$groupid"
            }
        }
    ]
}
"@
```

6. Finally, post the assignment:

```
Invoke-MgGraphRequest -Uri $url -Method Post -Body $json
-ContentType "application/json"
```

We have now covered adding our first managed Google Play application and assigning it, as well as covering the assignment in PowerShell.

Configuring a device restrictions policy

While we can now enroll a device, it will lack any configuration, and the user experience will be the same as any off-the-shelf device. For the full corporate experience, we need to configure a policy to manage them.

Android policies have yet to migrate to Settings catalog, so for this example, we are going to configure a device restrictions policy with some basic settings to set you on your way. The PowerShell script and included JSON will contain further settings.

How to do it...

Follow these steps:

1. First, click on **Devices** in the Intune menu.
2. Then, click **Android**.
3. Now, click **Configuration profiles**.
4. Finally, add a profile by clicking **+Create | +New policy**.
5. Select **Android Enterprise** and then **Device restrictions** under **Fully Managed, Dedicated and Corporate-Owned Work-Profile**. Then, click **Create**.
6. Give your policy a name and a description, and click **Next**.

   This next screen lists every setting available for Android devices. Make a note of the headers, as some settings only apply to particular device types (Kiosk settings are only for dedicated devices, for example).

   A list of every setting and their descriptions can be found here: `https://learn.microsoft.com/en-us/mem/intune/configuration/device-restrictions-android-for-work`.

   For our fully managed, user-assigned devices, these are some suggested settings. For additional suggestions, review the NCSC and CIS guidance in the *Chapter materials* section:

   • **Wi-Fi access point configuration**: Block.

   • **Tethering and access to hotspots**: Block.

   • **USB file transfer**: Block.

   • **External media**: Block.

- **Factory reset protection emails**: This allows you to restrict factory reset to approved admins only.

- **Factory reset**: Block.

- **Notification windows**: Disable.

- **Locate device**: Allow.

- **Threat scan on apps**: Require.

- **Enrollment profile type – fully managed**: This loads additional settings to configure the device using Microsoft Launcher. Ensure Microsoft Launcher is a required application (covered later in this chapter).

- **Password**: Set this to whatever suits your environment. It is always recommended to disable everything from the lock screen.

- **Add new users**: Block.

- **User removal**: Block.

- **Personal Google accounts**: Block.

- **Lock screen message**: Set this to something for lost devices as an extra protection layer.

7. When you have configured your settings, click **Next**.

8. Assign it to either your Intune users group or **All Users/All Devices** as required, then click **Next**.

9. Check that everything looks OK and click **Create**.

Automating it

Now that we know how to manually configure the policy, we can look at how to automate it. We have not covered device restrictions before, but it is more straightforward than a Settings catalog policy. Most settings are configured inline with either a numeric or Boolean value with the occasional nested array, in this case for the likes of password settings or Microsoft Launcher:

1. As always, we start with our variables:

    ```
    $name = "Android Device Restrictions"
    $description = "Android Device Restrictions"
    $groupid = "00000000-0000-0000-0000-000000000000"
    ```

2. Set the URL:

    ```
    $url = "https://graph.microsoft.com/beta/deviceManagement/
    deviceConfigurations"
    ```

3. The full JSON is available in this book's GitHub repository, so for this example, we will only
    add a couple of settings here to get a feel for how it looks:

```
$json = @"
{
    "@odata.type": "#microsoft.graph.
androidDeviceOwnerGeneralDeviceConfiguration",
    "alreadySetPassword": "********",
    "appsRecommendSkippingFirstUseHints": true,
    "cellularBlockWiFiTethering": true,
    "certificateCredentialConfigurationDisabled": true,
    "crossProfilePoliciesAllowDataSharing": "notConfigured",
    "description": "$description",
    "displayName": "$name",
    "enrollmentProfile": "fullyManaged",
    "factoryResetBlocked": true,
    "googleAccountsBlocked": true
}
"@
```

4. Create the profile:

```
$androidprofile = Invoke-MgGraphRequest -Method POST -Uri $url
-Body $json -ContentType "application/json" -OutputType PSObject
```

5. Grab the ID and populate the URL:

```
$androidprofileid = $androidprofile.id
$assignurl = "https://graph.microsoft.com/beta/deviceManagement/
deviceConfigurations/$androidprofileid/assign"
```

6. Add the group ID to the assignment JSON:

```
$assignjson = @"
{
    "assignments": [
        {
            "target": {
                "@odata.type": "#microsoft.graph.
groupAssignmentTarget",
                "groupId": "$groupid"
            }
        }
    ]
}
"@
```

7. Finally, assign the policy:

```
Invoke-MgGraphRequest -Method POST -Uri $assignurl -Body
$assignjson -ContentType "application/json" -OutputType PSObject
```

That completes this recipe, where we created our Android device restrictions policy in both the GUI and code.

Configuring an OEM policy

Most large Android manufacturers also provide the option to configure device-specific settings using a mixture of a Google Play application and a corresponding OEM policy. You can then use device filters (which we will cover in *Chapter 13*) to restrict these applications and policies to the correct devices.

For this example, we are going to configure a policy for the Microsoft Surface Duo range of devices, but some other manufacturer applications are as follows:

- Microsoft Surface: `https://play.google.com/store/apps/details?id=com.microsoft.surface.config`

  Settings: `https://learn.microsoft.com/en-us/surface-duo/surface-duo-2-manage-oemconfig`

- Zebra: `https://play.google.com/store/apps/details?id=com.zebra.oemconfig.common`

  Settings: `https://techdocs.zebra.com/oemconfig/11-5/about/`

- Samsung: `https://play.google.com/store/apps/details?id=com.samsung.android.knox.kpu`

  Settings: `https://docs.samsungknox.com/admin/uem/intune-configure-ksp-oemconfig-2.htm`

- Motorola: `https://play.google.com/store/apps/details?id=com.motorola.oemconfig.rel`

  Settings: `https://en-gb.support.motorola.com/app/answers/detail/a_id/160503/~/moto-oemconfig-guide`

- Datalogic: `https://play.google.com/store/apps/details?id=com.datalogic.settings.oemconfig`

  Settings: `https://datalogic.github.io/oemconfig/overview/`

- Nokia: `https://play.google.com/store/apps/details?id=com.hmdglobal.app.oemconfig`

  Settings: `https://solutions.hmdglobal.com/knowledgehub/what-benefits-does-the-oemconfig-app-offer`

The available settings will depend on the hardware manufacturer and have been provided here.

Getting ready

As we mentioned previously, we are using the Surface Duo OEM configuration for this example, so deploy the Microsoft Surface OEM application to your environment and assign it, as we covered previously.

Once the application has been approved and assigned, continue to the next steps to configure the policy.

How to do it...

Follow these steps:

1. First, navigate to **Devices**.
2. Then, click **Android**.
3. Then, click **Configuration profiles**.
4. Click **+Create | +New policy** to start the process.
5. Finally, select **Android Enterprise** and **OEMConfig**, then click **Create**.
6. As usual, add a name and a description. You also need to select the OEM Config app you deployed earlier by clicking the blue **Select an OEM Config app** text.
7. Select the application and click **Select**.
8. Once configured, click **Next**.
9. On the next screen, you can decide whether to configure the settings in a GUI or by editing the JSON.

   As the Microsoft settings are all user-friendly, we will continue with the configuration designer, but it is always worth checking which option is best for your manufacturer.

10. In this example, we will block Bluetooth and NFC for added security. Once you have configured the settings for your environment, click **Next**:

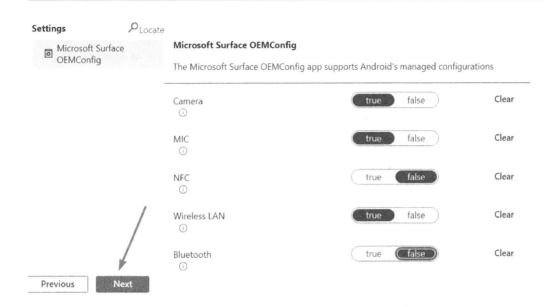

Figure 5.3 – OEM settings configuration

11. Click **Next** to skip the **Scope tags** page.

12. For assignments, choose the one that works best with a filter. So, pick **All Devices** and then filter to just your Surface devices. While we will cover this properly in *Chapter 13*, this is what a Surface filter looks like:

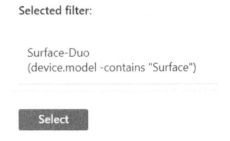

Figure 5.4 – Example Surface filter

13. For now, we will simply assign to **All Devices** and click **Next**.

14. Check that everything looks correct and click **Create**.

Automating it

Automating an OEM policy is slightly more complicated than previous ones, as we are passing both the application details as well as the configuration in JSON.

As JSON can include special characters, a lot will be encoded into Base64 content before it is uploaded. A useful website for encoding and decoding Base64 is `https://www.base64decode.org/`. Follow these steps:

1. We will start with the basics, only this time, we are including the application ID, which can be found at the following Google Play Store URL:

    ```
    $name = "Surface Duo Config"
    $description = "OEMConfig policy for Surface Duo"
    $packageid = "com.microsoft.surface.config"
    ```

2. Now, set the URL, which in this case is `mobileAppConfigurations`:

    ```
    $url = "https://graph.microsoft.com/beta/deviceAppManagement/
    mobileAppConfigurations"
    ```

3. With that, we have come to the first slightly tricky part. As well as the package ID, the payload also needs the application ID, which is specific to the application within your tenant, so we will run a command to grab it.

    This queries all `mobileApps` (that is, all apps) in the tenant, filters on the package ID, and returns the application ID (and just the ID by using the `-expandproperty` object):

    ```
    $appid = (Invoke-MgGraphRequest -Uri "https://graph.microsoft.
    com/beta/deviceAppManagement/mobileApps" -Method GET -OutputType
    PSObject).value | Where-Object { $_.packageId -eq $packageid } |
    select-object -ExpandProperty id
    ```

4. Now, we must configure the raw JSON with the values we picked earlier:

    ```
    $configjson = @"
    {
        "kind": "androidenterprise#managedConfiguration",
        "productId": "app:com.microsoft.surface.config",
        "managedProperty": [
            {
                "key": "CAM",
                "valueBool": true
            },
            {
                "key": "MIC",
                "valueBool": true
            },
    ```

```
            {
                "key": "NFC",
                "valueBool": false
            },
            {

                "key": "WLAN",
                "valueBool": true
            },
            {

                "key": "BT",
                "valueBool": false
            }
        ]
    }
    "@
```

5. As we mentioned previously, this needs to be in Base64 format, so we need to convert it:

```
$configjsonbase64 = [Convert]::ToBase64String([System.Text.
Encoding]::UTF8.GetBytes($configjson))
```

6. Next, we must add everything we have configured to the JSON and create the policy:

```
$json = @"
{
    "@odata.type": "#microsoft.graph.
androidManagedStoreAppConfiguration",
    "description": "$description",
    "displayName": "$name",
    "id": "00000000-0000-0000-0000-000000000000",
    "packageId": "com.microsoft.surface.config",
    "payloadJson": "$configjsonbase64",
    "roleScopeTagIds": [
        "0"
    ],
    "targetedMobileApps": [
        "$appid"
    ]
}
"@
$oempolicy = Invoke-MgGraphRequest -Method POST -Uri $url -Body
$json -ContentType "application/json" -OutputType PSObject
```

7. Grab the new policy ID:

```
$oempolicyid= $oempolicy.id
```

8. Add the policy to the URL. You will notice that it has an additional option to specify the application type:

```
$assignurl = "https://graph.microsoft.com/beta/
deviceAppManagement/mobileAppConfigurations/$oempolicyid/
microsoft.graph.managedDeviceMobileAppConfiguration/assign"
```

9. Finally, set our all devices target and assign it:

```
$assignjson = @"
{
    "assignments": [
        {
            "target": {
                "@odata.type": "#microsoft.graph.
allDevicesAssignmentTarget"
            }
        }
    ]
}
"@
Invoke-MgGraphRequest -Method POST -Uri $assignurl -Body
$assignjson -ContentType "application/json" -OutputType PSObject
```

With that, we have learned how to configure an OEM policy for device-specific configuration profiles, including automating how they are created.

Configuring a Wi-Fi policy

In an enterprise/office setup, you want a secure wireless network that the users both should not and cannot connect to themselves, whether this is using a certificate-based connection or just a secure code that is not shared with staff.

To do this, we need to deploy a Wi-Fi policy to our mobile devices. Remember, however, that unless you are using a zero-touch enrollment such as Samsung Knox, the devices will not pick up this new policy until *after* enrollment. Therefore, you will need an initial internet connection to enroll and set up new devices. This could be a 4G/5G connection, a guest network, or a basic enrollment network with strict security policies applied.

This example will cover a more simple WPA2 network configuration as an Enterprise configuration will require certificate deployments. If this is more appropriate for your environment, you can follow the guide here: https://learn.microsoft.com/en-us/mem/intune/configuration/ wi-fi-settings-android-enterprise.

Getting ready

For this recipe, you will need a secured wireless network and access to the WPA key. If you would rather use an Enterprise wireless network, you will need to configure the certificate policies beforehand:

- `https://learn.microsoft.com/en-us/mem/intune/protect/certificates-pfx-configure`

- `https://learn.microsoft.com/en-us/mem/intune/protect/certificates-profile-scep`

- `https://learn.microsoft.com/en-us/mem/intune/protect/certificates-scep-configure`

How to do it...

Follow these steps:

1. To create our policy, navigate to **Configuration profiles** within **Devices**, then **Android**.

2. Then, click **+Create** | **+New policy**.

3. Select **Android Enterprise** and the **Wi-Fi** profile type and click **Create**.

4. Add a name and description, then click **Next**.

5. Select your Wi-Fi type from the dropdown. Depending on your environment, you can choose **Basic** for a WEP/WPA key-based authentication or **Enterprise** for certificate-based EAP/PEAP authentication. For this example, we are deploying a **Basic** network.

6. Fill in the details as appropriate and click **Next**.

7. Now, assign the policy as appropriate. If you have one network across the estate, **All Devices** or **All Users** will be fine, but if you have different networks, it may be worth using group-based assignments (IT could have a less restricted network). Once configured, click **Next**.

8. Review the settings and click **Create**.

Automating it

Now, let's learn how to automate this process. Fortunately, this is easier than the OEM profile and just consists of a few extra variables:

1. We will start with the normal variables:

```
$name = "Android-Wi-Fi"
$description = "Android-Wi-Fi"
$groupid = "00000000-0000-0000-0000-000000000000"
```

2. Now, add the Wi-Fi-specific settings:

```
$ssid = "mobilewifi"
$wpakey = "12345678"
```

3. Add the URL:

```
$url = "https://graph.microsoft.com/beta/deviceManagement/
deviceConfigurations"
```

4. You will notice that the JSON is the same for both Basic and Enterprise, with certain settings simply switched off. Populate our variables in the JSON:

```
$json = @"
{
    "@odata.type": "#microsoft.graph.
androidDeviceOwnerWiFiConfiguration",
    "authenticationMethod": null,
    "connectAutomatically": true,
    "connectWhenNetworkNameIsHidden": false,
    "description": "$description",
    "displayName": "$name",
    "eapType": null,
    "id": "00000000-0000-0000-0000-000000000000",
    "innerAuthenticationProtocolForEapTtls": null,
    "innerAuthenticationProtocolForPeap": "none",
    "networkName": "Android-Devices",
    "outerIdentityPrivacyTemporaryValue": null,
    "preSharedKey": "$wpakey",
    "proxyAutomaticConfigurationUrl": null,
    "proxyExclusionList": null,
    "proxyManualAddress": null,
    "proxyManualPort": null,
    "proxySettings": "none",
    "roleScopeTagIds": [
        "0"
    ],
    "ssid": "$ssid",
    "trustedServerCertificateNames": [],
    "wiFiSecurityType": "wpaPersonal"
}
"@
```

5. Create the profile and grab the ID, then add it to the assignment URL:

```
$policy = Invoke-MgGraphRequest -Method POST -Uri $url -Body
$json -ContentType "application/json" -OutputType PSObject
$policyid = $policy.id
$assignurl = "https://graph.microsoft.com/beta/deviceManagement/
deviceConfigurations/$policyid/assign"
```

6. Finally, add the group ID to the JSON and assign the profile:

```
$assignjson = @"
{
    "assignments": [
        {
            "target": {
                "@odata.type": "#microsoft.graph.
groupAssignmentTarget",
                "groupId": "$groupid"
            }
        }
    ]
}
"@
Invoke-MgGraphRequest -Method POST -Uri $assignurl -Body
$assignjson -ContentType "application/json" -OutputType PSObject
```

By following this recipe, we have configured a Wi-Fi profile for our Android devices, both in the UI and using PowerShell.

Adding an app protection policy

We have now configured policies for our corporate-owned devices to keep them secured and managed, but what about devices owned by users who want to access their email and other corporate apps on their personal devices? One option is to block this completely, but for most, that is not ideal, and we will just end up with a much larger list of corporate devices to purchase and manage.

Another option is to do nothing and let them add the apps completely unmanaged, but from a data protection perspective, this is a security concern as you have no control over your corporate data.

For this, we can use app protection policies and enroll devices into **Mobile Application Management** (**MAM**) instead of **Mobile Device Management** (**MDM**). Both can be used for additional security, but this would be unusual as it will add extra steps for the users on their devices, and we can assume a managed device is secure at the device layer. We do not want users fully enrolling personal devices into the Intune tenant, so it is sensible to block personal devices; this will be covered in *Chapter 13*. We will also want to link this to an Entra conditional access policy to ensure unmanaged applications will not be able to access any data. Sending a **remote wipe** to these devices will also wipe corporate data from the managed apps, but not wipe the rest of the device.

We configured the MAM enrollment scopes in *Chapter 1*, so now, we need to configure the app protection policy and Entra conditional access policy.

App protection policies can be targeted at all applicable applications, be they Microsoft applications, core applications, or specific applications.

A list of the applications included in each is available here: `https://learn.microsoft.com/en-us/mem/intune/apps/apps-supported-intune-apps`.

How to do it...

We will start with the application protection policy and then move on to conditional access.

Adding an app protection policy

For this example, we will protect all Microsoft applications. If a different option is more suitable for your environment, it is a simple drop-down selection to change your choice as required:

1. First, we need to click on **Apps**.
2. Then, **App protection policies**.
3. Then, click **Create policy**.
4. Select **Android** from the dropdown.
5. Set your name and description, and then click **Next**. You will notice that the platform has been pre-configured for you.
6. On the next screen, we can select which apps to protect. If you want to protect selected apps, you need to click **+Select Public Apps** or **+Select Custom Apps**. Otherwise, change the dropdown so that it matches your needs.
7. In this case, we will select **All Microsoft Apps** and click **Next**.

   On the next screen, we must set the data protection settings for our data protected within these applications. You can set these as per your organization's requirements. As a general rule, the following settings are good to start with:

   - **Back up org data to Android backup services**: Block (one less breach to worry about)
   - **Send org data to other apps**: Policy-managed apps (we do not want data leaving our corporate *bubble* on the device)
   - **Save copies of org data**: Block with OneDrive and SharePoint selected (it is an unmanaged device, so we do not want data on the device; select Box if it is approved in your environment)

- **Transfer telecommunication data to**: Any policy-managed dialer app (again, keep things managed)

- **Open data into org documents**: Block with OneDrive for Business and SharePoint selected (this is for copying into documents, so it can be loosened if required)

- **Restrict cut, copy, and paste between other apps**: Policy-managed apps with paste-in (restrict within the bubble)

- **Screen capture and Google Assistant**: Block

- **Encrypt org data**: Require

- **Encrypt org data on enrolled devices**: Require

- **Sync policy-managed app data with native apps or add-ins**: Block (note that this blocks Outlook from adding to the native contacts, so be careful with this setting)

- **Printing org data**: Block (this is a little point-restricting if they can just print it)

- **Restrict web content transfer with other apps**: Microsoft Edge (this is a personal preference, but managing one browser across platforms is easier)

8. Once you have configured your settings, click **Next**.

9. The next screen (**Access requirements**) lets you specify access requirements for the applications themselves. As you cannot force the device to require a PIN, you can force the application itself to request one. Set these as preferred; it is often best to match the corporate device PIN requirements to make it easier to explain to end users.

10. The next page (**Conditional launch**) allows you to set further conditions for accessing the application, including the following

- **Max PIN attempts**: How many times an incorrect PIN can be entered. You can then either force a PIN reset or wipe the data.

- **Offline grace period**: After how many minutes you block access and after how many days you wipe the data.

- **Disabled account**: Block or allow access.

- **Minimum app version**: Oldest version of the app allowed (numeric)

You can also set restrictions on the device itself:

- **Jailbroken/rooted devices**: Block access or wipe data.

- **Minimum or Maximum OS version**: Warn, block, or wipe data (make sure you keep on top of this one if you are setting it).

- **Minimum patch version**: Warn, block, or wipe data.

- **Device manufacturer(s)**: Block or wipe anything not specified. This is an allow list, not a block list, so make sure you populate it carefully.

- **SafetyNet device attestation**: Warn, block, or wipe data (an API will confirm if the app and operating system are genuine).

- **Require threat scan on apps**: Warn or block.

- **Required SafetyNet evaluation type**: Hardware-backed key.

- **Require device lock** (low, medium, or high complexity): Warn, block, or wipe data.

- **Minimum Company Portal version** or **Maximum Company Portal age**: Warn, block, or wipe data (this is another one to keep on top of; otherwise, it will soon be useless if your minimum is out of date anyway).

- **Maximum allowed device threat level** (secured, low, medium, or high): Block or wipe data – this needs a Defender for Endpoint connection.

- **Primary MTD Service**: Either Defender for Endpoint or Mobile Threat Defense (non-Microsoft) – your device's antivirus.

11. Once you have configured your settings, click **Next**. See the following screenshot for the settings that were used in this example:

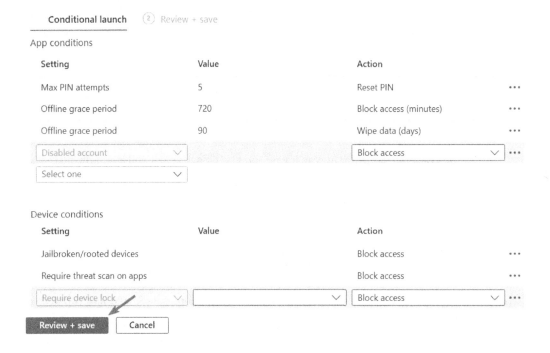

Figure 5.5 – Conditional launch settings

12. On the next screen, you will notice that we cannot assign this to the **All Users** or **All Devices** virtual groups. This is also a user-based policy as we have no information on the devices themselves, so we will assign it to the **Intune Users** group. Then, click **Next.**

13. Finally, double-check your settings and click **Create**.

Creating the conditional access policy

At this point, we have our app protection policy with all of the lovely **Block Access** settings, but Intune itself cannot block access to Microsoft 365 applications. For that, we need to use conditional access. There are new policy templates for most requirements, but in this case, we will manually create the policy so that you can understand the settings.

To find out more about conditional access policies, visit this page: `https://learn.microsoft.com/en-us/azure/active-directory/conditional-access/overview`.

One important thing to note is that when you are setting up conditional access policies, make sure you have a break-glass account configured that is excluded from all policies. If you accidentally set a policy that locks everyone out, you can use this to access the environment and fix the issue. A break-glass account should be a non-user account with a very secure password stored on paper in a secure location (ideally a fireproof safe). If possible, also link it to a FIDO2 security key stored in another safe. Remember that this account has full access to your environment without any of your conditional access protections, so it needs to be secured accordingly.

To access conditional access policies, follow these steps:

1. You can either use the Entra portal or, within **Endpoint security**, click **Conditional access**.

2. Click **Polices | +New policy**.

3. Give your policy a name and then click **0 users and groups selected**.

4. Select **All Users** under **Include** and then **Exclude** your break-glass account.

5. Now, click **No cloud apps, actions, or authentication contexts selected**.

6. Select **All Cloud apps** – we want this policy to protect everything.

7. Click **0 conditions selected**.

8. Then, click **Device Platforms Not Configured**.

9. Set **Configure** to **Yes**. As app protection is only supported on Android, Windows, and iOS, we need to restrict the platforms for this policy. While we are currently configuring for Android, *Chapter 6* covers iOS, so it makes sense to use the same policy for both. Windows has different requirements, so policy will be covered in *Chapter 11*.

10. Select **Android** and **iOS** and click **Done**:

Figure 5.6 – Device platforms

11. Click **0 controls selected** underneath **Grant**.

12. Tick **Require app protection policy** and click **Select**:

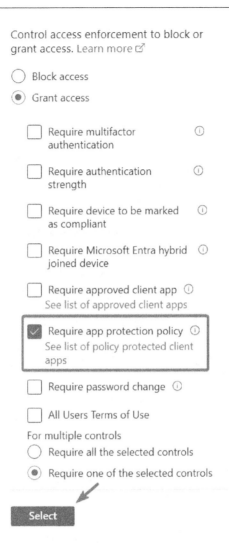

Figure 5.7 – Selecting grant controls

Session controls allows you to set a sign-in frequency and other session-based settings. We do not need those here.

13. At the bottom of the page, you can set the policy to **Off**, **Report-Only**, or **On**. For most policies, it is best to check the impact by setting it to **Report-Only**, but as this is a security-related policy, we can switch it straight to **On** as we do not want users accessing apps that are not protected anyway. Then, click **Create**.

Let us move on to the next subsection.

Automating it

These two policies are slightly different when it comes to automation – they are still JSON, but their structure is slightly different.

App protection policy

Starting with the app protection policy, the first thing you will notice is that the assignment is part of the policy creation and not a second POST request afterward. It is stored in an array within the JSON.

You will also notice that all settings are available within the JSON, so in that respect, it is easier to configure and amend:

1. As usual, we will start with the name, description, and group ID:

   ```
   $name = "Android App Protection Policy"
   $description = "Microsoft Apps Only"
   $groupid = "00000000-0000-0000-0000-000000000000"
   ```

2. Now, we need to set the URL. This one is in the deviceAppManagement category and androidManagedAppProtections sub-category:

   ```
   $url = "https://graph.microsoft.com/beta/deviceAppManagement/
   androidManagedAppProtections"
   ```

3. Finally, we must add the variables to the JSON with the settings we configured earlier. The full JSON is available in this book's GitHub repository, so we will just include a few settings here as an example:

   ```
   $json = @"
   {
       "@odata.type": "#microsoft.graph.
   androidManagedAppProtection",
       "allowedAndroidDeviceManufacturers": "",
       "allowedDataIngestionLocations": [
           "oneDriveForBusiness",
           "sharePoint"
       ],
       "allowedDataStorageLocations": [
           "oneDriveForBusiness",
           "sharePoint"
       ],
   ```

```
    "allowedInboundDataTransferSources": "managedApps",
    "allowedOutboundClipboardSharingExceptionLength": 0,
    "allowedOutboundClipboardSharingLevel":
"managedAppsWithPasteIn",
    "allowedOutboundDataTransferDestinations": "managedApps",
    "apps": [],
    "assignments": [
        {
            "target": {
                "@odata.type": "#microsoft.graph.
groupAssignmentTarget",
                "deviceAndAppManagementAssignmentFilterId":
null,
                "deviceAndAppManagementAssignmentFilterType":
"none",
                "groupId": "$groupid"
            }
        }
    ],
    "biometricAuthenticationBlocked": false,
    "description": "$description",
    "deviceComplianceRequired": true,
    "deviceLockRequired": false,
    "dialerRestrictionLevel": "managedApps",
    "disableAppEncryptionIfDeviceEncryptionIsEnabled": false,
    "disableAppPinIfDevicePinIsSet": false,
    "displayName": "$name",
    "encryptAppData": true
}
"@
```

4. We need to create the policy, but as we have already assigned it, we do not need the output in a variable:

    ```
    Invoke-MgGraphRequest -Method POST -Uri $url -Body $json
    -ContentType "application/json"
    ```

Next, we will configure our conditional access policy.

Conditional access policy

Conditional access policies also do not need assigning as we select which users are applied in the policy configuration.

These use nested arrays to hold the settings for each of the areas we configured earlier (apps, session, grant, and so on):

1. First, set the name:

   ```
   $name = "Require App Protection Policy"
   ```

2. Set the URL. While we accessed this through Endpoint Security, it has an Entra ID configuration underneath, so the URL is within the identity category:

   ```
   $url = "https://graph.microsoft.com/v1.0/identity/
   conditionalAccess/policies"
   ```

3. As we mentioned earlier, the full code is in this book's GitHub repository, so the code here is only to give you an example. Each category/array has an included/excluded option (a further array) that is configured accordingly:

   ```
   "conditions": {
       "applications": {
           "excludeApplications": [],
           "includeApplications": [
               "All"
           ],
           "includeAuthenticationContextClassReferences": [],
           "includeUserActions": [],
           "networkAccess": null
       },
       "clientApplications": null,
       "clientAppTypes": [
           "all"
       ],
       "clients": null,
       "devices": null,
       "locations": null,
       "platforms": {
           "excludePlatforms": [],
           "includePlatforms": [
               "android",
               "iOS"
           ]
       },
   ```

This policy is an everything policy, so no exclusions are included.

4.   Finally, create the policy:

```
Invoke-MgGraphRequest -Method POST -Uri $url -Body $json
-ContentType "application/json" -OutputType PSObject
```

There's more...

Similar to the OEM Config policy, you can also configure an app configuration policy via **Apps** | **App Configuration Policies**.

For supported apps, app configuration policies allow you to configure application-specific settings such as home screen settings for Microsoft Launcher or Exchange settings for Microsoft Outlook.

These can be configured using a GUI or raw JSON, as with the OEM policy we created earlier.

You have now completed this recipe and configured an app protection policy and conditional access policy to protect your personally owned devices.

Enrolling an Android device – managed device

Now that our policies have been fully configured, we can start enrolling our devices, starting with fully managed, corporate accounts. To do this, we will need an Android device that can be wiped for enrollment.

Getting ready

Wipe your Android device to the screen where you are prompted to enter your Gmail account and have your previously created QR code ready.

How to do it...

Follow these steps:

1.   On the screen where you must enter your credentials, you have two options, depending on the age of the device. For older devices, you will need to enter **afw#setup**; on newer devices, repeatedly tap the same screen:

Figure 5.8 – Android's Sign in screen

Click **Accept and Continue** on the **Let's set up your work device** screen.

2.   Scan your QR code (or enter it manually) and click **Accept & Continue**.

3.   Click **Next** on the privacy screen.

4.   Click **ACCEPT & CONTINUE** on the Chrome screen.

5.   Enter your email and password to sign in.

6.   Set up your screen lock.

7.   Set up notification settings and click **Next**. The settings are not important here as we have configured it via policy anyway.

8.   Click **Install** on the **Install work apps** screen.

9.   Click **Done** to confirm the required apps (these will vary, depending on your environment).

10. Click **Set up** on the **Register your device** screen.

11. Click **Sign In** on the Intune screen.

12. Click **Done**.

You will be taken to your device's home screen. Congratulations – you have enrolled your Android device!

Enrolling an Android device – BYOD

The preceding recipe was for corporate-owned devices. However, you cannot reset and enroll a personally owned device without many complaints. So, for these devices, we will use the Company Portal app to install our deployed apps into the secure work profile. As you will recall from earlier, personally owned devices with a work profile are enabled without any further configuration.

There are two ways of doing this, depending on your configuration – you can either allow or block personal devices to enroll with a work profile (covered in *Chapter 13*). The enrollment process is slightly different for each, so we will run through both here.

Getting ready...

For this recipe, you will need a current Android device with a connection to the Play Store and a signed-in account.

How to do it...

First, let us check what happens if you have personal enrollment *allowed* within your tenant.

Enrolling with personal enrollment allowed

Follow these steps:

1. Within the Google Play Store, find **Intune Company Portal** and click **Install**.

2. Once complete, click **Open**.

3. Once loaded, click **Sign In**.

4. After entering your credentials, you will be prompted to configure and activate your work profile. Click **Begin**.

5. Review the permissions settings and click **Continue**.

6. You then have another set of terms to **Accept & continue**.

7. The phone will now configure the work profile, which can take a couple of minutes. Once it is finished, you will see the following screen; click **Next**:

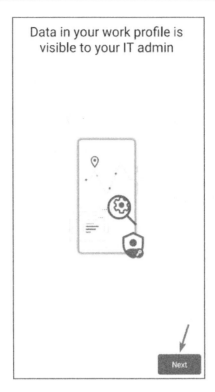

Figure 5.9 – Work profile permissions

8. This will configure and return you to Company Portal. After re-authenticating, you will be taken back to the original screen, this time to activate the work profile. Click **Continue**.

9. After a minute or so, you will return to the screen where everything should be configured. Click **Done**.

10. You will now be given a quick overview of how a work profile works. Click **Got It**.

11. To see the available apps, click **Open** in the notification at the bottom. Alternatively, you can click the Play Store icon with a briefcase next to it:

Figure 5.10 – Work profile – Play Store

As you can see, we published Outlook as an available app that now appears here. If we install this, it will be installed in the work profile, where we can control the data inside it. All work profile applications have a briefcase on the icon.

Now, let us see what happens if you have personal enrollment blocked.

Enrolling with personal enrollment blocked

This process still uses Company Portal to enforce our app protection policies. The application itself does nothing else – you cannot install applications from within it; it just serves as a broker:

1. Find and install **Microsoft Outlook** (or Word, Excel, or something else).

2. After installing it, click **Open**.

3. After logging in, you will be presented with the following screen. Click **GO TO STORE**:

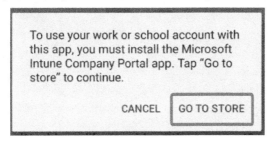

Figure 5.11 – GO TO STORE

4. This will take you to Company Portal. Click **Install**.

5. After installing it, click **Open**.

You will then be taken back to Outlook to continue as normal. All data within the application is secured via the app protection policy.

That completes this recipe on enrolling your Android BYOD.

6
iOS Device Management

We have covered Windows and Android enrollment, so the next logical step is iOS devices. This chapter looks at iOS device management, configuring policies to manage enterprise-owned and managed devices, and app protection policies for protecting your user-owned **Bring Your own Device** (**BYOD**). For our enterprise devices, we will be using **Apple Business Manager** (**ABM**) (or Apple Education). Configuring this is explained in the *Technical requirements* section.

We will also run through the process of configuring Intune to work with ABM and deploying applications using the **Volume Purchase Program** (**VPP**).

Finally, we will enroll both a managed device and a BYOD.

This chapter will include the following recipes:

- Configuring a connector between Apple and Intune
- Configuring an Apple VPP token
- Adding enrollment profile tokens
- Configuring iOS policies using the settings catalog
- Configuring iOS policies using device restrictions
- Deploying applications via Apple VPP
- Configuring iOS update settings
- Configuring an app protection policy
- Enrolling your device: corporate
- Enrolling your device: BYOD

Chapter materials

As with *Chapters 2* and *5*, this chapter will not cover all available policy types, so we will run through them all now to get a better understanding of what is available for iOS devices. You will notice more similarities with Windows profile types than with Android here, including the migration to the unified settings catalog.

The available profile types are as follows:

- **Settings catalog**: The unified settings catalog is the more modern way to deploy settings. We will cover this in the *Configuring iOS policies using the settings catalog* section.

- **Derived credential**: This is used for certificate authentication within apps. You can read more at https://learn.microsoft.com/en-gb/mem/intune/protect/derived-credentials.

- **Device restrictions**: This is an alternative to the settings catalog for your standard restrictions. We will cover it in the *Configuring iOS policies using device restrictions* section.

- **Device features**: Device restrictions are used to protect and lock down devices. Device features provide more custom settings, such as lock-screen messages, home screen layouts, and so on.

- **Edition upgrade and mode switch**: While sharing the name with the Windows profile type, this actually just sets dates and times for updates to be installed.

- **Email**: This configures email settings for the built-in mail client.

- **PKCS certificate**: This configures a public key pair certificate for authentication.

- **PKCS imported certificate**: This sets up an imported PKCS for S/MIME email authentication.

- **SCEP certificate**: This is used for certificate-based device authentication.

- **Secure assessment (Education)**: This is used to configure student and teacher certificates for the classroom app. You can read more at https://learn.microsoft.com/en-us/mem/intune/fundamentals/education-settings-configure-ios.

- **Trusted certificate**: This imports a trusted root certificate from an on-prem certificate authority server.

- **VPN**: This configures a VPN connection for your iOS devices.

- **Wi-Fi**: This configures Wi-Fi profiles, both basic and enterprise-supported, and can be used with certification profiles where applicable.

Important notes

It is important when dealing with Apple devices to keep an eye on the certificate renewal dates and to record them somewhere with a reminder. You could also use Azure Automation to automate the reminders for you. See more at `https://andrewstaylor.com/2022/06/07/alerting-when-my-apple-certificates-expire-in-intune-using-azure-automation/`.

The MDM push certificate connects your devices to the Intune MDM service. If this one expires, you can contact Apple directly within 30 days of expiry to renew it. If they cannot, or if 30 days have passed, your only option is to wipe and re-enroll all your devices. *Yes, this is a full wipe, data destruction, everything.*

An enrollment token is used to enroll your devices initially. If this one expires, you must create a new enrollment profile and transfer your devices to it. It is not quite as bad as a wipe, but it can result in the devices looking less healthy within the Intune portal itself.

The Apple VPP certificate is used to deploy applications to devices. If that one expires, users will not be able to download and install any new applications until it is renewed. This is not a massive issue and they are easy to replace, but you could waste time troubleshooting an app install issue and not consider this as the issue.

When looking at your device restrictions/settings catalog policy, the settings you configure need to be tailored to your specific needs to provide the best security without ruining the end user experience. Blocking the App Store, iCloud, and so on is a good starting point.

The official CIS benchmarks for iOS can be found at `https://www.cisecurity.org/benchmark/apple_ios`.

The NCSC guidance can be found at `https://github.com/ukncsc/Device-Security-Guidance-Configuration-Packs/tree/main/Apple/iOS`.

While these should not be used as the only way to configure your settings, they are an excellent starting point, as iOS does not offer pre-configured security baselines like with Windows.

Some rough guidance to start with can be found here:

`https://github.com/PacktPublishing/Microsoft-Intune-Cookbook/blob/main/Chapter-6/Recommended_iOS_Config.txt`

Technical requirements

For this chapter, you will need a modern web browser and a PowerShell code editor such as Visual Studio Code or the PowerShell ISE. You will also need to be connected to Microsoft Graph, as outlined in *Chapter 1*.

All of the scripts referenced can be found here: `https://github.com/PacktPublishing/Microsoft-Intune-Cookbook`

You will need an ABM account set up and ready to be configured with Intune. You can find instructions for setting up your ABM account at `https://www.apple.com/business/docs/site/Apple_Business_Manager_Getting_Started_Guide.pdf` and `https://www.intuneirl.com/onboarding-to-abm/`.

Your hardware supplier or service provider should be able to add your devices to ABM, but you can also use Apple Configurator on a device running macOS or iOS: `https://support.apple.com/en-gb/apple-configurator`

Alternatively, you can follow these videos:

`https://www.youtube.com/watch?v=G_9bPrsJHGY&t=34s`

`https://www.youtube.com/watch?v=G-rvHUY4iA0`

For enrolling devices, you will need an iOS device enrolled in ABM and a standard iOS device for BYOD enrollment.

Configuring a connector between Apple and Intune

Before we can enroll or configure devices, we need to set up a connector to link Intune to ABM or Apple Education. We will cover that here.

Getting started

Before starting this recipe, log in to your ABM account and navigate to your account preferences. From here, we can add an MDM server.

It is worth having Intune in a different tab, as we will be switching between the two when configuring the certificates.

How to do it...

Follow these instructions:

1. In the Intune portal, navigate to **Devices** and then **iOS.**

2. Next, click on **iOS/iPadOS Enrollment.**

3. You will notice there is only one option available here, which is **Apple MDM Push certificate**, so click on that.

4. In the popup, check the box and download the CSR certificate.

5. Then, click on the **Create your MDM push Certificate** link, which will take you to the Apple portal.

6. Click **Create a certificate.**

7. Check the box and click **Accept.**

8. Upload the CSR we downloaded from the Intune portal.

9. Make a note of the expiry date, add a reminder somewhere, and then click **Download.**

Figure 6.1 – Downloading the certificate

10. Enter your Managed Apple ID (do not use a personal Apple ID), upload the certificate, and click **Upload.**

11. You should now see a success message in the same panel.

Figure 6.2 – Intune MDM certificate status

Intune is now connected to ABM and the status should change to **Active**, as shown in *Figure 6.2*, which is the first step to deploying devices. In the next section, we will look at the Apple VPP token used to deploy applications.

Configuring an Apple VPP token

Now we have our environments linked, we need to configure our VPP token for application deployment.

Getting started

Open two tabs, one on Apple Business Manager and one in the Intune portal. We will again be switching between them for certificates.

How to do it...

Follow these instructions:

1. Within Apple Business Manager's preferences, click **Payments and Billing**.
2. At the bottom of the page, download the content token.
3. Now return to Intune, navigate to **Tenant administration**, and click on **Connectors and tokens**.
4. Click on **Apple VPP Tokens**.
5. Click **Create** at the top.
6. Enter a name and your Apple ID, upload the certificate from before, and click **Next**.
7. This is our only MDM server, so we can leave the top option as **No**.
8. Set the region, set the account type (usually **Business**, unless you are configuring for an education establishment), and select whether you want to allow automatic app updates. Finally, agree to the permissions and click **Next**:

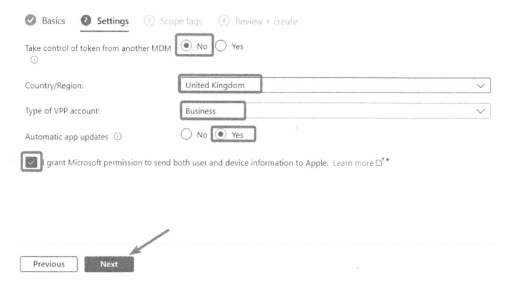

Figure 6.3 – VPP token settings

9. Click **Next** when on the **Scope tags** tab.

10. Check that everything is correct and click **Create**.

Automating it

This is the first step we can fully automate using Graph, but only after downloading the token from ABM:

1. First, we need to set our basic variables, including the path to the VPP token:

    ```
    $url = "https://graph.microsoft.com/beta/deviceAppManagement/
    vppTokens"
    $tokenpath = "c:\temp\vpptoken.vpp"
    $appleid = "APPLEID"
    $tokentype = "business"
    $name = "Apple VPP"
    ```

2. Now, obviously, we cannot upload a file, so we need to convert it to base64:

    ```
    $token = [System.Convert]::ToBase64String([System.
    Text.Encoding]::UTF8.GetBytes([System.
    IO.File]::ReadAllText($tokenpath)))
    ```

3. Populate the JSON, note the country code, and enable automatic app updates:

    ```
    $json = @"
    {
        "@odata.type": "#microsoft.graph.vppToken",
        "appleId": "$appleid",
        "automaticallyUpdateApps": true,
        "claimTokenManagementFromExternalMdm": false,
        "countryOrRegion": "gb",
        "dataSharingConsentGranted": true,
        "displayName": "$name",
        "roleScopeTagIds": [
            "0"
        ],
        "token": "$token",
        "vppTokenAccountType": "$tokentype"
    }
    "@
    ```

4. Finally, create the token:

    ```
    Invoke-MgGraphRequest -Uri $url -Method Post -body $json
    -ContentType "application/json"
    ```

Let us move on to the next recipe.

Adding enrollment profile tokens

The last step before we can enroll devices is to configure an enrollment profile token. We then configure ABM to use this token when deploying devices.

How to do it...

Follow these instructions:

1. Start by clicking **Devices** and then **iOS/iPadOS**.
2. Then, click **iOS/iPadOS enrollment**.
3. Click **Enrollment program tokens**.
4. Click **Add** at the top.
5. Check **Agree** and download the public key, as we will need that in Apple Business Manager.
6. Navigate to Apple Business Manager via the link:

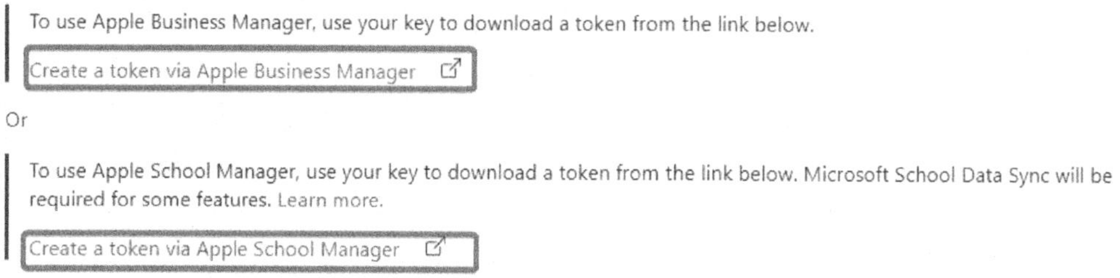

To use Apple Business Manager, use your key to download a token from the link below.

Create a token via Apple Business Manager   ⬚

Or

To use Apple School Manager, use your key to download a token from the link below. Microsoft School Data Sync will be required for some features. Learn more.

Create a token via Apple School Manager   ⬚

Figure 6.4 – The Apple Business Manager and Apple School Manager links

7. In Apple Business Manager, within your profile, click **Add** next to **Your MDM Servers**.

8. Enter a name, upload the certificate, and click **Save**.

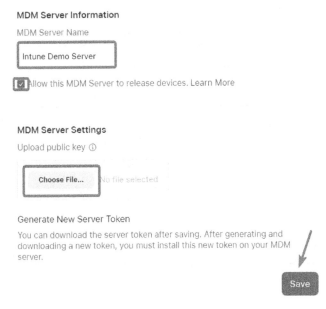

MDM Server Information

MDM Server Name

Intune Demo Server

☑ Allow this MDM Server to release devices. Learn More

MDM Server Settings

Upload public key ⓘ

Choose File...   No file selected

Generate New Server Token

You can download the server token after saving. After generating and downloading a new token, you must install this new token on your MDM server.

Save

Figure 6.5 – Uploading the server token

9. Click **Download Token**.

10. Back in the Intune portal, enter the Apple ID, select the certificate just downloaded, and click **Next**:

Save the Apple ID used in Apple Business Manager or Apple School Manager to create this token for future reference. You must log in to the portal to renew enrollment tokens annually.

Apple ID *

Upload your token. Intune will automatically sync devices from your Apple Business Manager or Apple School Manager account assigned to the MDM server associated with this token

Apple token *   "Intune_Token_2022-08-30T12-40-34Z_smime.p7m"

Previous   Next

Figure 6.6 – Adding the ABM enrollment token

11. Finally, check that everything is correct and click **Create**.

12. There are now two steps to complete for enrollment. First, in the Apple Business Manager portal, click **MDM Server Assignment**.

13. Click **Edit**.

14. Select your MDM server for each applicable hardware type and click **Save**.

15. Now return to the Intune portal and click on your new enrollment program token:

Token name	↑	Status	Program type	↑	Apple ID	↑	Devices synced
Intune		✓ Active	Apple Business Manager				1

Figure 6.7 – Intune enrollment program tokens

16. Click **Profiles**.

17. Click **Create profile** and select **iOS/iPadOS**.

18. Enter the basic details and click **Next**.

    There are options on the next screen:

    - **User affinity**: Here, you can select whether devices are enrolled to a specific user (**Enroll with User Affinity**), without a user, such as a kiosk (**Enroll without User Affinity**), or as a shared device (**Enroll with Microsoft Entra shared mode**). We are configuring a standard user device, so we select **Enroll with User Affinity**.

19. This will load some new options to pick from. First is the authentication method: you can either deploy and use **Company Portal** to authenticate the users or use **Setup Assistant with modern authentication**.

20. **Setup Assistant with modern authentication** is often more reliable, so we are going to use that one for this example. This also allows required authentication using Entra ID credentials during the **out-of-box experience** (**OOBE**) prior to accessing the device's home screen. It is also a requirement for **Just in Time enrollment** (covered in the *Enrolling your device: corporate* section).

21. We want to use the VPP to install the app, so the user does not require an Apple ID.

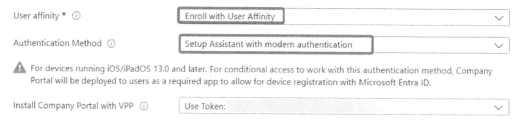

User Affinity & Authentication Method

User affinity * ⓘ	Enroll with User Affinity ⌄
Authentication Method ⓘ	Setup Assistant with modern authentication ⌄

⚠ For devices running iOS/iPadOS 13.0 and later. For conditional access to work with this authentication method, Company Portal will be deployed to users as a required app to allow for device registration with Microsoft Entra ID.

Install Company Portal with VPP ⓘ	Use Token: ⌄

Figure 6.8 – Authentication methods

Whichever authentication method has been chosen, make sure **Supervised** is set to **Yes** to allow for more device configuration for an unsupervised device.

22. Locked enrollment stops users from removing the profile from the device. Unless you are using Apple Configurator, set **Sync with computers** to **Deny All**:

Figure 6.9 – Locked enrollment

Finally, you can set **Device Name Template**, which supports the `{{SERIAL}}` and `{{DEVICETYPE}}` variables as well as any plain text.

23. **Activate cellular data** is for any compatible eSim devices (you will need the server URL from your carrier if you set this to **Yes**). Click **Next**.

24. On the next screen, you can select what options are available during setup and input IT contact details in case of issues.

25. It is recommended to hide as many setup screens as possible to speed up the process for your users and protect devices. Generally, just leaving **Passcode** and **Touch ID** and **Face ID** enabled should be all that is required.

26. Once you have configured your settings, click **Next**.

27. Now review the settings and click **Create**.

28. Finally, click **Set default profile**.

29. Select the profile just created and click **OK**. After configuring all of these settings, any devices now added to Apple Business Manager will automatically be assigned to Intune and configured with the enrollment profile token created.

30. If needed, you can assign a profile directly to a device by clicking **Devices** within the token, selecting the device, and clicking the **Assign profile** button.

Automating it

The JSON for this is reasonably straightforward (although as a restrictions policy contains all available settings whether configured or not, the code is long), but first, we need to populate the URL with the ID of the Apple token:

1. First, set the variables:

```
$name = "iOS Enrollment"
$description = "Corporate Managed iOS Devices"
```

2. Now we need to run a GET command to grab the ID of the token. It is within the `Value` array within the output, as with most graph objects, to allow pagination. We are looking for the ID setting:

```
$settingsurl = "https://graph.microsoft.com/beta/
deviceManagement/depOnboardingSettings/"
$tokenid = (Invoke-MgGraphRequest -Method GET -Uri $settingsurl
-OutputType PSObject).value.id
```

3. Now we populate that in the URL:

```
$url = "https://graph.microsoft.com/beta/deviceManagement/
depOnboardingSettings/$tokenid/enrollmentProfiles"
```

4. Add the variables into the JSON. You can see that every setting is configured with either a `true` or `false` value (the full JSON is available on the GitHub repository; the following has been shortened for brevity):

```
$json = @"
{
    "@odata.type": "#microsoft.graph.depIOSEnrollmentProfile",
    "appearanceScreenDisabled": true,
    "configurationEndpointUrl": "",
    "configurationWebUrl": true,
    "description": "$description",
    "deviceNameTemplate": "{{DEVICETYPE}}-{{SERIAL}}",
    "deviceToDeviceMigrationDisabled": true,
    "diagnosticsDisabled": true,
    "displayName": "$name",
    "enabledSkipKeys": [
        "Location"
    ],
    "enableSharedIPad": false,
    "zoomDisabled": true
}
"@
```

5. Finally, create the profile. There is no need to assign this one, but we still need to store it in a variable to set it as our default profile:

```
$iosprofile = Invoke-MgGraphRequest -Method POST -Uri $url -Body
$json -ContentType "application/json" -OutputType PSObject
```

6. To set the default profile, we send a POST request with an empty body, as the URL does the configuration for us. Grab the ID:

```
$profileid = $iosprofile.id
```

7. Now populate the URL and send the request:

```
$defaulturl = "https://graph.microsoft.com/beta/
deviceManagement/depOnboardingSettings/$tokenid/
enrollmentProfiles/$profileid/setDefaultProfile"
Invoke-MgGraphRequest -Method POST -Uri $defaulturl -ContentType
"application/json" -OutputType PSObject
```

Let us move on to the next recipe.

Configuring iOS policies using the settings catalog

Our connection between ABM and Intune is now complete. We could enroll devices now if we wanted, but we have not configured any policies or applications yet, so we want to configure those first. Policies can be configured using either the **settings catalog** or **device restrictions**. Both configure the same settings. Using the settings catalog is more modern, but either will work. For this recipe, we will use the settings catalog, and in the next one, we will use device restrictions.

How to do it...

Follow these instructions:

1. In the Intune console, select **Devices** and then **iOS/iPadOS**.
2. Click **Configuration profiles** and click **New policy**.
3. In the flyout menu, select **Settings catalog** and click **Create**.
4. As usual, provide a name and description and click **Next**.

   You will now see the settings picker we covered earlier during Windows profile creation (*Chapter 2*). Here, you can select the settings applicable to your environment. This list will continue to expand, so what is listed currently may increase as new settings are added. For this example, we are going to configure a couple of device restrictions to match the device restrictions policy we will set up in the next recipe.

5. Once you have configured your settings, click **Next**:

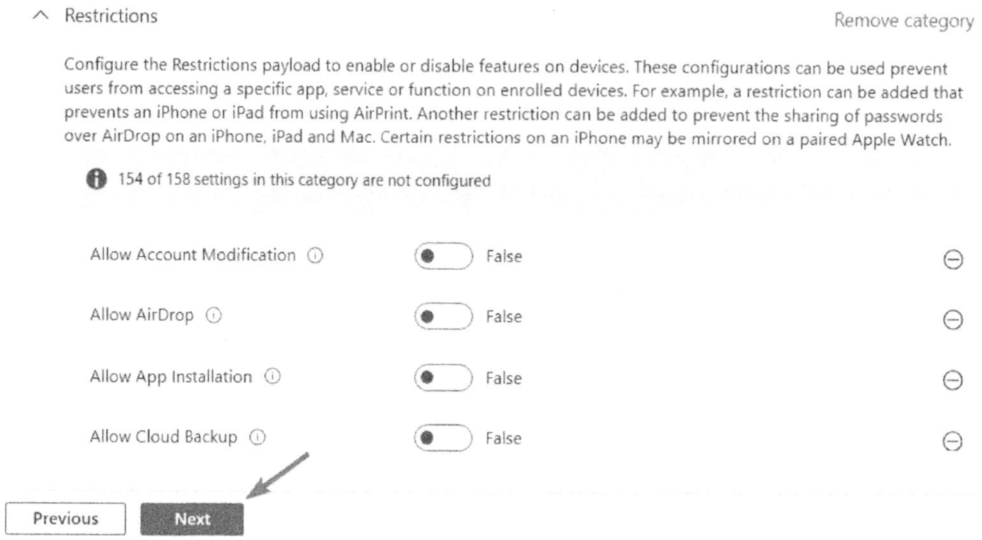

∧ Restrictions   Remove category

Configure the Restrictions payload to enable or disable features on devices. These configurations can be used prevent
users from accessing a specific app, service or function on enrolled devices. For example, a restriction can be added that
prevents an iPhone or iPad from using AirPrint. Another restriction can be added to prevent the sharing of passwords
over AirDrop on an iPhone, iPad and Mac. Certain restrictions on an iPhone may be mirrored on a paired Apple Watch.

ℹ 154 of 158 settings in this category are not configured

Allow Account Modification ⓘ   (●) False   ⊖

Allow AirDrop ⓘ   (●) False   ⊖

Allow App Installation ⓘ   (●) False   ⊖

Allow Cloud Backup ⓘ   (●) False   ⊖

[Previous]   [**Next**]

Figure 6.10 – Profile configured settings

6. We do not need scope tags, so click **Next**.

    We can assign this depending on our preference. For device restrictions, you could select all
    devices and filter on iOS devices, create a dynamic group, or just use a static user or device-
    based group. These types of settings will usually apply across the estate, so using a dynamic
    group or using filters will save time managing the groups and reduce the risk of a device being
    issued without the restrictions applied.

    If using a dynamic group, you could use `enrollmentProfileName equals xxx`, where
    xxx is the profile name we configured earlier, or `deviceOSType equals iOS`. For a filter,
    you can also use the enrollment profile name and select the filter for just iOS/iPadOS devices.

7. Click **Next** after assignment.

8. Finally, check that everything looks correct and click **Create**.

Automating it

This follows the same setup as the Windows settings catalog policies, though there are a few small differences:

1. The first difference is the category. To find all of the settings applicable to iOS, you need to run a GET request against this URL:

```
https://graph.microsoft.com/beta/deviceManagement/
configurationCategories?=&`$filter=(platforms has
'iOS') and (technologies has 'mdm' or technologies has
'appleRemoteManagement')
```

You can see not only are we looking at the platform but we are also extending the technologies to include `appleRemoteManagement`. This is similar to how we had to expand it for the security policies.

The other important thing to note is that many of the iOS settings have dependent parent settings. You can find out if the setting you are configuring has a dependency by looking at the **Options** field on the policy itself.

We can take `AllowNFC` as an example and expand the policy options:

```
itemId        : com.apple.applicationaccess_allownfc_false
description   :
helpText      :
name          : Disabled
displayName   : False
optionValue   : @{@odata.type=#microsoft.graph.
deviceManagementConfigurationStringSettingValue;
settingValueTemplateReference=; value=false}
dependentOn   : {@{dependentOn=com.apple.applicationaccess_
com.apple.applicationaccess; parentSettingId=com.apple.
applicationaccess_com.apple.applicationaccess}}
dependedOnBy : {}
```

You can see that this particular policy setting requires `com.apple.applicationaccess`.

Now, when we create our JSON, we do not jump straight into configuring the settings as follows:

```
"settingInstance": {
              "@odata.type": "#microsoft.graph.
deviceManagementConfigurationChoiceSettingInstance",
              "settingDefinitionId": "$policysettingid",
              "choiceSettingValue": {
                  "@odata.type": "#microsoft.graph.
deviceManagementConfigurationChoiceSettingValue",
                  "value": "$selectedvalue",
                  "children": []
```

```
            }
        }
```

We instead need to use `GroupSettingsCollectionInstance` and add child items and the parent ID:

```
"settingInstance": {
    "@odata.type": "#microsoft.graph.
deviceManagementConfigurationGroupSettingCollectionInstance",
    "groupSettingCollectionValue": [
        {
            "children": [
                {
                    "@odata.type": "#microsoft.graph.
deviceManagementConfigurationChoiceSettingInstance",
                    "choiceSettingValue": {
                        "@odata.type": "#microsoft.graph.
deviceManagementConfigurationChoiceSettingValue",
                        "children": [],
                        "value": "$selectedvalue"
                    },
                    "settingDefinitionId": "$policyid"
                }
            ]
        }
    ],
    "settingDefinitionId": "$dependancy"
}
```

2. Now, to look at the policy we created earlier, we set our variables, including the URL, which you will notice is the same as for any other settings catalog policy:

```
$name = "iOS Settings Catalog"
$description = "Blocks iCloud, App Store and AirDrop"
$groupid = "00000000-0000-0000-0000-000000000000"
$url = "https://graph.microsoft.com/beta/deviceManagement/
configurationPolicies"
```

3. Now we populate the JSON using the additional parent/child settings as discussed. Unlike the Windows settings where the value was usually a Boolean value of 0 or 1 for true or false, the iOS settings actually use the text `True` and `False` to differentiate them. Again, this has been shortened for brevity and the full JSON is available in the GitHub repository:

```
$json = @"
{
    "description": "$description",
    "name": "$name",
```

```
        "platforms": "iOS",
        "roleScopeTagIds": [
            "0"
        ],
        "settings": [
            {
                "@odata.type": "#microsoft.graph.
deviceManagementConfigurationSetting",
                "settingInstance": {
                    "@odata.type": "#microsoft.graph.
deviceManagementConfigurationGroupSettingCollectionInstance",
                    "groupSettingCollectionValue": [
                        {
                            "children": [
                                {
                                    "@odata.type": "#microsoft.
graph.deviceManagementConfigurationChoiceSettingInstance",
                                    "choiceSettingValue": {
                                        "@odata.type": "#microsoft.
graph.deviceManagementConfigurationChoiceSettingValue",
                                        "children": [],
                                        "value": "com.apple.
applicationaccess_allowaccountmodification_false"
                                    },
                                    "settingDefinitionId": "com.
apple.applicationaccess_allowaccountmodification"
                            "settingDefinitionId": "com.apple.
applicationaccess_com.apple.applicationaccess"
                        }
                    }
            ],
        "technologies": "mdm,appleRemoteManagement"
    }
"@
```

4. Now we just need a standard policy creation and assignment, the same as with any other policy:

```
$createprofile = Invoke-MgGraphRequest -Uri $url -Method Post
-body $json -ContentType "application/json" -OutputType PSObject
$profileid = $createprofile.id
$assignurl = "https://graph.microsoft.com/beta/deviceManagement/
configurationPolicies/$profileid/assign"
$assignjson = @"
{
    "assignments": [
        {
```

```
                        "target": {
                            "@odata.type": "#microsoft.graph.
            groupAssignmentTarget",
                            "groupId": "$groupid"
                        }
                    }
                ]
            }
            "@
            Invoke-MgGraphRequest -Method POST -Uri $assignurl -Body
            $assignjson -ContentType "application/json"
```

Let us move on to the next recipe.

Configuring iOS policies using device restrictions

The preceding recipe demonstrated how to use the new settings catalog to create a new profile for your iOS devices, but there is also the option to use a device restrictions policy, which is similar to that used with the Android devices in the previous chapter.

This recipe will demonstrate how to configure and automate your policy using the device restrictions profile type.

How to do it...

Follow these instructions:

1. As before, in the Intune console, select **Devices** and then **iOS/iPadOS**.
2. Click **Configuration profiles** and click **New policy**.
3. This time, instead of settings catalog, pick **Templates** and then **Device restrictions**. Click **Create**.
4. As usual, populate the basic details and click **Next**.

    Here, you can find all of the device restrictions grouped, but without the useful search functionality found in the settings catalog.

    We are going to configure the same three settings as earlier to block iCloud backups (found in **Cloud and Storage**), the App Store (found in the App Store), and AirDrop (found under **Connected devices**). Then, click **Next**:

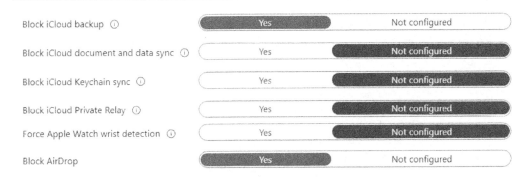

Figure 6.11 – Device restriction settings

5. You cannot set a scope tag on a device restrictions policy, so we are taken directly to the assignments page. The same applies to the earlier policy. You can use filtering here as well. Once you have created the assignment, click **Next**.

6. Finally, check that everything is correct and click **Create**.

Automating it

Being a device restrictions profile, this recipe is easier than the settings catalog recipe, as it has a finite number of settings. Even if we configure all of them, the underlying JSON will be a lot more manageable. If you try to configure every settings catalog setting, especially with Windows, you will soon find it almost impossible to manage (not to mention your browser will struggle with it). Take the following steps:

1. First, we set our standard variables:

```
$name = "iOS Device Restrictions"
$description = "Block App Store, iCloud and AirDrop"
$groupid = "0000000-0000-0000-0000-000000000000"
$url = "https://graph.microsoft.com/beta/deviceManagement/
deviceConfigurations"
```

2. There are a couple of things to note with the JSON itself. First, the cellular settings can only be True or False and are required; therefore, even if we do not configure them, they will still default to False in the JSON. The same is true for Safari cookie settings.

You will also see the scope tags nested array is present, even though you cannot set a scope tag within the GUI itself. As with the settings catalog, these settings are largely true/false values with the exception of any plain text fields, such as a password policy, or amending installed apps.

As with all JSON, note the case of the settings. These are case-sensitive and always start with a lowercase letter (`camelCase`):

```
$json = @"
{
    "@odata.type": "#microsoft.graph.
iosGeneralDeviceConfiguration",
    "airDropBlocked": true,
    "appStoreBlocked": true,
    "appsVisibilityListType": "none",
    "compliantAppListType": "none",
    "description": "$description",
    "displayName": "$name",
    "iCloudBlockBackup": true,
    "id": "00000000-0000-0000-0000-000000000000",
    "networkUsageRules": [
        {
            "cellularDataBlocked": false
        },
        {
            "cellularDataBlockWhenRoaming": false
        }
    ],
    "passcodeRequiredType": "deviceDefault",
    "roleScopeTagIds": [
        "0"
    ],
    "safariCookieSettings": "browserDefault"
}
"@
```

3. As usual, we now create the policy, grab the ID, and assign it:

```
$newprofile = Invoke-MgGraphRequest -Uri $url -Method Post -Body
$json -ContentType "application/json" -OutputType PSObject
$profileid = $newprofile.id
$assignurl = "https://graph.microsoft.com/beta/deviceManagement/
deviceConfigurations/$profileid/assign"
$assignjson = @"
{
    "assignments": [
        {
            "target": {
                "@odata.type": "#microsoft.graph.
groupAssignmentTarget",
                "groupId": "$groupid"
```

```
            }
        }
    ]
}
"@
Invoke-MgGraphRequest -Method POST -Uri $assignurl -Body
$assignjson -ContentType "application/json"
```

Let us move on to the next recipe.

Deploying applications via Apple VPP

We now have our restrictions configured so we know the devices are secure, but our users will not be happy if they cannot access the App Store and do not have any applications available centrally.

This recipe is going to concentrate on Apple VPP applications, as they are the preferred choice for application deployment in an enterprise environment. It is worth covering the other application options for awareness of what is available:

- **iOS store app**: This adds applications that are effectively shortcuts to the App Store. Users will need an Apple ID and you will need your restrictions policy configured to leave the store unblocked, which obviously means users can install anything they want.

- **iOS/iPadOS web clip**: This adds a shortcut to a web app to the device's home screen.

- **Web link**: This deploys a web link to devices to the home screen.

- **Built-in app**: These are pre-approved and curated applications that can be deployed without using the App Store. They are also pre-configured for app protection (covered in the *Configuring an app protection policy* section later in this chapter).

- **Line-of-business apps**: These are the way to deploy custom `ipa` applications to your managed devices (up to 2 GB in size). You can find out more at `https://learn.microsoft.com/en-us/mem/intune/apps/lob-apps-ios`.

Getting started

The first step here is to log in to your Apple Business Manager portal and make sure you have all of your details configured, including a payment method if you are adding any applications that are not free.

Then, click on **Apps and Books**.

Once on this screen, continue to follow the recipe.

How to do it...

First, search for your application. In this case, we are going to deploy **Microsoft Authenticator** to ensure our users are configured for **multi-factor authentication** (**MFA**). Then, follow these steps:

1. Click on the app in the results pane.

2. Select your MDM server in the drop-down menu, enter the number of licenses you require, and click **Get**. At the top, notice it says **Device Assignable**. This is important to note during application assignment.

    For less than 5,000 licenses, the application should appear almost straight away within the Intune console. Between 5,000 and 19,999 orders are processed daily at 13:00 (PST) and over 20,000 are processed at 16:00 (PST).

    Just to be on the safe side, we will speed this along by giving the VPP a sync.

3. Within the Intune console, navigate to **Tenant administration** and then **Connectors and tokens**.

4. Click **Apple VPP Tokens**.

5. Click the three dots to the right of the token (you may have to scroll across) and then click **Sync**:

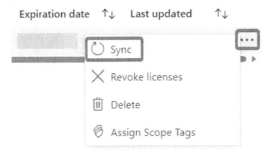

Figure 6.12 – Sync VPP token

6. Now, click on **Apps** and **iOS/iPadOS**.

7. You should see your application in the list but not assigned. Click on the application.

8. Click **Properties**.

9. Click **Edit** next to **Assignments**.

    You will see that you do not have the **Available for unenrolled devices** option like with Android. This is due to the licensing mentioned earlier.

    You can pick between **Required** (forced installation), **Available** (self-service), or forced **Uninstall**. In this case, we are going to force installation on all devices, as we want all users to have the application straight away.

10. After adding the assignment, some further options will be displayed:

License type	Prevent automatic app upda...	Uninstall on device removal	Prevent iCloud app backup
Device	No	No	No

Figure 6.13 – Assignment options

The important one here is the license type. We have made it so that our users do not require an Apple ID. Therefore, we need to make sure we use **Device licensing** (as we noted during the application purchase earlier).

Clicking on any of the blue text links will load a fly-out panel with further options.

11. You can configure these settings as required. In this case, we want the application to be forced, updated, not backed up (as this stores credentials), and not deleted unless the device is removed from management. When you have configured your requirements, click **OK**:

App settings

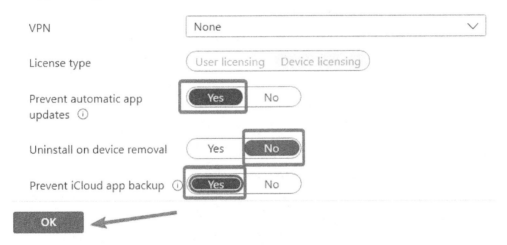

Figure 6.14 – App-specific settings

12. Now click **Review & Save**.

13. Check that everything looks okay and click **Save**.

We use **Save** rather than **Create** because we are updating an application assignment rather than creating something new.

Automating it

While you cannot automate adding the application itself, you can automate the assignment of it. We do this by finding the application ID and then assigning it:

1. First, set the name we are looking for. We will let PowerShell and Graph do the hard work for us:

    ```
    $appname = "Microsoft Authenticator"
    ```

2. Now we can run a GET request against all of the mobile apps in the tenant. We then only want Apple VPP-deployed applications using the @odata.type variable #microsoft.graph. iosVppApp. Once we have the VPP apps, we can find just those that match the name. Finally, we just want the ID (nested within Value):

    ```
    $appid = ((Invoke-MgGraphRequest -Uri "https://graph.
    microsoft.com/beta/deviceAppManagement/mobileApps" -Method Get
    -ContentType "application/json" -OutputType PSObject).value |
    Where-Object {$_.'@odata.type' -eq '#microsoft.graph.iosVppApp'}
    | Where-Object {$_.displayName -eq $appname}).id
    ```

3. Populate the URL with $appid:

    ```
    $url = "https://graph.microsoft.com/beta/deviceAppManagement/
    mobileApps/$appid/assign"
    ```

4. Now we need the JSON, which we configured for all devices earlier with the custom settings:

    ```
    $json = @"
    {
        "mobileAppAssignments": [
            {
                "@odata.type": "#microsoft.graph.
    mobileAppAssignment",
                "intent": "Required",
                "settings": {
                    "@odata.type": "#microsoft.graph.
    iosVppAppAssignmentSettings",
                    "isRemovable": false,
                    "preventAutoAppUpdate": false,
                    "preventManagedAppBackup": true,
                    "uninstallOnDeviceRemoval": true,
                    "useDeviceLicensing": true,
                    "vpnConfigurationId": null
                },
                "target": {
                    "@odata.type": "#microsoft.graph.
    allDevicesAssignmentTarget"
                }
    ```

```
            }
        ]
    }
    "@
```

5. Finally, we use POST for the assignment:

    ```
    Invoke-MgGraphRequest -Url $url -Method Post -Body $json
    -ContentType "application/json"
    ```

Now we can move on to the next recipe.

Configuring iOS update settings

We may also want to manage software updates on our iOS and iPadOS devices in a similar way to feature updates on Windows devices. This could be ensuring they are always up to date, restricting devices to a certain version, or specifying when to install an update. To do this, we use an update policy.

One important thing to note is that this does not stop users from manually searching for and installing updates, but you can set a deferral of up to 90 days using device restrictions (either in a device restrictions policy or the settings catalog).

How to do it...

Follow these instructions:

1. To create the new policy, navigate to **Devices** and then **iOS/iPadOS**.
2. Now select **Update policies for iOS/iPadOS** and click **Create profile**.
3. As usual, input a basic name and description and click **Next**.

    On the next screen, we set the policy itself. The first option lets you select which OS version to install on your devices. If you leave it set to **Latest update**, it will install whatever the newest version supported on the device is. You can also restrict this to older versions should you have specific application requirements.

4. You can also schedule options to install when the device next checks in to Intune or set a schedule that can either be inclusive or exclusive. You could set your active hours from 8:00 to 18:00 to align with a standard working day and decide you want the updates to only install out of hours, and in this case, set to **Update outside of scheduled time**. Alternatively, these may be on-call devices, in which case you would want them to be installed during the day so they are fully available out of hours. In this case, you would select **Update during scheduled time**. In our case, we are going to install the latest update at the next check-in.

5. Once you have configured for your environment, click **Next**.

6. We are not using scope tags in this environment, so on the next screen, click **Next**.

    When considering your assignments, look at your estate and user base carefully. You can have multiple update policies, so a one-size-fits-all approach may not be best for you. If all devices have the same configuration and use, you can use **All Users** or **All Devices** here, but it may be best to target groups. As per our earlier example, staff who are on call or who work shifts may require a different schedule from an office worker who only uses the device during the working day.

    Remember to use **Exclusions** as well. You could have a catch-all assigned to **All Users** but with exceptions for those who need slightly different configurations (but never mix user and device assignments).

    Do not forget to carefully consider your executives here, as well as those who may require the device both during and outside of working hours. For any high-impact policies and changes, it is often best to check first, especially when introducing new systems such as Intune. Winning over your user base is sometimes as tricky as the configuration itself.

7. In our case, we are assigning configurations to the **Intune-Users** group. Then, click **Next**.

8. Finally, review the settings to ensure they are correct and click **Create**.

Automating it

Automating an update policy may have a few additional settings and arrays depending on the iOS version and schedule settings selected during policy creation:

1. We can start with our standard variables:

    ```
    $name = "iOS Update Policy"
    $description = "Forces update to latest version on check-in"
    $groupid = "00000000-0000-0000-0000-000000000000"
    $url = "https://graph.microsoft.com/beta/deviceManagement/
    deviceConfigurations"
    ```

2. Now, when we look at the JSON, we have a simple setting called `desiredOsVersion`, which we can use to restrict the version deployed. To use the latest version, this is just set to `null`.

    There are also variables for `activeHoursStart` and `End`, which, to make things more confusing, are not actually used in this policy.

    Instead, when using a schedule, we use the `customUpdateTimeWindows` array, which will be demonstrated later.

    You can also use `utcTimeOffsetInMinutes` to set your time zone as required.

3. We will start with a standard update at the next check-in:

```
$json = @"
{
    "@odata.type": "#microsoft.graph.iosUpdateConfiguration",
    "activeHoursEnd": "00:00:00.0000000",
    "activeHoursStart": "00:00:00.0000000",
    "customUpdateTimeWindows": [],
    "description": "$description",
    "desiredOsVersion": null,
    "displayName": "$name",
    "id": "",
    "roleScopeTagIds": [
        "0"
    ],
    "scheduledInstallDays": [],
    "updateScheduleType": "alwaysUpdate",
    "utcTimeOffsetInMinutes": null
}
"@
```

4. If we want to use a schedule, we set updateScheduleType to either update
    DuringTimeWindows or updateOutsideOfTimeWindows and then set the
    customUpdateTimeWindows array accordingly:

```
$jsonscheduled = @"
{
    "@odata.type": "#microsoft.graph.iosUpdateConfiguration",
    "activeHoursEnd": "00:00:00.0000000",
    "activeHoursStart": "00:00:00.0000000",
    "customUpdateTimeWindows": [
        {
            "@odata.type": "#microsoft.graph.
customUpdateTimeWindow",
            "endDay": "friday",
            "endTime": "18:00:00.0000000",
            "startDay": "monday",
            "startTime": "07:00:00.0000000"
        }
    ],
    "description": "$description",
    "desiredOsVersion": null,
    "displayName": "$name",
    "id": "",
    "roleScopeTagIds": [
```

```
        "0"
    ],
    "scheduledInstallDays": [],
    "updateScheduleType": "updateDuringTimeWindows",
    "utcTimeOffsetInMinutes": 0
}
"@
```

5. Then, as usual, create the policy, grab the ID, and assign it:

```
$policy = Invoke-MgGraphRequest -Uri $url -Method Post -Body
$json -ContentType "application/json" -OutputType PSObject
$policyid = $policy.id
$url = "https://graph.microsoft.com/beta/deviceManagement/
deviceConfigurations/$policyid/assign"
$assignjson = @"
{
    "assignments": [
        {
            "target": {
                "@odata.type": "#microsoft.graph.
groupAssignmentTarget",
                "groupId": "$groupid"
            }
        }
    ]
}
"@
Invoke-MgGraphRequest -Uri $url -Method Post -Body $assignjson
-ContentType "application/json"
```

Now we will move on to the next recipe.

Configuring an app protection policy

For our BYOD devices, we cannot rely on device restrictions, as they are limited to corporate devices that have been fully enrolled. As with Android devices, which were covered in *Chapter 5*, we want to implement app protection policies to ensure the data is securely stored on user-owned devices.

Unlike Android, iOS does not support multiple profiles, so while the data is protected in the same way, it is less segregated on the device.

Getting started

The Conditional access policy configured in the Android app protection policy in *Chapter 5* was configured for both Android and iOS devices, so rather than run through the same steps in this recipe (if you have not configured that yet), read the Android recipe and configure the policy appropriately. This is used to force your devices to only connect if the application is policy-managed.

How to do it...

Follow these instructions:

1. First, we need to navigate to **Apps** and click **App protection policies**.
2. Click **Create policy** and select **iOS/iPadOS** in the drop-down menu.
3. As usual, name and describe your policy. The platform is pre-selected based on the drop-down menu selection before. Then, click **Next**.
4. Here, we can select which apps to protect. If you want to protect selected apps, you need to click the +**Select public apps** or +**Select custom apps** text. Otherwise, change the drop-down menu to match your needs.
5. In this case, we will select **All Microsoft Apps** and click **Next**.

   On the next screen, we set the data protection settings for our data protected within these applications. You can set these as per your organization's requirements. As a general rule, these settings are good to start with:

   - **Backup org data to iTunes and iCloud backups**: Set this to **Block** (one less breach to worry about).

   - **Send org data to other apps**: This should be set to **Policy managed apps** (we do not want data leaving our corporate bubble on the device). You can add exemptions here if required.

   - **Save copies of org data**: Set this to **Block** with **OneDrive** and **SharePoint** selected (it is an unmanaged device, so we do not want data on the device; select **Box** if it is approved in your environment).

   - **Transfer telecommunication data to**: Ideally, you should set this to **None**, but users may complain about being unable to copy and paste a telephone number, so it is worth considering this.

   - **Receive data from other apps**: Either **Policy managed apps** or **All Apps with incoming org Data** should be set here.

   - **Restrict cut, copy, and paste between other apps**: This should be set to **Policy managed apps with paste in** (restrict within the bubble).

- **Encrypt org data**: Set this option to **Require**.

- **Sync policy managed app data with native apps or add-ins**: Configure this setting to **Block** (note that this blocks Outlook from adding contacts into the native contacts application, so be careful with this setting).

- **Printing org data**: Set this to **Block** (there is little point restricting if they can just print it).

- **Restrict web content transfer with other apps**: This should ideally be set to **Microsoft Edge.** This is a personal preference, but managing one browser across platforms is easier.

6. Once you have configured your settings, click **Next**.

    The next screen lets you specify access requirements for the applications themselves. As you cannot force the device to require a PIN, you can instead force the application itself to request one. Set these as per your requirements, as it is often best to match the corporate device PIN requirements to make it easier to explain to end users. One to watch here is the **Work or school account credentials for access** setting. If you set this to **Require** and also **Require biometrics**, users will be prompted for both.

7. Set as required and click **Next**.

    This next page allows you to set further conditions for accessing the application, including the following:

- **Max PIN attempts**: This is how many times an incorrect PIN can be entered. You can either force a PIN reset or wipe the data.

- **Offline grace period**: This is after how many minutes you block access and after how many days you wipe the data.

- **Disabled account**: You can block or allow access.

- **Minimum app version:** The minimum allowed version, you can **Block access**, **Wipe data** or **simply Warn**.

- **Min SDK version :** Can be set to **Block access**, **Wipe data** or **Warn**.

You can also set restrictions on the device itself, including the following:

- **Jailbroken/rooted devices**: You can **Block access** or **Wipe data**.

- **Minimum or Maximum OS version**: Either **Warn**, **Block access**, or **Wipe data** (make sure you keep on top of this one if you set it).

- **Minimum patch version**: **Warn**, **Block access**, or **Wipe data**.

- **Device models(s)**: Block or wipe anything not specified. It is an allow list, not a block list, so make sure you populate it carefully.

- **Maximum allowed device threat level (Secured, Low, Medium,** or **High):** Block or wipe data. This needs a Defender for Endpoint connection.

- **Primary MTD service:** Set to either **Defender for Endpoint** or **Mobile Threat Defense** (non-Microsoft) – Your device anti-virus.

8. Once you have configured your settings, click **Next.** See the following screenshot for the settings used in this example:

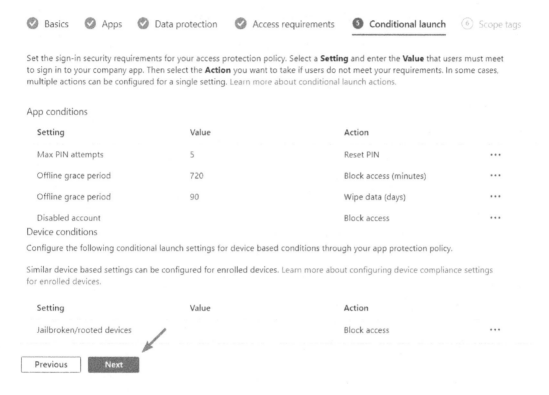

Figure 6.15 – Conditional launch settings

9. Click **Next** on the **Scope tags** page.

10. You will notice on the next screen that we cannot assign this policy to the **All Users** or **All Devices** virtual groups. This is also a user-based policy, as we have no information on the devices themselves. Assign it to the **Intune Users** group. Then, click **Next.**

11. Finally, check that everything looks okay. The policy will automatically have added key links to include and exclude. Then, click **Create.**

Automating it

As with the Android app protection policy, the first thing to note with this is that the assignment is included in the policy creation instead of having to be created and assigned, as was done in most recipes so far.

The JSON is fairly clear to follow, with a few nested arrays, such as the **Allowed locations** setting where we selected multiple options in the UI earlier.

Due to the large number of links included, we will not include the full JSON here, but it is of course available at the GitHub repository.

A list of all available settings and their relevant JSON can be found here:

```
https://learn.microsoft.com/en-us/graph/api/intune-shared-
iosmanagedappprotection-create?view=graph-rest-beta
```

Follow these steps to create your script:

1. First, we start with the policy's name, `description`, and `groupid`:

   ```
   $name = "iOS App Protection"
   $description = "Protect Microsoft Apps"
   $groupid = "00000000-0000-0000-0000-000000000000"
   $url = "https://graph.microsoft.com/beta/deviceAppManagement/
   iosManagedAppProtections"
   ```

2. Now we populate the JSON. Remember to include the assignment inside the array here:

   ```
   $json = @"
   {
       "appActionIfDeviceComplianceRequired": "block",
       "appActionIfIosDeviceModelNotAllowed": "block",
       "appActionIfMaximumPinRetriesExceeded": "block",
       "appActionIfUnableToAuthenticateUser": "block",
       "appDataEncryptionType": "whenDeviceLocked",
       "appGroupType": "allMicrosoftApps",
       "apps": [],
       "assignments": [
           {
               "target": {
                   "@odata.type": "#microsoft.graph.
   groupAssignmentTarget",
                   "deviceAndAppManagementAssignmentFilterId":
   null,
                   "deviceAndAppManagementAssignmentFilterType":
   "none",
                   "groupId": "$groupid"
   ```

```
            }
        }
    ],
    "blockAfterCompanyPortalUpdateDeferralInDays": 0,
    "description": "$description",
    "deviceComplianceRequired": true,
    "dialerRestrictionLevel": "blocked",
    "disableAppPinIfDevicePinIsSet": false,
    "disableProtectionOfManagedOutboundOpenInData": false,
    "displayName": "$name",
    "printBlocked": true,
    "protectInboundDataFromUnknownSources": false,
    "roleScopeTagIds": [
        "0"
    ],
    "saveAsBlocked": true,
    "shareWithBrowserVirtualSetting": "anyApp",
    "simplePinBlocked": true,
    "targetedAppManagementLevels": "unspecified",
    "thirdPartyKeyboardsBlocked": false,
    "warnAfterCompanyPortalUpdateDeferralInDays": 0,
    "wipeAfterCompanyPortalUpdateDeferralInDays": 0
}
"@
```

3. As the assignment is already done, we do not need any further details after creation. We can run the Graph request without adding the output into a variable:

```
Invoke-MgGraphRequest -Method POST -uri $url -Body $json
-ContentType "application/json"
```

There's more...

You may have noticed some other settings underneath **App protection policies** in the menu, so we will cover those now for greater understanding.

Looking at app configuration policies

App configuration policies can be applied at either the device or application level to set application-specific configurations (where supported by the application itself).

Some examples would be to configure the Outlook application or line-of-business applications. Depending on the application, you will have the choice to use a configuration designer or type in the raw text, whether that is S/MIME/XML, JSON, or something else.

For some apps, such as Outlook, the configuration designer includes comprehensive settings, while others include only textboxes. You need to be sure you know what to enter into them.

If we use Outlook as an example, the designer looks as follows:

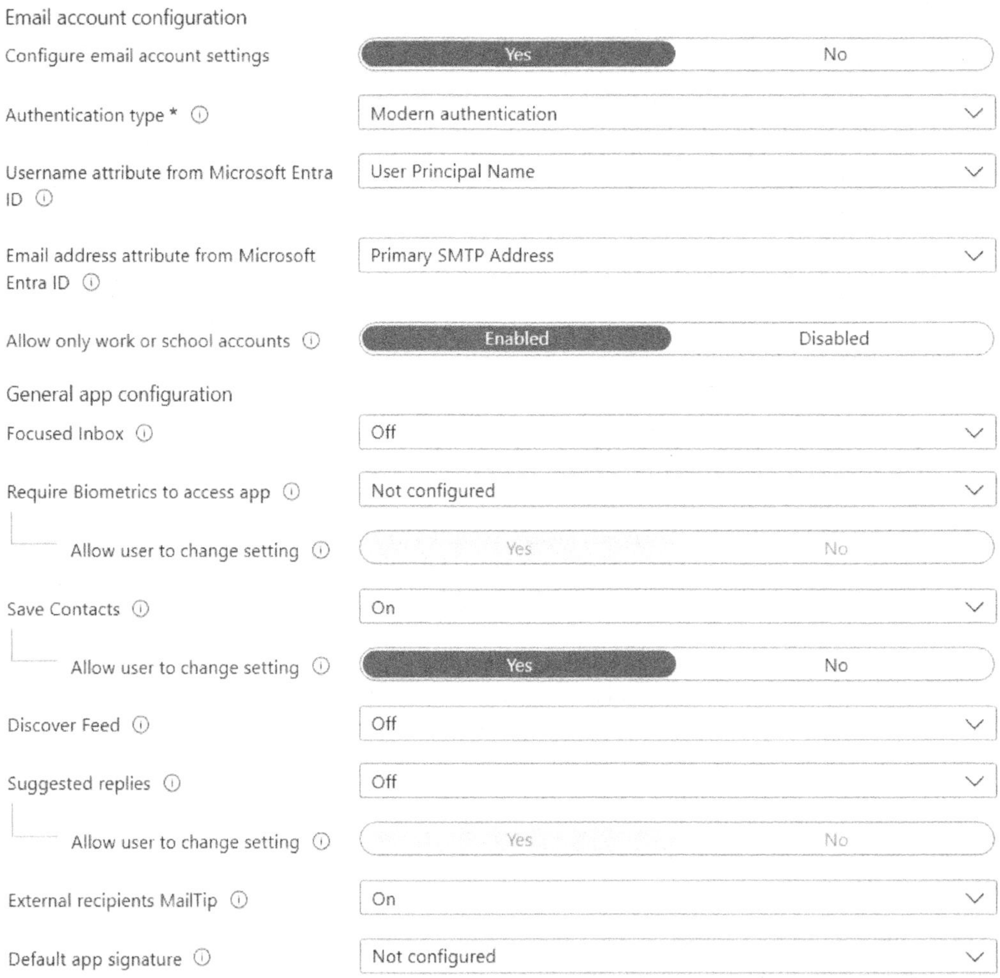

Email account configuration

Configure email account settings   Yes   No

Authentication type * ⓘ   Modern authentication   ⌄

Username attribute from Microsoft Entra   User Principal Name   ⌄
ID ⓘ

Email address attribute from Microsoft   Primary SMTP Address   ⌄
Entra ID ⓘ

Allow only work or school accounts ⓘ   Enabled   Disabled

General app configuration

Focused Inbox ⓘ   Off   ⌄

Require Biometrics to access app ⓘ   Not configured   ⌄

        Allow user to change setting ⓘ   Yes   No

Save Contacts ⓘ   On   ⌄

        Allow user to change setting ⓘ   Yes   No

Discover Feed ⓘ   Off   ⌄

Suggested replies ⓘ   Off   ⌄

        Allow user to change setting ⓘ   Yes   No

External recipients MailTip ⓘ   On   ⌄

Default app signature ⓘ   Not configured   ⌄

Figure 6.16 – Outlook app configuration settings

For Microsoft Word, for example, you have to enter the settings manually:

Configuration key	Value type	Configuration value
	Select one ⌄	

Figure 6.17 – Microsoft Word app configuration settings

Selecting the settings in Outlook simply populates the values for you:

Configuration key	Value type	Configuration value	
com.microsoft.outlook.EmailProfi...	String	ModernAuth	•••
com.microsoft.outlook.EmailProfi...	String	{{userprincipalname}}	•••
com.microsoft.outlook.EmailProfi...	String	{{mail}}	•••
IntuneMAMAllowedAccountsOnly	String	Enabled	•••
IntuneMAMUPN	String	{{userprincipalname}}	•••
com.microsoft.outlook.Mail.Focu...	Boolean	false	•••
com.microsoft.outlook.Contacts....	Boolean	true	•••
com.microsoft.outlook.Mail.Offic...	Boolean	false	•••
com.microsoft.outlook.Mail.Sugg...	Boolean	false	•••
com.microsoft.outlook.Mail.Exter...	Boolean	true	•••
com.microsoft.outlook.Mail.Orga...	Boolean	false	•••
com.microsoft.outlook.Mail.TextP...	Boolean	false	•••
	Select one ⌄		

Figure 6.18 – Outlook configured settings

In terms of automation, if we use the Outlook example, we are sending a POST request to https://graph.microsoft.com/beta/deviceAppManagement/mobileAppConfigurations.

The JSON would be as follows:

```
{
    "@odata.type": "#microsoft.graph.iosMobileAppConfiguration",
    "description": "",
    "displayName": "Outlook Configuration",
    "encodedSettingXml": "",
```

```
    "id": "00000000-0000-0000-0000-000000000000",
    "roleScopeTagIds": [
        "0"
    ],
    "settings": [
        {
            "appConfigKey": "com.microsoft.outlook.EmailProfile.
AccountType",
            "appConfigKeyType": "StringType",
            "appConfigKeyValue": "ModernAuth"
        },
        {
            "appConfigKey": "com.microsoft.outlook.EmailProfile.
EmailUPN",
            "appConfigKeyType": "StringType",
            "appConfigKeyValue": "{{userprincipalname}}"
        },
        {
            "appConfigKey": "com.microsoft.outlook.EmailProfile.
EmailAddress",
            "appConfigKeyType": "StringType",
            "appConfigKeyValue": "{{mail}}"
        }
    ],
    "targetedMobileApps": [
        "40957e67-f032-44b8-9eda-3d2312b3e142"
    ]
}
```

As you can see, you will need the application ID, but we can reuse the code used when assigning an application earlier to let PowerShell automate that part for you.

Learning about iOS app provisioning profiles

App provisioning profiles are used for your line-of-business applications, which need custom configuration suppliers. You simply upload the profile supplied with the application and assign it accordingly.

You can read more about them here:

```
https://learn.microsoft.com/en-gb/mem/intune/apps/app-provisioning-
profile-ios?WT.mc_id=Portal-Microsoft_Intune_Apps
```

Enrolling your device – corporate

We have our environment configured, so now we can start enrolling our devices, starting with corporate-owned and managed devices.

Getting started

First, make sure you have a factory reset iOS/iPadOS device enrolled in either ABM or Apple Education Manager.

How to do it...

Follow these instructions:

1. First, set your language and region on your device.
2. On the **Quick Start** screen, click **Set Up Manually**.
3. Connect to your Wi-Fi network, if required, or use mobile data.
4. You will then see the **Remote Management** screen. Click **Next**.
5. Sign in with your credentials and click **Next**.

If your policy requires a passcode, you will be asked to set and confirm it after signing in.

Finally, after a couple of minutes, you will see your home screen with any required applications deployed.

There's more

A recent addition to Intune is the availability of **Just in Time** enrollment for iOS and iPadOS. This uses the **single sign-on** (**SSO**) extension and leverages signing in to any compatible application to trigger a compliance check and complete enrollment.

You can learn more about Just in Time enrollment, including how to configure it and a user experience video, at the following link:

```
https://techcommunity.microsoft.com/t5/intune-customer-success/just-
in-time-registration-and-compliance-remediation-for-ios/ba-p/3660843
```

Enrolling your device – BYOD

Due to the differences between Android and iOS (no work profile, VPP, and Google Play differences), there are no real advantages to be gained from allowing personal devices to be enrolled over simply using app protection policies. Therefore, in this recipe, we will just demonstrate how to enroll using app protection only.

Getting started

For this recipe, you will need an Apple iOS/iPadOS device set up and signed into with an Apple ID to access Microsoft Store applications.

How to do it...

Follow these instructions:

1. Load up the App Store and search for an application. In this case, we are using Microsoft Word. After installing, click **Open**.

2. Click **Existing Microsoft 365 Users? Sign In**.

3. Enter your email address and click **Next**.

4. Enter your password and click **Sign In**.

5. After signing in, you will see the message in *Figure 6.19*. Click **OK** to restart the app:

Figure 6.19 – Click OK to restart

6. When you perform any action in the application (open a document, create a document), you will be prompted to set a PIN. You will also be told about any PIN restrictions set in your app protection policy.

7. Complete the same steps with any other organization apps.

7
macOS Device Management

The last of the different platforms covered in this book (at the time of writing, Linux and ChromeOS management are still too limited) is macOS. We will look at configuring and then deploying a corporate device. For this, we will use the **Apple Business Manager** (or **Apple Education**) configuration, which is explained in the *Technical requirements* section (as well as in the previous chapter on iOS).

The chapter will cover the configuration of profiles for your macOS devices as well as their enrollment.

We will also run through the process of configuring Intune to work with Apple Business Manager and deploy applications, using the **Volume Purchase Program**.

In this chapter, we will cover the following recipes:

- Configuring a macOS Settings catalog policy
- Deploying shell scripts to macOS
- Configuring update policies for macOS
- Deploying apps to macOS
- Configuring a macOS enrollment profile
- Enrolling your corporate device

Chapter materials

As with *Chapters 2, 5*, and *6*, this will not cover all available policy types, so we will run through them all now to get a better understanding of what is available for macOS devices. As with Windows and iOS, macOS policy settings have now been largely migrated to the settings catalog.

The available profile types are as follows:

- **Settings catalog**: The unified settings catalog is a more modern way to deploy settings.
- **Custom**: This lets you upload a `.mobileconfig` file created in Profile Manager to configure settings not yet available elsewhere. We will cover this briefly in the following shell scripts recipe. Some examples can be found here: `https://github.com/microsoft/shell-intune-samples/tree/master/macOS`.
- **Device restrictions**: These are an alternative to the settings catalog for your standard restrictions.
- **Device features**: Device restrictions are used to protect and lock down devices. Device features set various custom settings, such as lock-screen messages and home screen layout.
- **Endpoint protection**: You can use this to set a firewall, FileVault, or GateKeeper.
- **Extensions**: This configures kernel and system extensions, both allowed and blocked.
- **Preference file**: Configure application or device preferences using a `.plist` file.
- **Public-Key Cryptography Standards (PKCS) certificate**: This configures a public key pair certificate for authentication.
- **PKCS imported certificate**: This sets up an imported PKCS for **Secure/Multipurpose internet Mail Extensions (S/MIME)** email authentication.
- **Simple Certificate Enrollment Protocol (SCEP) certificate**: This is used for certificate-based device authentication.
- **Software updates**: This is the same as an update policy, which we will cover in the following recipe.
- **Trusted certificate**: Import the trusted certificate needed for SCEP.
- **VPN**: Configure a VPN connection for your macOS devices.
- **Wi-Fi**: Configure Wi-Fi profiles, both basic and enterprise-supported. This can be used with certification profiles where applicable.
- **Wired network**: Same as a Wi-Fi profile but with a wire. Set which network adapter to use and your network settings.

Important notes

When dealing with Apple devices, there are some very important things to consider throughout the initial setup and continued management, which we will run through here.

It is important when dealing with Apple devices to keep an eye on the certificate renewal dates and record them somewhere, with a renewal reminder. You could also use Azure Automation to automate the reminders for you; see more here: `https://andrewstaylor.com/2022/06/07/alerting-when-my-apple-certificates-expire-in-intune-using-azure-automation/`.

The **MDM Push Certificate** connects your devices to the Intune MDM Service. If this expires, you can sometimes contact Apple directly if it is within 30 days of expiry to renew it. If they cannot, or 30 days have passed, your only option is to wipe and re-enroll all your devices. Yes, it is a full wipe – data destruction, everything.

The enrollment token is used to initially enroll your devices. If this expires, you must create a new enrollment profile and transfer your devices to it. It is not quite as bad as a wipe, but it can result in the devices looking less healthy within the Intune portal itself.

The Apple VPP certificate is used to deploy applications to devices. If this expires, users will not be able to download and install any new applications from the App Store until it is renewed. It is not a massive issue, and the certificate is easy to replace, but you could waste time troubleshooting an app installation issue and not consider this the issue.

When looking at your device restrictions/settings catalog policy, the settings you configure need to be tailored to your specific needs, providing the best security without ruining the end-user experience.

The official CIS benchmarks for macOS can be found here: `https://www.cisecurity.org/benchmark/apple_os`.

The NCSC guidance can be found here: `https://www.ncsc.gov.uk/collection/device-security-guidance/platform-guides/macos`.

While these should not be used as the only way to configure your settings, they are an excellent starting point, as macOS does not offer pre-configured security baselines like Windows.

macOS management is constantly evolving and improving with Intune. One recently announced addition is Entra ID Single Sign-On, which you can learn about here: `https://techcommunity.microsoft.com/t5/microsoft-intune-blog/now-is-the-time-manage-your-mac-endpoints-with-microsoft-intune/ba-p/3974449`.

It is also worth keeping an eye on the latest Intune developments planned by following the following link: `https://www.microsoft.com/en-gb/microsoft-365/roadmap?rtc=3&filters=Mac%2CMicrosoft%20Intune`.

If you are managing a fleet of macOS devices, the Microsoft Mac Admins community is also worth joining at the following link: `https://github.com/microsoft/shell-intune-samples/wiki/Microsoft-Mac-Admins-Community`.

Technical requirements

For this chapter, you will need a modern web browser and a PowerShell code editor, such as Visual Studio Code or PowerShell ISE.

All of the scripts referenced can be found here: `https://github.com/PacktPublishing/Microsoft-Intune-Cookbook`.

You will need an **Apple Business Manager** (**ABM**) account set up and ready to be configured with Intune. You can find instructions to set up your ABM account at `https://www.apple.com/business/docs/site/Apple_Business_Manager_Getting_Started_Guide.pdf` and `https://www.intuneirl.com/onboarding-to-abm/`.

Your hardware supplier should be able to add your devices to ABM, but you can also use Apple Configurator on a device running macOS or iOS: `https://support.apple.com/en-gb/apple-configurator`.

Alternatively, you can watch these videos:

- `https://www.youtube.com/watch?v=G_9bPrsJHGY&t=34s`
- `https://www.youtube.com/watch?v=G-rvHUY4iA0`

To enroll devices, you will need a macOS device enrolled into ABM.

Configuring a macOS Settings catalog policy

We have looked at the different policy types available, but the most expanded option is the settings catalog, which is constantly being updated with new settings and, therefore, is the recommended method to deploy settings to your macOS device. You can now also export and import settings catalog directly in the UI, which is a further advantage over other policy options.

Follow this recipe to find out how to configure your devices.

How to do it...

Here, we will learn how to use the settings catalog to configure our first macOS policy:

1. First, navigate to **Devices**, and then click on **macOS**.

Figure 7.1 – The macOS Devices msenu

2. Now, click on **Configuration profiles**, and click **Create** and select **New policy**.
3. Select **Settings catalog**, and click **Create**.
4. Enter a name and an (optional) description, and then click **Next**.

   As with our Windows and iOS devices, we need to add settings.

Here, you can pick the settings applicable to your environment. Adopt the same *less is more* approach we used with Windows; it is better to have multiple small policies than a few unmanageable ones. In this case, we will set some basic device restrictions, forcing encryption and enabling OneDrive **Known Folder Move (KFM)** and Files On-Demand.

Again, refer to the CIS and NCSC baselines (more details can be found by following the link in the *Important notes* section) for some general security guidance.

Note that, in our settings, a lot of the macOS settings default to allow instead of block. Pay attention to the wording; you do not want to deploy a policy that accidentally allows everything you actually wanted to block.

5. When you have configured the settings, click **Next**:

FileVault   Remove subcategory

Configure the FileVault payload to manage FileVault disk encryption settings on devices.

ⓘ 10 of 11 settings in this subcategory are not configured

Enable * ⓘ | On   ⌄ |

‣ Microsoft Office   Remove category

Microsoft OneDrive   Remove subcategory

ⓘ 21 of 23 settings in this subcategory are not configured

Enable Files On-Demand ⓘ   ●◯ True   ⊖

Automatically and silently enable the | 12345678   ✓ |
Folder Backup feature (Known Folder   ⊖
Move) ⓘ

‣ Restrictions   Remove category

Configure the Restrictions payload to enable or disable features on devices. These configurations can be used prevent users from accessing a specific app, service or function on enrolled devices. For example, a restriction can be added that prevents an iPhone or iPad from using AirPrint. Another restriction can be added to prevent the sharing of passwords over AirDrop on an iPhone, iPad and Mac. Certain restrictions on an iPhone may be mirrored on a paired Apple Watch.

ⓘ 68 of 72 settings in this category are not configured

Allow Game Center ⓘ   ●◯ False   ⊖

Allow USB Restricted Mode ⓘ   ●◯ False   ⊖

Allow iTunes File Sharing ⓘ   ●◯ False   ⊖

Allow Find My Friends ⓘ   ●◯ False   ⊖

| revious | **Next** |

Figure 7.2 – The configured settings

6.   Click **Next** on the **Scope tags** page.

As this is a device restrictions policy, we have picked settings that will apply to all devices without exceptions, so we can use the **All Devices** assignment and could go one step further, applying a filter to just macOS devices.

> **Important note**
>
> As with any other policies, I suggest that if there are any settings that may need different configurations for different user groups, leave these out of the baseline policies. This way, you can have a single baseline across the estate and then use the smaller, easier policies to handle on/off exceptions.

7.   When you have configured your assignment, click **Next**.

8.   Finally, check that everything looks correct, and then click **Create**.

Automating it

Now that we have learned how to configure in the UI, we can look at how to automate this policy using PowerShell.

Similar to automating iOS settings in the previous chapter, there is a mix of settings here, some of which are child items and some of which are direct assignments:

1.   We can start by looking at the URL to find all macOS available settings:
      `https://graph.microsoft.com/beta/deviceManagement/`
      `configurationCategories?=&`$filter=(platforms has`
      `'macOS') and (technologies has 'mdm' or technologies has`
      `'appleRemoteManagement').`

      If we pick a couple of settings, we can have a look at the differences.

2.   We will first run a GET command against the preceding URL to retrieve all of the categories available.

      Our returned ID for full disk encryption is `3f56adc1-2207-4033-a6e2-07f64c08e3ff`.

3.   Now, we run a GET command to find the policies within the category against this URL: `https://graph.microsoft.com/beta/deviceManagement/configurationSettings?&$filter=categoryId+eq+'3f56adc1-2207-4033-a6e2-07f64c08e3ff'`.

      In the output, we can see that this setting depends on a parent setting ID:

```
"dependentOn": [
    {
            "dependentOn": "com.apple.mcx.filevault2_
com.apple.mcx.filevault2",
```

```
                    "parentSettingId": "com.apple.mcx.
    filevault2_com.apple.mcx.filevault2"
                }
```

This means it is a child setting and uses `groupSettingCollectionValue` with children in the JSON.

For OneDrive KFM, we will use the category ID `19ba782c-3594-45da-b829-72b5 4f6d45c7`.

Running a GET command on this URL then returns the available settings: `https://graph. microsoft.com/beta/deviceManagement/configurationSettings?&$fi lter=categoryId+eq+'19ba782c-3594-45da-b829-72b54f6d45c7'`.

In this output, both `dependentOn` and `dependedOnBy` are empty arrays, which means the JSON for these is more standard, as found in the Windows settings catalog:

```
            "dependentOn": [],
            "dependedOnBy": []
```

4. Now, we can use this knowledge and look at the JSON for our configured policy.

Set the name, description, and URL:

```
$name = "macOS Settings"
$description = "Baseline settings for macOS devices"
$url = "https://graph.microsoft.com/beta/deviceManagement/
configurationPolicies"
```

We will not include the full JSON here, as that is available on GitHub, and instead use two of the example settings, one with a child item (OneDrive KFM) and one without (Enabling FileVault):

```
$json = @"
{
    "description": "$description",
    "name": "$name",
    "platforms": "macOS",
    "roleScopeTagIds": [
        "0"
    ],
    "settings": [
        {
            "@odata.type": "#microsoft.graph.
deviceManagementConfigurationSetting",
            "settingInstance": {
                "@odata.type": "#microsoft.graph.
deviceManagementConfigurationGroupSettingCollectionInstance",
                "groupSettingCollectionValue": [
                    {
```

```
                        "children": [
                            {
                                "@odata.type": "#microsoft.
graph.deviceManagementConfigurationChoiceSettingInstance",
                                "choiceSettingValue": {
                                    "@odata.type": "#microsoft.
graph.deviceManagementConfigurationChoiceSettingValue",
                                    "children": [],
                                    "value": "com.apple.mcx.
filevault2_enable_0"
                                },
                                "settingDefinitionId": "com.
apple.mcx.filevault2_enable"
                            }
                        ]
                    }
                ],
                "settingDefinitionId": "com.apple.mcx.
filevault2_com.apple.mcx.filevault2"
            }
        },
        {
            "@odata.type": "#microsoft.graph.
deviceManagementConfigurationSetting",
            "settingInstance": {
                "@odata.type": "#microsoft.graph.
deviceManagementConfigurationSimpleSettingInstance",
                "settingDefinitionId": "com.apple.managedclient.
preferences_kfmsilentoptin",
                "simpleSettingValue": {
                    "@odata.type": "#microsoft.graph.
deviceManagementConfigurationStringSettingValue",
                    "value": "123456789"
                }
            }
        }
    ],
    "technologies": "mdm,appleRemoteManagement"
}
"@
```

5. Create the policy, and copy the policy ID:

```
$policy = Invoke-MgGraphRequest -Method POST -Uri $url -Body
$json -OutputType PSObject -ContentType "application/json"
$policyid = $policy.id
```

6. Populate the URL with the ID:

```
$assignurl = "https://graph.microsoft.com/beta/deviceManagement/
configurationPolicies/$policyid/assign"
```

7. Finally, assign the ID to all devices:

```
$json = @"
{
    "assignments": [
        {
            "target": {
                "@odata.type": "#microsoft.graph.
allDevicesAssignmentTarget"
            }
        }
    ]
}
"@
Invoke-MgGraphRequest -Method POST -Uri $assignurl -Body $json
-OutputType PSObject -ContentType "application/json"
```

Deploying shell scripts to macOS

With Windows devices, you can use PowerShell scripts to make changes not currently supported by other methods, such as the settings catalog or a custom OMA-URI. We will cover these in *Chapter 12, PowerShell Scripting across Intune*.

For devices that run macOS, the alternative is shell scripts. These can be configured to run at either the system or user level, and as macOS is Unix-based, it can configure almost anything on a device.

Getting started

There are some prerequisites and things to watch with shell scripts; we will start with the prerequisites:

- **Prerequisites**:

    - You must be running at least macOS 11.0

    - Your devices must have a direct connection to the internet (no proxy server)

    - Scripts must begin with # !

- **Considerations**:

  - Shell scripts run in parallel, so if you deploy multiple scripts, they will run at the same time

  - Scripts deployed as the signed-in user will run on *all* signed-in accounts on the device at the point the script runs

  - A user has to be signed on for user-level scripts

  - Users will need root access for any user-level scripts that are running elevated commands

  - While you can specify how often a script will run, should something change on the device, it may run more regularly (clearing the cache, device restart, etc.)

  - A script that runs for more than 60 minutes will time out, be stopped, and be reported as failed

  - Shell scripts can be a maximum of 200 KB

Now we have these out of the way, we can create our first shell script.

We will not be running through the process of creating shell scripts here but, instead, cover how to deploy them to your devices.

Before starting this recipe, you will need a shell script in the `.sh` format. Some examples from Microsoft can be found here: `https://github.com/microsoft/shell-intune-samples/tree/master/macOS`.

In this example, we will deploy a wallpaper image using the script here: `https://github.com/microsoft/shell-intune-samples/tree/master/macOS/Config/Wallpaper`.

The two scripts used will also be available on GitHub.

To gain an understanding of how to deploy a custom profile (which is used to run your script on devices), we will also include those steps.

How to do it...

We need to start by deploying the shell script itself, and then we can configure the policy to deploy it.

Deploying a Shell script

Follow these steps to deploy a shell script into Intune:

1. First, we need to navigate to **Devices** and then **macOS**.

2. In **macOS policies**, click **Shell scripts** and **Add**, set the name and description, and then click **Next**:

3. Click the folder icon, and select your script.

   This will display the script contents in the read-only editor below the script path on-screen. If you need to make changes, the file will need re-uploading:

```
# Define variables
usebingwallpaper=true # Set to true to have script fetch wallpaper from Bing
wallpaperurl="https://numberwang.blob.core.windows.net/numberwang/macOSWallpaper.jpg"
wallpaperdir="/Library/Desktop"
wallpaperfile="Wallpaper.jpg"
log="/var/log/fetchdesktopwallpaper.log"

# start logging

exec 1>> $log 2>&1
```

Figure 7.3 – The shell script content

Below the script name, you can see the details.

4. In our case, as shown in *Figure 7.3*, we want the script to run elevated, so **Run script as signed-in user** is set to **No**.

   We do not want notifications, and we want the script to run every day so that we can update the background.

5. Once you have configured the settings for your script, click **Next**:

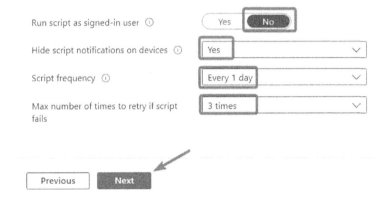

Figure 7.4 – The shell script settings

6. We are not setting scope tags at this point, so click **Next**.

7. Assign as appropriate; we will use Intune users so that we have the option to have different images for different user groups, but if it is a fixed corporate background, all devices with a filter will also work well. After configuring your assignments, click **Next**.

8. Finally, confirm everything is correct, and then click **Add**.

Deploying a custom profile

The script we have just created will download the wallpaper image to the device, but we also need to tell the device to use it. To do what, we are going to deploy a custom profile:

1. Click **Configuration Profiles**, and then click click **Create** and select **New policy**.

2. In the flyout, click **Templates | Custom**, and then click **Create**.

3. Give your new profile a name and description.

4. Give the setting a name, and select whether it runs in the **User** or **Device** context. This cannot be changed after the profile has been created, so if you select the wrong option here, the only option is to recreate the profile.

5. Upload your file, and it will be displayed in the read-only editor below.

6. In this example, the file needs to run in the device context. After configuring your settings, click **Next**:

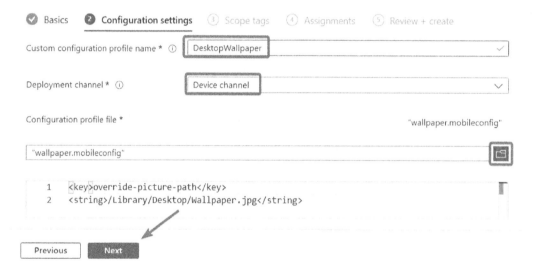

Figure 7.5 – Custom profile settings

7. Again, we do not need scope tags here, so press **Next**.

8. It is worth matching the assignment here to the custom script deployed earlier, and then click **Next**.

9. Confirm everything looks okay, and then click **Create**.

To take things one step further, you can then restrict users from changing the background by setting **Allow Wallpaper Modification** to **False** in the settings catalog (as covered earlier):

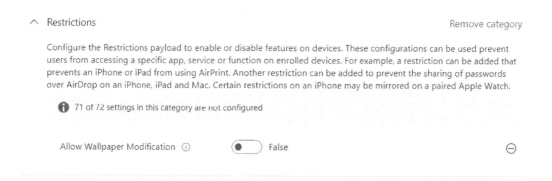

Restrictions   Remove category

Configure the Restrictions payload to enable or disable features on devices. These configurations can be used prevent users from accessing a specific app, service or function on enrolled devices. For example, a restriction can be added that prevents an iPhone or iPad from using AirPrint. Another restriction can be added to prevent the sharing of passwords over AirDrop on an iPhone, iPad and Mac. Certain restrictions on an iPhone may be mirrored on a paired Apple Watch.

71 of 72 settings in this category are not configured

Allow Wallpaper Modification   False

Figure 7.6 – Wallpaper modification in the settings catalog

Automating it

Now, we can look at automating both the shell script and the custom profile. As both involve a file upload, we will again let PowerShell do the heavy lifting and convert to Base64 for upload.

Deploying the shell script

We can start with the shell script:

1. We will start with the default settings and also include the path to the script itself. We will use the `deviceShellScripts` area of Microsoft Graph for this command:

```
$url = "https://graph.microsoft.com/beta/deviceManagement/
deviceShellScripts"
$name = "Download Wallpaper Background"
$description = "Downloads the wallpaper background to be used
with Custom Profile"
$groupid = "000000-0000-0000-0000-000000000000"
$scriptpath = "c:\temp\downloadwallpaper.sh"
```

2. Now, we want to convert the script to Base64:

```
$shellscript = [System.Convert]::ToBase64String([System.
Text.Encoding]::UTF8.GetBytes([System.
IO.File]::ReadAllText($scriptpath)))
```

3. We also need to pass the filename, which we will get using the `[System.IO.Path]::GetFileName` function:

```
$filename = [System.IO.Path]::GetFileName($scriptpath)
```

4. Next, populate the JSON. Note that we can also set the retry count (up to 3) and the frequency, which in this case is P1D (**Period 1 Day**).

The notifications are set via a simple `true`/`false` Boolean, and `runAsAccount` can be `system` or `user`:

```
$json = @"
{
    "blockExecutionNotifications": true,
    "description": "$description",
    "displayName": "$name",
    "executionFrequency": "P1D",
    "fileName": "$filename",
    "retryCount": 3,
    "roleScopeTagIds": [
        "0"
    ],
    "runAsAccount": "system",
    "scriptContent": "$shellscript"
}
"@
```

5. As usual, create the policy and grab the ID:

```
$policy = Invoke-MgGraphRequest -Uri $url -Method Post -Body
$json -ContentType "application/json" -OutputType PSObject
$policyid = $policy.id
```

6. Add the profile ID to the assignment URL, and assign it:

```
$assignurl = "https://graph.microsoft.com/beta/deviceManagement/
DeviceShellScripts/$policyid/assign"
$assignjson = @"
{
    "deviceManagementScriptAssignments": [
        {
            "target": {
                "@odata.type": "#microsoft.graph.
groupAssignmentTarget",
                "groupId": "$groupid"
            }
        }
    ]
}
"@
Invoke-MgGraphRequest -Uri $assignurl -Method Post -Body
$assignjson -ContentType "application/json"
```

This has created our shell script and then added and assigned it to Intune.

Deploying a custom profile

The same applies to the custom profile, where we need to upload a file and grab the filename:

1. As usual, start with the basics. Along with the file path, we also need a name for the setting itself:

    ```
    $url = "      https://graph.microsoft.com/beta/deviceManagement/
    deviceConfigurations"
    $name = "Configure Desktop Wallpaper"
    $description = "Forces wallpaper to /Library/Desktop/Wallpaper.
    jpg\nAs downloaded in Shell Script"
    $settingname = "DesktopWallpaper"
    $groupid = "000000-0000-0000-0000-000000000000"
    $configpath = "c:\temp\wallpaper.mobileconfig"
    ```

2. Convert our image to Base64:

    ```
    $configscript = [System.Convert]::ToBase64String([System.
    Text.Encoding]::UTF8.GetBytes([System.
    IO.File]::ReadAllText($configpath)))
    ```

3. Grab the filename:

    ```
    $filename = [System.IO.Path]::GetFileName($configpath)
    ```

4. Populate the JSON, and the only additional setting here is the deployment context, where you can have either deviceChannel or userChannel:

    ```
    $json = @"
    {
        "@odata.type": "#microsoft.graph.macOSCustomConfiguration",
        "deploymentChannel": "deviceChannel",
        "description": "$description",
        "displayName": "$name",
        "id": "00000000-0000-0000-0000-000000000000",
        "payload": "$configscript",
        "payloadFileName": "$filename",
        "payloadName": "$settingname",
        "roleScopeTagIds": [
            "0"
        ]
    }
    "@
    ```

5. Create the profile and grab the ID:

```
$policy = Invoke-MgGraphRequest -Uri $url -Method Post -Body
$json -ContentType "application/json" -OutputType PSObject
$policyid = $policy.id
```

6. Populate our URL with the policy ID, and assign the policy:

```
$assignurl = "https://graph.microsoft.com/beta/deviceManagement/
deviceConfigurations/$policyid/assign"

$assignjson = @"
{
    "deviceManagementScriptAssignments": [
        {
            "target": {
                "@odata.type": "#microsoft.graph.
groupAssignmentTarget",
                "groupId": "$groupid"
            }
        }
    ]
}
"@
Invoke-MgGraphRequest -Uri $assignurl -Method Post -Body
$assignjson -ContentType "application/json"
```

By following this script, you have created a custom profile and added your custom script to it.

Configuring update policies for macOS

As with our Windows and iOS devices, we want to make sure they run the latest available OS version to increase security across the estate. For macOS, this is accomplished using an update policy, which can either be created within the **Software updates** template in **Profiles**, the **Software Update** category in the settings catalog, or by using a specific menu item. To keep things standardized across platforms, in this example, we will use the specific update policies menu so you always know where to look for your updates. As with Windows devices, for a large macOS estate, it is worth using deployment rings so that updates can be tested prior to large-scale deployment.

How to do it...

Follow the following steps:

1. Start by clicking on **Devices** and then **macOS**.

2. Then, click **Update policies for macOS**.

3. Click **Create profile**.

4. As usual, we will start with a name and description, and then click **Next**.

5. On the next screen, you can select what happens with **Critical updates**, **Firmware updates**, **Configuration file updates**, and **All other updates**.

    The options available are as follows:

    *   **Not Configured**: Do nothing.

    *   **Download and install**: Download or install, depending on the current state.

    *   **Download only**: Download but do not install.

    *   **Install immediately**: Download and trigger a restart notification (this is best for userless devices).

    *   **Notify only**: Download the updates and notify in system settings.

    *   **Install later**: Download and defer installation (not for major OS upgrades). Selecting this option will then display the maximum user deferrals before installation and the priority (low or high) on all other updates only.

6. You can also set the schedule with options to simply install when the device next checks in to Intune, or set a schedule that can either be inclusive or exclusive, similar to with iOS. You could set your active hours to 08:00–18:00 to catch the standard working day, or you could decide you want the updates to only be installed outside active hours and set it to **Update outside of scheduled time**. Alternatively, your users may power off devices at the end of the working day, so you need to force updates during the working day to ensure they have been installed. In this case, you would select **Update during scheduled time**.

    In our case, we are going to install the latest update at the next check-in.

7. Once you have configured your environment, click **Next**:

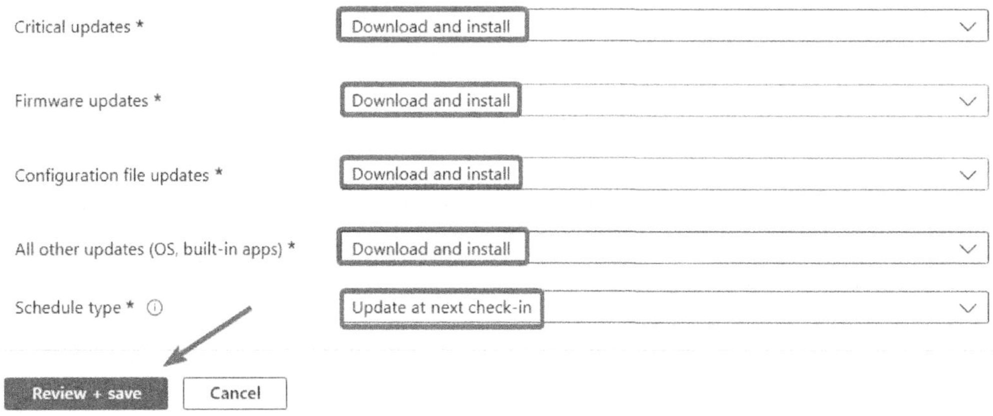

Critical updates *	Download and install	
Firmware updates *	Download and install	
Configuration file updates *	Download and install	
All other updates (OS, built-in apps) *	Download and install	
Schedule type * ⓘ	Update at next check-in	

Review + save   Cancel

Figure 7.7 – Update policy settings

8. We do not need scope tags, so again, click **Next**.

Now, consider your assignments, depending on what you have selected for the update policy. You may wish to create multiple policies with different settings for different user groups or device types (for example, your non-user kiosk-style devices may need different settings, or you could have shift workers).

In our case, we will assign to Intune users, giving us the flexibility to exclude other groups as required. Unlike Windows devices, you do not have the option to pick different deployment rings, and also note that you cannot set the OS version as with Windows and iOS.

9. Once everything is configured, click **Next**.

Finally, check that everything looks correct, and then click **Create**.

We have now created our update policy in the Intune UI.

Automating it

As mentioned at the start of this recipe, updates can be configured using the dedicated option, update templates, or the settings catalog. When deploying with the dedicated menu, the underlying JSON uses the update template and not the settings catalog, which does make it slightly easier to configure:

1. Start with the basics as usual:

```
$url = "https://graph.microsoft.com/beta/deviceManagement/
deviceConfigurations"
$name = "macOS Updates"
$description = "Managed updates on macOS devices"
$groupid = "000000-0000-0000-0000-000000000000"
```

2. In our example, we have set the updates to install at the next check-in, so `updateScheduleType` is set to `alwaysUpdate`, and the `customUpdateTimeWindows` array is empty. You can also see the update behavior options selected earlier – `installLater`, `installASAP`, and `default`.

With installations at the next check-in, our JSON looks like this:

```
$jsonimmediate = @"
{
    "@odata.type": "#microsoft.graph.
macOSSoftwareUpdateConfiguration",
    "allOtherUpdateBehavior": "installLater",
    "configDataUpdateBehavior": "default",
    "criticalUpdateBehavior": "installASAP",
    "customUpdateTimeWindows": [],
    "description": "$description",
    "displayName": "$name",
    "firmwareUpdateBehavior": "default",
    "id": "",
    "maxUserDeferralsCount": 3,
    "priority": "low",
    "roleScopeTagIds": [
        "0"
    ],
    "updateScheduleType": "alwaysUpdate",
    "updateTimeWindowUtcOffsetInMinutes": null
}
"@
```

If we opt to install updates during scheduled hours, it looks like this:

```
$jsonwindow = @"
{
    "@odata.type": "#microsoft.graph.
macOSSoftwareUpdateConfiguration",
    "allOtherUpdateBehavior": "installLater",
    "configDataUpdateBehavior": "default",
    "criticalUpdateBehavior": "installASAP",
    "customUpdateTimeWindows": [
        {
            "@odata.type": "#microsoft.graph.
customUpdateTimeWindow",
            "endDay": "Friday",
            "endTime": "18:00:00.0000000",
            "startDay": "Monday",
            "startTime": "08:00:00.0000000"
```

```
            }
        ],
        "description": "$description",
        "displayName": "$name",
        "firmwareUpdateBehavior": "default",
        "id": "",
        "maxUserDeferralsCount": 3,
        "priority": "low",
        "roleScopeTagIds": [
            "0"
        ],
        "updateScheduleType": "updateDuringTimeWindows",
        "updateTimeWindowUtcOffsetInMinutes": 0
    }
    "@
```

3. Finally, create and assign the policy:

```
$policy = Invoke-MgGraphRequest -Uri $url -Method Post -Body
$jsonimmediate -ContentType "application/json" -OutputType
PSObject
$policyid = $policy.id
$assignurl = "https://graph.microsoft.com/beta/deviceManagement/
deviceConfigurations/$policyid/assign"
$assignjson = @"
{
    "assignments": [
        {
            "target": {
                "@odata.type": "#microsoft.graph.
groupAssignmentTarget",
                "groupId": "$groupid"
            }
        }
    ]
}
"@
Invoke-MgGraphRequest -Uri $assignurl -Method Post -Body
$assignjson -ContentType "application/json"
```

We have now created and assigned an update policy for our macOS devices using PowerShell and Graph.

Deploying apps to macOS

We have configured and protected our devices, but the end users are going to want to have some applications deployed as well. Within Intune, there are a number of options available:

- **Microsoft 365 Apps**: A GUI to deploy M365 apps (covered later)
- **Microsoft Edge**: To deploy Edge version 77 and later (Chromium) (covered later)
- **Microsoft Defender for Endpoint**: To protect your devices (covered later)
- **Web link**: Deploy a URL to the desktop
- **Line-of-business app**: Deploy a custom pkg application
- **macOS app (DMG)**: Upload and deploy a DMG-based application (covered later)
- **App Store app**: Similar to iOS, this deploys a VPP app from the App Store (covered later)

Getting started

For this recipe, make sure you have a DMG file available to deploy, and also access to either ABM or Apple Education to deploy applications from the App Store.

How to do it...

All of these instructions will be from **Apps** and then **macOS apps** in the Intune portal.

App Store

Follow the following steps:

1. Within ABM, click **Apps and Books**.
2. Search for the application you want, and make sure it is a macOS app. In this case, we will use **GarageBand**:

Figure 7.8 – App selection

3. After clicking on the application, purchase licenses for your MDM, and then click **Get**:

Figure 7.9 – Getting an app

4. This application should appear almost instantly in Intune, but you can follow the application instructions in *Chapter 6, Apple iOS Device Management*, to force a sync if not.

5. Back in the Intune portal, you can see the application, which is unassigned. Click on it to configure assignments:

Figure 7.10 – The app in Intune

6. Click **Properties**, and under **Assignments**, click **Edit**.

7. Assign the application as required. For an application such as this, it is normally suggested to create application-specific install and uninstall groups, which is what we have done here. For a standard app such as M365 or Edge, the assignments can be more broad. You can also set the application as a forced install (**Required**) or self-service (**Available**).

    For free applications that do not require a license, one option is to force an installation on members of the group (those who need it for their role) and allow it as self-service for others to install as required.

8. After adding the assignment, some further options will be displayed:

License type	Uninstall on device ...	Prevent iCloud app ...	Prevent automatic a...
Device	No	No	No

Figure 7.11 – Assignment options

The important option here is the license type. We do not want our users to need an Apple ID to install applications, and therefore, we need to make sure we choose **Device** licensing.

9. Clicking on any of the blue text links will load a fly-out panel with further options.

You can configure these settings as required; in this case, we want the application to be forced, updated, and not backed up, as it stores credentials and should not be deleted unless the device is removed from Intune management. When you have configured your requirements, click **OK**:

Figure 7.12 – Further app settings

10. Once you have configured your assignments and settings, click **Review and Save**. We are editing an existing application, which is why there is no **Create or Add** option.

11. Check that everything looks acceptable, and then click **Save**.

DMG applications

When Intune first supported macOS, you had to wrap applications into the `.intunemac` format, similar to Windows Win32 apps and the `intunewin` packaging. Fortunately, in early 2022, the ability to deploy `.dmg` files directly was added.

To follow this recipe, you will need a DMG file to deploy to your devices; in this example, we will use Adobe Acrobat Reader, available at the following link (if you are downloading from a Windows machine, click **More Options** to select the macOS version): `https://get.adobe.com/uk/reader/`.

Now, follow the following steps:

1. Return to the Intune portal in Apps/macOS, and then click **Add**.
2. In the flyout, select **macOS App (DMG)**, and then click **Select**.
3. Click **Select app package file**.
4. In the flyout, select the DMG file downloaded earlier, and click **OK**
5. Complete the application details. If you are allowing this for self-service, supplying an image and category will make the company portal easier for end users to navigate. Once you have entered the necessary information, click **Next**:

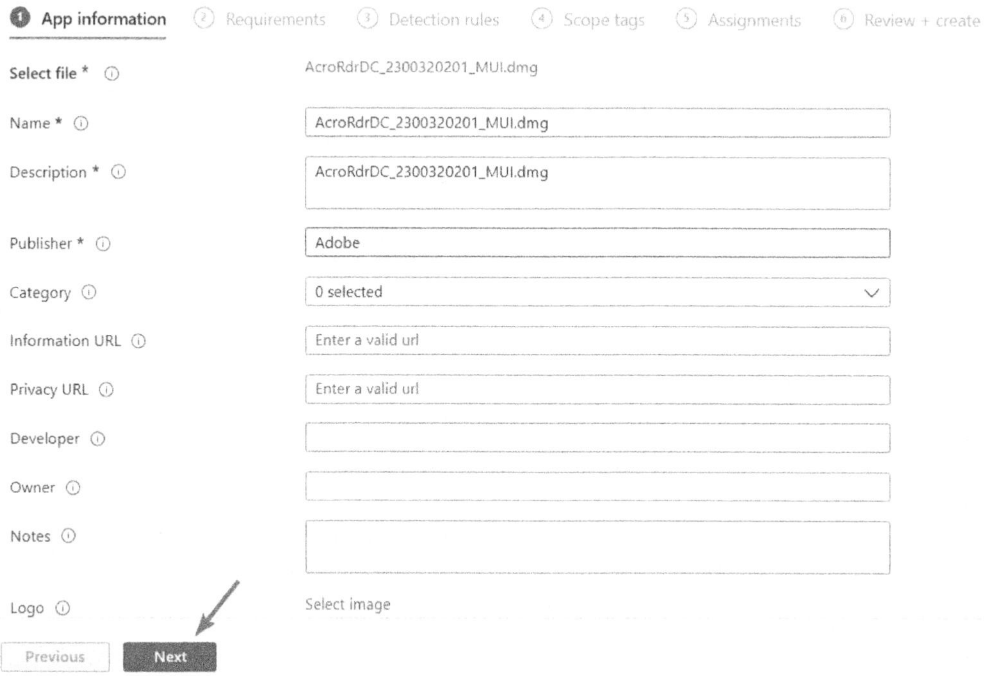

Figure 7.13 – The application details

6. On the next screen, you can specify a minimum OS version for the software to install on. In this case, the installer works on all of the available options, so we will select the oldest OS version.

7. If you have a mixed estate, you can deploy multiple versions of the same application, and then when assigning, simply use device filters to only install on applicable devices.

   Once you have selected a version, click **Next**.

8. We now have to look at application detection. The first thing is to check or ignore the app version. If the application automatically updates, you want to leave **Ignore app version** as **Yes** so that the application continues to be detected after an update.

9. When you set **Ignore app version** as **No**, the app bundle ID and version must match before the application is uninstalled (when a user/device is added to the uninstall group). If it is set to **Yes**, Intune only checks the bundle ID and ignores the version.

   To find the bundle ID, install the application on a test machine, and run the following command in Terminal (replace `Adobe Acrobat Reader` with the exact name of the application):

   ```
   osascript -e 'id of app "Adobe Acrobat Reader"'
   ```

   Note that the app list is case-sensitive, so pay close attention to the name.

10. We need to enter an app version, but it will not actually be used, as we have **Ignore app version** set to **Yes**. Once configured, click **Next**.

Figure 7.14 – App detection rules

11. We can skip past the **Scope tags** page, so click **Next**.

12. As with the store application, we are going to use groups for **Required** and **Uninstall** assignment. There is no self-service option for DMG-deployed applications. Once you have added your groups, click **Next**.

13. Finally, check that everything looks okay, and click **Create**.

Microsoft 365 apps

Now we have covered the more complex applications, we can look at the more simple GUI-driven ones for your key Microsoft applications. For Windows devices, we will look at something similar in *Chapter 11*, but it is often preferred to deploy Microsoft 365 apps as a Win32 application packaged with the **Office Deployment Tool** (**ODT**), due to the way applications and policies are processed.

On macOS, however, the GUI works well and does not have the same drawbacks:

1. Within macOS apps, create a new application, select **macOS** under **Microsoft 365 Apps**, and then click **Select**.

2. On the next screen, you have the familiar application details; conveniently, it is all pre-populated for you.

3. With Windows deployments, you have more options to select here, but for macOS, it is a simple configuration.

4. Make any changes to your environment, and click **Next**.

5. We do not need scope tags at this point, so again, click **Next**.

6. Assign the application as required. Generally, these apps are required by everyone, but you could also create a dynamic group to include only users who have an Office desktop apps license with this dynamic rule:

    ```
    (user.assignedPlans -any (assignedPlan.servicePlanId -eq
    "43de0ff5-c92c-492b-9116-175376d08c38" -and assignedPlan.
    capabilityStatus -eq "Enabled"))
    ```

7. The deployment options here are either required or available. There is no uninstall option, but you can utilize self-service with available assignments unlike with a DMG application.

8. In our case, we are going to use the **Intune-Users** group, and then click **Next**.

9. Finally, confirm everything is correct, and then click **Create**.

Microsoft Edge

Another Microsoft app you may want to deploy to your macOS devices is Microsoft Edge for easier management, cross-platform continuity, and also integration with Defender for Endpoint.

Fortunately, this is another straightforward GUI configuration.

1. Create a new application. This time, in the dropdown, select **macOS** under **Microsoft Edge, version 77 and later** (version 77 was the switch to the new Edge Chromium version). Then, click **Select**.

2. Note that, as with M365 apps, the details here are pre-populated, but this time, there is no option to add or change the image. This is because the image is selected depending on which channel is chosen on the next screen. Change anything if needed, and then click **Next**.

3. On the next screen, you can select which version of Edge to deploy, **Dev**, **Beta**, or **Stable**. While you should use **Stable** as the default for the majority of your users, it is worth deploying both the **Dev** and **Beta** versions to test users, similar to how we handle OS updates. This gives you a chance to confirm that all web-based applications work correctly before updates apply. It also gives you advance notice of any UI changes that you may want to notify your users about.

    You can find out more about the different Edge channels here: `https://learn.microsoft.com/en-us/deployedge/microsoft-edge-channels`.

    In this case, we are going to deploy the **Stable** version:

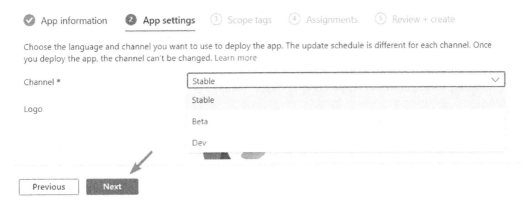

Figure 7.15 – Edge app settings

4. As usual, press **Next** on the **Scope tags** screen.

5. While this is an application that you will undoubtedly want to have across your entire estate and could potentially use for all users or devices, as mentioned earlier, you may prefer to utilize deployment rings for testing purposes. Therefore, assigning the application to a group gives you greater control.

    Note that, again, there is no uninstall group option, but you can add it for self-service along with a standard **Required** installation.

    In our case, we are going to use **Intune-Users** group.

6. Finally, check that everything looks okay, and then click **Create**. Note that the logo has now been added to match the channel chosen earlier.

Microsoft Defender for Endpoint

The final application we may wish to deploy is Microsoft Defender for Endpoint. We can use this to both protect against malware and, if you are licensed, use some of the extra features, such as web filtering.

> **Important note**
>
> There are prerequisites before deploying the application that need to be deployed to your environment. You can find out what they are and how to deploy them at the following link: `https://learn.microsoft.com/en-us/microsoft-365/security/defender-endpoint/mac-install-with-intune?view=o365-worldwide`.

Follow these steps to deploy Microsoft Defender for Endpoint for macOS:

1. As with the other Microsoft applications, it is another simple GUI. Create a new application, and this time, select **macOS** under **Microsoft Defender for Endpoint**. Then, click **Select**.

2. Again, all of the information is pre-populated, including the image (which you cannot change). Click **Next** after making any changes as required.

3. There are not any settings or further configuration options for Defender for Endpoint, so we are taken straight to the **Scope tags** page. Click **Next**.

4. Again, we have the option to deploy as required or available, but there is no uninstall option. As this is a security application, we really want to be sure it is installed everywhere, so we are going to select **All Devices**. As mentioned earlier, you could add a filter to only include macOS devices in order to keep things more tidy. Once you have added your assignment, click **Next**.

5. Finally, confirm everything looks correct, and then click **Create**.

Automating it

Now that we have added our application to the UI, we can look at which parts can be automated.

App Store

While you cannot automate adding the application itself, you can automate the assignment of it. We do this by finding the application ID and then assigning it:

1. First, set the name we are looking for. We will let PowerShell and Graph do the hard work for us:

   ```
   $appname = "GarageBand"
   ```

2. Now, we can run a GET request against all of the mobile apps in the tenant. We then only want Apple VPP-deployed applications so to limit the results, we filter the query using the `@odata.type` variable as `#microsoft.graph.macOSVppApp`. Once we have the VPP apps, we can find just those that match the name, and finally, we just want the ID (nested within the `value` attribute):

   ```
   $appid = ((Invoke-MgGraphRequest -Uri "https://graph.
   microsoft.com/beta/deviceAppManagement/mobileApps" -Method
   Get -ContentType "application/json" -OutputType PSObject).
   value | Where-Object {$_.'@odata.type' -eq '#microsoft.graph.
   macOSVppApp'} | Where-Object {$_.displayName -eq $appname}).id
   ```

3. Populate the URL with `$appid`:

```
$url = "https://graph.microsoft.com/beta/deviceAppManagement/
mobileApps/$appid/assign"
```

4. Now, we need the JSON, which you can see we have configured with the Required, Uninstall, and Available assignments:

```
$json = @"
{
    "mobileAppAssignments": [
        {
            "@odata.type": "#microsoft.graph.
mobileAppAssignment",
            "intent": "Required",
            "settings": {
                "@odata.type": "#microsoft.graph.
macOsVppAppAssignmentSettings",
                "preventAutoAppUpdate": false,
                "preventManagedAppBackup": false,
                "uninstallOnDeviceRemoval": false,
                "useDeviceLicensing": true
            },
            "target": {
                "@odata.type": "#microsoft.graph.
groupAssignmentTarget",
                "groupId": "$installgroupid"
            }
        },
        {
            "@odata.type": "#microsoft.graph.
mobileAppAssignment",
            "intent": "Available",
            "settings": {
                "@odata.type": "#microsoft.graph.
macOsVppAppAssignmentSettings",
                "preventAutoAppUpdate": false,
                "preventManagedAppBackup": false,
                "uninstallOnDeviceRemoval": false,
                "useDeviceLicensing": true
            },
            "target": {
                "@odata.type": "#microsoft.graph.
allLicensedUsersAssignmentTarget"
            }
        },
```

```
            {
                "@odata.type": "#microsoft.graph.
mobileAppAssignment",
                "intent": "Uninstall",
                "settings": {
                    "@odata.type": "#microsoft.graph.
macOsVppAppAssignmentSettings",
                    "useDeviceLicensing": true
                },
                "target": {
                    "@odata.type": "#microsoft.graph.
groupAssignmentTarget",
                    "groupId": "$unistallgroupid"
                }
            }
        ]
    }
"@
```

5. Finally, send a POST request to add the assignment:

```
Invoke-MgGraphRequest -Uri $url -Method Post -Body $json
-ContentType "application/json"
```

DMG applications

At present, DMG applications cannot be added using Graph and PowerShell, as the file encryption information seems to be hidden during the Azure Blob upload process.

Microsoft 365 apps

Deploying M365 apps is as straightforward using PowerShell as it is via the GUI. This is more of a policy than an application, so the JSON is just references to the applications rather than having to deal with file uploads or finding app information from the store:

1. As usual, we will start with the basics, name, description, URL, and group ID:

```
$url = "https://graph.microsoft.com/beta/deviceAppManagement/
mobileApps/"
$appname = "Microsoft 365 Apps"
$appdesc = "Microsoft 365 Apps for Enterprise"
$groupid = "00000000-0000-0000-0000-000000000000"
```

2. As this is a pre-configured application, the JSON already includes the Base64 code for the image, but if you want to add a custom image, you can just grab a file and convert it using this code, and then reference the variable in the JSON:

```
$imagepath = "c:\temp\yourimage.jpg"
$imagebase64 = [System.Convert]::ToBase64String([System.
Text.Encoding]::UTF8.GetBytes([System.
IO.File]::ReadAllText($imagepath)))
```

For our M365 apps, the JSON is as follows:

```
$json = @"
{
    "@odata.type": "#microsoft.graph.macOSOfficeSuiteApp",
    "description": "$appdesc",
    "developer": "Microsoft",
    "displayName": "$appname",
    "informationUrl": "https://products.office.com/explore-
office-for-home",
    "isFeatured": false,
    "largeIcon": {
        "type": "image/png",
        "value": "iVBORw0KGgoAAAANSUhEUgAAAF0AAAAeCAMAAAEOZN
```
```
KlAAAAAXNSR0IArs4c6QAAAARnQU1BAACxjwv8YQUAAAJhUExURf////7z7/
i9qfF1S/KCW/i+qv3q5P/9/PrQwfOMae1RG+s8AOxGDfBtQPWhhPvUx/759/
zg1vWgg+9fLu5WIvKFX/rSxP728/nCr/FyR+tBBvOMaO1UH+1RHOs+AvSScP
3u6f/+/v3s5vzg1+xFDO9kNPOOa/i7pvzj2/vWyes9Af76+Pzh2PrTxf/6+f
7y7vOGYexHDv3t5+1SHfi8qPOIZPvb0O1NFuxDCe9hMPSVdPnFs/3q4/vaz/
STcu5VIe5YJPWcfv718v/9/e1MFfF4T/F4TvF2TP3o4exECvF0SexIEPONav
zn3/vZze1QGvF3Te5dK+5cKvrPwPrQwvKAWe1OGPexmexKEveulfezm/BxRf
amiuxLE/apj/zf1e5YJfSXd/OHYv3r5feznPakiPze1P7x7f739f3w6+xJEf
nEsvWdf/Wfge1LFPe1nu9iMvnDsfBqPOs/BPOIY/WZevJ/V/zl3fnIt/vTxu
xHD+xEC+9mN+5ZJv749vBpO/KBWvBwRP/8+/SUc/etlPjArP/+vOLZ/F7Uv
Wae/708e1OF/aihvSWdvi8p+tABfSZefvVyPWihfSVde91Nvami+9jM/zi2f
KEXvBuQvOKZvalifF5UPJ/WPSPbbe9eLfrKuvvd0uxBB/7w7Pzj2vrRw/rOv+
1PGfi/q/eymu5bKf3n4PnJuPBrPf3t6PWfgvWegOxCCO9nOO9oOfaskvSYeP
i5pPi2oPnGtO5eLPevlvKDXfrNvv739Pzd0/708O9gL+9lNfJ9VfrLu/OPbP
nDsPBrPus+A/nArfarkQAAAGr5HKgAAADLdFJOU//////////////////////
///////////////////////////////////////////////////////////
///////////////////////////////////////////////////////////
///////////////////////////////////////////////////////////
////////8AvuakogAAAAlwSFlzAAAOwwAADsMBx2+oZAAAAz5JREFUOE+tVT
tu4zAQHQjppmWzwIJbEVCzpTpjbxD3grQHSOXKRXgCAT6EC7UBVAmp3KwBnm
vfzNCyZTmxgeTZJsXx43B+HBHRE34ZkXgkerXFTheeiCkRrbB4UXmp4wsWz5
raaQEMTM5TZwuiXoaKgV+6FsmkZQcSy0kA71yMTMGHanX+AzMMGLAQCxU1F/
```

```
ZwjULPugaz182GM0NEKm/U8EqFwEkO3/EAT4grgl0nucwlk9pcpTTJ4VPA4g/
Rb3yIRhhp507e9nTQmZ1OS5RO4sS7nIRPEeHXCHdkw9ZEW2yVE5oIS7peD58
Avs7CN+PVCmHh21oOqBdjDzIs+FldPJ74TFESUSJEfVzy9U/dhu+AuOT6eBp
6gGKyXEx8euO450ZE4CMfstMFT44broWw/itkYErWXRx+fFArt9Ca9os78TF
ed0LVIUsmIHrwbwaw3BEOnOk94qVpQ6Ka2HjxewJnfyd6jUtGDQLdWlzmYNY
LeKbbGOucJsNabCq1Yub0o92rtR+i30V2dapxYVEePXcOjeCKPnYyit7BtKe
NlZqHbr+gt7i+AChWA9RsRs03pxTQc67ouWpxyESvjK5Vs3DVSy3IpkxPm5X
+wZoBi+MFHWW69/w8FRhc7VBe6HAhMB2b8Q0XqDzTNZtXUMnKMjwKVaCrB/C
SUL7WSx/HsdJC86lFGXwnioTeOMPjV+szlFvrZLA5VMVK4y+4ll4e1xfx7Z8
8o4hkilRUH/qKqwNVlgDgpvYCpH3XwAy5eMCRnezIUxffVXoDql2rTHFDO+p
jWnTWzAfrYXn6BFECblUpWGrvPZvBipETjS5ydM7tdXpH41ZCEbBNy/+wFZu
71QO2t9pgT+iZEf657Q1vpN94PQNDxUHeKR103LV9nPVOtDikcNKO+2naCw7
yKBhOe9Hm79pe8C4/CfC2wDjXnqC94kEeBU3WwN7dt/2UScXas7zDl5GpkY+
M8WKv2J7fd4Ib2rGTk+jsC2cleEM7jI9veF7B0MBJrsZqfKd/81q9pR2NZfw
JK2JzsmIT1Ns8jUH0UusQBpU8d2JzsHiXg1zXGLqxfitUNTDT/nUUeqDBp2H
ZVr+Ocqi/Ty3Rf4Jn82xxfSNtAAAAElFTkSuQmCC"
    },
    "notes": "",
    "owner": "Microsoft",
    "privacyInformationUrl": "https://privacy.microsoft.com/
privacystatement",
    "publisher": "Microsoft",
    "roleScopeTagIds": []
}
"@
```

The important thing to note here is @odata.type, which tells Graph which app to deploy. For M365 apps, it is #microsoft.graph.macOSOfficeSuiteApp.

3. We then need to create the application and grab the ID:

```
$mobileapp = Invoke-MgGraphRequest -Url $url -Method Post -Body
$json -ContentType "application/json" -OutputType PSObject
$mobileappid = $mobileapp.id
```

4. Finally, we populate the URL and send our POST command with the JSON to assign it:

```
$assignurl = "https://graph.microsoft.com/beta/
deviceAppManagement/mobileApps/$mobileappid/assign"

$assignjson = @"
{
    "mobileAppAssignments": [
        {
            "@odata.type": "#microsoft.graph.
mobileAppAssignment",
```

```
            "intent": "Required",
            "settings": null,
            "target": {
                "@odata.type": "#microsoft.graph.
groupAssignmentTarget",
                "groupId": "$groupid"
            }
        }
    ]
}
"@
Invoke-MgGraphRequest -Uri $assignurl -Method Post -Body
$assignjson -ContentType "application/json"
```

Microsoft Edge

Very similar to M365 apps, the only differences are the different #odata.type "#microsoft.
graph.macOSMicrosoftEdgeApp" attributes and the option to select the channel. The Base64
code for this application is quite substantial, so it has been removed from the JSON here, but it is
available in the script within the GitHub repository:

1. First, we need to set the URL and group ID for assignment and the channel to deploy. The name
    and description are preconfigured, but you could replace these with variables if you wanted:

    ```
    $url = https://graph.microsoft.com/beta/deviceAppManagement/
    mobileApps/
    $channel = "stable"
    $groupid = "00000000-0000-0000-0000-000000000000"
    ```

2. Now, populate the JSON:

    ```
    $json = @"
    {
        "@odata.type": "#microsoft.graph.macOSMicrosoftEdgeApp",
        "channel": "$channel",
        "description": "Microsoft Edge is the browser for business
    with modern and legacy web compatibility, new privacy features
    such as Tracking prevention, and built-in productivity tools
    such as enterprise-grade PDF support and access to Office and
    corporate search right from a new tab.",
        "developer": "Microsoft",
        "displayName": "Microsoft Edge for macOS",
        "informationUrl": "https://www.microsoft.com/windows/
    microsoft-edge",
    ```

```
        "isFeatured": false,
        "largeIcon": {
            "type": "image/png",
            "value": BASE64 HERE
    },
        "notes": "",
        "owner": "",
        "privacyInformationUrl": "https://privacy.microsoft.com/
privacystatement",
        "publisher": "Microsoft",
        "roleScopeTagIds": []
}
"@
```

3. No doubt you have guessed what is coming next – send the POST request to create the application, grab the ID, and assign it:

```
$mobileapp = Invoke-MgGraphRequest -Url $url -Method Post -Body
$json -ContentType "application/json" -OutputType PSObject

$mobileappid = $mobileapp.id

$assignurl = "https://graph.microsoft.com/beta/
deviceAppManagement/mobileApps/$mobileappid/assign"

$assignjson = @"
{
    "mobileAppAssignments": [
        {
            "@odata.type": "#microsoft.graph.
mobileAppAssignment",
            "intent": "Required",
            "settings": null,
            "target": {
                "@odata.type": "#microsoft.graph.
groupAssignmentTarget",
                "groupId": "$groupid"
            }
        }
    ]
}
"@
Invoke-MgGraphRequest -Uri $assignurl -Method Post -Body
$assignjson -ContentType "application/json"
```

Microsoft Defender for Endpoint

This is another simple deployment, only without the channel we saw with Edge.

Again, `@odata.type` is the main difference here, which in this case is `#microsoft.graph.MacOSMicrosoftDefenderApp` (note the capital M found on MacOS here, which is not present in the previous examples).

The Base64 image is also sizeable again, so it is removed from the example but is still available in the GitHub script:

1. This time, we only need to set the URL and group ID unless you want to change any of the text:

    ```
    $url = "https://graph.microsoft.com/beta/deviceAppManagement/
    mobileApps/"
    $groupid = "00000000-0000-0000-0000-000000000000"
    ```

2. Set the JSON, which is fairly standard:

    ```
    $json = @"
    {
        "@odata.type": "#microsoft.graph.MacOSMicrosoftDefenderApp",
        "description": "Microsoft Defender for Endpoint is a unified
    platform for preventative protection, post-breach detection,
    automated investigation, and response. Microsoft Defender for
    Endpoint protects endpoints from cyber threats; detects advanced
    attacks and data breaches, automates security incidents and
    improves security posture.",
        "developer": "Microsoft",
        "displayName": "Microsoft Defender for Endpoint (macOS)",
        "informationUrl": "https://docs.microsoft.com/en-us/windows/
    security/threat-protection/microsoft-defender-atp/microsoft-
    defender-advanced-threat-protection",
        "isFeatured": false,
        "largeIcon": {
            "type": "image/png",
            "value":
    },
        "notes": "",
        "owner": "Microsoft",
        "privacyInformationUrl": "https://docs.microsoft.com/en-us/
    windows/security/threat-protection/microsoft-defender-atp/
    mac-privacy",
        "publisher": "Microsoft",
        "roleScopeTagIds": []
    }
    "@
    ```

3.   Again, create and assign:

```
$mobileapp = Invoke-MgGraphRequest -Url $url -Method Post -Body
$json -ContentType "application/json" -OutputType PSObject
$mobileappid = $mobileapp.id
$assignurl = "https://graph.microsoft.com/beta/
deviceAppManagement/mobileApps/$mobileappid/assign"
$assignjson = @"
{
    "mobileAppAssignments": [
        {
            "@odata.type": "#microsoft.graph.
mobileAppAssignment",
            "intent": "Required",
            "settings": null,
            "target": {
                "@odata.type": "#microsoft.graph.
groupAssignmentTarget",
                "groupId": "$groupid"
            }
        }
    ]
}
"@
Invoke-MgGraphRequest -Uri $assignurl -Method Post -Body
$assignjson -ContentType "application/json"
```

We have now deployed the Microsoft Defender for Endpoint application using PowerShell and Graph.

Configuring a macOS enrollment profile

Before we enroll our first macOS device, we have one last task to complete – we need to configure an enrollment profile, the same as we completed in the previous chapter for iOS.

Getting started

For this recipe, you will need your Intune instance linked to ABM with an enrollment token configured. If you did not complete this in *Chapter 6*, complete the following recipes before continuing:

*   Configuring a connector between Apple and Intune
*   Adding enrollment profile tokens

How to do it...

Follow the following steps:

1. First, select **Devices** and then **macOS**.

2. Click **macOS enrollment**.

3. Now, click on **Enrollment program tokens**.

4. Click on the token created earlier:

Token name	↑↓	Status	Program type	↑↓
Intune		✅ Active	Apple Business Manager	

Figure 7.16 – An Apple token

5. Next, click on **Profiles**, and if you set up an iOS profile earlier, you should see it here now.

6. Select the drop-down arrow next to **Create profile**, and choose **macOS**.

7. Enter a name and description, and then click **Next**.

8. Similar to our iOS profiles, we need to set a couple of settings:

    *   **User affinity**: This is whether the device will be associated with a user. For non-kiosk devices, you need to select **Enroll with User Affinity**.

    *   After selecting this, you will see an additional option for **Authentication Method**. We want to select **Setup Assistant with modern authentication** here.

    *   **Locked enrollment** specifies whether the user has the ability to remove the profile. For corporate devices, you want this set to **Yes** to stop users from unenrolling their devices.

9. Once we have set this, click **Next**.

10. On the next screen, you can specify what is and is not available on the setup screen. Unless there are any you particularly need, you can just toggle all of them to **Hidden**. You do need to set the department details at the top. Once your settings have been configured, click **Next**.

11. Now, we need to review and create the profile. Check that everything is okay, and then click **Create**.

    Now, we need to set it as our default profile, which will default all new macOS devices imported from ABM to use it.

12. Back on your profiles screen, select **Default Profile Set default profile**.

13. Select your newly created profile under **macOS Enrollment profile**, and then click **OK**.

We have created our first macOS profile within Intune using the UI.

Automating it

The JSON for this is reasonably straightforward (although with all of the available settings, it runs to many lines of code), but first, we need to populate the URL with the ID of the Apple token, and if you have followed the previous chapter, it is basically the same with a slightly different JSON set:

1. First, set the variables:

    ```
    $name = "macOS Enrollment"
    $description = "Corporate Managed macOS Devices"
    ```

2. Now, we need to run a GET command to grab the ID of the token. It is nested within the Value array within the output as with most Graph objects which allows for pagination, and we are looking for the ID setting:

    ```
    $settingsurl = "https://graph.microsoft.com/beta/
    deviceManagement/depOnboardingSettings/"
    $tokenid = (Invoke-MgGraphRequest -Method GET -Uri $settingsurl
    -OutputType PSObject).value.id
    ```

3. Now, we populate that in the URL:

    ```
    $url = "https://graph.microsoft.com/beta/deviceManagement/
    depOnboardingSettings/$tokenid/enrollmentProfiles"
    ```

4. Add the variables to the JSON. You can see that every setting is configured with either a true or false value:

    ```
    $json = @"
    {
        "@odata.type": "#microsoft.graph.depMacOSEnrollmentProfile",
        "accessibilityScreenDisabled": true,
        "adminAccountFullName": "",
        "adminAccountUserName": "",
        "appleIdDisabled": true,
        "applePayDisabled": true,
        "autoUnlockWithWatchDisabled": true,
        "chooseYourLockScreenDisabled": true,
        "configurationEndpointUrl": "",
        "configurationWebUrl": true,
        "description": "$description",
        "diagnosticsDisabled": true,
        "displayName": "$name",
        "displayToneSetupDisabled": true,
        "dontAutoPopulatePrimaryAccountInfo": true,
    ```

```
    "enableAuthenticationViaCompanyPortal": false,
    "enabledSkipKeys": [
        "Location",
        "TOS",
        "Biometric",
        "Payment",
        "Siri",
        "Privacy",
        "AppleID",
        "DisplayTone",
        "ScreenTime",
        "Diagnostics",
        "Restore",
        "TermsOfAddress",
        "Registration",
        "FileVault",
        "iCloudDiagnostics",
        "iCloudStorage",
        "Appearance",
        "Accessibility",
        "UnlockWithWatch"
    ],
    "enableRestrictEditing": false,
    "fileVaultDisabled": true,
    "hideAdminAccount": false,
    "iCloudDiagnosticsDisabled": true,
    "iCloudStorageDisabled": true,
    "id": "",
    "isMandatory": true,
    "locationDisabled": true,
    "primaryAccountFullName": "",
    "primaryAccountUserName": "",
    "privacyPaneDisabled": true,
    "profileRemovalDisabled": true,
    "registrationDisabled": true,
    "requireCompanyPortalOnSetupAssistantEnrolledDevices":
false,
    "requiresUserAuthentication": true,
    "restoreBlocked": true,
    "screenTimeScreenDisabled": true,
    "setPrimarySetupAccountAsRegularUser": false,
    "siriDisabled": true,
    "skipPrimarySetupAccountCreation": true,
    "supervisedModeEnabled": true,
```

```
                "supportDepartment": "IT Dept",
                "supportPhoneNumber": "12345",
                "termsAndConditionsDisabled": true,
                "touchIdDisabled": true
            }
        "@
```

5. Finally, create the profile; there is no need to assign this one, but we still need to store it in a variable to set it as our default profile:

    ```
    $macosprofile = Invoke-MgGraphRequest -Method POST -Uri $url
    -Body $json -ContentType "application/json" -OutputType PSObject
    ```

6. To set the default profile, we send a POST request but with an empty body, as the URL does the configuration for us:

7. Grab the ID:

    ```
    $profileid = $macosprofile.id
    ```

8. Now, populate the URL and send the request:

    ```
    $defaulturl = "https://graph.microsoft.com/beta/
    deviceManagement/depOnboardingSettings/$tokenid/
    enrollmentProfiles/$profileid/setDefaultProfile"
    Invoke-MgGraphRequest -Method POST -Uri $defaulturl -ContentType
    "application/json" -OutputType PSObject
    ```

    This script has used PowerShell and Graph to automate the configuration and assignment of our macOS profile.

Enrolling your corporate device

Now, we have our environment configured to support and manage macOS devices, and we can enroll our first device. As these are generally corporate-owned machines, this recipe will only cover full ABM enrollment, and it is suggested to turn off personal enrollment of macOS devices.

If, however, you need to allow **Bring Your own Device (BYOD)** for macOS, you can find instructions here: https://learn.microsoft.com/en-us/mem/intune/user-help/enroll-your-device-in-intune-macos-cp.

Getting started

For this recipe, you will need a factory reset device that is already enrolled into either ABM or Apple Education and connected to the internet. If you wish to use Apple Configurator on an iPhone to register your applications, follow the guide at the following link: https://support.apple.com/en-gb/guide/apple-configurator/apd65c9ff558/ios.

How to do it...

Use the following steps:

1. Upon booting your device, you will first be presented with a screen to select your language. Select as appropriate, and click **Continue**:

Figure 7.17 – Selecting an OS country or region

2. macOS will now configure the language settings according to your country selection, but if necessary, click **Customize Settings** and change them accordingly. Then, click **Continue**.

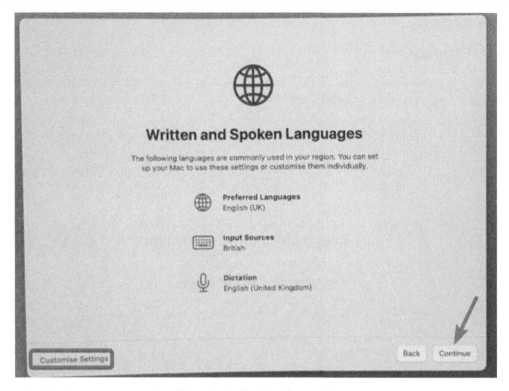

Figure 7.18 – Setting a language

3. Depending on the settings used in your enrollment profile, you may see other screens here, such as **Accessibility** settings:

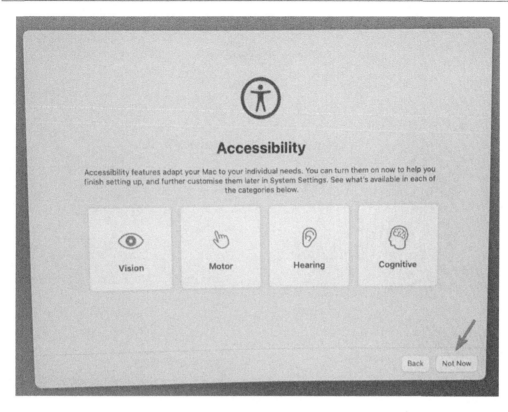

Figure 7.19 – Accessibility options

4. Once you have completed any additional settings, you will be prompted to connect to a wireless network (unless the device has a hardwired connection). Select your network, enter the password, and click **Continue**.

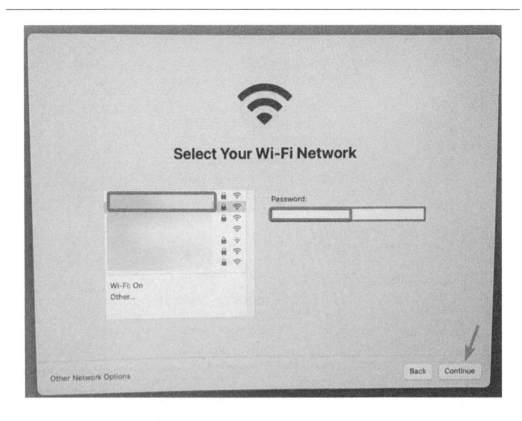

Figure 7.20 – Connecting to a wireless network

5. This is where setup differs from an unmanaged device; you will be prompted to enable remote management. Click **Continue**.

Figure 7.21 – Enabling remote management

6. Enter your Microsoft credentials (username and password).

7. If prompted, create a user account on the device, and click **Continue**.

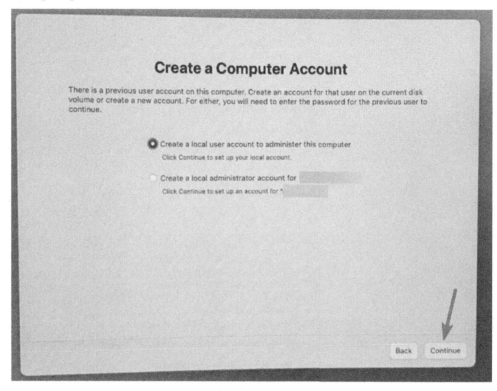

Figure 7.22 – Creating a user account

8. Enter the details of the account:

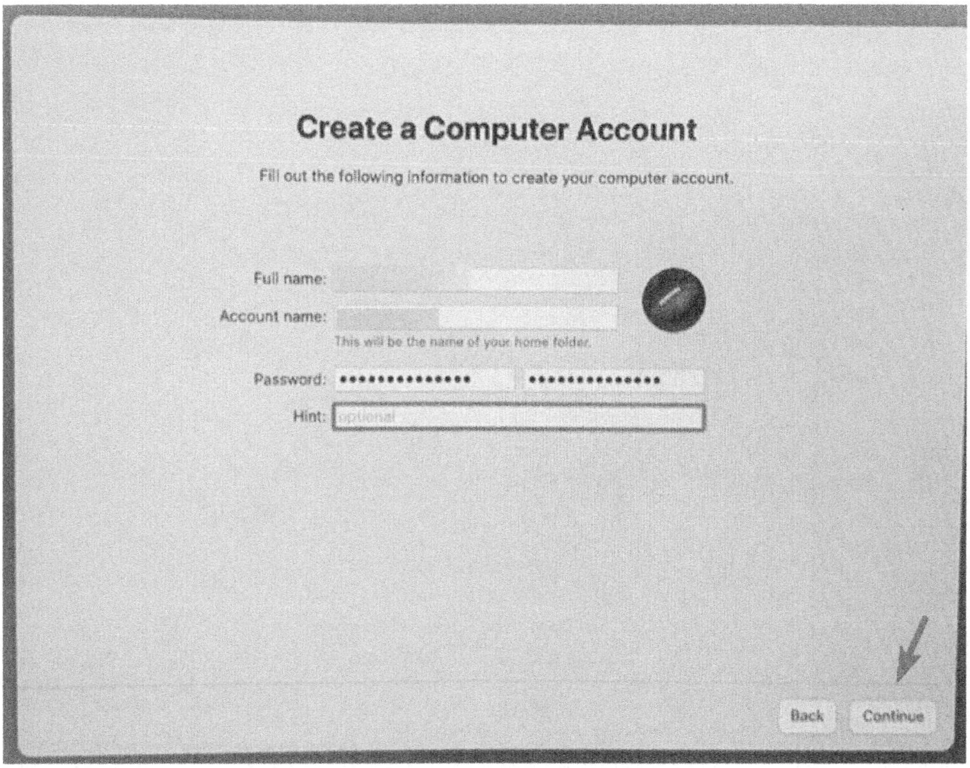

Figure 7.23 – Confirming the account details

9.   Finally, set your time zone, and then click **Continue**:

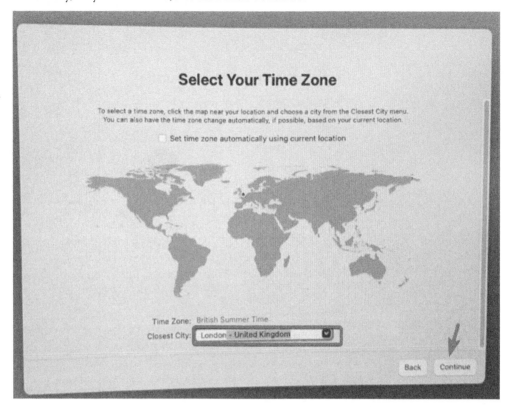

Figure 7.24 – Setting the time zone

Congratulations! You have enrolled your first macOS device on Intune.

8

Setting Up Your Compliance Policies

Now that we have successfully enrolled a device from all of the major platforms (Windows, macOS, iOS, and Android), we need a method of ensuring they are always managed, updated, and compliant with our own requirements. For that, we can use **compliance policies**. These allow us to configure a set of requirements that devices must meet to be classed as compliant within the environment. Then, we can add a **conditional access** policy on top to restrict access to corporate data from any devices that do not meet the criteria. This increases your security posture and also gives you the ability to quickly monitor your estate for any major issues.

In addition to showing you how to deploy these policies, we will also look at what each of the settings requires on the device. We will also cover the more advanced custom compliance policy for Windows.

Finally, we will look at how to restrict access from non-compliant machines using conditional access.

In this chapter, we will cover the following recipes:

- Configuring notification templates
- Deploying a Windows compliance policy
- Deploying an Android compliance policy
- Deploying an iOS compliance policy
- Deploying a macOS compliance policy
- Deploying a Linux compliance policy
- Configuring and deploying a Windows custom compliance policy
- Using conditional access to restrict access based on compliance

Technical requirements

For this chapter, you will need a modern web browser and a PowerShell code editor such as Visual Studio Code or PowerShell ISE.

All of the scripts that will be referenced in this chapter can be found here: `https://github.com/PacktPublishing/Microsoft-Intune-Cookbook`.

If you wish to test the policies, you will need a corporate-managed device running each device platform for testing. For Linux, it will need to be running Ubuntu.

Chapter materials

Before we begin configuring our policies, there is one setting that we want to configure for the tenant that tells Intune what to do with devices that do not have any compliance policies assigned.

For this, navigate to **Devices** and then **Compliance**. Then, click on **Compliance policy settings**.

We have two settings here:

- **Mark devices with no compliance policy assigned as**: A device without a policy assigned is a potential security risk as it could potentially be non-compliant with multiple settings. The best practice is always to set this to non-compliant.

- **Compliance status validity period (days)**: This sets how long you will accept a prior status report – put another way, if a device has not checked into Intune, after how many days should it be flagged as non-compliant? At a very basic level, consider Windows updates; if a machine has not been seen for 30 days or more, assume it is missing at least one set of updates, possibly including antivirus updates and definitions.

    In our case, we are leaving the second setting set to **30 days** and setting devices without a policy to **Not Compliant**. Once these have been set, click **Save**.

There is also one configuration that applies to all compliance policies and that is the action to take on non-compliant devices.

Actions for noncompliance

After configuring the compliance settings, we also need to tell Intune what to do when it detects devices that do not meet the criteria:

- **Mark device non-compliant**: Set the number of days before a device is marked as non-compliant. As mentioned earlier, **immediately** may cause issues with some attestation rules, but setting it too long increases the security risk.

- **Send email to end user**: Here, you can also set the number of days, after which an email is sent to the user informing them the device is not compliant. You can configure the message that is sent and also send a copy elsewhere, such as to your IT department. You could set multiple templates here with different warnings to the user before you simply block access. We will look at this in the first recipe.

- **Add device to retire list**: After the number of days has been selected, the device will be added to a retirement list. Nothing will happen until the administrator retires the devices via the **Retire non-compliant devices** menu within **Compliance Policies**:

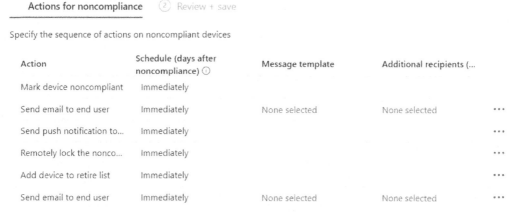

Figure 8.1 – Retire non-compliant devices

- **Send push notification to end user (Android and iOS only)**: This is similar to email, but the message appears on-screen and cannot be customized.

- **Remotely lock the non-compliant device (iOS and Android only)**: This option locks the user out of the device:

Actions for noncompliance   ② Review + save

Specify the sequence of actions on noncompliant devices

Action	Schedule (days after noncompliance) ⓘ	Message template	Additional recipients (...	
Mark device noncompliant	Immediately			
Send email to end user	Immediately	None selected	None selected	•••
Send push notification to...	Immediately			•••
Remotely lock the nonco...	Immediately			•••
Add device to retire list	Immediately			•••
Send email to end user	Immediately	None selected	None selected	•••

Figure 8.2 – Actions for noncompliance

Configuring notification templates

All supported platforms can send an email to the end user (and copy it to any other distribution lists), informing them that they are using a non-compliant device. This can be used to provide warnings before the device is blocked.

As these are cross-platform, this first recipe will cover how to create your template.

How to do it...

Follow these steps:

1. First, navigate to **Devices** and then **Compliance**.

2. Now, click on **Notifications** and create a new notification.

3. First, you must set a name for the template and select how corporate you want it to look. The corporate details are grabbed from **Tenant details**, which we will cover in *Chapter 13*. Once selected, click **Next**.

4. On the next screen, you can configure your message and language. If you are multi-national, you can have multiple notifications. One has to be set as the default before you can click **Next** to continue.

5. Click **Next** to progress past **Scope tags**.

6. Finally, review that everything looks correct and click **Create**.

Automating it

Now that we have created a template, we can look at how to automate this process.

Creating notification templates is an unusual one to automate as while we do not have to assign it, it is still a two-step process:

1. First, though, we need to set the subject and message. Note that any line breaks need \n in the code:

   ```
   $subject = "First Warning"
   $message = "Your device is now showing as non-compliant. Please
   contact IT to resolve the issue.\nYour access will be blocked in
   xx days"
   $displayname = "First Alert"
   ```

   All these notifications use the following URL for POST and GET requests:

   ```
   https://graph.microsoft.com/beta/deviceManagement/
   notificationMessageTemplates
   ```

2. Now, we need to set the URL:

```
$createnotificationurl = "https://graph.microsoft.com/beta/
deviceManagement/notificationMessageTemplates"
```

3. Next, we need to create the initial policy with the display name and the corporate branding settings, which are simply comma-separated values in the setting:

```
$createnotificationjson = @"
{
    "brandingOptions": "includeCompanyLogo,includeCompanyName,
includeContactInformation",
    "displayName": "$displayname",
    "roleScopeTagIds": [
        "0"
    ]
}
"@
$createnotification = invoke-mggraphrequest -uri
$createnotificationurl -json $createnotificationjson -method
post -contenttype "application/json" -outputtype PSObject
```

4. We have output the policy creation as we still need the policy ID for the next step:

```
$createnotificationid = $createnotification.id
```

5. Add the policy ID to the URL:

```
$createnotificationmessageurl = "https://
graph.microsoft.com/beta/deviceManagement/
notificationMessageTemplates/$createnotificationid/
localizedNotificationMessages"
```

6. Now, we can populate the JSON and add the template to the policy:

```
$createnotificationmessagejson = @"
{
    "isDefault": true,
    "locale": "en-GB",
    "messageTemplate": "$message",
    "subject": "$subject"
}
"@
$createnotificationmessage = invoke-mggraphrequest
-uri $createnotificationmessageurl -json
$createnotificationmessagejson -method post -contenttype
"application/json" -outputtype PSObject
```

If you have multiple templates for different languages, then each template is a separate POST request, not a nested array.

Deploying a Windows compliance policy

There are two ways to configure compliance policies for Windows devices. Both will be covered in this chapter, but we will start with the easier of the two, which is GUI-driven.

Getting started

As mentioned earlier, before we start creating our policy, we should look at the available settings and what they do.

Compliance settings

We will start with the available compliance settings.

Custom compliance

We will cover this in a later recipe (*Configuring and deploying a Windows custom compliance policy*), but to summarize, you can deploy a custom PowerShell script to monitor anything on the device and feed it into a compliance policy.

Device Health

Device health rules use the **Device Health Attestation** service. One important thing to note is that they require a reboot to report back as they are querying the BIOS, among other things. Therefore, if you set these settings, make sure you do not set devices as non-compliant immediately; otherwise, your fresh devices will lose access. Let us run through the available settings under **Device Health**:

- **Bitlocker**: Checks that drives are encrypted using BitLocker
- **Secure Boot**: Checks that Secure Boot is enabled within UEFI
- **Code integrity**: Checks drivers and firmware for signs of corruption or malicious activity

Device Properties

Under the **Device Properties** sub-heading, we have the following options:

- **Minimum OS version**: The operating system version in `major.minor.build.revision` format. For example, if we wanted the Windows 11 22H2 May 2023 release, it would be `10.0.22621.1702`.

> **Important note**
>
> You can check which versions are available at `https://support.microsoft.com/en-us/topic/windows-11-version-23h2-update-history-59875222-b990-4bd9-932f-91a5954de434`.

- **Maximum OS version**: The same as **Minimum OS version**, but if you want to restrict to non-preview builds, for example, you can also set a maximum version.

- **Minimum and Maximum OS version for mobile devices**: This is for Windows Mobile, so it can be ignored.

- **Valid operating system builds**: You can use this to specify multiple minimum and maximum builds. For example, if you want to support Windows 10 and Windows 11, but only on supported versions, you could add one entry for each with the minimum set to the last supported revision.

Configuration Manager compliance

If you are running in a co-managed environment with **Configuration Manager**, setting **Require device compliance from Configuration Manager** to **Require** will force devices to use the device compliance set within **Configuration Manager**.

System Security

Under the **System Security** heading, we have these options:

- **Require a password to unlock mobile devices**: Unlike mobile devices, this one is actually for Windows and is related to the PIN for Windows Hello for Business.

- **Simple passwords**: This will block simple PINs such as `1234` or `0000`.

- **Password type**: It can be one of the following:

  - **Device Default**: Password, numeric PIN, or alphanumeric PIN

  - **Numeric**: Password or numeric PIN only

  - **Alphanumeric**: Password or alphanumeric only

  The recommended option is alphanumeric to add some extra complexity.

- **Minimum password length**: Number of digits for the PIN (make sure this follows company policy and matches with your other PIN configuration policies).

- **Maximum minutes of activity before password is required**: This can be anything from **Not Configured**, to 8 hours, down to 1 minute. 15 minutes is recommended for a good compromise between security and user experience.

- **Password expiration**: After how many days the user will need to reset (1-730).

- **Number of previous passwords to prevent reuse**: How many passwords must have been used before an old one can be re-used (1-24).
- **Require password when device returns from idle state**: This is only for Windows Mobile and Holographic.

These configurations will not force the settings; they will simply check whether the device is compliant with them. If you do not have additional policies (Settings catalog and so on) configured, a user could still set a simple four-digit PIN, but the device would be marked as non-compliant.

Encryption

Let us look at the settings under the **Encryption** heading:

- **Require encryption of data storage on device**: This is a more simple encryption check compared to the **Require BitLocker** option but does not require a reboot

Device Security

Our next heading is **Device Security**, which contains the following settings:

- **Firewall**: Requires Windows Firewall to be enabled and monitoring traffic
- **Trusted Platform Module (TPM)**: Requires a TPM to be present (this is a prerequisite for Windows 11 installations anyway, so it is only applicable for Windows 10 devices)
- **Antivirus**: Requires antivirus software to be present. This can be Windows Defender or a third party, so long as it is registered and recognized by Security Centre. If you are using a third party, a custom compliance policy may give you more options.
- **Antispyware**: The same as **Antivirus** but for anti-spyware.

Defender

Within the **Defender** heading, we have the following settings:

- **Microsoft Defender antimalware**: Checks that the antimalware service is enabled and running.
- **Microsoft Defender Antimalware minimum version**: The minimum version of the antimalware product – for example, 4.11.0.0. This can be found here: `https://www.microsoft.com/en-us/wdsi/defenderupdates`.
- **Microsoft Defender Antimalware security intelligence up-to-date**: Checks that the signatures have been updated.
- **Real-time protection**: Checks that the real-time protection service is enabled and running.

Microsoft Defender for Endpoint

Note that to use these settings, you will require licensing for Defender for Endpoint. Double-check you have the correct licenses before enabling this option:

- **Require the device to be at or under the machine risk score**: The options are as follows:

  - **Not Configured**: No setting will be applied

  - **Clear**: The device cannot have any threats at all

  - **Low**: The device can only have low-level threats

  - **Medium**: The device can have low or medium-level threats

  - **High**: This allows all threat levels

  You can find out more about these risk levels at `https://learn.microsoft.com/en-us/microsoft-365/security/defender-endpoint/alerts-queue?view=o365-worldwide`.

How to do it...

Now that we know what all of the settings do, we can create our policy. For this example, we will keep it fairly simple, but amend it as appropriate for your environment:

1. First, navigate to **Devices** and then **Compliance**.

2. Within **Policies**, click **Create policy**.

3. In the fly-out, select **Windows 10 and Later** and then click **Create**.

4. As with any other policy/profile, we start with **Name** and **Description** values and click **Next**.

5. Now, we need to configure our settings based on the information we covered earlier. In this example, we are going to require all **Device Health** options as well as **Antivirus**, **Antimalware**, **Firewall**, and **TPM**.

6. Once configured, click **Next**.

7. Now for the noncompliance actions. As mentioned earlier, our device health rules require a restart, so we will set that to 0 . 5 days. We are going to assume a machine not seen for 180 days no longer exists and add it to the retire list. Once configured for your environment, click **Next**.

> **Important note**
>
> Adding to the retire list does not retire the device; this is only for reporting. To retire these devices, follow the steps in the *Chapter materials* section.

8. We do not want to set **Scope tags**, so click **Next**.

> **Important note**
>
> When looking at assignments, for user-based devices, it is important to assign the policy to a user group. If assigned to a device group, the policy will run against both the user and system account and if either flags as non-compliant, the device will fail compliance.
>
> Device-based assignment should only be used for non-user-based machines, such as kiosks.

9. In our case, we are going to use the **Intune-Users** group. Once set, click **Next**.

10. Finally, check that everything looks correct and click **Create**.

With that, we have configured a Windows compliance policy in the UI.

Automating it

Now, we can look at using PowerShell and Graph to automate our Windows compliance configuration.

The first thing to note when automating compliance policies is that the POST requests are sent to the same URL for all device platforms:

```
https://graph.microsoft.com/beta/deviceManagement/
deviceCompliancePolicies
```

The difference between them is the @odata.type field, which for this Windows policy is as follows:

```
#microsoft.graph.windows10CompliancePolicy
```

At the time of writing, compliance policies use *Settings catalog*, so the JSON is a more simple setting: value configuration, with the values either being Boolean or plain text.

The non-compliance actions are also a nested array within the main settings. Let us take a look:

1. As usual, start with the basics:

    ```
    $name = "Windows Compliance Policy"
    $description = "Windows Compliance Policy using GUI settings"
    $groupid = "0000000-0000-0000-0000-000000000000"
    $url = "https://graph.microsoft.com/beta/deviceManagement/
    deviceCompliancePolicies"
    ```

2. Now, we can look at the JSON:

    ```
    $json = @"
    {
        "@odata.type": "#microsoft.graph.windows10CompliancePolicy",
    ```

```
    "activeFirewallRequired": true,
    "antiSpywareRequired": true,
    "antivirusRequired": true,
    "bitLockerEnabled": true,
    "codeIntegrityEnabled": true,
    "defenderEnabled": true,
    "description": "$description",
    "deviceThreatProtectionEnabled": false,
    "deviceThreatProtectionRequiredSecurityLevel":
"unavailable",
    "displayName": "$name",
    "id": "00000000-0000-0000-0000-000000000000",
    "passwordRequiredType": "deviceDefault",
    "roleScopeTagIds": [
        "0"
    ],
    "rtpEnabled": true,
    "scheduledActionsForRule": [
        {
            "ruleName": "PasswordRequired",
            "scheduledActionConfigurations": [
                {
                    "actionType": "block",
                    "gracePeriodHours": 12,
                    "notificationMessageCCList": [],
                    "notificationTemplateId": ""
                },
                {
                    "actionType": "retire",
                    "gracePeriodHours": 4320,
                    "notificationMessageCCList": [],
                    "notificationTemplateId": ""
                }
            ]
        }
    ],
    "secureBootEnabled": true,
    "signatureOutOfDate": true,
    "tpmRequired": true
}
"@
```

Anything not configured is not included in the JSON, so the majority are `true`. The `deviceThreatProtectionRequiredSecurityLevel` setting is `unavailable` in this case as the tenant does not have licensing for Defender for Endpoint, so there is no risk of non-compliance when licensing is not in place.

3. We covered notification templates in the previous recipe, but to find the ID, simply run a GET request against this URL: `https://graph.microsoft.com/beta/deviceManagement/notificationMessageTemplates`.

4. Finally, we need to create the policy and assign it:

```
$compliance = invoke-mggraphrequest -uri $uri -json $json
-method post -contenttype "application/json" -outputtype
PSObject
$complianceid = $compliance.id
$assignurl = "https://graph.microsoft.com/beta/deviceManagement/
deviceCompliancePolicies/$complianceid/assign"
$assignjson = @"
{
    "assignments": [
        {
            "target": {
                "@odata.type": "#microsoft.graph.
groupAssignmentTarget",
                "groupId": "527ee8b8-b3e7-4bbf-9abf-
45bdced10a0d"
            }
        }
    ]
}
"@
invoke-mggraphrequest -uri $assignurl -json $assignjson -method
post -contenttype "application/json" -outputtype PSObject
```

That concludes this recipe on deploying a Windows compliance policy using PowerShell and Graph.

Deploying an Android compliance policy

Now, we can look at our Android corporate devices. While BYOD is handled by App Protection policies (as we have no control over the device itself), we can force our managed devices to remain compliant to access corporate data. In this recipe, we are only going to be looking at corporate-owned and managed devices. Settings for other device types can be found here: `https://learn.microsoft.com/en-gb/mem/intune/protect/compliance-policy-create-android-for-work#system-security-settings`.

Getting started

As with the Windows policy, we will start by looking at the available options and what they do.

Compliance settings

We can run through the various compliance settings for our Android devices.

Microsoft Defender for Endpoint

Note that for these settings, you will require licensing for Defender for Endpoint. Double-check you have the correct licenses before enabling. It also requires the application to be deployed to and running on the device:

- **Require the device to be at or under the machine risk score**: The options are as follows:

  - **Not configured**: Take no action

  - **Clear**: The device cannot have any threats at all

  - **Low**: The device can only have low-level threats

  - **Medium**: The device can have low or medium-level threats

  - **High**: This allows all threat levels

  You can find out more about these risk levels at `https://learn.microsoft.com/en-us/microsoft-365/security/defender-endpoint/alerts-queue?view=o365-worldwide`.

Device Health

Under the **Device Health** heading, we have the following settings:

- **Require the device to be at or under the Device Threat Level**: The options are as follows:

  - **Not configured**

  - **Secured**

  - **Low**

  - **Medium**

  - **High**

  This uses a Mobile Threat Defense partner and feeds back into Intune. If you do not use Mobile Threat Defense, leave this as **Not configured**. A list of partners can be found here: `https://learn.microsoft.com/en-us/mem/intune/protect/mobile-threat-defense#mobile-threat-defense-partners`.

- **Play Integrity Verdict**: The options are as follows:

  - **Not configured**

  - **Check basic integrity**: The application has not been tampered with

  - **Check basic integrity & device integrity**: The application and device have not been tampered with

  These leverage the Google Play API. More information can be found here: `https://support.google.com/googleplay/android-developer/answer/11395166?hl=en-GB`.

Device Properties

Under **Device Properties**, we have the following settings:

- **Minimum and Maximum OS version**: These are self-explanatory. Remember that these are just for compliance and will not force a version or restrict enrollment (we will cover this in *Chapter 13*). A list of version numbers can be found here: `https://source.android.com/docs/setup/about/build-numbers`.

- **Minimum security patch level**: Similar to Windows updates, Android has security patches as well as larger operating system updates. These are generally released each month and you can use a compliance policy to specify a minimum version allowed. This can be useful in the case of any zero-day exploits. It has to be in YYYY-MM-DD format. To find the version numbers, check the bulletin here: `https://source.android.com/docs/security/bulletin/asb-overview`.

System Security

We have the following settings under **System Security**:

- **Require a password to unlock mobile devices**: Enable this to require users to configure a password. Remember, this will not force a password and if you do nothing with your non-compliant devices, they can continue to use a device without a password.

- **Required password type**: The options are as follows:

  - **Device default**: This cannot be used to evaluate compliance, so it is not recommended.

  - **Password required, no restrictions**: Any password; you cannot set further restrictions.

  - **Weak biometric**: More information can be found at `https://android-developers.googleblog.com/2018/06/better-biometrics-in-android-p.html`.

  - **Numeric**: Can only be numbers. It also presents the option for a minimum length (4-16).

  - **Numeric complex**: Can only be numbers and there cannot be patterns. It also presents the option for a minimum length (4-16).

- **Alphabetic**: Can only be letters in the alphabet. It also presents the option for a minimum length (4-16).

- **Alphanumeric** – Uppercase letters, lowercase letters, and numbers only. It also presents the option for a minimum length (4-16).

- **Alphanumeric with symbols**: Uppercase letters, lowercase letters, numeric characters, punctuation marks, and symbols. This also presents the minimum password length (4-16), number of characters required (1-16), number of lowercase characters required (1-16), number of uppercase characters required (1-16), number of non-letter characters required (1-16), number of numeric characters required (1-16), and number of symbol characters required (1-16).

- **Maximum minutes of inactivity before password is required**: Try and balance security and usability here. The value can be 1 minute to 8 hours.

- **Number of days until password expires**: This is an optional field. The values can be 1-365 days or left blank so that it is disabled.

- **Number of passwords required before user can reuse a password**: This is also optional and can be set from 1-24 previous passwords if required. Again, consider security implications as well as potential user issues.

Encryption

Under the **Encryption** heading, we have these settings:

- **Require encryption of data storage on device**: Android Enterprise forces encryption on enrollment, so this is not necessarily required, but an extra layer of protection is not a bad thing.

Device Security

Finally, we have a single setting under **Device Security**:

- **Intune app runtime integrity**: This checks that Intune App (previously Company Portal) has the default runtime environment installed, is correctly signed, and is not in debug mode.

How to do it...

Now that we understand the settings, we can configure the policy. In this example, we will set a few key setting:

1. First, click **Devices** and then **Android**.
2. Click **Compliance policies**.
3. Now, click **Create policy**.

In the fly-out, select **Android Enterprise** and select **Fully managed, decidated and corporate-owned work profile**.

4. Once these options have been selected, click **Create**.

5. Set **Name** and **Description** values and click **Next**.

6. Configure your settings as required and click **Next**. In this example, we have configured the following:

    *   **Play Integrity Verdict** – Check basic integrity and device integrity

    *   **Required password type** – **Alphanumeric with symbols**; **Length = 6, Characters = 6**, and one of each of the available options

    *   Require **Encryption**

7. Now, we need to set the noncompliance actions, as covered at the beginning of this chapter. As this is a mobile device, we have a few extra options that we will enable. After configuring them, click **Next**.

8. We do not need scope tags in this example, so click **Next**.

9. Set your assignments. As with Windows, for non-kiosk devices, it is sensible to configure with user-based assignment. In this case, we are using Intune users, but you could also use **All Users** and an Android filter. You may wish to have different policies, depending on the devices. Once your assignments have been set, click **Next**.

10. Finally, confirm that everything looks correct and click **Create**.

With that, we have configured our Android compliance policy in the UI.

Automating it

Now, we can look at replicating the previous steps but automating them in PowerShell and Graph.

As with Windows, the JSON is similar and we are sending a POST request to the same URL with a different @odata.type. In this case, this is as follows:

```
#microsoft.graph.androidDeviceOwnerCompliancePolicy
```

This book's GitHub repository contains an example with all the settings configured, but for this example, we will use the policy we created previously: https://github.com/PacktPublishing/Microsoft-Intune-Cookbook/blob/main/Chapter-8/create-android-compliance-allsettings.ps1. Follow these steps:

1. As usual, we start with the standard variables:

    ```
    $name = "Android-Compliance-FullyManaged"
    $description = "Android Compliance Policy for Fully Managed
    ```

```
Devices"
$groupid = "000000-0000-0000-0000-000000000000"
$url = "https://graph.microsoft.com/beta/deviceManagement/
deviceCompliancePolicies"
```

2. Now, populate the JSON. Again, it is mostly Boolean and string values, and the noncompliance actions are included in a nested array. As this is a new policy, the ID is clear. If we were updating another policy, the ID would be included and we would be running a PATCH command:

```
$json = @"
{
    "@odata.type": "#microsoft.graph.
androidDeviceOwnerCompliancePolicy",
    "advancedThreatProtectionRequiredSecurityLevel":
"unavailable",
    "description": "$description",
    "deviceThreatProtectionEnabled": false,
    "deviceThreatProtectionRequiredSecurityLevel":
"unavailable",
    "displayName": "$name",
    "id": "00000000-0000-0000-0000-000000000000",
    "localActions": [],
    "passwordMinimumLength": 6,
    "passwordMinimumLetterCharacters": 6,
    "passwordMinimumLowerCaseCharacters": 1,
    "passwordMinimumNonLetterCharacters": 1,
    "passwordMinimumNumericCharacters": 1,
    "passwordMinimumSymbolCharacters": 1,
    "passwordMinimumUpperCaseCharacters": 1,
    "passwordMinutesOfInactivityBeforeLock": 5,
    "passwordRequired": true,
    "passwordRequiredType": "alphanumericWithSymbols",
    "roleScopeTagIds": [
        "0"
    ],
    "scheduledActionsForRule": [
        {
            "ruleName": "PasswordRequired",
            "scheduledActionConfigurations": [
                {
                    "actionType": "block",
                    "gracePeriodHours": 0,
                    "notificationMessageCCList": [],
                    "notificationTemplateId": ""
                },
```

```
                    {
                        "actionType": "pushNotification",
                        "gracePeriodHours": 120,
                        "notificationMessageCCList": [],
                        "notificationTemplateId": ""
                    },
                    {
                        "actionType": "remoteLock",
                        "gracePeriodHours": 240,
                        "notificationMessageCCList": [],
                        "notificationTemplateId": ""
                    }
                ]
            }
        ],
        "securityRequireSafetyNetAttestationBasicIntegrity": true,
        "securityRequireSafetyNetAttestationCertifiedDevice": true,
        "storageRequireEncryption": true
    }
    "@
```

3. Create the policy and grab the ID:

```
$androidpolicy = Invoke-MgGraphRequest -uri $url -Method Post
-Body $json -ContentType "application/json" -OutputType PSObject
$androidpolicyid = $androidpolicy.id
```

4. Now, populate the URL and assign the policy:

```
$assignurl = "https://graph.microsoft.com/beta/deviceManagement/
deviceCompliancePolicies/$androidpolicyid/assign"
$assignjson = @"
{
    "assignments": [
        {
            "target": {
                "@odata.type": "#microsoft.graph.
groupAssignmentTarget",
                "groupId": "$groupid"
            }
        }
    ]
}
"@
Invoke-MgGraphRequest -uri $assignurl -Method Post -Body
$assignjson -ContentType "application/json" -OutputType PSObject
```

This completes the steps to automate the creation of our Android compliance policy.

Deploying an iOS compliance policy

After setting up our Android policy, we can now look at iOS devices. As with other policies, we will start by looking at the available settings and what they require before looking at configuring the policy and how it works.

Getting started

We will start by looking at all of the available settings and what they require.

Compliance settings

Let us run through all of the settings available for iOS devices.

Email

We will start with the single setting under the **Email** heading:

- **Unable to set up email on the device**: The device must use a managed account configured via Intune. Any accounts that were manually added previously will need to be removed before the device can be marked as compliant.

Device Health

Now, we can review the options for **Device Health**:

- **Jailbroken devices**: Any jailbroken devices will be blocked on iOS 8.0 and above.
- **Require the device to be at or under the Device Threat Level**: The options are as follows:

  - Not configured
  - Secured
  - Low
  - Medium
  - High

  This uses a Mobile Threat Defense partner and feeds back into Intune. If you do not use Mobile Threat Defense, leave this as **Not configured**. A list of partners can be found here: https://learn.microsoft.com/en-us/mem/intune/protect/mobile-threat-defense#mobile-threat-defense-partners.

Device Properties

Under **Device Properties**, we have these options:

- **Minimum and Maximum OS version**: These are self-explanatory. Remember that these are just for compliance and will not force a version or restrict enrollment (we will cover this in *Chapter 13*). A list of version numbers can be found here: `https://iosref.com/ios`.

- **Minimum and Maximum OS build version**: Here you can set the build versions and, optionally, the supplemental build number. Apple security updates can be found here: `https://support.apple.com/en-us/HT201222`.

Microsoft Defender for Endpoint

Note that this setting requires licensing for Defender for Endpoint. Double-check that you have the correct licenses before enabling it. It also requires the application to be deployed to and running on the device:

- **Require the device to be at or under the machine risk score**: The options are as follows:

  - **Not configured**

  - **Clear**: The device cannot have any threats at all

  - **Low**: The device can only have low-level threats

  - **Medium**: The device can have low or medium-level threats

  - **High**: This allows all threat levels

  You can find out more about the risk levels here: `https://learn.microsoft.com/en-us/microsoft-365/security/defender-endpoint/alerts-queue?view=o365-worldwide`.

System Security

Onto the **System Security** options, we have the following:

- **Password**:

  - **Require a password to unlock mobile devices**: This marks a device as non-compliant if no password of any sort is set. The next settings only apply for devices enrolled using Apple Business Manager or Apple School Manager and do not apply for BYOD. These will also force the setting rather than just report on it, so be extra careful:

    - **Simple passwords**: Block sequences such as 1111 or 1234

    - **Minimum password length**: 4-14 digits, digits or characters

- **Required password type**: Can be **Not configured**, **Numeric**, or **Alphanumeric**

- **Number of non-alphanumeric characters in password**: Can be set to **Not configured** or from 0-4 characters

- **Maximum minutes after screen lock before password is required**: Can be set to one of the following options:

  - **Immediately**

  - **1 minute**

  - **5 minutes**

  - **15 minutes**

  - **1 hour**

  - **4 hours**

As the screen is locked, **Immediately** is the safest option and should not cause too much disruption.

- **Maximum minutes of inactivity until screen locks**: Can be anything from **Immediately** up to **15 minutes**. While immediate is the most secure, that may cause disruption for your users. 2-3 minutes should be a good balance of security and usability.

- **Password expiration (days)**: Can be 1 to 730 days. Depending on your password complexity, pick the most balanced for your environment.

- **Number of previous passwords to prevent reuse**: 1-24 passwords. Again, if you set it to 24, users are going to struggle to think of a new password and will just add numbers to old ones, or worse still, write it down.

- **Device Security**:

  - **Restricted apps**: A list of apps that, if detected, will be marked as non-compliant. The policy will take no action; just mark it as non-compliant. You can configure a **Device restrictions** policy to remove these apps.

How to do it...

Now that we have covered the settings, we can set up our policy:

1. First, navigate to **Devices** and then **Compliance**.

2. Click **Policies** and **Create policy**.

3. In the fly-out, select **iOS/iPadOS** and click **Create**.

4. Specify your policy's **Name** and **Description**, then click **Next**.

5. Configure your settings as required. In this case, we are blocking user-configured email and jailbroken devices and configuring the password settings. Once you have configured your environment, click **Next**.

6. Now, set the actions for non-compliant devices. Again, as with Android, you can specify push notifications as well as email.

7. We are not setting **Scope tags** in this example, so click **Next**.

8. Again, we are using a user-based assignment for a better experience, and in this example, we are using the **Intune-Users** group we created in *Chapter 1*. Often, your executive users will have iOS devices, so you may find yourself needing different compliance policies for different user groups. Once you have configured everything, click **Next**.

9. Finally, review that everything looks correct and click **Create**.

We have now configured our iOS Compliance Policy in the UI and can now look at automating it using PowerShell and Graph.

Automating it

As with our Android policy, for this example, we will cover the preceding settings, but in this book's GitHub repository, there is an example with all the settings configured: `https://github.com/PacktPublishing/Microsoft-Intune-Cookbook/blob/main/Chapter-8/create-ios-compliance-allsettings.ps1`.

This is similar to previous policies, only with `@odata.type` set to the following:

```
#microsoft.graph.iosCompliancePolicy
```

Again, the MDE components are marked as unavailable due to licensing:

1. First, we will start with the basics, including the standard Compliance Policy URL:

```
$name = "iOS Compliance"
$description = "iOS Compliance Policy"
$groupid = "00000-00000-00000-00000"
$url = "https://graph.microsoft.com/beta/deviceManagement/
deviceCompliancePolicies"
```

2. Now, we must populate the JSON. Note that again, the actions are a nested JSON within the primary policy:

```
$json = @"
{
    "@odata.type": "#microsoft.graph.iosCompliancePolicy",
    "advancedThreatProtectionRequiredSecurityLevel":
"unavailable",
```

```
    "description": "$description",
    "deviceThreatProtectionEnabled": false,
    "deviceThreatProtectionRequiredSecurityLevel":
"unavailable",
    "displayName": "$name",
    "id": "00000000-0000-0000-0000-000000000000",
    "managedEmailProfileRequired": true,
    "passcodeBlockSimple": true,
    "passcodeExpirationDays": 30,
    "passcodeMinimumCharacterSetCount": 1,
    "passcodeMinimumLength": 6,
    "passcodeMinutesOfInactivityBeforeLock": 0,
    "passcodeMinutesOfInactivityBeforeScreenTimeout": 2,
    "passcodePreviousPasscodeBlockCount": 3,
    "passcodeRequired": true,
    "passcodeRequiredType": "alphanumeric",
    "roleScopeTagIds": [
        "0"
    ],
    "scheduledActionsForRule": [
        {
            "ruleName": "PasswordRequired",
            "scheduledActionConfigurations": [
                {
                    "actionType": "block",
                    "gracePeriodHours": 0,
                    "notificationMessageCCList": [],
                    "notificationTemplateId": ""
                },
                {
                    "actionType": "pushNotification",
                    "gracePeriodHours": 48,
                    "notificationMessageCCList": [],
                    "notificationTemplateId": ""
                },
                {
                    "actionType": "remoteLock",
                    "gracePeriodHours": 120,
                    "notificationMessageCCList": [],
                    "notificationTemplateId": ""
                },
                {
                    "actionType": "retire",
                    "gracePeriodHours": 720,
```

```
                              "notificationMessageCCList": [],
                              "notificationTemplateId": ""
                    }
               ]
          }
     ],
     "securityBlockJailbrokenDevices": true
}
"@
```

3. Create the policy and grab the ID:

```
$iospolicy = Invoke-MgGraphRequest -uri $url -Method Post -Body
$json -ContentType "application/json" -OutputType PSObject
$policyid = $iospolicy.id
```

4. Populate the URL and JSON, then assign the policy:

```
$assignurl = "https://graph.microsoft.com/beta/deviceManagement/
deviceCompliancePolicies/$policyid/assign"
$assignjson = @"
{
    "assignments": [
        {
            "target": {
                "@odata.type": "#microsoft.graph.
groupAssignmentTarget",
                "groupId": "$groupid"
            }
        }
    ]
}
"@
Invoke-MgGraphRequest -uri $assignurl -Method Post -Body
$assignjson -ContentType "application/json" -OutputType PSObject
```

That completes this recipe on deploying an iOS compliance policy.

Deploying a macOS compliance policy

Now that we have looked at Apple devices, we can look at making sure our corporate-managed macOS device is compliant.

One important thing to note with macOS is that unlike our other policies (except iOS), if you configure the PIN setting within a macOS compliance policy, it will enforce the setting on the device rather than just reporting on it.

Getting started

As with the other recipes, we will start by looking at the settings available to us.

Compliance settings

Now, let us run through the settings available for macOS devices.

Device Health

We will start with the single setting available under **Device Health**:

- **Require system integrity protection**: This stops protected files and folders from being changed by malicious software and was introduced in El Capitan. More information can be found here: `https://support.apple.com/en-gb/HT204899`.

Device Properties

Now, we will look at the settings for **Device Properties**:

- **Minimum and Maximum OS version**: In standard format, which can be found here: `https://support.apple.com/en-gb/HT201260`

- **Maximum and Minimum OS build version**: These are the build numbers and rapid response numbers, as found in brackets here: `https://developer.apple.com/news/releases/`

System Security

Within **System Security**, we have the following settings:

- **Password**: Our password options are as follows:

  - **Require a password to unlock mobile devices**: Marks a device as non-compliant if no password of any sort is set. We have the following options underneath:

    - **Simple passwords**: Block sequences such as 1111 or 1234

    - **Minimum password length**: 4-14 digits, digits or characters

    - **Required password type**: Can be **Not configured**, **Numeric**, or **Alphanumeric**

    - **Number of non-alphanumeric characters in password**: Can be set to **Not configured** or from 0-4 characters

    - **Maximum minutes of inactivity before password is required**: Can be set to one of the following values:

      - **1 minute**

      - **5 minutes**

- **15 minutes**
- **1 hour**
- **4 hours**

As with your Windows devices, you want a balance of security and usability here. Anything more than 15 minutes is going to leave you more open to security issues.

- **Password expiration (days)**: Can be 1 to 730 days. Depending on your password complexity, pick the most balanced for your environment.

- **Number of previous passwords to prevent reuse**: 1-24 passwords. Again, if you set it to 24, users are going to struggle to think of a new password and will just add numbers to old ones, or worse still, write it down.

- **Encryption**: Our encryption compliance option is as follows:

  - **Require encryption of data storage on device**: This will mark machines not encrypted with FileVault as non-compliant

- **Device Security**: Here, we have the following options:

  - **Firewall**: Requires the firewall to be enabled.

  - **Incoming connections**: This will block any connections that are not required for basic internet services. This includes blocking sharing services.

  - **Stealth Mode**: This blocks ping requests or connection attempts from closed TCP or UDP networks.

- **Gatekeeper**: Within **Gatekeeper**, we have these options:

  - **Allow apps downloaded from these locations**: This restricts application installations to trusted software. The options are as follows:

    - **Not configured**
    - **Mac App Store**
    - **Mac App Store and identified developers**
    - **Anywhere**

More information can be found here: `https://support.apple.com/en-gb/guide/security/sec5599b66df/web`.

Keep in mind that if you deploy apps via Company Portal that are not identified developers, the installation will be blocked unless set to **Anywhere**, so it is worth reviewing your application requirements before configuring this setting.

How to do it...

Now that we have covered the settings, we can set up our policy:

1. Start with **Devices** and then **Compliance**.

2. Click **Policies** and then **Create policy**.

3. In the fly-out select **macOS** and click **Create**.

4. Add **Name** and **Description** values and click **Next**.

5. Configure the settings as required using the preceding details as a reference point. Once configured, click **Next**.

6. Next, set the actions for noncompliance. We still have the option to remotely lock the device, but as this is not iOS or Android, we cannot send a push notification.

7. As usual, we are not setting any **Scope tags** in this example, so click **Next**.

8. As mentioned in other recipes, assigning to users gives better results, so we are assigning to our **Intune-Users** group.

9. Finally, check everything looks correct and click **Create**.

That completes this recipe on how to configure a macOS compliance policy in the UI. Now, let's automate it.

Automating it

When looking at automating this policy, it is very similar to the previous recipes we covered earlier. Again, we will include an example with all the settings configured in this book's GitHub repository: https://github.com/PacktPublishing/Microsoft-Intune-Cookbook/blob/main/Chapter-8/create-macos-compliance-allsettings.ps1.

The @odata.type property that is used for a macOS compliance policy is as follows:

```
#microsoft.graph.macOSCompliancePolicy
```

Follow these steps:

1. As with all the other scripts, we will start with the basic variables:

```
$name = "macOS Compliance"
$description = "Compliance Policy for macOS Devices"
$groupid = "00000000-0000-0000-0000-000000000000"
$url = "https://graph.microsoft.com/beta/deviceManagement/
deviceCompliancePolicies"
```

2.   Then, populate the JSON. Again, the noncompliance actions are a nested array within the main JSON with everything else as string or Boolean values:

```
$json = @"
{
    "@odata.type": "#microsoft.graph.macOSCompliancePolicy",
    "description": "$description",
    "displayName": "$name",
    "firewallEnabled": true,
    "firewallEnableStealthMode": true,
    "gatekeeperAllowedAppSource":
"macAppStoreAndIdentifiedDevelopers",
    "id": "00000000-0000-0000-0000-000000000000",
    "passwordBlockSimple": true,
    "passwordExpirationDays": 41,
    "passwordMinimumCharacterSetCount": 1,
    "passwordMinutesOfInactivityBeforeLock": 5,
    "passwordPreviousPasswordBlockCount": 3,
    "passwordRequired": true,
    "passwordRequiredType": "alphanumeric",
    "roleScopeTagIds": [
        "0"
    ],
    "scheduledActionsForRule": [
        {
            "ruleName": "PasswordRequired",
            "scheduledActionConfigurations": [
                {
                    "actionType": "block",
                    "gracePeriodHours": 0,
                    "notificationMessageCCList": [],
                    "notificationTemplateId": ""
                },
                {
                    "actionType": "remoteLock",
                    "gracePeriodHours": 480,
                    "notificationMessageCCList": [],
                    "notificationTemplateId": ""
                },
                {
                    "actionType": "retire",
                    "gracePeriodHours": 1080,
                    "notificationMessageCCList": [],
                    "notificationTemplateId": ""
```

```
                        }
                    ]
                }
            ],
            "storageRequireEncryption": true,
            "systemIntegrityProtectionEnabled": true
        }
    "@
```

3. Assign the policy and grab the ID:

```
$assignpolicy = Invoke-MgGraphRequest -Uri $url -Method POST
-Body $json -ContentType "application/json" -OutputType PSObject
$policyid = $assignpolicy.id
```

4. Add the ID to the URL:

```
$assignurl = "https://graph.microsoft.com/beta/deviceManagement/
deviceCompliancePolicies/$policyid/assign"
```

5. Populate the JSON and assign our policy:

```
$assignjson = @"
{
    "assignments": [
        {
            "target": {
                "@odata.type": "#microsoft.graph.
groupAssignmentTarget",
                "groupId": "$groupid"
            }
        }
    ]
}
"@
Invoke-MgGraphRequest -Uri $assignurl -Method POST -Body
$assignjson -ContentType "application/json" -OutputType PSObject
```

That completes the automated process of creating our macOS compliance policy.

Deploying a Linux compliance policy

This is a relatively new addition to Intune. While we cannot currently deploy configuration or applications to Linux devices, we can configure compliance policies, primarily for Ubuntu-based devices to ensure that any devices accessing corporate data meet the same standards across platforms.

Getting started

Again, we will start by looking at the available settings. One of the first things to note is that Linux compliance uses Settings catalog to configure as it is a much newer addition.

Allowed Distributions

Under **Allowed Distributions**, we have the following option:

- **Type**: At the time of writing, the only option is **Ubuntu**, but you can set minimum and maximum versions. The version numbers can be found here: `https://wiki.ubuntu.com/Releases`.

Custom Compliance

Within **Custom Compliance**, we have the following single setting:

- **Require custom compliance**: This will be covered in greater depth in the next recipe, but instead of using PowerShell to capture the settings, it uses Bash. An example policy is available here: `https://github.com/petripaavola/Intune/tree/master/Linux`.

Device Encryption

Under **Device Encryption**, we can select from the following options:

- **Require device encryption**: Requires Ubuntu **Full Disk Encryption** (FDE). Any encryption that uses `dm-crypt` is recognized and the following directories are ignored:

  - Read-only files

  - Pseudosystem files

  - Boot partitions

Password Policy

Finally, under **Password Policy**, we have the following options:

- **Password policy**: Forces specific password formats:

  - **Minimum uppercase**

  - **Minimum lowercase**

  - **Minimum length**: The total length of the password

  - **Minimum digits**: Numeric digits in the password

How to do it...

Now that we know about the different settings, we can create our policy. This should all be familiar as it is a Settings catalog policy, which we covered in *Chapter 2*:

1. First, navigate to **Devices** and then **Compliance**.

2. Click on **Policies** and then **Create policy**.

3. In the fly-out, select **Linux**; the bottom dropdown will automatically switch to **Settings catalog**. Then, click **Create**.

4. As usual, start with **Name** and **Description** values, then click **Next**.

5. Click **Add settings**.

6. Add your settings as required. If you are looking at versions, check the Ubuntu version URL and see which are currently in support and exclude those that are out of support as a start. In this recipe, we require encryption and will only set a password.

7. In the non-compliance options, we can only email the user. The devices are not fully managed, so you cannot retire them and Linux does not support push notifications. In our case, we will simply mark it as not compliant and let the conditional access policy sort the rest.

8. As usual, we are skipping **Scope tags** in this example, so click **Next**.

9. As with other policies, we are assigning at the user level. Compliance is less of a risk with a Linux device, but often, you will find these are used by developers and other IT staff, so you may need slightly different policies accordingly. In this case, we are using our **Intune-Users** Entra group. When you have selected your assignment, click **Next**.

10. Finally, review that everything looks correct and click **Create**.

Automating it

As with the previous recipe, we are only creating the Linux compliance policy here, but this book's GitHub repository contains a policy example with all the settings configured: `https://github.com/PacktPublishing/Microsoft-Intune-Cookbook/blob/main/Chapter-8/create-linux-compliance-allsettings.ps1`.

Unlike the others, however, this policy uses **Settings catalog** underneath, so the JSON is different.

When setting the variables, you can see that the URL is still the same as it was for the previous policies:

```
https://graph.microsoft.com/beta/deviceManagement/compliancePolicies
```

To find the available categories, we need to run a GET request against this URL:
`https://graph.microsoft.com/beta/deviceManagement/complianceCategories?$filter=technologies eq 'linuxMdM'`.

As an example, the allowed distributions fall under the category ID:

```
f2c81665-b10b-4fa2-b177-7781b8650292
```

The individual settings can be found here: `https://graph.microsoft.com/beta/ deviceManagement/compliancesettings`.

For allowed distributions, go to `https://graph.microsoft.com/beta/deviceManagement/ compliancesettings?$filter=categoryId eq 'f2c81665-b10b-4fa2-b177- 7781b8650292'`.

Now, we can get back to our example:

1. As usual, we start with the basics:

    ```
    $name = "Linux Compliance"
    $description = "Linux Compliance, non-custom"
    $url = "https://graph.microsoft.com/beta/deviceManagement/
    compliancePolicies"
    $groupid = "00000000-0000-0000-0000-000000000000"
    ```

2. Populate the newly discovered JSON (reduced for brevity; the full code is available on GitHub):

    ```
    $json = @"
    {
        "description": "$description",
        "name": "$name",
        "platforms": "linux",
        "roleScopeTagIds": [
            "0"
        ],
        "settings": [
            {
                "@odata.type": "#microsoft.graph.
    deviceManagementConfigurationSetting",
                "settingInstance": {
                    "@odata.type": "#microsoft.graph.
    deviceManagementConfigurationChoiceSettingInstance",
                    "choiceSettingValue": {
                        "@odata.type": "#microsoft.graph.
    deviceManagementConfigurationChoiceSettingValue",
                        "children": [],
                        "value": "linux_deviceencryption_required_
    true"
                    },
                    "settingDefinitionId": "linux_deviceencryption_
    required"
    ```

```
            }
        }
    ],
    "technologies": "linuxMdm"
}
"@
```

3. Create the policy and grab the ID:

```
$linuxpolicy = Invoke-MgGraphRequest -uri $url -Method POST
-Body $json -ContentType "application/json" -OutputType PSObject
$policyid = $linuxpolicy.id
```

4. Update the URL and assign the policy:

```
$assignurl = "https://graph.microsoft.com/beta/deviceManagement/
compliancePolicies/$policyid/assign"
$assignjson = @"
{
    "assignments": [
        {
            "target": {
                "@odata.type": "#microsoft.graph.
groupAssignmentTarget",
                "groupId": "$groupid"
            }
        }
    ]
}
"@
Invoke-MgGraphRequest -uri $assignurl -Method POST -Body
$assignjson -ContentType "application/json" -OutputType PSObject
```

That completes this recipe on automating a Linux compliance policy.

Configuring and deploying a Windows custom compliance policy

Sometimes, you will find that your compliance may not meet what is available with the built-in settings. For example, you may have third-party products that you need to monitor or want to block machines with particular software installed. You could also restrict your environment to a specific hardware type, manufacturer, and amount of RAM – anything that can be detected by PowerShell can be used for compliance.

Once the script has been configured, you can set a JSON policy within Intune that looks at the output from PowerShell and compares it to the settings we specified in the JSON and their values. If the expected value meets the actual value, that setting is compliant. If not, it is non-compliant.

One non-compliant setting is enough to mark a device as non-compliant.

Now that we know how it works, we can configure our scripts.

Getting started

Before we create the policy, we need to create the two files we will use in them. These scripts are both available in this book's GitHub repository.

Compliance JSON: `https://github.com/PacktPublishing/Microsoft-Intune-Cookbook/blob/main/Chapter-8/custom-compliance-json.json`.

Compliance PowerShell: `https://github.com/PacktPublishing/Microsoft-Intune-Cookbook/blob/main/Chapter-8/custom-compliance-script.ps1`.

You can also find some pre-configured compliance templates at `https://github.com/JayRHa/Custom-Compliance-Scripts`.

PowerShell script

First, we need the PowerShell script so that we can set the output we will be looking for within the JSON.

The most important thing here is the export, which must be in this format:

```
return $hash | ConvertTo-Json -Compress
```

What `$hash` contains is up to you, but it must be returned as a compressed JSON.

The JSON supports these operators:

- `IsEquals`
- `NotEquals`
- `GreaterThan`
- `GreaterEquals`
- `LessThan`
- `LessEquals`

It also supports these data types:

- `Boolean`
- `Int64`
- `Double`
- `String`
- `DateTime`
- `Version`

The options here are massive, so in this example, we will demonstrate them with a few settings.

First, we can query the device manufacturer:

```
$biosinfo = Get-CimInstance -ClassName Win32_ComputerSystem
$manufacturer = $biosinfo.Manufacturer
```

Now, we can return $manufacturer to query in the JSON.

We will also check whether the domain firewall is enabled:

```
$domainfirewall= ((Get-NetFirewallProfile | select Name, Enabled |
where-object Name -eq Domain | select Enabled).Enabled).ToString()
```

Notice that we are converting that into a string value so that we can query it later.

We will also check for malware:

```
$noactivemalware = Get-MpThreatDetection
if ($null -eq $noactivemalware) {
    $noactivemalware = "True"
}
else {
    $noactivemalware = "False"
}
```

Finally, we will check whether Bitlocker is enabled and the drive is encrypted:

```
$bitlockerprotected = (get-bitlockervolume).ProtectionStatus
$bitlockerencryption = (get-bitlockervolume).VolumeStatus
if (($bitlockerprotected -eq "On") -and ($bitlockerencryption -eq
"FullyEncrypted")) {
    $bitlocker = "True"
}
```

```
else {
    $bitlocker = "False"
}
```

As mentioned previously, we need to add these to $hash. In this case, we will use an array:

```
$hash = @{
    Manufacturer = $manufacturer
    DomainFirewall = $domainfirewall
    NoActiveMalware = $noactivemalware
    Bitlocker = $bitlocker
}
```

We need to make a note of the headings that are passed through to the $hash array as these are what are queried in the JSON.

Then, we must take our array and return it as compressed JSON:

```
return $hash | ConvertTo-Json -Compress
```

JSON file

Now that we have our PowerShell script, we need to write the JSON to query it. We covered the data types and operators earlier. We must configure rules for each setting, telling them what to look for, and also an error message if the value is not found. This is multi-language if required as well.

We can also use the {ActualValue} option in the error message so that the user knows not only if the device is non-compliant, but also why.

More information about the JSON composition can be found here: https://learn.microsoft.com/en-us/mem/intune/protect/compliance-custom-json.

For our example, the JSON looks like this:

```
{
"Rules":[
    {
        "SettingName":"Manufacturer",
        "Operator":"IsEquals",
        "DataType":"String",
        "Operand":"Dell",
        "MoreInfoUrl":"https://www.google.com",
        "RemediationStrings":[
            {
                "Language":"en_US",
                "Title":"This machine is not a Dell.",
```

```
                    "Description": "We only support Dell devices, please
contact us for more information. You are on an {ActualValue}"
                }
            ]
        },
        {
            "SettingName":"DomainFirewall",
            "Operator":"IsEquals",
            "DataType":"String",
            "Operand":"True",
            "MoreInfoUrl":"https://support.microsoft.com/en-us/windows/
turn-microsoft-defender-firewall-on-or-off-ec0844f7-aebd-0583-67fe-
601ecf5d774f",
            "RemediationStrings":[
                {
                    "Language": "en_US",
                    "Title": "Domain Firewall is Off",
                    "Description": "Your domain firewall is switched off,
please re-enable."
                }
            ]
        },
        {
            "SettingName":"NoActiveMalware",
            "Operator":"IsEquals",
            "DataType":"String",
            "Operand":"True",
            "MoreInfoUrl":"https://support.microsoft.com/en-us/windows/stay-
protected-with-windows-security-2ae0363d-0ada-c064-8b56-6a39afb6a963",
            "RemediationStrings":[
                {
                    "Language": "en_US",
                    "Title": "Active Malware Detected",
                    "Description": "Active Malware detected, please
remediate."
                }
            ]
        },
        {
            "SettingName":"Bitlocker",
            "Operator":"IsEquals",
            "DataType":"String",
            "Operand":"True",
            "MoreInfoUrl":"https://support.microsoft.com/en-us/windows/turn-
on-device-encryption-0c453637-bc88-5f74-5105-741561aae838",
```

```
        "RemediationStrings":[
            {
                "Language": "en_US",
                "Title": "Unencrypted",
                "Description": "Your device is not fully encrypted, please
  encrypt."
            }
        ]
    }
  ]
}
```

We are grabbing `SettingName` from the PowerShell array, telling it what to look for, which in our case is `Equals`, all items that have been converted into strings to make `DataType` easier, and then simply what we are looking for in the operand.

Then, we provide a URL for more information and the error message to display on non-compliant devices.

How to do it...

We now have our scripts so that we can create the policy. This has been split into two parts – one for the PowerShell script and one for the policy itself.

PowerShell script

The first part is to create and upload our PowerShell script to Intune. Follow these steps to complete this:

1. First, click **Devices** and then **Compliance**.

2. Now, select **Scripts**, click **Add**, and select **Windows 10 and later**.

3. Set your **Name** and **Description**. You also have a **Publisher** field which you can configure to your name or organization name if required. Then, click **Next**.

4. Paste your script into the box (there is no upload functionality here). We have not signed the script, so we need to leave that set to **No**. We also want this to run at the system level as we are querying to BIOS. Finally, while 32/64-bit should not make a difference for our queries, it is best to leave it set to **Yes**. Then, click **Next**.

5. Now, confirm that everything looks correct and click **Create**.

Compliance policy

Now that we have the script, we can create the policy (the JSON is added in the policy section):

1. Click the **Policies** tab and then click **Create policy**.

2. In the fly-out, select **Windows 10 and later** and click **Create**.

3. Enter **Name** and **Description** values and click **Next**.

4. Now, we can see the familiar settings we covered earlier. This time, we are just setting **Custom compliance**.

5. Expand **Custom compliance**, click **Require**, and then click the blue text labeled **Click to select** to select the script.

6. Pick your script from the list and click **Select**.

7. Now, select your JSON; you will see that it populates not only the script (this box is read-only) but also what it is looking for. Click **Next** if you are happy that everything looks correct.

8. Set your non-compliance actions, as we covered in the *Actions for noncompliance* section, then click **Next**.

9. We are not setting **Scope tags** in this example, so click **Next**.

10. As with other policies, we want to assign at the user level to avoid issues. In this case, we are using **Intune-Users**. Once you have configured your assignment, click **Next**.

11. Finally, review your policy and click **Create**.

That completes the configuration of our custom Windows compliance policy in the UI.

Automating it

Now that we have created the policy in the UI, we can look at creating our custom policy using PowerShell and Graph.

While two different UI areas were required to create it graphically, when automating, we can run both steps within the same script, including embedding the PowerShell and JSON scripts within the same file.

As we already know the content of these scripts, they are not included in this example but are available on GitHub (links can be found in this recipe's *How to do it...* section).

We will start by creating the PowerShell script:

1. First, configure the settings. Here, we are also including the run-as context (`system` or `user`) and whether to run in the 32-bit context (`true` or `false`):

    ```
    $name = "Windows Custom Compliance"
    $description = "Checks Manufacturer, Firewall, Malware and
    Bitlocker"
    $publisher = "Publisher"
    $loggedonuser = "system"
    $runas32 = "false"
    ```

2. Now, set the URL for the script upload:

    ```
    $url = "https://graph.microsoft.com/beta/deviceManagement/
    deviceComplianceScripts"
    ```

3. At this point, we can add the PowerShell script (this has been cut down here to give you an idea):

```
$psscript = @'
$biosinfo = Get-CimInstance -ClassName Win32_ComputerSystem
$manufacturer = $biosinfo.Manufacturer
'@
```

4. We need to convert this into Base64 so that we can upload it:

```
$scriptcontent = [System.Text.Encoding]::UTF8.
GetBytes($psscript)
$scriptcontent = [System.
Convert]::ToBase64String($scriptcontent)
```

5. Populate the configured variables into the JSON to upload the script:

```
$json = @"
{
    "description": "$description",
    "detectionScriptContent": "$scriptcontent",
    "displayName": "$name",
    "enforceSignatureCheck": false,
    "id": "",
    "publisher": "$publisher",
    "runAs32Bit": $runas32,
    "runAsAccount": "$loggedonuser"
}
"@
```

6. Upload and grab the ID; we will need this later:

```
$psscript = Invoke-MgGraphRequest -Uri $url -Method Post -Body
$json -ContentType "application/json" -OutputType PSObject
$scriptid = $psscript.id
```

7. Now, we can move on to the policy itself, starting with the standard basics:

```
$policyname = "Windows Custom Compliance"
$policydescription = "Custom Compliance ONLY"
$groupid = "000000-0000-0000-0000-000000000000"
```

8. As with the PowerShell script, we include the JSON here (again, this has been reduced):

```
$compliancejson = @'
{
    "Rules":[
        {
            "SettingName":"Manufacturer",
```

```
                         "Operator":"IsEquals",
                         "DataType":"String",
                         "Operand":"Dell",
                         "MoreInfoUrl":"https://www.google.com",
                         "RemediationStrings":[
                             {
                                 "Language":"en_US",
                                 "Title":"This machine is not a Dell.",
                                 "Description": "We only support Dell devices,
         please contact us for more information. You are on an
         {ActualValue}"
                             }
                         ]
                     }
                 ]
             }
         '@
```

9. This needs to be Base64 as well:

```
$jsoncontent = [System.Text.Encoding]::UTF8.
GetBytes($compliancejson)
$jsoncontent = [System.Convert]::ToBase64String($jsoncontent)
```

10. Set the URL:

```
$policyurl = "https://graph.microsoft.com/beta/deviceManagement/
deviceCompliancePolicies"
```

11. Populate the JSON, including not only the JSON in Base64 but also the script ID:

```
$policyjson = @"
{
    "@odata.type": "#microsoft.graph.windows10CompliancePolicy",
    "description": "$policydescription",
    "deviceCompliancePolicyScript": {
        "deviceComplianceScriptId": "$scriptid",
        "rulesContent": "$jsoncontent",
    },
    "deviceThreatProtectionEnabled": false,
    "deviceThreatProtectionRequiredSecurityLevel":
"unavailable",
    "displayName": "$policyname",
    "id": "00000000-0000-0000-0000-000000000000",
    "passwordRequiredType": "deviceDefault",
    "roleScopeTagIds": [
```

```
                        "0"
            ],
            "scheduledActionsForRule": [
                {
                    "ruleName": "PasswordRequired",
                    "scheduledActionConfigurations": [
                        {
                            "actionType": "block",
                            "gracePeriodHours": 0,
                            "notificationMessageCCList": [],
                            "notificationTemplateId": ""
                        }
                    ]
                }
            ]
        }
"@
```

12. Now, let us get back to normal – create the policy, grab the ID, populate the URL, and assign the policy to our Entra group:

```
$compliancepolicy = Invoke-MgGraphRequest -Uri $policyurl
-Method Post -Body $policyjson -ContentType "application/json"
-OutputType PSObject
$policyid = $compliancepolicy.id
$assignmenturl = "https://graph.microsoft.com/beta/
deviceManagement/deviceCompliancePolicies/$policyid/assign"
$assignmentjson = @"
{
    "assignments": [
        {
            "target": {
                "@odata.type": "#microsoft.graph.
groupAssignmentTarget",
                "groupId": "$groupid"
            }
        }
    ]
}
"@
Invoke-MgGraphRequest -Uri $assignmenturl -Method Post -Body
$assignmentjson -ContentType "application/json" -OutputType
PSObject
```

This completes our recipe on configuring a custom compliance script for Windows using PowerShell and Graph.

Using conditional access to restrict access based on compliance

There is one final step when using compliance policies. While we have some non-compliance settings configured to lock mobile devices, we are mostly just warning users that their device is not compliant, but this does not stop them from using them. We do not want devices that do not meet our criteria to access corporate data, unencrypted devices, devices with active malware, and more. For that, we need to set up a conditional access policy.

> **Important note**
>
> This conditional access policy is just for restricting non-compliant devices. For full tenant security, you will need to deploy further policies. Common policies from Microsoft can be found at the following link: `https://learn.microsoft.com/en-us/microsoft-365/security/office-365-security/zero-trust-identity-device-access-policies-common?view=o365-worldwide`.
>
> You can also use some pre-configured templates directly from Entra, as covered here: `https://learn.microsoft.com/en-us/entra/identity/conditional-access/concept-conditional-access-policy-common?tabs=secure-foundation`.

Getting started

Before we set up this policy, make sure you have a breakglass account configured so that we can exclude it from any conditional access policies. This will give you access to the environment in case there is an issue with a policy that blocks all access.

How to do it...

Follow these steps to configure a conditional access policy to protect the environment from non-compliant devices:

1. Start by navigating to **Endpoint security**, then **Conditional access**.
2. Click **Create new policy**.
3. Give the policy a name and click **0 users and groups selected**.
4. Under **Include**, select **All Users**.

5. Click the **Exclude** tab and exclude your Break Glass account. Also, consider your IT staff, who may need to access these machines to make them compliant again. In this case, we are going to add the **Local Device Administrators** role to the exclusion as well.

6. Now, click **No target resources selected**.

7. We do not want these machines accessing anything, so click **All cloud apps** under the **Include** tab.

> **Important note**
>
> We also do not want an exclusion in this policy, but when looking at future policies, consider the *Microsoft Intune Enrollment* application for exclusion if you want to allow device provisioning on occasions where a conditional access policy would normally block it (such as location-based).

We need to watch that we do not block personal non-enrolled devices using MAM as they will not be compliant as they are not enrolled at all. For this, we will use **Device Based Filtering** under **Conditions**.

8. Click **0 conditions selected** and then **Not configured** under **Filter for devices**.

9. Set the rule to **DeviceOwnership Equals Company**. This will restrict the policy so that it can only be applied to corporate-owned devices. We created an additional policy in this book to restrict our BYOD devices to require app protection. These policies are in addition to MFA, not instead of; each is an additional layer of security. Now, click **Done**:

Figure 8.3 – Restricting to corporate devices

10. Click **0 controls selected** under **Access controls**.

11. Select **Grant access** as this is an allow rather than a block policy and tick the box for **Require device to be marked as compliant**.

If you configure more than one setting here, you can specify whether the requirement is any or all of the options. Once configured, click **Select**.

We do not require any session controls, so we can leave that option unconfigured.

The final consideration is the status of the policy, which depends on the status of your environment. If you have a large number of non-compliant devices, setting this to **On** will cause calls to your IT support line as users are blocked from accessing corporate data. In this case, set it to **Report-only** so that you can monitor who will be blocked and fix the issue. As soon as your devices are mostly compliant, switch the policy on and add your security.

12. In this example, we will switch the policy on.

This completes our conditional access policy configuration in the UI.

Automating it

We can now look at configuring our policy using Graph and PowerShell.

Conditional access policies are a single POST command as no assignment is required. All settings are contained within a nested array in the main JSON:

1. First, the only variables we need here are the name and URL:

```
$url = "https://graph.microsoft.com/v1.0/identity/
conditionalAccess/policies"
$name = "Block Non-Compliant Devices"
```

2. Then, we must configure the JSON with the values configured. For the user/role configuration, you need to use the ID rather than the display name.

For users, this can be obtained by running a GET request against this URL: https://graph.microsoft.com/v1.0/users.

We are grabbing this in the script with the following query:

```
$breakglassname = "Azure BreakGlass Account"
$breakglassid = (Invoke-MgGraphRequest -Uri "https://
graph.microsoft.com/v1.0/users?`$filter=displayName eq
'$breakglassname'" -Method Get -ContentType "application/json"
-OutputType PSObject).value.Id
```

The same applies for the role ID, which comes from this URL: https://graph.microsoft.com/v1.0/directoryRoles.

Again, we will include this in the script:

```
$rolename = "Azure AD Joined Device Local Administrator"
$roleid = (Invoke-MgGraphRequest -Uri "https://graph.microsoft.
com/v1.0/directoryRoles?`$filter=displayName eq '$rolename'"
-Method Get -ContentType "application/json" -OutputType
PSObject).value.Id
```

3. Now, we must populate the JSON:

```
$json = @"
{
    "conditions": {
        "applications": {
            "excludeApplications": [],
            "includeApplications": [
                "All"
            ],
            "includeAuthenticationContextClassReferences": [],
            "includeUserActions": [],
            "networkAccess": null
        },
        "clientApplications": null,
        "clientAppTypes": [
            "all"
        ],
        "clients": null,
        "devices": {
            "deviceFilter": {
                "mode": "include",
                "rule": "device.deviceOwnership -eq \"Company\""
            },
            "excludeDevices": [],
            "includeDevices": []
        },
        "locations": null,
        "platforms": null,
        "servicePrincipalRiskLevels": [],
        "signInRiskDetections": null,
        "signInRiskLevels": [],
        "times": null,
        "userRiskLevels": [],
        "users": {
            "excludeGroups": [],
            "excludeGuestsOrExternalUsers": null,
```

```
            "excludeRoles": [
                "$roleid"
            ],
            "excludeUsers": [
                "$breakglassid"
            ],
            "includeGroups": [],
            "includeGuestsOrExternalUsers": null,
            "includeRoles": [],
            "includeUsers": [
                "All"
            ]
        }
    },
    "displayName": "$name",
    "grantControls": {
        "authenticationStrength": null,
        "builtInControls": [
            "compliantDevice"
        ],
        "customAuthenticationFactors": [],
        "operator": "AND",
        "termsOfUse": []
    },
    "sessionControls": null,
    "state": "enabled"
}
"@
```

4. Finally, create the policy. We do not need to do anything further, so we can run the request without grabbing the output:

```
Invoke-MgGraphRequest -Method POST -Uri $url -Body $json
-ContentType "application/json" -OutputType PSObject
```

With that, we have created our conditional access policy via automation.

9

Monitoring Your New Environment

One of the best aspects of modern device management is that a well-configured environment can free up staff resources to work on being more proactive, spotting and resolving issues before the end users find them. To do that, we are going to use the tools included in Intune, starting in this chapter with a look at monitoring tools, and then continuing the theme in the next chapter when we will look at reporting.

In this chapter, we will cover the following recipes:

- Monitoring applications
- Monitoring device configuration
- Monitoring device compliance
- Monitoring device enrollment
- Monitoring updates across platforms
- Monitoring device actions
- Reviewing audit logs

Technical requirements

For this chapter, you will need a modern web browser and a PowerShell code editor such as Visual Studio Code or PowerShell ISE.

All the scripts referenced can be found here: `https://github.com/PacktPublishing/Microsoft-Intune-Cookbook`.

If you wish to test the policies, you will need a corporate-managed device running each supported platform (Windows, iOS, macOS, Linux, and Android). For Linux, it will need to be running Ubuntu OS.

Monitoring applications

In this recipe, we will be looking at application monitoring. There are a few options within this category, so we will cover each of them and then look at how to grab the same information via Graph. As these reports are all output-only, there is nothing to create, but we will cover the export functionality.

Getting ready

For all of the monitoring reports covered here, we need to navigate to **Apps** and then click on **Monitor**.

How to do it...

We will start by looking at monitoring application licenses and then run through the others in the order they appear within Intune:

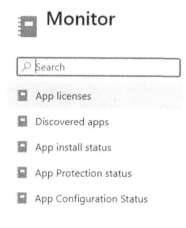

Figure 9.1 – Monitor apps menu

App licenses

Our first menu option is **App licenses**.

This is for store-based applications only (Apple, Microsoft, and Google Play Store). As we covered in *Chapter 6*, when deploying an application using Apple Volume Purchase, you select the number of licenses to make available for each application. If you have free applications, you can just order more than required, but for paid applications, you may want to restrict the licenses.

When you reach the license limit for any application, it will stop deploying; therefore, checking on license usage is a valuable thing to do.

At the top, you have the option to add additional columns (although most will not have any data), refresh, export to CSV, and usefully, kick off a VPP sync.

Clicking the three dots also gives you the option to delete the application, which can be useful.

Unfortunately, the apps are listed alphabetically with no option to sort, but you can filter with the free text field at the top. To sort (which is much more useful), be sure to check out the automation as that utilizes the `Out-GridView` command to give a similar display, but with better control.

Clicking on an application will take you to the application details.

Discovered apps

Next on the menu is **Discovered apps**.

This report is for all applications and lists every application found on Intune-managed devices, whether deployed by Intune or not. It is a powerful tool, but as each version is a separate entry, it can be unmanageable (a small tenant could have 1,000+ entries).

Again, we can export using the button at the top and search, but there is no option to sort.

The script available at the following URL will extend the functionality to then list the devices with the application installed:

`https://andrewstaylor.com/2022/11/08/quick-and-easy-application-inventory-with-intune/`

Clicking on an application takes you to the application details page where you can look further at the install lists.

As with app licenses, the script will give more sorting options.

App install status

Next on the list is the **App install status** option for all apps across platforms.

As with the other reports available in Intune, you have the option to **Filter**, **Search**, and **Export**.

This blade also adds the option to sort on the columns though, which is a welcome addition.

Clicking on the app name will take you to the main application details page. Clicking **Device** and **User failures** will take you directly to **Device install status** and **User install status** respectively.

This is a very useful place to keep an eye on and spot any troublesome or mispackaged apps before you start seeing support calls. Sorting by **Install failure** will cover both device and user installation and give you the best idea of what is causing issues in your estate.

App Protection status

An important one for any security team is to check the status of protected applications on personal and corporate devices.

Like in **App install status**, you can export, search, and sort on the headers.

There are a lot of columns here, so watch for the scroll bar across the bottom as some of the most important fields are toward the end where you can see **App protection status** and **Compliance state**.

As these are MAM devices, there is no further clickthrough enabled.

While Conditional access will protect your corporate data, monitoring your app protection status will help diagnose the issue when users are blocked from accessing resources.

App Configuration Status

The final application monitoring report is **App Configuration Status**.

This is for any application configuration policies you have deployed to managed devices or managed applications (MDM and MAM) and covers both Android and iOS device types at the device level.

As with other reports in this chapter, you can refresh and export as well as search here.

It also includes the ability to sort by header.

Again, there is a lot of content here so use the scrollbar, but fortunately, most of the important settings are earlier on.

While this usually will not have any significant security issues, it is worth monitoring for an optimal user experience.

Automating it

When automating these reports, we will again be dealing with Graph pagination for any larger results, so the scripts all include the following function, which takes in a URL and exports all data across multiple pages:

```
function getallpagination () {
[cmdletbinding()]
param
(
    $url
)
    $response = (Invoke-MgGraphRequest -uri $url -Method Get
-OutputType PSObject)
    $alloutput = $response.value
    $alloutputNextLink = $response."@odata.nextLink"
    while ($null -ne $alloutputNextLink) {
        $alloutputResponse = (Invoke-MGGraphRequest -Uri
$alloutputNextLink -Method Get -outputType PSObject)
        $alloutputNextLink = $alloutputResponse."@odata.nextLink"
```

```
        $alloutput += $alloutputResponse.value
    }
    return $alloutput
    }
```

We will also add a simple pop-up box to select whether to view or export the output using the Windows Forms functionality:

```
Add-Type -AssemblyName System.Windows.Forms
$form = New-Object System.Windows.Forms.Form
$form.Text = "Export or View"
$form.Width = 300
$form.Height = 150
$form.StartPosition = "CenterScreen"
$label = New-Object System.Windows.Forms.Label
$label.Text = "Select an option:"
$label.Location = New-Object System.Drawing.Point(10, 20)
$label.AutoSize = $true
$form.Controls.Add($label)
$exportButton = New-Object System.Windows.Forms.Button
$exportButton.Text = "Export"
$exportButton.Location = New-Object System.Drawing.Point(100, 60)
$exportButton.DialogResult = [System.Windows.Forms.DialogResult]::OK
$form.AcceptButton = $exportButton
$form.Controls.Add($exportButton)
$viewButton = New-Object System.Windows.Forms.Button
$viewButton.Text = "View"
$viewButton.Location = New-Object System.Drawing.Point(180, 60)
$viewButton.DialogResult = [System.Windows.Forms.DialogResult]::Cancel
$form.CancelButton = $viewButton
$form.Controls.Add($viewButton)
$result = $form.ShowDialog()
```

Now that we have covered the repeatable code blocks, we can look at the automation of the reports covered earlier.

App licenses

First, we will cover the app licenses report.

The full script, including the preceding code, is available on GitHub here: https://github.com/PacktPublishing/Microsoft-Intune-Cookbook/blob/main/Chapter-9/get-applicenses.ps1.

Follow the subsequent steps to create this report for your environment:

1. For our app licenses, we are going to present the option to either view or export the output, so the first thing to do is to set a path for the exported file:

    ```
    $exportpath = "c:\temp\applicenses.csv"
    ```

2. Now we need to set our URL, which filters the app types that are added from any of the stores. We then use this URL with our function to retrieve the results:

    ```
    $url = "https://graph.microsoft.com/beta/deviceAppManagement/
    mobileApps?`$filter=isof('microsoft.graph.macOsVppApp')
    or isof('microsoft.graph.iosVppApp') or isof('microsoft.
    graph.microsoftStoreForBusinessApp') or isof('microsoft.
    graph.androidManagedStoreApp') or isof('microsoft.graph.
    androidManagedStoreWebApp')"
    $allapps = getallpagination -url $url
    ```

3. Now, this simply dumps the entire application data, which is not much use for quickly checking the licenses. It also only includes total licenses and used licenses, but there is no option to see what is available. While we can do the sums ourselves, it would be nice to be able to sort on those running out of licenses, so we will add the calculation into the `select-object` query:

    ```
    $applist = $allapps | select-object DisplayName,
    totalLicenseCount, usedLicenseCount, @
    {Name="availableLicenseCount";Expression={$_.totalLicenseCount -
    $_.usedLicenseCount}}
    ```

4. Now, we grab the result of the popup. For export, simply save it as CSV, or for view, output with `gridview`, which gives you the option to both filter and sort:

    ```
    if ($result -eq [System.Windows.Forms.DialogResult]::OK) {
        $applist | export-csv $exportpath
    } elseif ($result -eq [System.Windows.Forms.
    DialogResult]::Cancel) {
        $applist | Out-GridView
    }
    ```

That completes the script for app licenses. We can now look at discovered apps.

Discovered apps

Now we can move on to discovered apps.

The full script can be found on GitHub here: `https://github.com/PacktPublishing/Microsoft-Intune-Cookbook/blob/main/Chapter-9/get-discoveredapps.ps1`.

Follow these steps to create your script for discovered apps:

1. This follows the same structure as the previous script, so again, we need to start with the output path:

   ```
   $exportpath = "c:\temp\discoveredapps.csv"
   ```

2. We will use the same pagination function, so we need to provide it with a URL:

   ```
   $url = "https://graph.microsoft.com/beta/deviceManagement/
   detectedApps"
   $allapps = getallpagination -url $url
   ```

3. There is less data retrieved here, but we only need a few fields:

   ```
   $applist = $allapps | select-object DisplayName, version,
   devicecount
   ```

4. Like before, run the popup and export or display as required:

   ```
   if ($result -eq [System.Windows.Forms.DialogResult]::OK) {
       $applist | export-csv $exportpath
   } elseif ($result -eq [System.Windows.Forms.
   DialogResult]::Cancel) {
       $applist | Out-GridView
   }
   ```

After viewing our discovered apps, we can move on to app install status.

App install status

This one is a lot trickier to automate as it does not support the GET command and instead only supports POST. Even then, it will not output into a variable and simply dumps raw JSON back, and therefore must be run with -OutputFilePath or it will throw an error.

To add to the fun, it supports pagination but within the JSON request, so you must get creative with a while loop and temp files. Follow the subsequent steps to create your script:

1. We will start with the easy part, the export path and URL:

   ```
   $exportpath = "c:\temp\appinstallstatus.csv"
   $url = "https://graph.microsoft.com/beta/deviceManagement/
   reports/getAppsInstallSummaryReport"
   ```

2. Then, we need to do a first run to grab the total number of rows and the first 50 results. We do this with a POST request, specifying the fields we want to retrieve:

```
$json = @"
{
    "filter": "",
    "orderBy": [],
    "select": [
        "DisplayName",
        "Publisher",
        "Platform",
        "AppVersion",
        "FailedDevicePercentage",
        "FailedDeviceCount",
        "FailedUserCount",
        "ApplicationId"
    ],
}
"@
```

3. Send the request, noting the all-important -OutputFilePath:

```
$tempfilepath = $env:TEMP + "\appinstallstatus.txt"
Invoke-MgGraphRequest -Method POST -Uri $url -Body $json
-ContentType "application/json" -OutputFilePath $tempfilepath
```

4. Next, we need to read that JSON into a variable:

```
$parsedData = get-content $tempfilepath | ConvertFrom-Json
```

5. We also need the total rows:

```
$allrows = $parsedData.TotalRowCount
```

6. Also, we need the values for the first 50 results, which we are storing inside an array to use later:

```
$fullvalues = $parsedData.Values
```

7. Now, we need to loop through and send a request incrementing every 50 results until we hit the total count. Each time we run, we export to a .txt file with an incremented name and then drop the values into our array:

```
$n = 0
while ($n -lt $allrows) {
    $n += 50
    $tempfilepath2 = $env:TEMP + "\appinstallstatus-$n.txt"
    $url = "https://graph.microsoft.com/beta/deviceManagement/
```

```
reports/getAppsInstallSummaryReport"
    $json = @"
{
    "filter": "",
    "orderBy": [],
    "select": [
        "DisplayName",
        "Publisher",
        "Platform",
        "AppVersion",
        "FailedDevicePercentage",
        "FailedDeviceCount",
        "FailedUserCount",
        "ApplicationId"
    ],
    "skip": $n,
    "top": 50
}
"@
    Invoke-MgGraphRequest -Method POST -Uri $url -Body $json
-ContentType "application/json" -OutputFilePath $tempfilepath2
    $tempdata = get-content $tempfilepath2 | ConvertFrom-Json
    $fullvalues += $tempdata.Values

}
```

8. Once that is done, we have a lot of `.txt` files and a very messy, unorganized array. Now we need to loop through that, grab the values, clean them, and drop them into a new array.

    Now, we can create a new array:

    ```
    $outputarray = @()
    ```

9. Loop through each item, add it to a custom PowerShell object with a useful title, and then populate the array:

    ```
    foreach ($value in $fullvalues) {
        $id = $value[0]
        $version = $value[1]
        $appname = $value[2]
        $devicefailure = $value[3]
        $installfailure = $value[4]
        $userfailure = $value[5]
        $platform = $value[7]
        $publisher = $value[8]
        $objectdetails = [pscustomobject]@{
            ID = $id
    ```

```
                    Version = $version
                    AppName = $appname
                    DeviceFailure = $devicefailure
                    InstallFailurePercent = $installfailure
                    UserFailure = $userfailure
                    Platform = $platform
                    Publisher = $publisher
                }
                $outputarray += $objectdetails
            }
```

10. Now, we use the same popup as earlier and either display or export the data:

```
if ($result -eq [System.Windows.Forms.DialogResult]::OK) {
    $outputarray | export-csv $exportpath -NoTypeInformation
} elseif ($result -eq [System.Windows.Forms.
DialogResult]::Cancel) {
    $outputarray | Out-GridView
}
```

11. Finally, clean up those .txt files:

```
Remove-Item $tempfilepath
$allrows = $parsedData.TotalRowCount
$n = 0
while ($n -lt $allrows) {
    $n += 50
    $tempfilepath2 = $env:TEMP + "\appinstallstatus-$n.txt"
    Remove-Item $tempfilepath2
}
```

That completes the recipe for app install status. Now we can cover the important app protection status.

App Protection status

This report uses the same process as the previous one, so rather than copying the entire code, we will just look at the differences.

The full script is available on GitHub here: https://github.com/PacktPublishing/Microsoft-Intune-Cookbook/blob/main/Chapter-9/get-appprotectionstatus.ps1.

Follow these steps to create a script to review your app protection status:

1. First, set the export path:

```
$exportpath = "c:\temp\appprotectstatus.csv"
```

2. This also has a different URL, which we need to set:

```
$url = "https://graph.microsoft.
com/beta/deviceManagement/reports/
getMobileApplicationManagementAppRegistrationSummaryReport"
```

3. Again, we are grabbing the total number of results and then looping through into temporary text files. The JSON request is different though, with more items to select. This has been shortened for brevity (the full JSON can be found on GitHub):

```
$json = @"
{
    "filter": "",
    "orderBy": [],
    "select": [
        "User",
        "Email"      ]
}
"@
```

4. The array also changes accordingly (again, shortened):

```
$outputarray = @()
foreach ($value in $fullvalues) {
    $platform = $value[0]
    $objectdetails = [pscustomobject]@{
        Platform = $platform
    }
    $outputarray += $objectdetails
}
```

5. Then, either output or export the data:

```
if ($result -eq [System.Windows.Forms.DialogResult]::OK) {
    $outputarray | export-csv $exportpath -NoTypeInformation
} elseif ($result -eq [System.Windows.Forms.
DialogResult]::Cancel) {
    $outputarray | Out-GridView
}
```

6. Clean up the `.txt` files we have created during our loop:

```
Remove-Item $tempfilepath
$allrows = $parsedData.TotalRowCount
$n = 0
while ($n -lt $allrows) {
    $n += 50
    $tempfilepath2 = $env:TEMP + "\appinstallstatus-$n.txt"
    Remove-Item $tempfilepath2
}
```

Now that we have learned how to programmatically view app protection status reports, we will cover app configuration reporting.

App Configuration Status

This report is almost the same as the app protection status report, only without the compliance setting, as configuration policies cannot be used to measure compliance. Therefore, rather than duplicate from before, we will just include the initial differences.

Follow these steps to create your script:

1. First, obviously we need a different output path:

```
$exportpath = "c:\temp\appconfigstatus.csv"
```

2. We also need a different URL:

```
$url = "https://graph.microsoft.com/beta/deviceManagement/
reports/getMobileApplicationManagementAppConfigurationReport"
```

3. And the only other change is a different POST request:

```
$json = @"
{
    "filter": "",
    "orderBy": [],
    "select": [
        "User",
        "Email",
        "App",
        "AppVersion",
        "AppInstanceId",
        "DeviceType",
        "AADDeviceID",
        "_Platform",
        "Policy",
```

```
        "LastSync",
        "DeviceName",
        "DeviceManufacturer",
        "DeviceModel",
        "AndroidPatchVersion",
        "MDMDeviceID",
        "PlatformVersion",
        "SdkVersion"
    ]
 }
"@
```

This completes the application monitoring recipe. We can now look at device monitoring.

Monitoring device configuration

Now that we know how to monitor our applications, we can look at monitoring the devices themselves, starting with the configuration profiles applied to them.

Getting ready

At the time of writing, the New Devices Experience view is in preview and is available via opt-in. As it is expected that this will become the default, we have used the New Devices Experience view throughout. To enable it, click on **Devices**, then **Overview**, and then click the text at the top:

Figure 9.2 – Devices overview screen

In the fly-out, click **Try it now**.

How to do it...

There are three available monitoring options for device configuration, which we will run through one at a time. To find them, click on **Devices** and then **Configuration** (under **Manage devices**).

In the new experience, you will then be taken to the **Monitor** tab where you can find our options, which we will now run through.

Devices with restricted apps

This option works alongside any **Device restriction** policies across operating systems. You can configure a policy to block certain applications, and any device with these applications discovered will be flagged in the report.

In this case, we have a macOS restrictions profile configured to restrict the use of Apple Calculator (to ensure it triggers):

Figure 9.3 – Device restrictions – restricted apps policy

When looking at the monitoring output, the device is flagged as having a prohibited app:

Device name	Email address	Profile name	Platform	State	Restricted apps
		macOS Restrictions	macOS	Prohibited apps	▪1

Figure 9.4 – Monitor devices with restricted apps

Clicking on the row will tell you which apps have been discovered.

At the top you have the usual **Export** button, search functionality (although this only searches on user email address), and the useful ability to sort on column headers.

Encryption report

This is an important one to keep an eye on, although hopefully, you have well-curated compliance policies backed by Conditional access to at least offer some protection. While that protects these devices from accessing M365 data, if an unencrypted device is lost or stolen with locally stored files, there is still a risk. Therefore, monitoring your unencrypted devices is a very important task.

It is worth noting that this only applies to Windows and macOS devices, so do not expect to see any Android or iOS devices present.

Frustratingly, you cannot sort on the column headers here and the search is only on either device or username, so finding your unencrypted devices is not as straightforward in a large environment (use the script in the automation section instead). You can, however, use the filter button at the top to restrict the results accordingly.

One useful header available is **Readiness**, which will quickly tell you if a device is not encrypted and whether the issue is at the policy or device level. If the device is **Not ready** and without active **Trusted Platform Module (TPM)**, it would suggest a hands-on look at the hardware itself rather than a hands-off remote session.

We can now move on to our next report, monitoring certificates.

Certificates

The final monitoring option for device configuration is certificates. This is only relevant if you are pushing certificates to your devices via Intune for authentication, app packaging, and so on.

There are a large number of headings available and again, the most important two are right at the end, **Certificate expiry** and **Certificate status**, so if you are on a smaller screen, you may want to press the **Columns** button to remove some you do not need, or drag to reorder.

As well as the ability to search (free text too), you can export and sort by column heading, but you will notice that has come at the expense of the filter button. Sorting by **Expiry** should be your go-to view for general monitoring and then you can use the search for any additional troubleshooting.

After reviewing our certificates, we can move on to the hidden assignment failures report.

Assignment failures

While not listed with the other three monitoring options, there is one more option available when looking at device configuration, **Assignment failures**, which looks at failures at the policy level.

To get to this, navigate to **Devices** and click the blue text labeled **Configuration profile status**.

This will take you to a new screen where you can quickly look at your policies that have errors or conflicts across your devices.

You can sort by column headers here to quickly spot any policies with significant failures as well as be able to search on the profile name. There is also a more advanced filter to restrict by platform, profile type, or profile source.

Clicking on the profile name will take you to a second screen where you can see which devices are having issues with the profiles.

While in an ideal world, this report would be clear, there will always be issues on individual devices. When looking at this, start with devices with conflict as these are not device faults, but policy configuration or scoping faults where you have two conflicting policies on the same device (keep in mind, a policy can be in conflict even if the setting is the same across policies).

Once you have cleared your conflicting policies, you can then start on the errors. As a general rule, if the value is more than about one-third of your total estate, it is an issue with the policy itself (assuming a larger estate) rather than an issue on the device.

Automating it

After covering these reports within the UI, we can now look at each in turn and how we can automate them.

Devices with restricted apps

Fortunately, automating this one is reasonably straightforward as it is a simple GET request. As with our previous exports, we will be using the `getallpagination` function to grab all results as they will be paginated on a large estate. To save the additional click, we will also list the prohibited apps in the first output.

Follow these steps to automate your report:

1. As usual, we start with the output path and the URL we are grabbing:

    ```
    $exportpath = "c:\temp\restrictedapps.csv"
    $url = "https://graph.microsoft.com/beta/deviceManagement/
    deviceConfigurationRestrictedAppsViolations"
    ```

2. Then, run the function against the URL to grab all of the values (the function is in the script on GitHub):

    ```
    $allapps = getallpagination -url $url
    ```

3. The `appID` attribute is within a nested array called `restrictedApps`, so in our next command, we want to expand that array to grab the data from it. We then run a second `select-object` to remove some of the output such as `userID` or `deviceConfigurationID`, which do not add any real value:

    ```
    $applist = $allapps | select-object * -ExpandProperty
    restrictedapps | select-object userName, deviceName,
    managedDeviceID, deviceConfigurationName, platformType,
    restrictedAppsState, appId
    ```

4. As with our other scripts, we will use forms to provide a popup for the option to export or view the results.

5. We then look at the button clicked and action appropriately with either `export-csv` or `Out-GridView`:

    ```
    if ($result -eq [System.Windows.Forms.DialogResult]::OK) {
        $applist | export-csv $exportpath
    } elseif ($result -eq [System.Windows.Forms.
    DialogResult]::Cancel) {
        $applist | Out-GridView
    }
    ```

This completes the script covering reporting on devices with restricted apps.

Encryption report

Automating the encryption report is one of the more tricky ones, similar to app configuration status in the last recipe. It uses a POST request and the output is not in readable JSON format, so it needs exporting and re-importing again. We use the following steps:

1. First, we need the output path and URL:

```
$exportpath = "c:\temp\encryptionreport.csv"
$url = "https://graph.microsoft.com/beta/deviceManagement/
reports/getEncryptionReportForDevices"
```

The JSON is slightly simpler as there are fewer options to retrieve:

```
$json = @"
{
    "filter": "",
    "orderBy": [],
    "select": [
        "DeviceId",
        "DeviceName",
        "DeviceType",
        "OSVersion",
        "TpmSpecificationVersion",
        "EncryptionReadinessState",
        "EncryptionStatus",
        "UPN"
    ]
}
"@
```

2. We want to export the raw results into a temporary text file to grab the total number of rows and also the first 50 records by saving and then ingesting the data:

```
$tempfilepath = $env:TEMP + "\encryptionreport.txt"
Invoke-MgGraphRequest -Method POST -Uri $url -Body $json
-ContentType "application/json" -OutputFilePath $tempfilepath
$parsedData = get-content $tempfilepath | ConvertFrom-Json
$fullvalues = $parsedData.Values
$allrows = $parsedData.TotalRowCount
```

3. Now, we loop through the total number of rows, each time incrementing by 50, saving each to a new text file that we then ingest and add to the master array:

```
$n = 0
while ($n -lt $allrows) {
    $n += 50
```

```
        $tempfilepath2 = $env:TEMP + "\encryptionreport-$n.txt"
        $url = "https://graph.microsoft.com/beta/deviceManagement/
reports/getEncryptionReportForDevices"
        $json = @"
{
    "filter": "",
    "orderBy": [],
    "select": [
        "DeviceId",
        "DeviceName",
        "DeviceType",
        "OSVersion",
        "TpmSpecificationVersion",
        "EncryptionReadinessState",
        "EncryptionStatus",
        "UPN"
    ],
    "skip": $n,
    "top": 50
}
"@
        Invoke-MgGraphRequest -Method POST -Uri $url -Body $json
-ContentType "application/json" -OutputFilePath $tempfilepath2
        $tempdata = get-content $tempfilepath2 | ConvertFrom-Json
        $fullvalues += $tempdata.Values
}
```

4. Add these to a new array to use in the output with meaningful headers. By default, the TPM reports either a version number or nothing at all, so we are also changing the blank to something a bit more useful (unknown to match the GUI):

```
$outputarray = @()
foreach ($value in $fullvalues) {
    $deviceid = $value[0]
    $devicename = $value[1]
    $OSType = $value[3]
    $readiness = $value[5]
    $encryption = $value[7]
    $OSVersion = $value[8]
    $TPMversion2 = $value[9]
    $username = $value[10]
    if ($TPMversion2 -eq "") {
        $TPMversion = "Unknown"
    }
```

```
else {
    $TPMversion = $TPMversion2
}
$objectdetails = [pscustomobject]@{
    DeviceID = $deviceid
    DeviceName = $devicename
    OSVersion = $OSVersion
    OS = $OSType
    TPMVersion = $TPMversion
    EncryptionReadiness = $readiness
    EncryptionStatus = $encryption
    Username = $username
}
$outputarray += $objectdetails
}
```

5. Then, after the popup, export or view the data retrieved:

```
if ($result -eq [System.Windows.Forms.DialogResult]::OK) {
    $outputarray | export-csv $exportpath -NoTypeInformation
} elseif ($result -eq [System.Windows.Forms.
DialogResult]::Cancel) {
    $outputarray | Out-GridView
}
```

6. Finally, clean up those text files:

```
Remove-Item $tempfilepath
$allrows = $parsedData.TotalRowCount
$n = 0
while ($n -lt $allrows) {
    $n += 50
    $tempfilepath2 = $env:TEMP + "\appconfigstatus-$n.txt"
    Remove-Item $tempfilepath2
}
```

This completes our script to view encryption reports programmatically.

Certificates

This is another export and import with a POST request, so rather than entering the same content here, we will just include the different URL and JSON. The full script is, of course, available on GitHub.

The URL for certificates is as follows:

```
$url = "https://graph.microsoft.com/beta/deviceManagement/reports/
getAllCertificatesReport"
```

The fields we are looking for are the following:

```
$json = @"
{
    "filter": "",
    "orderBy": [],
    "select": [
        "DeviceName",
        "UPN",
        "Thumbprint",
        "SerialNumber",
        "SubjectName",
        "IssuerName",
        "KeyUsage",
        "EnhancedKeyUsage",
        "ValidFrom",
        "ValidTo",
        "CertificateStatus",
        "PolicyId"
    ]
}
"@
```

After automating our certificates report, we can now cover assignment failures.

Assignment failures

Follow these steps to create your script:

1. This report is another POST request. Export and ingest the .txt files using this URL and JSON:

```
$url = "https://graph.microsoft.com/beta/deviceManagement/
reports/getConfigurationPolicyNoncomplianceSummaryReport"
$json = @"
{
    "filter": "",
    "orderBy": [],
    "select": [
        "PolicyName",
        "UnifiedPolicyType",
        "ProfileSource",
```

```
            "UnifiedPolicyPlatformType",
            "NumberOfNonCompliantOrErrorDevices",
            "NumberOfConflictDevices",
            "PolicyId",
            "PolicyBaseTypeName"
        ]
    }
    "@
```

2. To take this one step further, when using the view option, we want the ability to `drill-down` as we can on the web portal.

   For that, we are using the `-PassThru` parameter on `Out-GridView` and sending it to a variable:

   ```
       $selecteditems = $outputarray | Out-GridView -Title "Pick a
   policy to drill-down" -PassThru
   ```

3. We then want to loop through the selected policy to do another export and ingest, only using these options, not the policy ID within the JSON:

   ```
       $url = "https://graph.microsoft.com/beta/deviceManagement/
   reports/getConfigurationPolicyNonComplianceReport"
   $json = @"
   {
       "filter": "((PolicyBaseTypeName eq 'Microsoft.Management.
   Services.Api.DeviceConfiguration') or (PolicyBaseTypeName eq
   'DeviceManagementConfigurationPolicy') or (PolicyBaseTypeName eq
   'Microsoft.Management.Services.Api.DeviceManagementIntent')) and
   (PolicyId eq '$policyid2')",
       "orderBy": [],
       "select": [
           "DeviceName",
           "UPN",
           "PolicyStatus",
           "PspdpuLastModifiedTimeUtc",
           "UserId",
           "IntuneDeviceId",
           "PolicyBaseTypeName",
           "UnifiedPolicyPlatformType"
       ],
       "skip": 0,
       "top": 50
   }
   "@
   ```

4.   Then, we want to display the output of this second array in a second gridview:

```
$outputarray2 = @()
foreach ($value in $fullvalues2) {
$devicename = $value[0]
$deviceid = $value[1]
$policybasetype = $value[2]
$policystatus = $value[3]
$lastmodified = $value[4]
$policytype = $value[5]
$user = $value[6]
$userid = $value[7]

    $objectdetails = [pscustomobject]@{
        DeviceName = $devicename
        DeviceID = $deviceid
        PolicyBaseType = $policybasetype
        PolicyStatus = $policystatus
        LastModified = $lastmodified
        PolicyType = $policytype
        User = $user
        UserID = $userid
    }
    $outputarray2 += $objectdetails
}
}
$outputarray2 | Out-GridView
```

As always, the full script is on GitHub here: https://github.com/PacktPublishing/
Microsoft-Intune-Cookbook/blob/main/Chapter-9/get-noncompliantpolicies.
ps1.

That completes the scripts to monitor application reports, so now, we can look at device compliance.

Monitoring device compliance

After monitoring device configuration, we also need to keep an eye on device compliance, especially as this is going to cause the most complaints once users are restricted to non-compliant devices.

Getting ready

To access these reports, click on **Devices** and then **Compliance.**

You will then be taken to the **Monitor** tab where we can access our next six reports.

How to do it...

We will start by looking at non-compliant devices and then run through the other available reports.

Noncompliant devices

Starting with noncompliant devices, this report is fairly self-explanatory and displays any devices across all platforms (including Linux) that are failing any compliance policy applied. If a device has multiple policies, a single failure will send the whole device into non-compliance.

You have the standard columns and **Export** button, along with a search option to search device name, device ID, username, user email, user ID, IMEI, or serial number.

There is also the ability to filter on **Compliance status**, **OS**, **Ownership type**, and **Device type**, as well as being able to sort on the individual headings.

Clicking on a device will take you to the device details page rather than directly to the **Device compliance** panel within it.

If you have Conditional access set to block non-compliant devices, this is one you should regularly monitor so you can proactively resolve issues before the user becomes blocked and calls to complain.

Devices without compliance policy

Another straightforward one, this will show you any devices that do not have any policies assigned. If you have configured the global settings correctly, this will instantly mark the devices as non-compliant so this will help with troubleshooting.

If you have the setting to mark them as compliant, looking here is even more important to make sure your devices are all protected and monitored appropriately.

At the time of writing, it is a limited experience with an option to export, select columns (which cannot be sorted), or do a search. There are, however, plans to improve the experience in the future.

Setting compliance

This monitoring option looks at the settings configured across all of your compliance policies, including any custom Windows policies.

It expands upon the initial non-compliant devices by telling you exactly which settings within the policies are causing the non-compliance of the devices.

On the first launch, you may need to sync the results by clicking the **Sync report** button at the top.

You can export the information displayed as well as search or sort on the headers.

Clicking any of the rows will take you to further details, including the devices that are non-compliant due to the setting.

Ordering by non-compliant devices will quickly establish whether you have an issue with a particular setting or just device-specific issues.

The **Is active** setting works from the validity period in **Compliance settings** and may often feature toward the top of lists depending on the value you have set.

Policy compliance

We have so far been able to look at non-compliant devices and the individual settings that are causing the non-compliance, but that is per setting and does not specify the policy they are contained in.

For that, we have the **Policy compliance** option that lists each compliance policy and the number of compliant devices, non-compliant devices, and devices in an error state.

Again, on first access, you can run an initial synchronization of the report. Once it has run, you can export the data as well as search and sort on the headers. Compliant devices should not be of any concern, so sorting on non-compliance and error is the best approach here.

Clicking on a policy name will take you to the device status page for each policy to list each device and the compliance state.

Noncompliant policies

At the time of writing, this is in preview and is basically the same as the previous option, only it does not list anything that is compliant, so it concentrates entirely on non-compliance and error. It includes all device types and gives you the option to filter by platform.

On top of this, you have the usual options to search by policy name, export, and sort on the headers.

Clicking on a policy takes you to a list that displays the devices with issues rather than showing all devices, as with the previous option.

For day-to-day management, this is a more useful option than the previous one as it reduces the amount of information and concentrates on the parts you really want to look at.

Windows health attestation report

The final device compliance monitoring option is the Windows health attestation report, which is Windows-only and looks at the attestation settings configured on the device.

This can be used to quickly check for any hardware or firmware issues that could cause security concerns, such as BitLocker or Secure Boot.

There are a lot of fields so watch for the scrollbar at the bottom of the screen, or use the **Columns** button to remove any that are not applicable in your environment.

The output is fairly simple. There is no search option or the ability to sort by headers, but there is a filter available:

Select device type:

☐ Devices that support health attestation

Select data point status:

☐ BitLocker not enabled

☐ Secure Boot not enabled

☐ Code integrity not enabled

☐ Early launch anti-malware driver is not loaded

Figure 9.5 – Health attestation report filter

None of the output can be clicked, so it is strictly view-only here.

Automating it

After covering these reports in the UI, we can look at how to automate them.

Non-compliant devices

This works in the same way as the previous automations in this chapter with a POST request. Grab the output, save it to a .txt file, and then re-ingest it.

The full script is on GitHub at the following URL: https://github.com/PacktPublishing/ Microsoft-Intune-Cookbook/blob/main/Chapter-9/get-noncompliantdevices. ps1.

Follow these steps to create your non-compliant devices script:

1. Here, we will again stick to just the URL and JSON:

```
$url = "https://graph.microsoft.com/beta/deviceManagement/
reports/getDeviceNoncomplianceReport"
$json = @"
{
    "filter": "",
    "orderBy": [],
    "select": [
        "DeviceName",
        "UPN",
        "ComplianceState",
        "OS",
        "OSVersion",
```

```
            "OwnerType",
            "LastContact",
            "ManagementAgents",
            "IntuneDeviceId"
        ]
    }
    "@
```

2. We then work out the total number of rows, loop through to grab everything into a new array, and then tidy this into an output array.

> **Important note**
>
> The array values do not necessarily match so during the `foreach` loop, it is best to do a simple `write-output` for each array item to check what it corresponds to, for example `-- write-output $value[0]` will show the first value in the array.

3. In our case, the final array looks like this:

```
$outputarray = @()
foreach ($value in $fullvalues) {
$compliancestate = $value[1]
$devicename = $value[2]
$intunedeviceid = $value[3]
$lastcontact = $value[4]
$os = $value[7]
$osversion = $value[9]
$owner = $value[11]
$username = $value[12]
$objectdetails = [pscustomobject]@{
    ComplianceState = $compliancestate
    DeviceName = $devicename
    DeviceID = $intunedeviceid
    LastContact = $lastcontact
    OS = $os
    OSVersion = $osversion
    OwnerType = $owner
    Username = $username
}
$outputarray += $objectdetails
}
```

4. As with the other recipes, we send a pop-up question, then export or output as required and clean up the environment, removing all of the .txt files created:

```
if ($result -eq [System.Windows.Forms.DialogResult]::OK) {
    $outputarray | export-csv $exportpath -NoTypeInformation
} elseif ($result -eq [System.Windows.Forms.
DialogResult]::Cancel) {
    $outputarray | Out-GridView
}
Remove-Item $tempfilepath
$allrows = $parsedData.TotalRowCount
$n = 0
while ($n -lt $allrows) {
    $n += 50
    $tempfilepath2 = $env:TEMP + "\appconfigstatus-$n.txt"
    Remove-Item $tempfilepath2
}
```

We will now move on to finding any devices without a compliance policy assigned.

Devices without compliance policy

This is a more straightforward one to script as it is a simple GET command to retrieve the output in standard JSON format. The only thing to watch is that the URL includes a filter that uses the $ sign and therefore needs to be escaped with a backtick (`` ` ``).

We are going to use the pagination function as per the other scripts to ensure we grab all results in larger environments, although in this case, there should hopefully not be more than 50 devices without a policy assigned. Follow these steps to create your script:

1. First, we set the export path:

```
$exportpath = "c:\temp\nocompliancepolicy.csv"
```

2. Now, provide the URL:

```
$url = "https://graph.microsoft.com/beta/deviceManagement/
deviceCompliancePolicySettingStateSummaries/
DefaultDeviceCompliancePolicy.
RequireDeviceCompliancePolicyAssigned/
deviceComplianceSettingStates?`$filter=((state eq
'noncompliant') or (state eq 'error'))"
```

3. Run the function against the URL:

```
$allapps = getallpagination -url $url
```

4. Clean the data to remove fields we do not need:

```
$applist = $allapps | select-object deviceName, deviceID,
userName, userPrincipalName, deviceModel, state
```

5. Then, display the popup and either export or display the data:

```
if ($result -eq [System.Windows.Forms.DialogResult]::OK) {
    $applist | export-csv $exportpath
} elseif ($result -eq [System.Windows.Forms.
DialogResult]::Cancel) {
    $applist | Out-GridView
}
```

That completes the script for devices without a compliance policy, which should hopefully be empty. We will now look at the compliance of individual settings.

Setting compliance

Similar to the last one, this is also a GET request, and we want to return everything using the pagination function.

There is one small difference in this case as we cannot be sure a report has been generated, so to be on the safe side, we will initiate a sync and then wait for 60 seconds before grabbing any output. Follow the subsequent steps for your report:

1. As usual, we start with the export path:

```
$exportpath = "c:\temp\settingscompliance.csv"
```

2. Now, we want to initiate a sync, which is done via a POST request but without any JSON in the body:

```
$syncurl = "https://graph.microsoft.com/beta/
deviceManagement/deviceCompliancePolicies/
refreshDeviceComplianceReportSummarization"
Invoke-MgGraphRequest -Method POST -Uri $syncurl
```

3. Sleep for 60 seconds to wait for the report to generate:

```
Start-Sleep -Seconds 60
```

4. Then, set the URL and grab all of the results:

```
$url = "https://graph.microsoft.com/beta/deviceManagement/
deviceCompliancePolicySettingStateSummaries?`
$orderby=nonCompliantDeviceCount%20desc"
$fulloutput = getallpagination -url $url
```

5. Grab the items we want to display (generally, the ID is just an extra field to skip past):

```
$selectedoutput = $fulloutput | select-object settingName,
platformType, unknownDeviceCount, notApplicableDeviceCount,
nonCompliantDeviceCount, compliantDeviceCount,
remediatedDeviceCount, errorDeviceCount, conflictDeviceCount
```

6. After displaying the usual popup, either export or display the output.

7. In this case, we also want to drill down to match the GUI, so we add the -PassThru parameter on the gridview command and pipe it into an array. We then loop through that array, sending a second Graph GET request to a new URL to grab the details of each device. This URL uses deviceCompliancePolicySettingSummaries and then passes the displayName attribute of the policy rather than the usual ID:

```
if ($result -eq [System.Windows.Forms.DialogResult]::OK) {
    $selectedoutput | export-csv $exportpath
} elseif ($result -eq [System.Windows.Forms.
DialogResult]::Cancel) {
    $selection = $selectedoutput | Out-GridView -PassThru
    foreach ($item in $selection) {
        $policyname = $item.settingName
        $url = "https://graph.
microsoft.com/beta/deviceManagement/
deviceCompliancePolicySettingStateSummaries/$policyname/
deviceComplianceSettingStates"
        $fulloutput = getallpagination -url $url
        $selectedoutput = $fulloutput | select-object
deviceName, deviceID, userName, userPrincipalName, deviceModel,
state, platformType | Out-GridView
    }
}
```

That completes the script for setting compliance. Now, we can discover which policies have compliance issues.

Policy compliance

This is very similar to the last one, just with an extremely complicated URL (watch for the escaped $ characters). Follow these steps to create your report:

1. First, we set the export path for saving the report content:

```
$exportpath = "c:\temp\policycompliance.csv"
```

2. Send a sync and wait for the report to generate:

```
$syncurl = "https://graph.microsoft.com/beta/
deviceManagement/deviceCompliancePolicies/
refreshDeviceComplianceReportSummarization"
```

```
Invoke-MgGraphRequest -Method POST -Uri $syncurl
Start-Sleep -Seconds 60
```

3.   Grab the output:

```
$url = "https://graph.microsoft.com/beta/deviceManagement/
deviceCompliancePolicies?`$select=id,displayName,
lastModifiedDateTime,roleScopeTagIds,
microsoft.graph.androidCompliancePolicy/
deviceThreatProtectionRequiredSecurityLevel,
microsoft.graph.androidWorkProfileCompliancePolicy/
deviceThreatProtectionRequiredSecurityLevel,
microsoft.graph.iosCompliancePolicy/
deviceThreatProtectionRequiredSecurityLevel,
microsoft.graph.windows10CompliancePolicy/
deviceThreatProtectionRequiredSecurityLevel,
microsoft.graph.iosCompliancePolicy/
advancedThreatProtectionRequiredSecurityLevel,
microsoft.graph.androidWorkProfileCompliancePolicy/
advancedThreatProtectionRequiredSecurityLevel,
microsoft.graph.androidDeviceOwnerCompliancePolicy/
advancedThreatProtectionRequiredSecurityLevel,
microsoft.graph.androidDeviceOwnerCompliancePolicy/
deviceThreatProtectionRequiredSecurityLevel,
microsoft.graph.androidCompliancePolicy/
advancedThreatProtectionRequiredSecurityLevel&
`$expand=deviceStatusOverview,assignments"
$fulloutput = getallpagination -url $url
$selectedoutput = $fulloutput | select-object -Property
id, displayName, @{Name="Name"; Expression={$_.
deviceStatusOverview.Name}}, @{Name="pendingCount";
Expression={$_.deviceStatusOverview.pendingCount}}, @
{Name="notApplicableCount"; Expression={$_.deviceStatusOverview.
notApplicableCount}}, @{Name="notApplicablePlatformCount";
Expression={$_.deviceStatusOverview.
notApplicablePlatformCount}}, @{Name="successCount";
Expression={$_.deviceStatusOverview.successCount}}, @
{Name="errorCount"; Expression={$_.deviceStatusOverview.
errorCount}}, @{Name="failedCount"; Expression={$_.
deviceStatusOverview.failedCount}}, @{Name="conflictCount";
Expression={$_.deviceStatusOverview.conflictCount}}
```

After the prompt, either export the results to the .csv set earlier or display them in the gridview UI and pass through the policy ID to drill down further:

```
if ($result -eq [System.Windows.Forms.DialogResult]::OK) {
    $selectedoutput | export-csv $exportpath
} elseif ($result -eq [System.Windows.Forms.
```

```
DialogResult]::Cancel) {
    $selection = $selectedoutput | Out-GridView -PassThru
    foreach ($item in $selection) {
        $policyid = $item.id
        $url = "https://graph.microsoft.com/beta/
deviceManagement/deviceCompliancePolicies/$policyid/
deviceStatuses"
        $fulloutput = getallpagination -url $url
        $selectedoutput = $fulloutput | select-object
deviceDisplayName, userName, status, userPrincipalName,
deviceModel, lastReportedDateTime | Out-GridView
    }
}
```

After covering policy compliance, we can now look at non-compliant policies.

Noncompliant policies

Automating this is almost identical to the assignment failures script we created in the previous recipe. Again, it uses a POST request with JSON, which we have to retrieve into a temporary text file and then ingest. Follow these steps to create your script:

1. We are looping through this URL with JSON attached:

    ```
    $url = "https://graph.microsoft.com/beta/deviceManagement/
    reports/getPolicyNoncomplianceSummaryReport"
    $json = @"
    {
        "filter": "((PolicyBaseTypeName eq 'Microsoft.Management.
    Services.Api.DeviceCompliancePolicy') or (PolicyBaseTypeName eq
    'DeviceManagementCompliancePolicy'))",
        "orderBy": [],
        "select": [
            "PolicyName",
            "UnifiedPolicyPlatformType",
            "NumberOfNonCompliantDevices",
            "NumberOfErrorDevices",
            "PolicyBaseTypeName",
            "PolicyId"
        ]
    }
    "@
    ```

2. The values are then transferred into this array (we need policyBaseType for the passthrough):

    ```
    $outputarray = @()
    foreach ($value in $fullvalues) {
    ```

```
$numberoferrordevices = $value[0]
$NumberOfNonCompliantDevices = $value[1]
$PolicyBaseTypeName = $value[2]
$policyid = $value[3]
$policyname = $value[4]
$unifiedpolicyplatformtype = $value[5]
    $objectdetails = [pscustomobject]@{
        PolicyName = $policyname
        NumberOfErrorDevices = $numberoferrordevices
        NumberOfNonCompliantDevices =
$NumberOfNonCompliantDevices
        UnifiedPolicyPlatformType = $unifiedpolicyplatformtype
        PolicyBaseTypeName = $PolicyBaseTypeName
        PolicyID = $policyid
    }
    $outputarray += $objectdetails
}
```

3.   We then export our report data or passthrough in the UI:

```
if ($result -eq [System.Windows.Forms.DialogResult]::OK) {
    $outputarray | export-csv $exportpath -NoTypeInformation
} elseif ($result -eq [System.Windows.Forms.
DialogResult]::Cancel) {
    $selecteditems = $outputarray | Out-GridView -Title "Pick a
policy to drill-down" -PassThru
foreach ($selected in $selecteditems) {
    $policyid2 = $selected.PolicyID
    $PolicyBaseTypeName2 = $selected.PolicyBaseTypeName
    $url = "https://graph.microsoft.com/beta/deviceManagement/
reports/getPolicyNoncomplianceReport"
$json = @"
{
    "filter": "((PolicyBaseTypeName eq '$PolicyBaseTypeName2')
and (PolicyId eq '$policyid2'))",
    "orderBy": [],
    "select": [
        "DeviceName",
        "UPN",
        "PolicyStatus",
        "PspdpuLastModifiedTimeUtc",
        "UserId",
        "IntuneDeviceId"
    ],
    "skip": 0,
```

```
        "top": 50
    }
    "@
```

4. And finally, we display our drill-down array in a second gridview:

```
$outputarray2 = @()
foreach ($value in $fullvalues2) {
$devicename = $value[0]
$deviceid = $value[1]
$policystatus = $value[2]
$lastmodified = $value[3]
$user = $value[4]
$userid = $value[5]
    $objectdetails = [pscustomobject]@{
        DeviceName = $devicename
        DeviceID = $deviceid
        PolicyStatus = $policystatus
        LastModified = $lastmodified
        User = $user
        UserID = $userid
    }
    $outputarray2 += $objectdetails
}
}
$outputarray2 | Out-GridView
```

This completes the recipe to view non-compliant policies.

Windows health attestation report

As this is view-only, it is more simple with a GET request and to retrieve the output in a JSON format. The output does contain a nested array though (and a lot of information we do not need), so we will do some data manipulation:

1. Start with the setting export file location and URL:

```
$exportpath = "c:\temp\windowsattestation.csv"
$url = "https://graph.microsoft.com/beta/deviceManagement/
managedDevices?`$filter=isof('microsoft.graph.
windowsManagedDevice')&`$select=deviceHealthAttestationState,
deviceName,operatingSystem,id"
```

2. Now, grab all results:

```
$allapps = getallpagination -url $url
```

3. Now ,we want to retrieve all output and expand the value of the `deviceAttestationState` array:

```
$applist2 = $allapps | select-object * -expandproperty
deviceHealthAttestationState
```

4. And then remove some items that take up too much screen estate:

```
$applist3 = $applist2 | select-object * -ExcludeProperty
pcr0, codeIntegrityPolicy, bootRevisionListInfo,
operatingSystemRevListInfo, deviceHealthAttestationState
```

5. After the popup, either export or display our final output:

```
if ($result -eq [System.Windows.Forms.DialogResult]::OK) {
    $applist3 | export-csv $exportpath
} elseif ($result -eq [System.Windows.Forms.
DialogResult]::Cancel) {
    $applist3 | Out-GridView
}
```

This completes our recipe for monitoring device compliance both in the UI and when using PowerShell and Graph.

Monitoring device enrollment

While we can now monitor our device compliance and configuration, that is of no use if the devices have failed to enroll. For that, we need to use the device enrollment monitoring options. These are especially useful when users are self-enrolling devices to look for any errors and to assist in troubleshooting.

Getting ready

To access these reports, click on **Devices** and then **Enrollment**.

This will take you to the **Monitor** panel where you can find our available options, which we will now cover in more detail.

How to do it...

We will start by looking at enrollment failures and then run through each report available.

Enrollment failures

We start with enrollment failures, which is a cross-platform report on all failed enrollments using any supported enrollment method. It also includes error details, which are especially useful.

The first thing to check is the powerful filter available here, which can look at the platform, error type, enrollment type, and date/time of the enrollment. This will help significantly to spot any spikes or repeated failures.

There is also the ability to export the output to CSV.

Another feature specific to this option is to select either a specific user (**Select user**) or display for **All users**. This is a very useful troubleshooting tool should a user have enrollment issues.

While you cannot sort by header, the powerful filter should negate that requirement.

Finally, there is the option to view a graphical representation, which is useful for a regular check to spot any enrollment failure spikes that could be caused by a firewall change or an outage somewhere.

Incomplete user enrollments

This section is only for Android and iOS devices enrolled using Company Portal, so does not include Android for Work, Zero Touch, or Apple Business Manager enrollments.

It displays a graph of enrollments that were not completed by the user, either by ending the wizard or the enrollment timing out.

This should normally be empty, but is worth monitoring to be able to offer assistance to any users on the list.

At the top is another powerful filter where you can filter by operating system, date/time, or the phase of enrollment at the time of cancellation/timeout.

Windows Autopilot deployments

The last option here is just for Windows devices and shows details of all Autopilot deployments for the previous 30 days, successes and failures.

As with the other reports covered, it includes another powerful filter.

Unlike the others, you also have the option to sort by header and even search, but there is no option to export data (you will have to use the automation for that).

Clicking on a device will show the Autopilot device details.

As Autopilot is usually a user-led enrollment, monitoring these events is always useful to keep an eye on. The last thing you want is a device being deployed with an incomplete deployment. You can also check the total time to see how the user experience is and whether there is anything that could be done to improve it.

Automating it

After reviewing these reports in the UI, we can now look at how to automate them.

Enrollment failures

This is a fairly easy one to automate as it is a GET request to one of two URLs, depending on the user selection. To keep things comparable, we will do the same here.

The full script can be found on GitHub at the following URL: `https://github.com/PacktPublishing/Microsoft-Intune-Cookbook/blob/main/Chapter-9/get-userenrollmentfailures.ps1`.

These steps will run through the key aspects:

1. As usual, start with the CSV path:

    ```
    $exportpath = "c:\temp\userenrollmentfailures.csv"
    ```

2. Now, we quickly grab all users into an array to store for later:

    ```
    $allusersurl = "https://graph.microsoft.com/beta/users"
    $allusers = getallpagination -url $allusersurl
    ```

3. After sending the popup, we then filter the URL on the response:

    *   For all users, the URL runs at the tenant level:

        ```
        $url = "https://graph.microsoft.com/beta/deviceManagement/
        troubleshootingEvents"
        ```

    *   If users has been selected, we need to pop up a list of users to make a selection. We then grab the user ID and populate the URL, which in this case is at the user level:

        ```
        $selecteditems = $allusers | select-object
        userPrincipalName, id | Out-GridView -Title "Pick a user to
        drill-down" -PassThru
            foreach ($selected in $selecteditems) {
                $userid = $selected.id
                $url = "https://graph.microsoft.com/beta/users/$userid/
        deviceManagementTroubleshootingEvents"
            }
        ```

4. Then, we are back to a normal script. Grab all of the data for the new URL:

    ```
    $fulloutput = getallpagination -url $url
    $selectedoutput = $fulloutput | select-object *
    ```

5. After a second popup, either display the output or export the data to CSV:

```
if ($result -eq [System.Windows.Forms.DialogResult]::OK) {
    $selectedoutput | export-csv $exportpath
} elseif ($result -eq [System.Windows.Forms.
DialogResult]::Cancel) {
$selectedoutput | Out-GridView
}
```

This completes the automation of the enrollment failures report. We will now look at incomplete user enrollments.

Incomplete user enrollments

Again, this is a relatively straightforward GET request, returning readable JSON.

> **Important note**
>
> The URL includes a date range that is 30 days by default, so it is something we will replicate here.

We will let PowerShell do the work for us to calculate dates automatically:

1. First, set the export path:

```
$exportpath = "c:\temp\userenrollmentfailures.csv"
```

2. Now, get today's date and the date 30 days ago using the AddDays functionality:

```
$todaydate = Get-Date -Format "yyyy-MM-ddTHH:mm:ss.fffZ"
$lastmonthdate = (Get-Date).AddDays(-30).ToString("yyyy-MM-ddTHH:mm:ss.fffZ")
```

3. Add these dates to the URL and grab the results:

```
$url = "https://graph.microsoft.com/beta/reports/
managedDeviceEnrollmentAbandonmentSummary(
skip=null,top=null,filter='eventDateUTC%20ge%20
dateTime''$lastmonthdate''%20and%20eventDateUTC%20le%20
dateTime''$todaydate''',
skipToken=null)/content"
$fulloutput = getallpagination -url $url
$selectedoutput = $fulloutput | select-object -Property
id, displayName, @{Name="Name"; Expression={$_.
deviceStatusOverview.Name}}, @{Name="pendingCount";
Expression={$_.deviceStatusOverview.pendingCount}}, @
{Name="notApplicableCount"; Expression={$_.deviceStatusOverview.
notApplicableCount}}, @{Name="notApplicablePlatformCount";
Expression={$_.deviceStatusOverview.
notApplicablePlatformCount}}, @{Name="successCount";
```

```
Expression={$_.deviceStatusOverview.successCount}}, @
{Name="errorCount"; Expression={$_.deviceStatusOverview.
errorCount}}, @{Name="failedCount"; Expression={$_.
deviceStatusOverview.failedCount}}, @{Name="conflictCount";
Expression={$_.deviceStatusOverview.conflictCount}}
```

4. Finally, after a popup, export the data to CSV or output in a `gridview` UI:

    ```
    if ($result -eq [System.Windows.Forms.DialogResult]::OK) {
        $selectedoutput | export-csv $exportpath
    } elseif ($result -eq [System.Windows.Forms.
    DialogResult]::Cancel) {
        $selectedoutput | Out-GridView -PassThru
    }
    ```

After completing incomplete user enrollments, we can cover the final script in this recipe, looking at autopilot deployments.

Windows Autopilot deployments

This is another GET request, but in the URL, we are adding the date to check from. Unlike the previous script, this is simply retrieving all data from the date specified rather than between a range of dates.

We will also drill down to pass through the device details:

1. As usual, we start with the export file:

    ```
    $exportpath = "c:\temp\policycompliance.csv"
    ```

2. Now, create the date to use (today minus 30 days):

    ```
    $lastmonthdate = (Get-Date).AddDays(-30).ToString("yyyy-MM-
    ddTHH:mm:ss.fffZ")
    ```

3. And populate the URL with the date:

    ```
    $url = "https://graph.microsoft.com/beta/deviceManagement/
    autopilotEvents?`$filter=microsoft.graph.
    DeviceManagementAutopilotEvent/enrollmentStartDateTime ge
    $lastmonthdate"
    ```

4. Grab the output:

    ```
    $fulloutput = getallpagination -url $url
    $selectedoutput = $fulloutput | select-object *
    ```

5. After the popup, look for **Export** or **View**. If **View** is selected, pass the `deviceid` variable through to a new URL to grab the specific device details. Then, output those into a second `gridview` UI:

```
if ($result -eq [System.Windows.Forms.DialogResult]::OK) {
    $selectedoutput | export-csv $exportpath
} elseif ($result -eq [System.Windows.Forms.
DialogResult]::Cancel) {
    $selection = $selectedoutput | Out-GridView -PassThru
    foreach ($item in $selection) {
        $deviceid = $item.deviceid
        $url = "https://graph.microsoft.com/beta/
deviceManagement/managedDevices('$deviceid')/
logCollectionRequests"
        $fulloutput = getallpagination -url $url
        $selectedoutput = $fulloutput | Out-GridView
    }
}
```

That completes the recipe. Now, we will look at monitoring device updates.

Monitoring updates across platforms

One key requirement for most environments is keeping your devices updated with the latest security patches. While Intune has systems to do the updating for you, there is always the chance that some devices will have issues installing the updates. To check these, we have the functionality to check the update status for Windows, iOS, and macOS (no Android at present).

Getting ready

To access these reports, we need to navigate to **Devices** in the Intune menu. Each is in a different location, which will be covered for each individual report.

How to do it...

We will start this recipe by looking at Windows updates before moving on to iOS and macOS.

Windows updates

Within **Devices**, click on **Windows 10 and later updates**.

This then gives you an overview of the following:

- **Update ring device status** – This shows any devices that have issues with the update ring policies themselves, not at the individual update level.

- **Feature update device errors** – This displays the number of devices across your policies having issues deploying feature updates.

- **Expedited update failures** – Same as before, but for expedited updates. This is one to keep a close eye on as expedited updates are often for urgent security issues.

- **Driver update failures** – If driver updates are enabled, this will show any devices with failed drivers.

Clicking on the three dots in the top right of any of the available reports will give you the option to navigate to the underlying report:

Figure 9.6 – Updating the ring status

Within the report, you can then click on rows to drill down further as required.

Within the report, there is the option to export your data.

Use the overview page as a general indication of the estate and then the individual reports to troubleshoot and repair issues. Start with policy errors; if a policy is not applying to a device, there is a chance that it is not receiving any updates. Once they are resolved, expedited updates are the next most important to look at.

The next chapter includes a look at reports that give further insight into your Windows updates.

iOS update status

This option can be found within **Devices**, then **Apple updates**. Finally, click on **iOS update status**.

Here you will find a familiar layout with a list of your iOS devices that have installation failures. It will only list those with issues, as Apple does not report on healthy devices.

As well as the option to export, there is a powerful filter that can look at both a date range and the installation status, which is a comprehensive list:

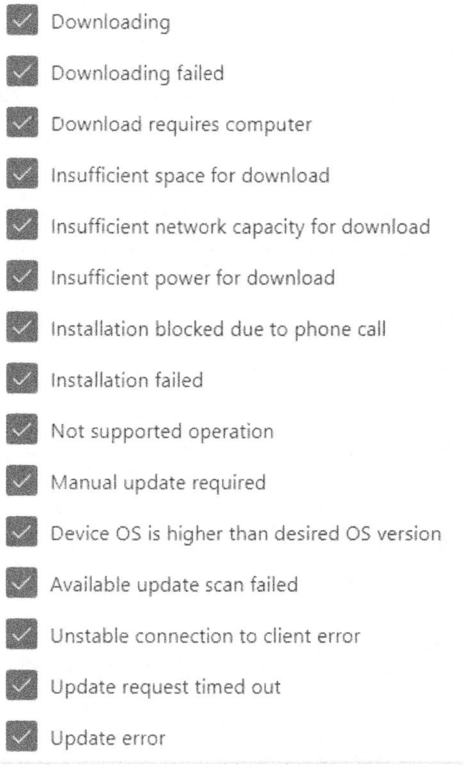

- ☑ Downloading
- ☑ Downloading failed
- ☑ Download requires computer
- ☑ Insufficient space for download
- ☑ Insufficient network capacity for download
- ☑ Insufficient power for download
- ☑ Installation blocked due to phone call
- ☑ Installation failed
- ☑ Not supported operation
- ☑ Manual update required
- ☑ Device OS is higher than desired OS version
- ☑ Available update scan failed
- ☑ Unstable connection to client error
- ☑ Update request timed out
- ☑ Update error

Figure 9.7 – iOS update status filter

The headers are sortable and there is also a free-text search.

With such a large selection of reasons why an update could fail, including receiving a telephone call, this is always worth keeping an eye on, especially as iOS devices are often used by C-level executives.

macOS update status

This one is accessed via **Devices | Apple updates | macOS update status**.

Clicking on it takes us to another report screen, similar to that for iOS but slightly less feature-rich.

The filter adds support for minimum and maximum OS versions but there are fewer update status options.

As well as the usual **Export** button, there is a search box that queries the main items, but the headers here cannot be clicked and sorted.

While not as thorough as that for Windows and iOS, there is enough data in here to spot any devices with issues and allow you to troubleshoot.

Automating it

After reviewing these reports within the portal, we can now cover the automation of them.

Windows updates

While in the web interface this looks straightforward, if you study the network logs, you will see it is sending a batch request. This means it is sending multiple requests (either POST or GET) in a single request and then grabbing the information back.

In this case, there are four different requests being sent. Three of them use the POST, export, ingest method, but fortunately with the same JSON and output. The fourth, however, is a GET request with different fields.

Therefore, we will combine the first three into a single output and split the expedited updates into a different output.

The full script is available on GitHub here: https://github.com/PacktPublishing/ Microsoft-Intune-Cookbook/blob/main/Chapter-9/get-windowsupdatestatus. ps1.

As there is a lot of repetition of POST requests in these reports, we have to run the same loop three times:

1. First, we need the first export path. We are also creating our empty array at the top as we are going to populate it with all three loops:

```
$exportpath = "c:\temp\windowsupdates.csv"
$outputarray = @()
```

2. Set the URL and JSON (this is for the policy status):

```
$url = "https://graph.microsoft.com/beta/deviceManagement/
reports/getWindowsUpdateAlertSummaryReport"
$json = @"
{
    "filter": "",
    "orderBy": [],
    "select": [
        "PolicyName",
        "NumberOfDevicesWithErrors",
        "PolicyId"
    ]
}
"@
```

3. Grab the data into a text file and ingest it. Count the total rows and loop through 50 at a time, exporting into a `.txt` file and then re-importing into our array. We are also clearing out the text files during the loops here so the files are removed for the next report:

```
$tempfilepath = $env:TEMP + "\summaryreport.txt"
Invoke-MgGraphRequest -Method POST -Uri $url -Body $json
-ContentType "application/json" -OutputFilePath $tempfilepath
$parsedData = get-content $tempfilepath | ConvertFrom-Json
$fullvalues = $parsedData.Values
Remove-Item $tempfilepath
$allrows = $parsedData.TotalRowCount
$n = 0
while ($n -lt $allrows) {
    $n += 50
    $tempfilepath2 = $env:TEMP + "\summaryreport-$n.txt"
    $url = "https://graph.microsoft.com/beta/deviceManagement/
reports/getWindowsUpdateAlertSummaryReport"
    $json = @"
{
    "filter": "",
    "orderBy": [],
    "select": [
        "PolicyName",
        "NumberOfDevicesWithErrors",
        "PolicyId"
    ],
    "skip": $n,
    "top": 50
}
"@
    Invoke-MgGraphRequest -Method POST -Uri $url -Body $json
-ContentType "application/json" -OutputFilePath $tempfilepath2
    $tempdata = get-content $tempfilepath2 | ConvertFrom-Json
    $fullvalues += $tempdata.Values
    Remove-Item $tempfilepath2
}
```

4. When adding to the output array, we have added an item to mark exactly which report it is from:

```
foreach ($value in $fullvalues) {
$numberoferrordevices = $value[0]
$policyid = $value[1]
$policyname = $value[2]
$type = "Policy Errors"
    $objectdetails = [pscustomobject]@{
```

```
                ReportType = $type
                PolicyName = $policyname
                ErrorDevices = $numberoferrordevices
                PolicyID = $policyid
            }
        $outputarray += $objectdetails
    }
}
```

For quality updates and driver updates, the process is the same only with these URLs:

- **Quality updates**:

This is the URL required for quality updates:

```
$url = "https://graph.microsoft.com/beta/deviceManagement/
reports/getWindowsQualityUpdateAlertSummaryReport"
```

- **Driver updates**:

If using driver updates, you require this URL:

```
$url = "https://graph.microsoft.com/beta/deviceManagement/
reports/getWindowsDriverUpdateAlertSummaryReport"
```

5. Then, after a popup, display or export the data retrieved from Graph:

```
if ($result -eq [System.Windows.Forms.DialogResult]::OK) {
    $outputarray | export-csv $exportpath -NoTypeInformation
} elseif ($result -eq [System.Windows.Forms.
DialogResult]::Cancel) {
    $outputarray | Out-GridView
}
```

For expedited updates, this is a single GET request. It has no pagination options and the output is not nested within the value array, so we have no need for the usual pagination function.

Therefore, we simply set the export path and URL and then grab the exact values:

```
$exportpath2 = "c:\temp\featureupdates.csv"
$url = "https://graph.microsoft.com/beta/deviceManagement/
softwareUpdateStatusSummary"
$fulloutput = Invoke-MGGraphRequest -Uri $url -Method Get
-outputType PSObject
$selectedoutput = $fulloutput | select-object *
```

Finally, again, export or view after a popup:

```
if ($result -eq [System.Windows.Forms.DialogResult]::OK) {
    $selectedoutput | export-csv $exportpath2 -NoTypeInformation
} elseif ($result -eq [System.Windows.Forms.
DialogResult]::Cancel) {
```

```
        $selectedoutput | Out-GridView
    }
```

This completes the automation of Windows update reporting. We can now cover iOS updates.

iOS update status

This is very straightforward to automate as it is a simple paginated GET request:

1. First, set the output path:

    ```
    $exportpath = "c:\temp\iosupdatestatus.csv"
    ```

2. Set the URL and grab the data:

    ```
    $url = "https://graph.microsoft.com/beta/deviceManagement/
    iosUpdateStatuses"
    $fulloutput = getallpagination -url $url
    $selectedoutput = $fulloutput | select-object *
    ```

3. The only change after this is that the output could be completely clear, which will block any export or gridview from displaying. Therefore, we inspect the output first, and if it is null, we simply output that to the screen:

    ```
    if ($result -eq [System.Windows.Forms.DialogResult]::OK) {
        if ($null -eq $selectedoutput) {
            write-host "Nothing to display"
        }
        else {
            $selectedoutput | export-csv $exportpath
        }
    } elseif ($result -eq [System.Windows.Forms.
    DialogResult]::Cancel) {
        if ($null -eq $selectedoutput) {
            write-host "Nothing to display"
        }
        else {
        $selectedoutput | Out-GridView
        }
    }
    ```

After reviewing iOS updates, we will now cover macOS updates.

macOS update status

This is exactly the same as the preceding iOS script, only with a different export path and URL. The full script is on GitHub, but these are the only values changed to grab macOS values:

```
$exportpath = "c:\temp\masosupdatestatus.csv"
$url = "https://graph.microsoft.com/beta/deviceManagement/
macOSSoftwareUpdateAccountSummaries"
```

It also uses pagination and has the possibility to be a null result, so it includes the same `if` statement.

That completes the recipe for monitoring updates. We will now look at device actions.

Monitoring device actions

As an Intune administrator, especially in a larger organization, it is essential to have an audit trail as there are buttons within the console that can have serious effects. Imagine someone accidentally clicks **Wipe** on the wrong device and you need to find out what happened for an incident report. Fortunately, these are all logged in **Device actions**, which we will cover now.

Getting ready

To access these logs, click on **Devices**, then **Overview**, and finally, click on the **Device actions** box.

How to do it...

On this screen, you will be presented with a list of all actions taken against all devices (cross-platform), including what was performed, when, and by whom.

There is no search functionality and you cannot sort on the headers (use the automated script to add this functionality), but it does have a powerful filter that includes every possible action across all device types:

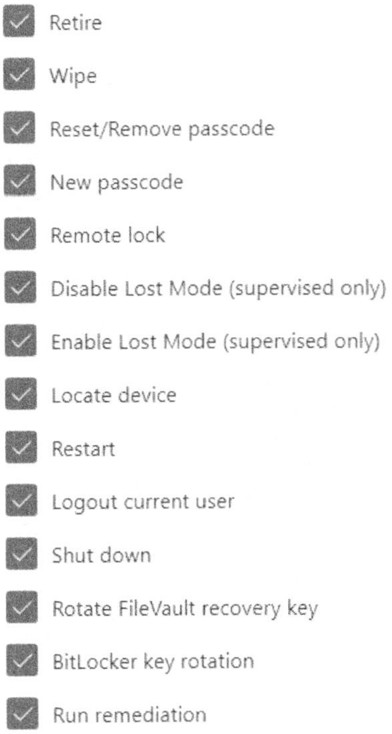

- ☑ Retire
- ☑ Wipe
- ☑ Reset/Remove passcode
- ☑ New passcode
- ☑ Remote lock
- ☑ Disable Lost Mode (supervised only)
- ☑ Enable Lost Mode (supervised only)
- ☑ Locate device
- ☑ Restart
- ☑ Logout current user
- ☑ Shut down
- ☑ Rotate FileVault recovery key
- ☑ BitLocker key rotation
- ☑ Run remediation

Figure 9.8 – Device actions filter

It is strictly view-only (or exportable if clicking the **Export** button). There is no functionality to drill down.

Hopefully, this is a report that is rarely required, but think of it as your insurance policy.

Automating it

This is a simple GET request, although if you watch the network in your browser, you will see that by default, the request only selects the first 25 entries, so clearly we are going to need pagination here. Follow these steps to create your script:

1. As usual, we start with the export path and URL:

```
$exportpath = "c:\temp\deviceactions.csv"
$url = "https://graph.microsoft.com/beta/deviceManagement/
remoteActionAudits"
```

2. We will use the same function as covered at the start of the chapter to grab all data:

```
$fulloutput = getallpagination -url $url
$selectedoutput = $fulloutput | select-object *
```

3. After presenting our popup, export or display the data. While it is unlikely the report will be completely empty, there is the possibility of such, so we will include the extra `if` statement and the associated output:

```
if ($result -eq [System.Windows.Forms.DialogResult]::OK) {
    if ($null -eq $selectedoutput) {
        write-host "Nothing to display"
    }
    else {
        $selectedoutput | export-csv $exportpath
    }
} elseif ($result -eq [System.Windows.Forms.
DialogResult]::Cancel) {
    if ($null -eq $selectedoutput) {
        write-host "Nothing to display"
    }
    else {
    $selectedoutput | Out-GridView
    }
}
```

This completes the recipe reviewing device actions. We will now look at the all-important audit logs.

Reviewing audit logs

In the last recipe, we covered auditing actions taken directly on devices, which, while they can have a high impact, are on an individual device level, so less likely to cause significant issues. If, however, policies are amended, deleted, or created, there is a far greater chance of issues at a larger level. To monitor for such changes, we need to delve into the audit logs.

Getting ready

To access audit logs, click on **Tenant administration | Audit logs**.

How to do it...

Once you are on the **Audit logs** page, you will be presented with a familiar report-type screen. Again, there is a powerful filter option at the top, including the ability to filter on the activity. Be warned, however, that this is a long list and does not have any search functionality built in, so make sure you are selecting the correct option when using it.

The search box allows you to find the person who made the change and you can also sort by date and activity (but not the other headers).

The export here just exports exactly what is onscreen and not the further information you can grab.

Clicking on a row shows further information about exactly what was changed, including the new and old value set, which is incredibly useful if you need to revert a change but do not have the previous value recorded anywhere (or use a backup/restore tool).

While the logs within the UI are comprehensive, they are much more manageable in Graph, which we will cover now.

Automating it

The basic view is easy to automate here as it is a basic GET request, but there is a lot more information available. So, in this script, we will amend the output to remove some unwanted settings and also provide the ability to drill down for further information:

1. We start with our export path:

    ```
    $exportpath = "c:\temp\auditlog.csv"
    ```

2. We then want to grab all results, expand the nested array called Actor, and remove some unwanted items via two select-object commands:

    ```
    $uri = "https://graph.microsoft.com/beta/deviceManagement/
    auditEvents"
    $eventsvalues = getallpagination -url $uri
    $eventsvalues = $eventsvalues | select-object * -ExpandProperty
    Actor
    $eventsvalues = $eventsvalues | select-object resources,
    userPrincipalName, displayName, category, activityType,
    activityDateTime, activityOperationType, id
    ```

3. Then, we drop these into our first array, which we will use to export or view the returned data:

    ```
    $listofevents = @()
    $counter = 0
    foreach ($event in $eventsvalues)
    {
        $counter++
        $id = $event.id
        Write-Progress -Activity ‹Processing Entries›
    -CurrentOperation $id -PercentComplete (($counter /
    $eventsvalues.count) * 100)
        $eventobject = [pscustomobject]@{
            changedItem = $event.Resources.displayName
            changedBy = $event.userPrincipalName
    ```

```
        change = $event.displayName
        changeCategory = $event.category
        activityType = $event.activityType
        activityDateTime = $event.activityDateTime
        id = $event.id
    }
    $listofevents += $eventobject
}
```

4. If we have selected export, we need a simple `export-csv` command here:

```
$listofevents | export-csv $exportpath
```

5. If we have selected view, we will present a gridview output, but we want to add the ability to look at individual items so are using the `-PassThru` parameter:

```
$selected = $listofevents | Out-GridView -PassThru
```

6. Create a new array to store this information in:

```
$selectedevents = @()
```

7. We then grab the ID of the selected item and retrieve the data associated:

```
$selectedid = $item.id
$uri = "https://graph.microsoft.com/beta/deviceManagement/
auditEvents/$selectedid"
$changedcontent = (Invoke-MgGraphRequest -Uri $uri -Method GET
-ContentType "application/json" -OutputType PSObject)
```

8. Add the item details to our array:

```
$eventobject = [pscustomobject]@{
    change = $changedcontent.displayName
    changeCategory = $changedcontent.category
    activityType = $changedcontent.activityType
    activityDateTime = $changedcontent.activityDateTime
    id = $changedcontent.id
    activity = $changedcontent.activity
    activityResult = $changedcontent.activityResult
    activityOperationType = $changedcontent.
activityOperationType
    componentName = $changedcontent.componentName
    type = $changedcontent.actor.type
    auditActorType = $changedcontent.actor.auditActorType
    userPermissions = $changedcontent.actor.userPermissions
    applicationId = $changedcontent.actor.applicationId
```

```
     applicationDisplayName = $changedcontent.actor.
applicationDisplayName
     userPrincipalName = $changedcontent.actor.userPrincipalName
     servicePrincipalName = $changedcontent.actor.
servicePrincipalName
     ipAddress = $changedcontent.actor.ipAddress
     userId = $changedcontent.actor.userId
     remoteTenantId = $changedcontent.actor.remoteTenantId
     remoteUserId = $changedcontent.actor.remoteUserId
     resourcedisplayname = $changedcontent.resource.displayName
     resourcetype = $changedcontent.resource.type
     auditResourceType = $changedcontent.resource.
auditResourceType
     resourceId = $changedcontent.resource.resourceId
}
```

The items changed within a policy could be basically unlimited so we still have one array left to present, which is modifiedproperties nested within resources.

To grab these and add them to the array, we need to make sure they all have different names, so we will use a numerical loop and append this to the name.

9. Start with setting our value:

    ```
    $i = 0
    ```

10. Loop through the array, and on each loop, add one to the value and append that to the name. Then, add this to our master array:

    ```
    foreach ($resource in $changedcontent.resources.
    modifiedproperties) {
         $name = "Name" + $i
         $oldvalue = "OldValue" + $i
         $newvalue = "NewValue" + $i
         $eventobject | Add-Member -MemberType NoteProperty -Name
    $name -Value $resource.displayName
         $eventobject | Add-Member -MemberType NoteProperty -Name
    $oldvalue -Value $resource.oldValue
         $eventobject | Add-Member -MemberType NoteProperty -Name
    $newvalue -Value $resource.newValue
         $i++
    }
    ```

11. Finally, add all looped items into the same array and output it:

```
$selectedevents += $eventobject
$selectedevents | Out-GridView
```

This gives you a fully filtered, searchable list of audit events, as well as the ability to quickly check exactly what has been changed, when, and by whom.

This completed the recipe for reviewing audit logs.

10

Looking at Reporting

After looking at the more basic monitoring in the last chapter, we will now continue to look at the out-of-the-box reports available. We will then extend that to demonstrate how to export the data to use in **Power BI** and **Azure** and look at the more advanced Windows Update reporting available using **Log Analytics**.

Reporting is an important part of any Intune environment for a **point-in-time** (**PIT**) snapshot of where you stand, especially if requested by executive members of the organization. This chapter will show you the reports available within Intune, how to run them manually, and how to automate them.

In this chapter, we will cover the following recipes:

- Checking device management reports
- Reviewing endpoint security reports
- Reviewing endpoint analytics reports
- Using Intune Data Warehouse with Power BI
- Checking Windows updates via reporting
- Expanding Windows Update reporting
- Exporting diagnostics to Azure

Technical requirements

For this chapter, you will need a modern web browser and a PowerShell code editor such as Visual Studio Code or **PowerShell Integrated Scripting Environment** (**PowerShell ISE**).

All scripts referenced can be found here: https://github.com/PacktPublishing/Microsoft-Intune-Cookbook.

If you wish to test the policies, you will need a corporate-managed device running each device platform for testing. For Linux, it will need to be running Ubuntu **Operating System** (**OS**)

Checking device management reports

We will start our review of available reports with those covering all aspects of device management.

> **Note**
> These reports are also available within the individual policies in Intune.

Getting ready

To access the device management reports, click the **Reports** button in the menu. We can find all these under **Device management**.

Now we have access to the reports, we can review each in turn.

How to do it...

Here, we will run through the large selection of reports available and the data within them.

Reviewing device compliance

We will use the following steps to review device compliance:

1. For device compliance reports, click on the **Device compliance** option and then click the **Reports** tab at the top.

   We will start by running through what each of the following reports offers and then how to run them. Apart from device compliance trends, they all have the same mechanism, so the guide to run the reports will apply to all others:

   - **Device compliance**: This displays a list of all devices and their compliance state. This will be a useful report that most executives will be interested in. You can export it, but you cannot click through to find out why devices are not compliant. It does have search functions as well as some good filtering.

   - **Device compliance trends**: This is a simple graph that displays device compliance over the last 60 days. It gives you the option to filter, but not to export or click through.

   - **Noncompliant devices and settings**: This report gives more depth to your **Device compliance** report from earlier, and in most cases is the most useful report. It displays the device name and then which particular setting(s) in the compliance policy (or policies) is causing the non-compliance. If you have a custom policy, this can look at each individual setting within it. It also reports whether the setting is simply non-compliant or if there is an error. It features filtering, search functionality, and the ability to sort on headings.

- **Devices without compliance policy**: This is a reasonably straightforward report that simply lists any devices that do not have any compliance policies assigned. This should ideally be empty, so it is always worth monitoring, more so if you have configured devices not listed as compliant (it will tell you what these are set to and how to change them). You can filter on OS and ownership, as well as sort and search on the device name. For a simple report, this should be more than sufficient.

- **Setting compliance**: This report lists all compliance settings across all policies and platforms and the compliance/non-compliance figures for each setting. As well as filtering and searching, all columns can be selected for sorting, and you can click through to find out which devices are compliant or non-compliant for each setting. This is a useful report for spotting trends across the estate, especially if you find a lot of non-compliant devices and want to look for any similarities.

- **Policy compliance**: Similar to the previous report, but rather than looking at individual settings, this looks at the policy level and shows device compliance and non-compliance per policy. Again, if you suddenly find numerous devices being blocked for non-compliance, you can use this to see which policy is triggering it. It is especially useful for estates with larger numbers of policies to help drill down which report a particular setting is in. As with the others, you can search, filter, and sort by column.

2. With the exception of **Device compliance trends**, running these reports is simply a matter of clicking the **Generate report** (or **Generate again**) button.

    It can take a few minutes to process, but the portal will inform you when the report is ready.

3. For the **Device compliance trends** report, you simply click the **Refresh** button to run it.

We have now reviewed and created our device compliance reports.

Checking device configuration

Now, we can look at the device configuration report to check the status of the policies assigned:

1. This report is accessed by clicking **Reports**, then **Device configuration**, and then the **Reports** tab at the top. Then, click on **Profile configuration status**.

2. Click **Generate report**, or click **Generate again** if you have previously run the report.

3. Once generated, you will receive this notification:

Figure 10.1 – Report success notification

This report displays a list of all profiles across operating systems, as well as a count of each status for every profile showing **Success**, **Error**, or **Conflict** totals for the profiles.

As well as exporting, you can filter on OS and profile type, as well as the ability to search on the profile name or sort on any header. Sorting is especially useful for spotting any trends in conflicting policies or policies with errors. Those with large success figures are of lesser concern.

> **Tip**
> None of the rows can be clicked on, so there is no way to drill down from within this report; it is view only.

That covers device configuration. We can now look at Group Policy analytics.

Reviewing Group Policy analytics

This report is used alongside **Group policy analytics**, as covered in *Chapter 2*, and simply displays the output of all of your imported group policies and the status of the settings within them. The **Summary** screen initially displayed will give an overview of the settings detected and their readiness for importing into Intune.

Follow these instructions to create your report:

1. To access it, navigate to **Reports** and then **Group policy analytics**. Once you are there, click the **Reports** tab and click **Group policy migration readiness**.

2. Once you are in the report, click **Generate** or **Generate again**, depending on whether you have run this before.

3. After the report has been generated, as well as the usual **Export** button, you have a useful overview and a fairly powerful filter:

Figure 10.2 – Group Policy analytics filter

You can also search on just about anything, as well as sort on each header.

Nothing can be clicked through here, but this report gives us an overview of what can and cannot be migrated. To perform any further steps, you would need to go back to the **Group policy analytics** page within **Devices**.

While bulk importing settings is never the best approach, this report will at least give an indication of any settings that may need to be reviewed and either replaced or configured using an alternative method such as policy ingestion, custom policy, or PowerShell scripting:

Setting Name ↑↓	Group Policy Setti... ↑↓	Migration Readiness ↑↓	Min OS Version ↑↓	Scope ↑↓	Profile Type ↑↓
Choose drive encryptio...	Windows Components/...	Ready for migration	15063	Computer	Device configuration: All
Choose drive encryptio...	Windows Components/...	Ready for migration	15063	Computer	Device configuration: All
Choose drive encryptio...	Windows Components/...	Ready for migration	15063	Computer	Device configuration: All
Choose drive encryptio...	Windows Components/...	Ready for migration	15063	Computer	Device configuration: All
Choose drive encryptio...	Windows Components/...	Not supported	0	Computer	Not supported
Choose drive encryptio...	Windows Components/...	Not supported	0	Computer	Not supported
Choose drive encryptio...	Windows Components/...	Not supported	0	Computer	Not supported
Choose drive encryptio...	Windows Components/...	Not supported	0	Computer	Not supported
Do not keep history of r...	Start Menu and Taskbar	Ready for migration	17755	Computer	Device configuration: All
Turn off File History	Windows Components/...	Ready for migration	18362	Computer	Device configuration: All

Figure 10.3 – Analytics report output

We have now reviewed the Group Policy analytics reports and can look at what is available for co-managed devices.

Cloud-attached devices

The **Co-Management Eligibility** and **Co-Managed Workloads** reports are only for environments currently using Configuration Manager and looking at co-management.

You can find out more about co-management here:

https://learn.microsoft.com/en-us/mem/configmgr/comanage/overview

To access these reports, within the Intune portal, navigate to **Reports | Cloud Attached Devices** and then click on the **Reports** tab.

Now, we can look at the content of these reports.

Co-Management Eligibility

This report shows the status of cloud-attached devices and whether they are eligible for co-management.

Run the report by clicking **Generate report** or **Generate again**.

Once run, this will show basic details about the devices and the eligibility status of each one. You can filter, export, search, and sort on the headers, as with the other reports.

Co-Managed Workloads

When configuring co-management, you can select which workloads are handled by Intune and which workloads Configuration Manager handles.

Running this report will list your devices and which workloads are configured on a per-device basis. This is a useful troubleshooting tool should you encounter any issues.

As with the previous report, click **Generate Report** or **Generate Again**.

As with the **Co-Management Eligibility** report, there is a powerful filter to quickly check for individual settings. You can only search and sort by device name and device ID, however, so use the filters instead.

That completes our overview of the information available in device management reports and how to run them. We can now look at how to automate these.

Automating reports

After learning about these reports in the GUI, we can now move on to automating them.

Reviewing device compliance

As with the *How to do it…* section, there are two different approaches here: one for **Device compliance trends** and one for the other reports.

As the **Device compliance trends** report is a more graphical experience, automating it will just produce numerical output that does not offer any value over the other reports available here, so we will concentrate on automating those as they all have a similar configuration.

The other reports all use a very similar method underneath, so we can get more clever here and have them all within the same script (you can, of course, split them if needed).

Some of these code blocks have been shortened for brevity. You can find the full script at the following link: `https://github.com/PacktPublishing/Microsoft-Intune-Cookbook/blob/main/Chapter-10/compliance-reports.ps1`.

Follow these steps to make your master report builder:

1. We start with the output path as usual:

    ```
    $exportpath = "c:\temp\userenrollmentfailures.csv"
    ```

2. Next, we are going to create an array with the different reports and their Graph API name. We use this in an Out-GridView cmdlet to select the value:

    ```
    $reporttypes = @()
        $reporttypes += "DeviceCompliance"
        $reporttypes += "NoncompliantDevicesAndSettings"
        $reporttypes += "DevicesWithoutCompliancePolicy"
        $reporttypes += "SettingComplianceAggReport"
        $reporttypes += "PolicyComplianceAggReport"

    $selectedreport = $reporttypes | Out-GridView -PassThru -Title
    "Select Report"
    ```

3. We add the selected array object to the full policy name:

    ```
    $fullreport = $selectedreport + "_00000000-0000-0000-0000-
    000000000001"
    ```

4. Now we have our policy name, we need to send a POST request to generate the report:

    ```
    $generateurl = "https://graph.microsoft.com/beta/
    deviceManagement/reports/cachedReportConfigurations"
            $json = @"
            {
                "filter": "",
                "id": "$fullreport",
                "metadata": null,
                "orderBy": [
                    "PolicyName asc"
                ],
                "select": []
            }
    "@
    Invoke-MgGraphRequest -Method POST -Uri $generateurl -Body $json
    -ContentType "application/json"
    ```

    As you can see, we use the ID to tell Graph which report to create.

5. We do not want to grab our results until the report is ready, so we run a GET request against a URL populated with the ID:

```
$url = "https://graph.microsoft.com/beta/deviceManagement/
reports/cachedReportConfigurations('$fullreport')"
```

6. We are looking for a status of Completed, so we grab the output and use a while loop to wait for the output to match:

```
$reportcheck = (Invoke-MgGraphRequest -uri $url -Method Get
-OutputType PSObject).status
while ($reportcheck -ne "Completed") {
    $reportcheck = (Invoke-MgGraphRequest -uri $url -Method Get
-OutputType PSObject).status
    Start-Sleep -Seconds 5
}
```

7. Now we can continue to grab the data, which uses the same format as the last chapter. We need to grab the output into a text file and, due to pagination, loop through to grab all values.

Before doing so, the JSON for each POST command is slightly different, so we are using the SWITCH command within PowerShell to check the output from the earlier selection and populate it accordingly:

```
switch ($selectedreport) {
    "DeviceCompliance" {
        $jsonselection = @"
        "Select": [
            "DeviceName",
            "ComplianceState"
        ],
"@
    }
    "NoncompliantDevicesAndSettings" {
        $jsonselection = @"
        "Select": [
            "DeviceName",
            "SettingName"
        ],
"@
    }
    "DevicesWithoutCompliancePolicy" {
        $jsonselection = @"
        "Select": [
            "DeviceId"
        ],
```

```
"@
        }
        "SettingComplianceAggReport" {
            $jsonselection = @"
            "Select": [
            ],
"@
        }
        "PolicyComplianceAggReport" {
            $jsonselection = @"
            "Select": [
            ],
"@
        }
    }
```

8. We then use this data to populate our final JSON:

```
$reportjson = @"
{
    "filter": "",
    "Id": "$fullreport",
    "OrderBy": [],
    "Search": "",
$jsonselection
    "Skip": 0,
    "Top": 50
}
"@
```

9. Grab the first set of results into a `.txt` file and then re-ingest it:

```
$tempfilepath = $env:TEMP + "\compliance-report.txt"
Invoke-MgGraphRequest -Method POST -Uri $reporturl -Body
$reportjson -ContentType "application/json" -OutputFilePath
$tempfilepath
$parsedData = get-content $tempfilepath | ConvertFrom-Json
$fullvalues = $parsedData.Values
```

10. Now, count the number of rows so that we can loop through accordingly:

```
$allrows = $parsedData.TotalRowCount
```

11. Set our variable and loop until we hit our total. We are doing the same grab and retrieve, only setting a filename with a number at the end to avoid overwriting the original file:

```
$n = 0
while ($n -lt $allrows) {
    $n += 50
    $tempfilepath2 = $env:TEMP + "\compliancereport-$n.txt"
    $json = @"
{
    "filter": "",
    "Id": "$fullreport",
    "OrderBy": [],
    "Search": "",
$jsonselection
    "skip": $n,
    "top": 50
}
"@
    Invoke-MgGraphRequest -Method POST -Uri $reporturl
-Body $json -ContentType "application/json" -OutputFilePath
$tempfilepath2
    $tempdata = get-content $tempfilepath2 | ConvertFrom-Json
    $fullvalues += $tempdata.Values
}
```

12. As we need to create a legible array and have different JSON requests, we need to use another SWITCH command to populate our array depending on the selection:

```
switch ($selectedreport) {
    "DeviceCompliance" {
        $outputarray = @()
        foreach ($value in $fullvalues) {
            $objectdetails = [pscustomobject]@{
                DeviceName = $value[2]
            }

            $outputarray += $objectdetails
        }
    }
    "NoncompliantDevicesAndSettings" {
        $outputarray = @()
        foreach ($value in $fullvalues) {
            $objectdetails = [pscustomobject]@{
                DeviceName = $value[1]
            }
```

```powershell
            $outputarray += $objectdetails
        }
    }
    "DevicesWithoutCompliancePolicy" {
        $outputarray = @()
        foreach ($value in $fullvalues) {
            $objectdetails = [pscustomobject]@{
                DeviceId = $value[1]
            }
            $outputarray += $objectdetails
        }
    }
    "SettingComplianceAggReport" {
        $outputarray = @()
        foreach ($value in $fullvalues) {
            $objectdetails = [pscustomobject]@{
            setting = $value[3]
            }
            $outputarray += $objectdetails
        }
    }
    "PolicyComplianceAggReport" {
        $outputarray = @()
        foreach ($value in $fullvalues) {
            $objectdetails = [pscustomobject]@{
            }
            $outputarray += $objectdetails
        }
    }
}
```

13. Then, as with all previous scripts, we send a popup, which is available in the main script within the GitHub repository. Depending on the response, either display or export the report:

```powershell
if ($result -eq [System.Windows.Forms.DialogResult]::OK) {
    # Export code here
    $outputarray | export-csv $exportpath -NoTypeInformation
} elseif ($result -eq [System.Windows.Forms.
DialogResult]::Cancel) {
    # View code here
    $outputarray | Out-GridView
}
```

14. Finally, we will clean up our files:

```
Remove-Item $tempfilepath
$allrows = $parsedData.TotalRowCount
$n = 0
while ($n -lt $allrows) {
    $n += 50
    $tempfilepath2 = $env:TEMP + "\compliancereport-$n.txt"
    Remove-Item $tempfilepath2
}
```

If selecting to view the output, an example would be this:

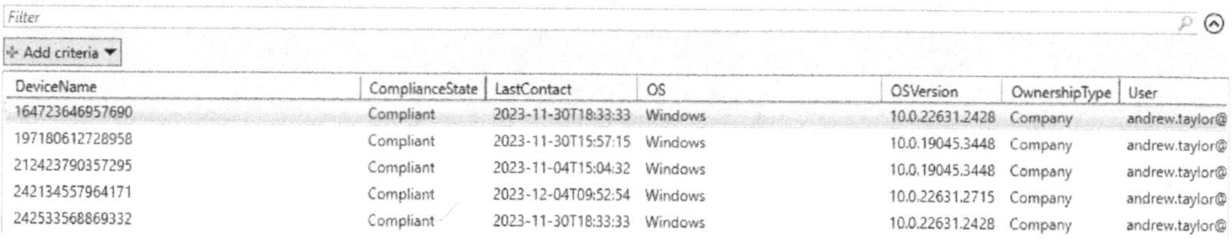

DeviceName	ComplianceState	LastContact	OS	OSVersion	OwnershipType	User
164723646957690	Compliant	2023-11-30T18:33:33	Windows	10.0.22631.2428	Company	andrew.taylor@
197180612728958	Compliant	2023-11-30T15:57:15	Windows	10.0.19045.3448	Company	andrew.taylor@
212423790357295	Compliant	2023-11-04T15:04:32	Windows	10.0.19045.3448	Company	andrew.taylor@
242134557964171	Compliant	2023-12-04T09:52:54	Windows	10.0.22631.2715	Company	andrew.taylor@
242533568869332	Compliant	2023-11-30T18:33:33	Windows	10.0.22631.2428	Company	andrew.taylor@

Figure 10.4 – Device compliance report

That completes the script for retrieving device compliance reports; we can now look at device configuration.

Reviewing device configuration

This one is very similar to the previous report, but as it is a single report, we do not need the array and associated `SWITCH` query. Follow these steps to automate the device configuration report:

1. First, we start with the `.csv` file:

```
$exportpath = "c:\temp\profileconfigurationreport.csv"
```

2. Next, set the report name and populate the URL:

```
$selectedreport = "ConfigurationPolicyAggregate"
$fullreport = $selectedreport + "_00000000-0000-0000-0000-
000000000001"
$generateurl = "https://graph.microsoft.com/beta/
deviceManagement/reports/cachedReportConfigurations"
```

3. Set the JSON and generate the report:

```
$json = @"
{
    "filter": "",
    "id": "$fullreport",
```

```
            "metadata": null,
            "orderBy": [
            ],
            "select": [
                "PolicyName",
                "UnifiedPolicyType",
                "UnifiedPolicyPlatformType",
                "NumberOfCompliantDevices",
                "NumberOfNonCompliantOrErrorDevices",
                "NumberOfConflictDevices"
                ]
        }
"@
Invoke-MgGraphRequest -Method POST -Uri $generateurl -Body $json
-ContentType "application/json"
```

4. As before, we need to run a GET request and wait for the status to be marked as Completed:

```
$url = "https://graph.microsoft.com/beta/deviceManagement/
reports/cachedReportConfigurations('$fullreport')"
$reportcheck = (Invoke-MgGraphRequest -uri $url -Method Get
-OutputType PSObject).status
while ($reportcheck -ne "Completed") {
    $reportcheck = (Invoke-MgGraphRequest -uri $url -Method Get
-OutputType PSObject).status
    Start-Sleep -Seconds 5
}
```

5. Once that is done, we run our command to grab the data, export to text, import back from JSON and count, then loop through the counted objects:

```
$url = "https://graph.microsoft.com/beta/deviceManagement/
reports/cachedReportConfigurations('$fullreport')"
$reportcheck = (Invoke-MgGraphRequest -uri $url -Method Get
-OutputType PSObject).status
while ($reportcheck -ne "Completed") {
    $reportcheck = (Invoke-MgGraphRequest -uri $url -Method Get
-OutputType PSObject).status
    Start-Sleep -Seconds 5
}
$reporturl = "https://graph.microsoft.com/beta/deviceManagement/
reports/getCachedReport"
$reportjson = @"
{
    "filter": "",
    "Id": "$fullreport",
```

```
        "OrderBy": [],
        "Search": "",
        "Select": [
            "PolicyName",
            "UnifiedPolicyType",
            "UnifiedPolicyPlatformType",
            "NumberOfCompliantDevices",
            "NumberOfNonCompliantOrErrorDevices",
            "NumberOfConflictDevices"
            ],
        "Skip": 0,
        "Top": 50
}
"@
$tempfilepath = $env:TEMP + "\configreport.txt"
Invoke-MgGraphRequest -Method POST -Uri $reporturl -Body
$reportjson -ContentType "application/json" -OutputFilePath
$tempfilepath
$parsedData = get-content $tempfilepath | ConvertFrom-Json
$fullvalues = $parsedData.Values
$allrows = $parsedData.TotalRowCount
$n = 0
while ($n -lt $allrows) {
    $n += 50
    $tempfilepath2 = $env:TEMP + "\configreport-$n.txt"
    $json = @"
{
    "filter": "",
    "Id": "$fullreport",
    "OrderBy": [],
    "Search": "",
    "Select": [
        "PolicyName",
        "UnifiedPolicyType",
        "UnifiedPolicyPlatformType",
        "NumberOfCompliantDevices",
        "NumberOfNonCompliantOrErrorDevices",
        "NumberOfConflictDevices"
        ],
    "skip": $n,
    "top": 50
}
"@
    Invoke-MgGraphRequest -Method POST -Uri $reporturl
```

```
-Body $json -ContentType "application/json" -OutputFilePath
$tempfilepath2
    $tempdata = get-content $tempfilepath2 | ConvertFrom-Json
    $fullvalues += $tempdata.Values


}
```

6. Now we have our array of values, we need to add them to an object so that we can tidy it to view or export:

```
$outputarray = @()
foreach ($value in $fullvalues) {
    $objectdetails = [pscustomobject]@{
        PolicyName = $value[3]
        PolicyType = $value[5]
        Platform = $value[4]
        CompliantDevices = $value[0]
        NonCompliantDevices = $value[2]
        ConflictDevices = $value[1]
    }
    $outputarray += $objectdetails
}
```

7. After running the popup, either export or display the content:

```
if ($result -eq [System.Windows.Forms.DialogResult]::OK) {
    # Export code here
    $outputarray | export-csv $exportpath -NoTypeInformation
} elseif ($result -eq [System.Windows.Forms.
DialogResult]::Cancel) {
    # View code here
    $outputarray | Out-GridView
}
```

8. Finally, clean everything up:

```
Remove-Item $tempfilepath
$allrows = $parsedData.TotalRowCount
$n = 0
while ($n -lt $allrows) {
    $n += 50
    $tempfilepath2 = $env:TEMP + "\configreport-$n.txt"
    Remove-Item $tempfilepath2
}
```

An example output for this report would look like this:

PolicyName	PolicyType	Platform	CompliantDevices	NonCompliantDevices	ConflictDevices
Audacity	Windows10	Windows10	7	3	0
Background and Lockscreen	Windows10	Windows10	0	10	0
Base Android Config	AndroidForWork	AndroidForWork	1	0	0
Baseline Device Restrictions	iOS	IOS	0	0	1
Baseline iOS Features	iOS	IOS	1	0	0
Browser Homepage	Windows10	Windows10	10	0	0
Cloud Site List	Windows10	Windows10	20	0	0
Cloud Trust	Windows10	Windows10	20	0	0
Command Prompt	Windows10	Windows10	7	3	0

Figure 10.5 – Device configuration report

Now we have completed automating our device configuration reports, we can look at Group Policy analytics.

Reviewing Group Policy analytics

This works in exactly the same way as the previous script, so we will just mention the differences in JSON and URL (the full script is in the GitHub repository):

https://github.com/PacktPublishing/Microsoft-Intune-Cookbook/blob/
main/Chapter-10/group-policy-analytics.ps1

Follow these steps to automate your report generation:

1. First, we need to set the path:

   ```
   $exportpath = "c:\temp\gpanalyticsreport.csv"
   ```

2. Set the report name:

   ```
   $selectedreport = "GPAnalyticsSettingMigrationReadiness"
   ```

3. Add that to the full report name:

   ```
   $fullreport = $selectedreport + "_00000000-0000-0000-0000-
   000000000001"
   ```

4. Run the initial POST request to generate the data output:

   ```
   $generateurl = "https://graph.microsoft.com/beta/
   deviceManagement/reports/cachedReportConfigurations"
           $json = @"
   ```

```
        {
            "filter": "",
            "id": "$fullreport",
            "metadata": null,
            "orderBy": [
            ],
            "select": [
                "SettingName",
                "SettingCategory",
                "MigrationReadiness",
                "OSVersion",
                "Scope",
                "ProfileType"
            ]
        }
"@
```

5. Using the same JSON, we wait for completion and then loop through all returned rows, incrementing 50 at a time.

6. Finally, we need to add these to our array:

```
$outputarray = @()
foreach ($value in $fullvalues) {
    $objectdetails = [pscustomobject]@{
        SettingName = $value[5]
        SettingCategory = $value[4]
        MigrationReadiness = $value[0]
        OSVersion = $value[1]
        Scope = $value[3]
        ProfileType = $value[2]
    }
    $outputarray += $objectdetails
}
```

7. Then, we do the usual display/export and cleanup:

```
if ($result -eq [System.Windows.Forms.DialogResult]::OK) {
    # Export code here
    $outputarray | export-csv $exportpath -NoTypeInformation
} elseif ($result -eq [System.Windows.Forms.
DialogResult]::Cancel) {
    # View code here
```

```
        $outputarray | Out-GridView
    }
    Remove-Item $tempfilepath
    $allrows = $parsedData.TotalRowCount
    $n = 0
    while ($n -lt $allrows) {
        $n += 50
        $tempfilepath2 = $env:TEMP + "\gpanalytics-$n.txt"
        Remove-Item $tempfilepath2
    }
```

The output of this script should look like this:

SettingName	SettingCategory	MigrationReadiness	OSVersi...	Scope	ProfileType	
Choose drive encryption method and cipher strength...	Windows Components/BitLocker Drive E...	Supported	15063	Computer	DeviceConfiguration: All	
Choose drive encryption method and cipher strength...	Windows Components/BitLocker Drive E...	Supported	15063	Computer	DeviceConfiguration: All	
Choose drive encryption method and cipher strength...	Windows Components/BitLocker Drive E...	Supported	15063	Computer	DeviceConfiguration: All	
Choose drive encryption method and cipher strength...	Windows Components/BitLocker Drive E...	Supported	15063	Computer	DeviceConfiguration: All	
Choose drive encryption method and cipher strength...	Windows Components/BitLocker Drive E...	Unsupported	0	Computer	Not Supported	
Choose drive encryption method and cipher strength...	Windows Components/BitLocker Drive E...	Unsupported	0	Computer	Not Supported	
Choose drive encryption method and cipher strength...	Windows Components/BitLocker Drive E...	Unsupported	0	Computer	Not Supported	
Choose drive encryption method and cipher strength...	Windows Components/BitLocker Drive E...	Unsupported	0	Computer	Not Supported	
Do not keep history of recently opened documents	Start Menu and Taskbar	Supported	17755	Computer	DeviceConfiguration: All	
Turn off File History	Windows Components/File History	Supported	18362	Computer	DeviceConfiguration: All	

Figure 10.6 – Group Policy analytics output

That completes the automation of the Group Policy analytics report. We will now look at cloud-attached devices.

Cloud-attached devices

Both the **Co-Management Eligibility** and **Co-Managed Workloads** reports use the same basic functionality as the previous recipes, so we will look only at the URL, JSON, and output array here. The full scripts are available on GitHub:

- https://github.com/PacktPublishing/Microsoft-Intune-Cookbook/blob/main/Chapter-10/co-managed-workloads.ps1

- https://github.com/PacktPublishing/Microsoft-Intune-Cookbook/blob/main/Chapter-10/co-management-eligibility.ps1

Co-Management Eligibility

We will start with the **Co-Management Eligibility** report.

1. First, this is the code for the URL and required variables:

```
$selectedreport = "ComanagementEligibilityTenantAttachedDevices"
$fullreport = $selectedreport + "_00000000-0000-0000-0000-
000000000001"
$generateurl = "https://graph.microsoft.com/beta/
deviceManagement/reports/cachedReportConfigurations"
```

2. The JSON looks like this:

```
$json = @"
{
    "filter": "",
    "id": "$fullreport",
    "metadata": null,
    "orderBy": [
    ],
    "select": [
        "DeviceName",
        "DeviceId",
        "Status",
        "OSDescription",
        "OSVersion"
        ]
}
"@
```

3. The output array looks like this:

```
$outputarray = @()
foreach ($value in $fullvalues) {
    $objectdetails = [pscustomobject]@{
        DeviceID = $value[0]
        DeviceName = $value[1]
        OSDescription = $value[2]
        OSVersion = $value[3]
        Status = $value[4]
    }
    $outputarray += $objectdetails
}
```

Now, we can look at the **Co-Managed Workloads** report for cloud-attached devices.

Co-Managed Workloads

These extracts will differentiate between the **Co-Management Eligibility** and **Co-Managed Workloads** report.

1. For this report, this is the code for the URL and variables:

```
$selectedreport = "ComanagedDeviceWorkloads"
$fullreport = $selectedreport + "_00000000-0000-0000-0000-
000000000001"
$generateurl = "https://graph.microsoft.com/beta/
deviceManagement/reports/cachedReportConfigurations"
```

2. The JSON looks like this:

```
$json = @"
{
    "filter": "",
    "id": "$fullreport",
    "metadata": null,
    "orderBy": [
    ],
    "select": [
        "DeviceName",
        "DeviceId",
        "CompliancePolicy",
        "ResourceAccess",
        "DeviceConfiguration",
        "WindowsUpdateforBusiness",
        "EndpointProtection",
        "ModernApps",
        "OfficeApps"
        ]
}
"@
```

3. This is the code for the output array:

```
$outputarray = @()
foreach ($value in $fullvalues) {
    $objectdetails = [pscustomobject]@{
        CompliancePolicy = $value[0]
        DeviceConfiguration = $value[1]
        DeviceID = $value[2]
        DeviceName = $value[3]
        EndpointProtection = $value[4]
```

```
          ModernApps = $value[5]
          OfficeApps = $value[6]
          ResourceAccess = $value[7]
          WindowsUpdateforBusiness = $value[8]
      }
      $outputarray += $objectdetails
  }
```

That completes the automation of cloud-attached device reports and device management reports. Now, we will look at endpoint security reports.

Reviewing endpoint security reports

We now move on to look at all-important security reports. Even if you do not monitor these yourself, you may have security teams or a **security operations center** (**SOC**) that need to keep an eye on the security status of your machines. Ideally, everything monitored here will be picked up in a compliance policy, but it is always useful to have reports to fall back on.

How to do it...

All endpoint security report references in this recipe are available under **Reports** and then **Endpoint security**.

Once we have accessed the **Reports** menu in the UI, we can run through each report.

Reviewing Microsoft Defender Antivirus

Within the **Endpoint security reports** section, click on **Microsoft Defender Antivirus** and then click the **Reports** tab, where you will find our two available reports. Here, we will cover them both in further detail.

Antivirus agent status

This report shows the full status of all aspects of the antivirus agent on all devices across your estate. You can use it to quickly spot any at-risk machines, find out exactly which component is at fault, and remediate the issue.

To generate the report, click **Generate report** or **Generate again**.

After running the report, you have a useful chart that should hopefully be mostly, if not all, green to show the status of your devices.

There is a good filter, as well as basic search functionality and the ability to sort by header:

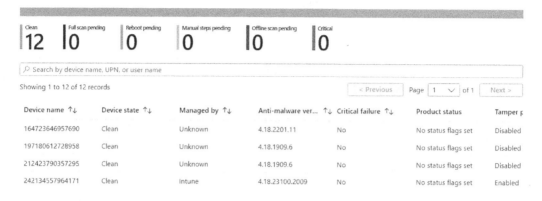

Figure 10.7 – Antivirus report

> **Important note**
> There is a lot of data to process with a large scroll bar at the bottom, so make sure it is all checked, especially if a device is reporting issues.

Detected malware

This report lists any infected devices (or devices that have previously been infected), as well as details about the malware found and the number of instances.

As usual, click **Generate report** or **Generate again**.

After running, you have filter, search, and sort by header options, and a useful graph to show the overall status. This report is a pretty critical one that allows you to keep on top of infected devices or repeat offenders.

After reviewing antivirus reports, the next logical step is firewall reports.

Reviewing firewall reports

The firewall report shows the status of Windows Firewall across your devices. It is a simple but useful report. Follow these steps to generate the report:

1. To access this report, click **Firewall** and then click **MDM Firewall status for Windows 10 and later**. You will notice there are no tabs within this report.

2. Click **Generate report** or **Generate again**.

After generating, you will see a similar screen to before with a chart showing the overall status, a filter that is powerful enough, and the ability to search and sort on any column. Realistically you will only be interested in those with the firewall disabled so that you can either filter or sort; either will have the same ultimate result.

By following these instructions, we have generated and reviewed endpoint security reports. Now, we can look at automating them.

Automating the reports

Endpoint security reports, especially antivirus reports, are often requested for a security review of the tenant, therefore automating them is a good option. We can now run through how to do so.

Reviewing Microsoft Defender Antivirus

Both Microsoft Defender Antivirus and Firewall reports use the same format as our previous scripts. The full content is available on GitHub; as with the others, we will just list the URLs, JSON, and arrays here.

Now, we can look at the individual reports.

Antivirus agent status

You can find the full script on GitHub here, as the code blocks shown next have been shortened:

`https://github.com/PacktPublishing/Microsoft-Intune-Cookbook/blob/main/Chapter-10/antivirus-status.ps1`

We start with the antivirus agent status report to check for any devices without active antivirus softwar:.

1. First, we set the report name:

    ```
    $selectedreport = "DefenderAgents"
    $fullreport = $selectedreport + "_00000000-0000-0000-0000-
    000000000001"
    ```

2. Then, we configure the URL, which in this case looks like this:

    ```
    $generateurl = "https://graph.microsoft.com/beta/
    deviceManagement/reports/cachedReportConfigurations"
    ```

3. Next, we add the JSON to tell Graph which fields we want to retrieve:

    ```
    $json = @"
    {
        "filter": "",
        "id": "$fullreport",
        "metadata": null,
        "orderBy": [
    ```

```
        ],
        "select": [
            "DeviceName",
            "DeviceState",
            "_ManagedBy",
            "AntiMalwareVersion"
            ]

    }
"@
```

4. We also want to configure the array to return the results in a readable format:

```
$outputarray = @()
foreach ($value in $fullvalues) {
    $objectdetails = [pscustomobject]@{
        _ManagedBy = $value[0]
        DeviceName = $value[4]
        DeviceState = $value[6]
    }
    $outputarray += $objectdetails

}
```

Detected malware

Now, we can look at the **Detected malware** report. Again, the full script can be found on GitHub: https://github.com/PacktPublishing/Microsoft-Intune-Cookbook/blob/main/Chapter-10/detected-malware.ps1.

1. First, as with the previous report, set the ID and URL:

```
$selectedreport = "Malware"
$fullreport = $selectedreport + "_00000000-0000-0000-0000-
000000000001"
$generateurl = "https://graph.microsoft.com/beta/
deviceManagement/reports/cachedReportConfigurations"
```

2. Set the JSON to retrieve from Graph:

```
$json = @"
{
    "filter": "",
    "id": "$fullreport",
    "metadata": null,
    "orderBy": [
    ],
    "select": [
```

```
            "DeviceName",
            "_ManagedBy",
            "DetectionCount",
            "ExecutionState",
            "Severity",
            "MalwareName",
            "MalwareCategory",
            "State"
            ]
        }
    "@
```

3. Set the output array:

```
$outputarray = @()
foreach ($value in $fullvalues) {
    $objectdetails = [pscustomobject]@{
        _ManagedBy = $value[0]
        DetectionCount = $value[1]
        DeviceName = $value[2]
        ExecutionState = $value[3]
        MalwareCategory = $value[4]
        MalwareName = $value[5]
        Severity = $value[6]
        State = $value[7]
    }
    $outputarray += $objectdetails
}
```

Now, we can move on to do this for the firewall report now.

Firewall report

As with all of the other reports, the report uses the same structure, and the full script is available on GitHub:

https://github.com/PacktPublishing/Microsoft-Intune-Cookbook/blob/main/Chapter-10/firewall-status.ps1

For brevity, we will just run through the differences her:.

1. For this, we need to first set the report name and URL:

```
$selectedreport = "FirewallStatus"
$fullreport = $selectedreport + "_00000000-0000-0000-0000-
000000000001"
```

```
$generateurl = "https://graph.microsoft.com/beta/
deviceManagement/reports/cachedReportConfigurations"
```

2. This is the different JSON we will be using:

```
$json = @"
{
    "filter": "",
    "id": "$fullreport",
    "metadata": null,
    "orderBy": [
    ],
    "select": [
        "DeviceName",
        "FirewallStatus",
        "_ManagedBy",
        "UPN"
        ]
}
"@
```

3. Finally, the output array will look like this:

```
$outputarray = @()
foreach ($value in $fullvalues) {
    $objectdetails = [pscustomobject]@{
        _ManagedBy = $value[0]
        DeviceName = $value[1]
        FirewallStatus = $value[2]
        UPN = $value[3]
    }
    $outputarray += $objectdetails
}
```

By following these steps, we have automated the creation and output of endpoint security reports.

Reviewing endpoint analytics reports

Endpoint analytics is a veritable treasure trove of information that displays not only information for your estate but also a baseline against similar-sized organizations.

As all of the endpoint analytics reports are display-and-export-type reports, which we have covered in the previous recipes in this chapter, rather than providing instructions on how to run them, we will instead cover what each individual report does and how it can help you.

We will then create a single automation script to grab the output from any of the reports quickly and easily.

Getting ready

To find these reports, navigate to **Reports** and click on **Endpoint analytics**.

Click on **Settings**, and make sure the **Intune data collection policy** setting is showing as **Connected**.

Now that we know where to find our endpoint analytics reports, we can run through what they all display.

Startup performance

This selection of reports looks at the startup performance, from pressing the button to a usable desktop. It then reviews this against an industry baseline to give an initial representation of how your devices and configuration compare.

Within here, you can drill down on:

- **Model performance**: All models within the tenant (minimum of 10 devices).
- **Device performance**: All devices within the tenant. This and the model performance also include drive type, which is an excellent way of viewing both the performance increases with an **Solid State Drive/nonvolatile memory express (SSD/NVMe)** compared with an old spinning HDD (to help with any business cases), but it can also help spot any drives that may be beginning to fail.
- **Startup processes**: A list of all discovered startup processes, including the number of devices discovered and how much time they are adding to the startup.
- **Restart frequency**: This is a particularly useful one as it lists the cause of restarts as well as trends over the last 30 days. If you release a software or driver update, this would be a good place to check for any spikes in reboots that could be caused by that. You could also look at **Anomaly Detection** in **Advanced Endpoint analytics**, which we cover in *Chapter 14*.

After reviewing startup performance, we can now review application reliability.

Application reliability

This set of reports digs down to the application level and looks at application crashes. The initial screen shows the reliability score compared to the baseline, as well as the main offenders over the last 14 days.

The reports include the following:

- **App performance**: A look at all discovered applications, how many devices use them (and for how long), and then how many times they have crashed in the last 14 days. This is a useful report as it includes usage figures, so an application that has crashed often but is heavily used is less of a concern than one that is rarely used but crashes each time.

- **Model performance**: This looks at application performance per device model to look for trends in application crashes that could potentially be linked to hardware issues, particularly useful for your more intensive apps such as **Computer-Aided Design (CAD)** or graphical packages.

- **Device performance**: This drills down even further to the device level and lists application crashes per machine, including the health status of the device itself. You may find this one useful when a user complains about device performance or application crashes. If you have one device with statistics that are considerably worse than others, it could also point to hardware issues.

- **OS versions performance**: A useful report when upgrading OS. Use this to monitor performance after deploying to your preview and pilot rings to see if there is any obvious performance degradation before deploying to the larger estate. Similarly, a noticeable performance improvement may help when convincing users to upgrade.

Our next reports to review are **Work from anywhere** reports.

Work from anywhere

These reports mainly look at the cloud management of your devices, whether they are Intune joined (or co-managed) or Autopilot builds. However, there is one important report here that displays the readiness of your devices for Windows 11, looking at all of the hardware requirements.

The reports include:

- **Model performance**: A count of each model and the results of the cloud management and Windows compatibility. This is a quick way to review which of your models will not support Windows 11 and to obtain a figure of the number of devices that will need replacing. You can obtain exact numbers in the Windows report.

- **Device performance**: As per the previous report, but at the individual device level. This is probably of less use, though, as the next reports look at the settings individually.

- **Windows**: An all-important report that looks at every discovered device and lists compatibility with Windows 11. As well as a pass/fail status, it will also list the reason for the failure in case it is something that can be more easily resolved. The key columns here are the last two, so make sure you scroll across.

- **Cloud identity**: This will show devices and their management type (Microsoft Entra Joined or Microsoft Entra hybrid joined). Probably less useful than other reports.

- **Cloud management**: This displays the management tool for devices (Intune, Configuration Manager) as well as the compliance policy assigned. For a split environment, it can be a quick way to grab metrics or for basic troubleshooting.

- **Cloud provisioning**: This shows your devices and the Autopilot details associated. It does give slightly more information than in the **Device Enrollment** screen and has filtering, which may be useful.

That completes the **Work from anywhere** reports. We can now look at **Resource performance** reports.

Resource performance

These two reports are for Windows 365 Cloud PCs to check how your assigned devices are running and whether you may need to increase the device spec with a higher license, or if the devices are underutilized, save money and run a lower license.

The available reports are as follows:

- **Model performance**: CPU and RAM score by device model. If you see one model struggling more, you may need to look at a license uplift across the estate.

- **Device performance**: This looks at each device so that you can look for any devices that may be struggling or underused and re-license as appropriate. To manage your costs, this is the one most worth keeping an eye on as you can always scale up again if required. It is often best to start with a lower spec and see how the users manage, especially as Windows 365 runs on the Microsoft network, so performance on web-based applications will be significantly improved.

After reviewing the Windows 365 **Resource performance** reports, we now have another Windows 365 report: **Remoting connection**.

Remoting connection

Again for your Windows 365 devices, this looks at performance when connecting to the cloud PC from a host machine, including the speed of the last connection, the median speed, and the overall rating.

It includes the following reports:

- **Model performance**: This shows the **round-trip time** (**RTT**) and sign-in time for cloud PCs. The RTT should not deviate significantly at the device level, so concentrate on the sign-in time in case a particular model is giving a significant drop in user experience.

- **Device performance**: This looks at the individual device level, where you may find some users have higher login requirements in terms of applications and may require a faster machine. The RTT is more useful here as it may indicate poor network connectivity from the host machine.

That completes our review of endpoint analytics reports. Now, we can look at how to automate them.

How to do it...

All of the reports in **Endpoint analytics** run automatically on loading, but we can still look at how to automate them.

Automating the reports

As mentioned earlier, all of these reports run a similar GET request, so rather than creating numerous scripts, we can concentrate on creating a single script with a simple menu to select which report to run.

The first important thing is this uses pagination, so we will again be using the `getallpagination` function as used in other scripts. Some code blocks have been shortened for brevity, therefore the full script including the function is available on GitHub at the following link: https://github.com/PacktPublishing/Microsoft-Intune-Cookbook/blob/main/Chapter-10/all-analytics-reports.ps1.

Follow these steps to create a single script for all of the reports in **Endpoint analytics**:

1. As usual, we start with the output path:

    ```
    $exportpath = "c:\temp\analytics-report.csv"
    ```

2. Then, we are going to create an array containing all available reports:

    ```
    $outputarray = @()
    $outputarray += "Startup Performance - Model Performance"
    $outputarray += "Startup Performance - Device Performance"
    $outputarray += "Startup Performance - Startup Processes"
    ```

3. Now, display the array in a `gridview` output with the all-important `-PassThru` parameter so that we can grab the output:

    ```
    $selectedreport = $outputarray | Out-GridView -Title "Select a
    report to export" -PassThru
    ```

4. Next, we need to run a `SWITCH` command on the selected report to populate the URL:

    ```
    switch ($selectedreport) {
        "Startup Performance - Model Performance" {
            $url = "https://graph.microsoft.com/beta/
    deviceManagement/userExperienceAnalyticsDevicePerformance/
    summarizeDevicePerformanceDevices(summarizeBy=microsoft.graph.
    userExperienceAnalyticsSummarizedBy>model>)
    ?dtFilter=all&`$expand=*"
        }
        "Startup Performance - Device Performance" {
            $url = "https://graph.
    microsoft.com/beta/deviceManagement/
    userExperienceAnalyticsDevicePerformance?dtFilter=all"
        }
        "Startup Performance - Startup Processes" {
            $url = "https://graph.microsoft.com/beta/
    deviceManagement/
    ```

```
userExperienceAnalyticsDeviceStartupProcessPerformance
?dtFilter=all"
    }
}
```

> **Important note**
> Watch for the $ signs in the URLs, which are escaped with the ` backtick.

5. Grab the data from the URL:

```
$allanalytics = getallpagination -url $url
```

6. After the usual popup, either display or export the report data. We are also adding some logic here to deal with empty reports:

```
if ($result -eq [System.Windows.Forms.DialogResult]::OK) {
    # Export code here
    if ($null -eq $allanalytics) {
       write-host "Nothing to display"
    }
    else {
        $allanalytics | export-csv $exportpath
    }
} elseif ($result -eq [System.Windows.Forms.
DialogResult]::Cancel) {
    # View code here
    if ($null -eq $allanalytics) {
       write-host "Nothing to display"
    }
    else {
    $allanalytics | Out-GridView
    }
}
```

That completes the automation of endpoint analytics reports.

Using Intune Data Warehouse with Power BI

Anyone experienced with Power BI will know that it is a very powerful reporting tool that adds a lot of extra functionality and the ability to customize what you can get out of the box with Intune.

Fortunately, you can use Power BI with **Intune Data Warehouse**, and, better still, there are preconfigured templates to get you started.

How to do it...

Follow these steps to configure Data Warehouse with your tenant:

1. Navigate to **Reports** and click on **Data warehouse**.

    On this screen, you can grab the URL for manual data ingestion, but in this example, we will use the preconfigured template instead.

    At the end of this section, we will include some links to useful blog posts and a video for more of a deep dive into the functionality.

2. For now, click on the **Get Power BI app** link.

3. In the **Intune Compliance (Data Warehouse)** application window, click **Get it now**.

4. This will transfer you to Power BI, and after a few minutes, it will display in your list of apps:

Figure 10.8 – Intune app

5. Click on the newly added application.

6. Now, click on **Compliance Overview**. This is using sample data, so do not be alarmed.

7. Click **Connect your data**.

8. On the **Connect to Intune Compliance (Data Warehouse)** screen, click **Next** as we do not have any parameters in this application.

9. Set the **Privacy Level** type and click **Sign in and connect**.

10. When prompted, authenticate in the pop-up window (you may need to allow popups).

    After a minute, you will see your data replace the same data

Now your data is connected, you can manipulate it as required.

The following are useful links for getting started with Power BI and Intune Data Warehouse:

*   `https://www.petervanderwoude.nl/post/super-easy-start-with-reporting-and-the-intune-data-warehouse/`

*   `https://jannikreinhard.com/2022/07/10/build-powerbi-dashboard-based-on-intune-data-warehouse/`

*   `https://www.youtube.com/watch?v=2ICPKRBIews`

By following the preceding steps, you have connected your Intune tenant to Data Warehouse.

Checking Windows updates via reporting

Windows Update reports are likely to be the most useful and most used reports within Intune, as tracking the status of Windows Updates is key to security across the estate. We will start by looking at the built-in reports, and then in the next recipe will take things further and introduce Log Analytics for finer control.

Due to the extra selections required to generate these reports, the inputs do not lend themselves to automation as it would be a similar number of textboxes and clicks to achieve the same result. Therefore, in this recipe, we will not cover automating them. If, however, this is of interest, it uses the same export/import POST requests as with many of the earlier reports here.

Getting ready

Within the Intune portal, click on **Reports**, then click **Windows updates**, and finally, click the **Reports** tab.

How to do it...

There are multiple reports available here, so we will start by looking at how to run them, and then we will cover what each report contains.

1. Select any of the reports available. In this case, we will use **Windows Feature Update Report**:

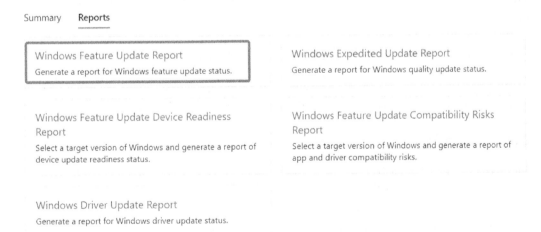

Figure 10.9 – Windows Update report options

2. In each report, you will have to make a selection to report on by clicking the blue text on the right-hand side. For this example, we need to click an update ring via the appropriate profile.

3. After making the selection, a **Generate report** button becomes available; click that.

4. You will be notified when the report is available to view.

Now we know how to run the reports, let us look at what each one displays:

- **Windows Feature Update Report**: As the name implies, when deploying feature updates such as 22H2, this will display the status of the update for all devices in the selected policy/ring.

- **Windows Expedited Update Report**: Similar to the previous report, but for **Quality updates** (if configured, as these do need additional licensing).

- **Windows Feature Update Device Readiness Report**: This report also needs additional licensing and license verification enabled, which you can find at the following link:

  `https://learn.microsoft.com/en-gb/mem/intune/protect/windows-update-compatibility-reports#prerequisites`

  Once enabled, you can select a **target OS** version, and it will report the readiness state of your devices to receive the update. This is a very useful report to use when planning updates.

- **Windows Feature Update Compatibility Risks Report**: Another extremely useful report when planning updates. This one will list any applications or drivers that are not compatible with the selected operating system. It also requires the same licensing and prerequisites as before.

- **Windows Driver Update Report**: If you are using the new driver update functionality, this will display the installation status of the selected driver across your estate.

Now we have learned what is in the built-in Windows update reports, we can look at improving this further by utilizing Log Analytics.

Expanding Windows Update reporting

While the built-in Intune reports are excellent, we can take this one step further by leveraging Log Analytics to give us further data and manipulation and real-time analytics.

Getting ready

For this recipe, we will need to create a Log Analytics workspace within Azure (there is no charge for Windows Update data, though).

How to do it...

Follow these steps to configure Windows Update for Business reports:

1. Navigate to `https://portal.azure.com` and search for **Log Analytics workspaces**.

2. Click **Create**.

3. Select your **Subscription** type and either select or create a new **Resource group** type.

4. Then, name your workspace and click **Review and Create**.

5. If all looks OK, click **Create**.

6. Back in the Azure portal, click **Monitor**.

7. Then, click on **View** under **Workbooks**.

8. Scroll down to **Insights** and select **Windows Update for Business Reports**.

9. Click **Get Started**.

10. Select your subscription and the workspace we created earlier, and then press **Save settings**.

11. Click **Save** to confirm.

12. You will be notified when this has completed.

After a few days, the workbook will contain data that you can manipulate and export.

To find out more, check out this Microsoft documentation:

`https://learn.microsoft.com/en-gb/windows/deployment/update/wufb-reports-workbook`

These steps have onboarded the tenant into Windows Update for Business reports.

Exporting diagnostics to Azure

The final recipe in this chapter also uses Azure, but this time to store Intune logs and diagnostic data in a variety of locations, listed as follows:

- A Log Analytics workspace

- Azure Blob storage

- An event hub: You can learn more about this at the following URL:

  `https://learn.microsoft.com/en-gb/azure/azure-monitor//partners?WT.mc_id=Portal-Microsoft_Azure_Monitoring`

- A partner solution: Learn more about this at the following URL:

  `https://learn.microsoft.com/en-us/azure/partner-solutions/overview`

In this example, we are going to use a Log Analytics workspace as it offers a greater feature set than Blob storage.

Getting ready

Again, for this one, we are going to need a Log Analytics workspace. This one will incur costs, though, so make sure you set up a cost warning if you deploy and then forget you have done so.

In the Azure portal, select **Log Analytics workspace** and press **Create new**. Create your workspace and make a note of the name.

In this example, we have created a workspace called `intunealerts` within the `rg-loganalytics` resource group.

Now we have our workspace, we can configure the diagnostics to export into it.

How to do it...

Follow these steps to configure the diagnostics to export:

1. Back in the Intune console, click **Reports** and then **Diagnostic Settings**.
2. Click **Add diagnostic setting**.
3. On the next screen, you can pick what to send to the workspace. Remember that there are data charges, so decide how much data you want in there and weigh this up against the potential costs. You can include the following data in your workspace:

    • **Audit Logs**: Anything amended or added within the Intune portal such as new policies, deleted policies, and so on

    • **Operational Logs**: User and device enrollment as well as non-compliant devices

    • **DeviceComplianceOrg**: Reports on device compliance and lists non-compliant devices

    • **Devices**: Device inventory and status

    You can find out more about exporting Intune logs here:

    ```
    https://learn.microsoft.com/en-us/mem/intune/fundamentals/
    review-logs-using-azure-monitor
    ```

4. After selecting the reports, check **Send to Log Analytics workspace,** and then select the workspace created earlier.
5. Once selected, click **Save**.
6. After a while, your logs will appear within **Log Analytics** under **Logs**.

That completes the recipe for configuring Intune diagnostic data exports.

11

Packaging Your Windows Applications

We have configured our Windows policies and enrolled our devices, but in most environments, we are going to need to deploy some applications.

In this chapter, we are going to run through the different application types that are available and how to deploy them into your environment.

When managing Windows devices, applications are critical, and packaging them correctly will ensure a smooth experience for end users. By following this chapter, you will learn how to package and deploy applications to your devices using the modern methods supported by Intune.

In this chapter, we will cover the following recipes:

- Using the Microsoft Store integration
- Packaging into MSIX
- Packaging Win32 applications
- Managing app supersedence and dependencies
- Deploying Office applications
- Updating Office applications
- Windows app protection

Chapter materials

Before starting, we will not be covering **MSI Line-of-business** applications as it is best practice to wrap these into a Win32 application, which is extremely straightforward. There are a couple of reasons for this:

- MSI Line-of-Business applications execute using the standard `msiexec` service, whereas Win32 uses the **Intune Management Extension** (**IME**) to deploy. This means that neither is aware of the other, which can lead to clashes during Autopilot provisioning, where the installer service is busy on the other application.

- Win32 applications give significantly more functionality around requirements, detection, and supersedence, none of which are available with an MSI Line-of-Business deployment.

Assigning applications

We also need to look at assignment options as they are the same across all app types. We have the following three options:

- **Required**: This will force an install and will only appear in Company Portal under **Installed Applications**

- **Available for enrolled devices**: This displays the application within Company Portal for user self-service

- **Uninstall**: This removes the application

Assignments depend on the application, but as a general rule, if the application is not required across the estate, configure Microsoft Entra groups for both installation and uninstallation. This gives added flexibility after deployment and is especially useful if you need to quickly remove an application as the group is already assigned and ready to use.

During assignment, you can also specify an installation deadline, a grace period for any restarts, and the ability to display or suppress the install/uninstall notifications.

A further consideration is around user versus device context, especially when deploying Win32 applications.

System context

Applications in the system context are run via the system user (you can test this on a standard device with the `psexec` tool by running the `psexec.exe -I -s cmd.exe` command). Your installations will have full administrative permissions to everything, but will not have user profiles. You can access the logged-in user with PowerShell scripts such as the one at `https://andrewstaylor.com/2023/11/07/enumerating-the-logged-on-user-when-running-as-system-with-azure-ad-entra-joined-devices/`.

You can also use `serviceui.exe` to provide user-level interaction with scripts and applications running at the system level.

In terms of paths and environmental variables, they are as follows:

- Temp points to `c:\Windows\Temp`
- Local app data: `C:\WINDOWS\system32\config\systemprofile\AppData\Local`
- App data: `C:\WINDOWS\system32\config\systemprofile\AppData\Roaming`
- User profile: `c:\users\Public`

This is most suitable for your standard Win32 applications, which you would traditionally require someone with elevated rights to install.

User context

These installations run at the level of the logged-in user, so they can only access files and folders the user can access during their day-to-day work, including the user profile and HKEY's current user registry hive. If you users do not have administrative rights, there is no access to program files, Windows, or anything that requires elevation.

In terms of paths and variables, they are as follows:

- Temp points: `c:\users\username\AppData\Local\Temp`
- Local app data: `c:\users\username\AppData\Local`
- App data: `c:\users\username\AppData\Roaming`
- User profile: `c:\users\username`

This is best suited for applications that target the user context, such as Teams, Visual Studio Code, OneDrive, which lives in `%LocalAppData%`, MSIX, AppX, and some MSI installers. Store apps also fall into this category as these are AppX or MSIX packages, although these can now be deployed in the system context, as covered in the first recipe (*Using the Microsoft Store integration*).

> **Important note**
> If you are wrapping MSI into Win32, you might come across occasions where the MSI itself is hard-coded and forces the user context. If you find one of these, you can either edit the MSI with something such as Orca or wrap it with an installation script, after which it will unlock the option to choose.

Technical requirements

For this chapter, you will need a modern web browser and a PowerShell code editor such as Visual Studio Code or PowerShell ISE.

All the scripts that will be referenced can be found here: `https://github.com/ PacktPublishing/Microsoft-Intune-Cookbook`.

If you wish to test the policies, you will need a corporate-managed device running each device platform for testing. For Linux, it will need to be running Ubuntu.

Using the Microsoft Store integration

We start by looking at the **Microsoft Store integration**, which no longer uses the Microsoft Store for Business and instead integrates directly into the store source within Winget. This is also how Windows applications such as Notepad and Calculator are deployed and updated.

> **Important note**
>
> Store apps that are deployed via Intune will continue to receive updates even if the Windows Store is blocked for end users via a policy.

Fortunately, this change has also reduced the number of steps to deploy an application!

How to do it...

Follow these steps to deploy your first Windows Store application:

1. To start, click **Apps** and then **Windows**.
2. Click **Add**.
3. In the fly-out, select **Microsoft Store app (new)** (it may just be called **Microsoft Store app**), and click **Select**.
4. Click **Search the Microsoft Store app (new)**.
5. In the fly-out, search for the application you are looking for.

Important note

It is worth noting that due to Intune being extensively used in Education, it will only search for applications with a rating suitable for children, so some apps may not be displayed.

For these applications, find them in the Microsoft Store online and make a note of the App ID (highlighted with a red rectangle in the following screenshot):

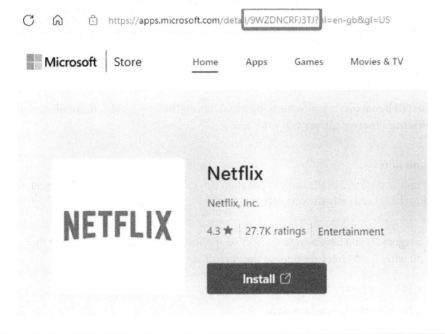

Figure 11.1 – App Store App ID

Now, search within Intune for that ID:

Figure 11.2 – Search by App ID

6. In this example, we will keep things simple and deploy **Company Portal** as we will need this for the demonstration later. Click **Select**.

    You will notice that the type is listed as **UWP**. This is a **Universal Windows Platform** application (APPX, MSIX, and so on), which means it is a traditional store app.

There are also a handful of Win32 apps available that can be pushed out this way instead of being packaged into a Win32 `intunewin` application.

7. The details will now be pre-populated for you (except the logo at the time of writing). If you want to add a logo, click **Select image** and upload one.

    You can edit any of the information on here as this is what will be displayed to the user if they self-service deploy.

    Among the options available, these three are worth paying attention to:

    • **Show this as a featured app in Company Portal**: This will pin the application to the home screen of the **Apps** page within Company Portal

    • **Install behavior**: If you want to block ESP until this app has been installed, change this to **System**; otherwise, **User** will work fine

> **Important note**
> Mixing user and system in the same application can cause issues in your environment, so make sure you select them early in your deployments.

    • **Category**: If you have a large number of applications available, categorizing them may assist you when your users are finding the correct app to deploy

8. Once you have confirmed the details, click **Next**.

9. Click **Next** on the **Scope tags** page.

10. Now, let us look at the assignment, which we covered at the start of this chapter. This application is one we want all users to have installed, so we are going to add the **Intune Users** group as a **Required** installation. Once configured, click **Next**.

11. Finally, check that everything looks correct and click **Create**.

With that, we have deployed a Microsoft Store app using the UI.

Automating it

When automating the deployment of store apps, we have to replicate the functionality of the GUI. So, while the actual deployment is a straightforward JSON request, we have to find the application details with which to populate. Follow this script to automate the deployment of Company Portal:

1. The first thing we need to do is set the application we are looking for and our install scope, as well as the assignment group ID:

    ```
    $appname = "Company Portal"
    $scope = "user" ##Can be user or system
    $groupid = "000-000-000-000"
    ```

2. Then, we need to search the store for that application and return the details:

```
$storeSearchUrl = "https://storeedgefd.dsx.mp.microsoft.com/
v9.0/manifestSearch"
$body = @{
    Query = @{
        KeyWord    = $appName
        MatchType = "Substring"
    }
} | ConvertTo-Json
$appSearch = Invoke-RestMethod -Uri $storeSearchUrl -Method POST
-ContentType 'application/json' -body $body
$exactApp = $appSearch.Data | Where-Object { $_.PackageName -eq
$appName }
```

This creates a JSON array with the query to pass to the store where we are looking for our app name. Then, we grab the output and restrict it to just the application we are looking for.

3. Now, we need to grab the application information by adding the **Package Identifier** to a store URL:

```
$appUrl = "https://storeedgefd.dsx.mp.microsoft.com/v9.0/
packageManifests/{0}" -f $exactApp.PackageIdentifier
```

4. Running a GET request will return an array containing all of the application information:

```
$app = Invoke-RestMethod -Uri $appUrl -Method GET
```

5. We can grab the values that are returned with the application details:

```
$appId = $app.Data.PackageIdentifier
$appInfo = $app.Data.Versions[-1].DefaultLocale
$appInstaller = $app.Data.Versions[-1].Installers
```

6. One advantage of scripting is that we can also grab the image directly from the Microsoft Store by grabbing the image on the store web page using the System.Net.Webclient functionality. Then, we can download and convert the file into Base64 format:

```
$imageUrl = "https://apps.microsoft.com/store/api/
ProductsDetails/GetProductDetailsById/{0}?hl=en-US&gl=US" -f
$exactApp.PackageIdentifier
$image = Invoke-RestMethod -Uri $imageUrl -Method GET
$wc = New-Object System.Net.WebClient
$wc.DownloadFile($image.IconUrl, "./temp.jpg")
$base64string = [Convert]::ToBase64String([IO.
File]::ReadAllBytes('./temp.jpg'))
```

7. As the details include escape characters, we want to tidy up before we populate our JSON. You can also set `Featured` to `$true` here if required:

```
$appdescription = ($appInfo.Shortdescription).ToString()
$appdescription2 = $appdescription.replace("`n","
").replace("`r"," ").replace("\n"," ").replace("\\n"," ")
$appdeveloper = $appInfo.Publisher
$appdisplayName = $appInfo.packageName
$appinformationUrl = $appInfo.PublisherSupportUrl
$apprunAsAccount = $scope
$appisFeatured = $false
$apppackageIdentifier = $appId
$appprivacyInformationUrl = $appInfo.PrivacyUrl
$apppublisher = $appInfo.publisher
```

8. Populate the JSON and send the `POST` request to the `MobileApps` part of Graph:

```
$deployUrl = "https://graph.microsoft.com/beta/
deviceAppManagement/mobileApps"
$json = @"
{
    "@odata.type": "#microsoft.graph.winGetApp",
    "categories": [],
    "description": "$appdescription2",
    "developer": "$appdeveloper",
    "displayName": "$appdisplayName",
    "informationUrl": "$appinformationUrl",
    "installExperience": {
        "runAsAccount": "$apprunAsAccount"
    },
    "isFeatured": false,
    "largeIcon": {
        "@odata.type": "#microsoft.graph.mimeContent",
        "type": "string",
        "value": "$base64string"
        },
    "notes": "",
    "owner": "",
    "packageIdentifier": "$apppackageIdentifier",
    "privacyInformationUrl": "$appprivacyInformationUrl",
    "publisher": "$apppublisher",
```

```
        "repositoryType": "microsoftStore",
        "roleScopeTagIds": []
}
"@
$appDeploy = Invoke-mggraphrequest -uri $deployUrl -Method POST
-Body $json -ContentType "application/JSON"
```

9. The assignment uses fairly typical JSON with a few added options for deadline, notification, and restart grace periods:

```
$appdeployid = $appDeploy.id
$JSON = @"
{
    "mobileAppAssignments": [
        {
            "@odata.type": "#microsoft.graph.
mobileAppAssignment",
            "intent": "Required",
            "settings": {
                "@odata.type": "#microsoft.graph.
winGetAppAssignmentSettings",
                "installTimeSettings": null,
                "notifications": "showAll",
                "restartSettings": null
            },
            "target": {
                "@odata.type": "#microsoft.graph.
groupAssignmentTarget",
                "groupId": "$groupid"
            }
        }
    ]
}
"@
$uri = "https://graph.microsoft.com/Beta/deviceAppManagement/
mobileApps/$appdeployid/assign"
Invoke-MgGraphRequest -Uri $uri -Method Post -Body $JSON
-ContentType "application/json"
```

That completes this recipe on deploying a Microsoft Store application in Intune.

Packaging into MSIX

MSIX is one of the newer packaging formats available and operates by monitoring an application installation, grabbing any changes to the filesystem, registry, and so on, and then wrapping them into a single file that can be installed at the user level. One advantage of MSIX is that you can use it as **AppAttach** on Azure Virtual Desktop environments to make applications available on a per-user level rather than having to install it directly onto the host machine in a multi-user environment.

> **Important note**
>
> An MSIX package can be reverted by the end user, do not package any applications that have a database included, as reverting will wipe any additions that have been made. Client-server apps are fine, but not those with databases built into them.

Getting started

There are some prerequisites for MSIX packages:

- **Code signing certificate**: All packages have to be signed before deployment. You have two options here – you can either purchase a public code signing certificate, which will be trusted by all devices automatically, or you can create a self-signing certificate and deploy it to your devices either via a **certificate authority** (**CA**) or using Intune. If you are using Intune, navigate to **Tenant administration** and click on **Connectors and tokens**.

  Within **Windows enterprise certificate**, select your certificate and upload it.

- **Packaging machine**: As MSIX monitors an installation, you will need a virtual machine to package on. Ideally, this should be as clear as possible to avoid any additional processes adding themselves to your final package. Make sure you enable snapshots/checkpoints as well so that you can quickly reuse them for the next package.

  If you have Hyper-V available on a Windows 10 or 11 machine, you can use **Quick Create**, which will configure the machine for you:

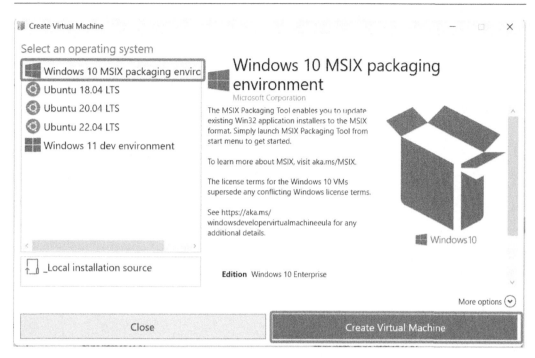

Figure 11.3 – Create Virtual Machine

Now that we have our four prerequisites in place, we can start the recipe.

How to do it...

We will start by packaging the application itself and then look at deploying it.

Packaging

Now that we have a packaging machine and a certificate, we can run through the packaging and deployment process. In this example, we will use Notepad++. Follow these steps to package your first MSIXL

1. Start MSIX Packaging Tool and click **Application Package**.

2. Select **Create package on this computer** and click **Next**.

3. Your machine will run some checks. Disable anything suggested by ticking the checkbox next to the item that has been flagged and clicking **Disable selected** (see *Figure 11.4*) for the best packaging experience. Then, click **Next**:

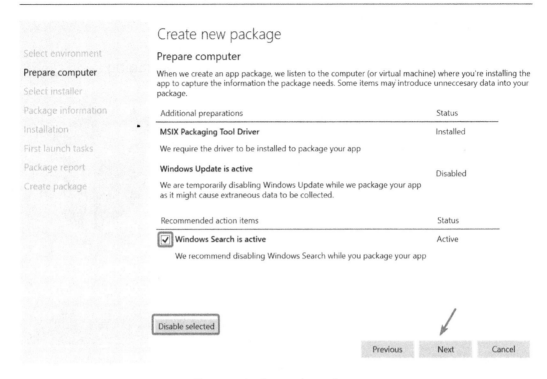

Figure 11.4 – Create new package

4. If you know the exact install commands, you can enter them on the next screen. However, in this example, we will do a full install from scratch, so we will leave the installer boxes empty.

    We need to sign our application here.

5. Select **Sign with a certificate (.pfx)**, point at the certificate you created, and enter the password.

> **Important note**
>
> The **Time stamp server URL** field is important. If you leave this blank, when your certificate expires, you will need to renew your packages with an updated certificate.
>
> If you specify a timestamp server, so long as the certificate was valid when the application was created and stamped, it will remain valid after the certificate has expired.
>
> One free server is `https://ca.signfiles.com/TSAServer.aspx`.

6. After filling in the details, as shown in the following screenshot, click **Next**:

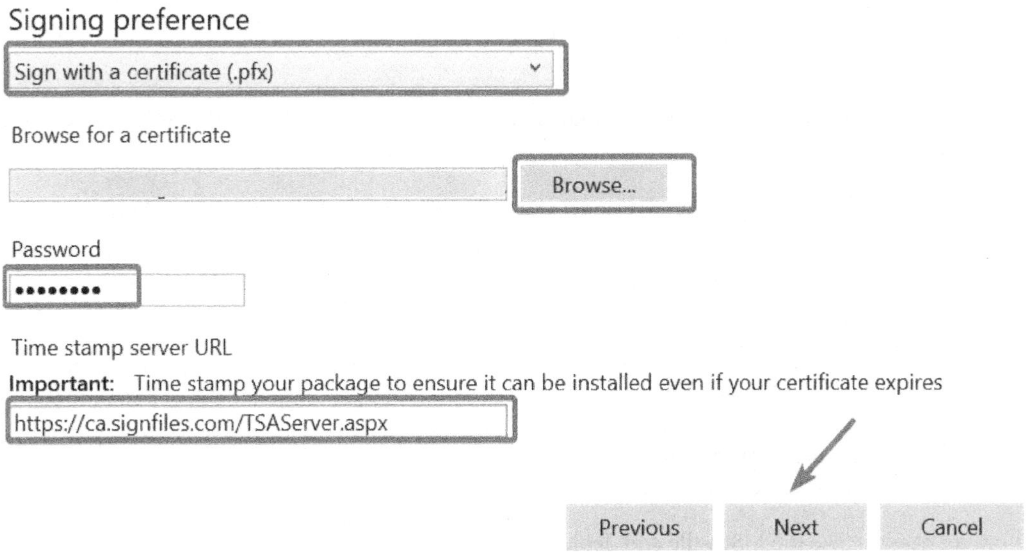

Signing preference

Sign with a certificate (.pfx)   ˅

Browse for a certificate

| | Browse... |

Password

••••••••

Time stamp server URL

Important: Time stamp your package to ensure it can be installed even if your certificate expires

https://ca.signfiles.com/TSAServer.aspx

| Previous | Next | Cancel |

Figure 11.5 – The Select installer screen

7. On the next screen (**Package information**), you need to enter the package details. As a naming convention, app name, platform, and version are usually a good start (for example, Notepad++_x64_8.5.8_001). Enter **Package name**, **Package display name**, and **Package description** details; these will be displayed in Company Portal. Also, choose your **Publisher display name** and **Version**. Then, click **Next**.

8. On the **Create new package** screen, install your application. If it needs to be restarted, click the button marked **Restart machine**; the sequencer will reload on startup.

    If possible, it is a good idea to turn off auto updates as users can revert a package that will wipe out any updates.

9. Once installed, click **Next**.

10. The next screen shows the executables that have been detected. Running the main installer will detect any first-run modifications so that it can disable updates, hints and tips, and so on.

    You can also remove any stubs to executables you do not want users to see, such as `uninstall.exe`.

    If any are missing, you can click **Browse** and manually add them here. Once you have set this up, click **Next**.

11. As this is the last monitoring step, you need to confirm you want to stop monitoring the device here. Click **Yes, move on**.

12. If the sequencer has detected any services, you can choose to exclude them here. Once you are done, click **Next**.

13. Finally, select a location to save the package and click **Create**. You can also access the package editor here should you wish to check the files and registry keys or make further amendments.

You can find out more about the package editor here: `https://learn.microsoft.com/en-us/windows/msix/packaging-tool/package-editor`.

Now, we need to take the MSIX file and deploy it.

Deploying our MSIX package

Now that we have packaged the application, we can deploy it to Intune:

1. Within Intune, select **Apps** and then **Windows**.

2. Click **Add**.

3. Choose **Line-of-business app** and click **Select**.

4. Click **Select app package file** and pick the MSIX file you created in the previous subsection. Then, click **OK**.

5. Amend any details and add an image if required, then click **Next**.

6. Click **Next** on the **Scope tags** page.

7. This is an application that lends itself to self-service, so we will set up **Required** and **Uninstall** groups for those who need or do not need the application and then make them available for everyone else. You can also switch between installing in the user and device context here. Once your assignments have been configured, click **Next**.

8. Finally, check that everything looks correct and click **Create**.

That completes this recipe on packaging an MSIX application. Now, we can look at Win32 applications.

Packaging Win32 applications

Packaging into Win32 will be your primary method of application deployment, so this recipe is an important one to follow.

Getting started

Before we do any packaging, we need to keep our application source code tidy so that we can easily work out what is what when we need to update that weird and wonderful application in 2 years!

> **Important note**
> The packaging tool will grab *every* file in the Source directory you point it to, so make sure that the directory *only has source files in it*. If you point it at your Downloads folder, for example, you will find yourself wondering why a 2 MB installer is showing as 45 GB when packaged!

The packaging tool creates an intunewin file, which is effectively an encrypted ZIP file that uploads with a manifest into Azure Blob storage. When installing, your computer downloads, decrypts, and runs the installation specified.

This is entirely personal preference, but this folder layout works well:

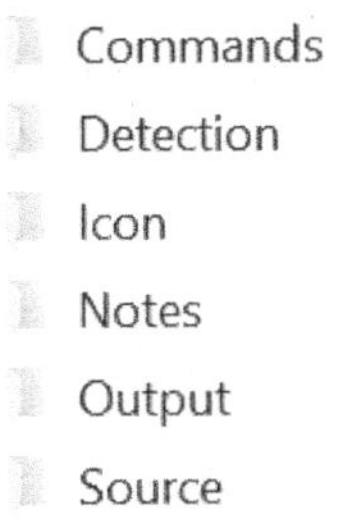

Commands

Detection

Icon

Notes

Output

Source

Figure 11.6 – Recommended folder structure

The Source folder contains the raw files, installer and config files, and more.

Output is where we will store the intunewin file.

The rest are pretty self-explanatory.

Once you have added your `intunewin` file to Intune, you cannot retrieve it, so always keep a copy of any source files.

Now, we need to look at the different ways of creating an installer.

Calling MSI/Exe directly

If it is a simple install, we could simply package up the MSI or executable on its own and then, in Intune, set the `install` command to run the file:

```
msiexec.exe /i myinstaller.msi /qn
myinstaller.exe /silent
```

This is perfectly acceptable but does not allow for any customization pre or post-install.

It is also worth noting that if the MSI has been written to install in the user context, Intune may force it to do the same and you will notice that the context is grayed out. If you want one of these to install in the system context, you will need to edit the MSI or wrap it using a method.

Batch script

While PowerShell is infinitely more powerful and modern, using a batch script will still work when you are packaging. If this is what you are more comfortable with, that is fine. In the long term, look at moving to PowerShell or **PowerShell Application Deployment Toolkit** (**PSADT**, covered later in this recipe), but for the time being, this will be more than adequate.

Simply create your installation batch script. When packaging, this is your install file:

```
For example:
rem Delete file
del c:\temp\myfile.txt
rem Stop Service
net stop myservice
rem Install App
my-installer.exe /verysilent /allusers /noreboot
rem Delete Shortcut
del %public%\desktop\myshortcut.lnk
```

Let us cover a few handy hints if you are using a batch script.

In a command prompt, type `SET` to get a list of variables on the machine. These can be referenced within `%`, as we have done with the public user environment, `%public%`.

If you want to reference the current directory, use %~dp0 but *do not* add a backslash:

```
%~dp0myinstaller.exe
```

Within Intune, simply set your install command to install.bat or whatever you have called your batch script.

PowerShell script

PowerShell scripts take installation one step further as you have greater control over the machine (and for something complex, it is just easier). You can put logic in and look at the underlying hardware – anything is available at this point.

As an example, for a PowerShell script to run an MSI, you must run the following code:

```
$MSIArguments = @(
"/i"
('"{0}"' -f $filelocation)
"/qn"
"/norestart"
"/L*v"
)
Start-Process "msiexec.exe" -ArgumentList $MSIArguments -Wait
-NoNewWindow
```

Of course, when using PowerShell, you can also add/remove features for apps that do not have an MSI.

Here, we are using DotNet as an example:

```
Enable-WindowsOptionalFeature -Online -FeatureName 'NetFx3' -Source .\
sxs\ -NoRestart -LimitAccess
```

The installation command within Intune would be as follows:

```
powershell.exe -ExecutionPolicy Bypass -file myinstaller.ps1
```

PSADT

PSADT (https://psappdeploytoolkit.com/) is a very powerful tool that leverages PowerShell but gives many built-in functions to take this process one step further.

For example, you could check whether applications are running and prompt the user to close them, run a particular file in the user context and have the rest in the system context, or add pre/post-install commands.

A full list of the functions can be found at https://psappdeploytoolkit.com/#functions-logic.

> **Important note**
>
> If you are deploying via Intune and you want user interaction, you will need to use the `ServiceUI` executable from the **Microsoft Deployment Tools (MDT)** toolkit.

When deploying a PSADT packaged application, for user interaction, the install command would be as follows:

```
.\ServiceUI.exe -Process:explorer.exe Deploy-Application.exe
```

Now that we have covered the different ways we can install an application, we can look at packaging one.

How to do it...

Now that we have our source files and installer, we need to package them using `IntuneWinAppUtil` from Microsoft, which is available here: `https://github.com/microsoft/Microsoft-Win32-Content-Prep-Tool/blob/master/IntuneWinAppUtil.exe`.

This takes the source files, encrypts and compresses them, and gives us our `intunewinfile`.

Follow these steps to package your application into `intunewin` format:

1. First, we must load the application (for ease, we are using 7-Zip). We will be prompted to **Please specify the source folder**. Point it to the `Source` folder we created earlier, which contains your installation media and setup file.

2. Then, enter the installation file's name (setup file).

3. Finally, tell `IntuneWinAppUtil` where to put the `intunewin` file (the `Output` folder).

After packaging the application, we need to find out how Intune can detect that the installation has been completed successfully.

Application detection

Before adding to Intune, it is worth grabbing the detection type so that it knows that the installation has been completed correctly. We can follow these steps to find our detection and then configure it within Intune:

1. For most applications, we can use Windows Sandbox as a temporary machine to look for a file or registry key to use for detection. However, if you have an MSI application, you can quickly grab the product code using this PowerShell script:

   ```
   $path = "PATH TO MSI"
   $comObjWI = New-Object -ComObject WindowsInstaller.Installer
   $MSIDatabase = $comObjWI.GetType().
   InvokeMember("OpenDatabase","InvokeMethod",$Null,$comObjWI,@
   ($Path,0))
   ```

```
$Query = "SELECT Value FROM Property WHERE Property =
'ProductCode'"
$View = $MSIDatabase.GetType().
InvokeMember("OpenView","InvokeMethod",
$null,$MSIDatabase,($Query))
$View.GetType().InvokeMember("Execute", "InvokeMethod", $null,
$View, $null)
$Record = $View.GetType().
InvokeMember("Fetch","InvokeMethod",$null,$View,$null)
$Value = $Record.GetType().
InvokeMember("StringData","GetProperty",$null,$Record,1)
write-host "Your MSI code is $Value" -ForegroundColor Green
```

This script will output the MSI code you can use for both detection and uninstallation.

2. Now that we have our file, we need to add it to Intune.

    Within the Intune portal, click on **Apps** and then **Windows**. Then, click **Add**.

3. In the fly-out, select **Windows app (Win32)** and click **Select**.

4. Click on the blue **Select app package file** text.

5. Now, browse to the `Intunewin` file we created earlier and click **OK**.

6. As we have packaged an executable, it will only populate the filename, so, at a minimum, we need to add a publisher, but ideally a name, description, version, and logo. Once these fields have been populated, click **Next**.

7. We have a few options to set on this next screen. First, populate the `Install` and `Uninstall` commands, depending on how the application was packaged. This could be a batch or PowerShell script, or simply point to the file. If the application is an MSI, both fields should auto-populate for you.

8. You can also specify how long before the installation times out as failed. This is more useful for larger or more complex applications. For 7-Zip, the default of 60 minutes will be more than adequate.

9. **Allow available uninstall** is for applications that are available for users to self-service install within Company Portal. Setting this to **Yes** will also give them the ability to uninstall the application themselves.

10. The install behavior for this application needs to be set to **System**. However, some apps may be user-based, so change this as required.

11. You can also specify what restart action to take if necessary.

12. Finally, if the application has unusual return codes, add them here. Generally, the default codes will be fine.

13. Once set, click **Next**.

14. Now, we need to set the minimum requirements for the application to be installed. If a device does not meet these, the installation will not continue.

    You can specify finer details at the device level, including RAM and processor speed for some more complex applications such as CAD software.

    If you want to take this further, you can also add a custom requirements script. For example, if you only want to install on laptops (for a VPN client), you could query the device chassis using **Windows Management Interface** (**WMI**) and query that here.

15. In the case of 7-Zip, we just want to check that the machine is 64-bit as that is the version we have packaged. Once configured, click **Next**.

16. The next step is to configure the detection rule, which is what Intune will use to check whether the application has been installed correctly.

    We have a few options here:

    - **MSI**: For any straight MSI files, this will auto-populate. You can also add the MSI **globally unique identifier** (**GUID**), which will look for the presence of that ID.

    - **File**: Look for a specific file, file date, file version, or file size (these are useful for upgrades). For example, you could point it to the executable that is launched. Note the 32/64-bit option here; if you set it to **Yes**, it will look in the 32-bit context on 64-bit machines (such as Program Files (x86)).

    - **Registry**: Look for a specific key, string, version, or integer in the registry. The same applies to 32/64-bit.

    - **Requirements script**: This lets you look for almost anything, be it a running service or a combination of different methods. Here, the key is for a successful detection, so the script must exit with an exit code of 0. An example of this is shown here:

    ```
    $service = get-service -name "MozillaMaintenance"
    if ($service.Status -eq "Running") {
        write-output "MozillaMaintenance detected and running,
    exiting"
        exit 0
    }
    else {
        exit 1
    }
    ```

    For 7-Zip, we are going to look for the presence of the 7z executable using a **File Rule** type with the path and file set accordingly.

17. Once we have configured the detection, click **Next**.

18. We will cover **Dependencies** and **Supersedence** in the next recipe, so we can press **Next** on both of these for now.

19. Click **Next** on the **Scope tags** page.

20. Now, we need to assign the application. As this is free software, once again, we will set **Available for enrolled devices** for **All Users** (or **All Devices**), but with specific groups for **Required** and **Uninstall** for better overall management. Once configured, click **Next**:

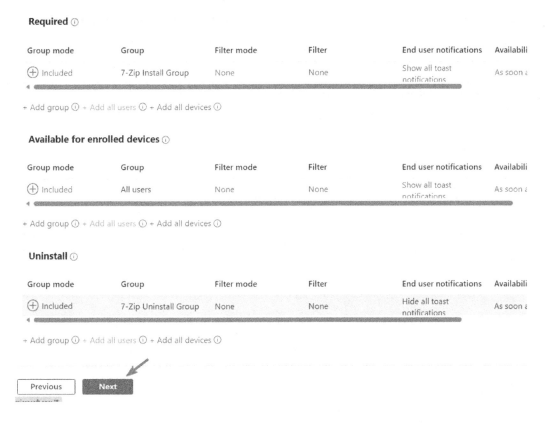

Figure 11.7 – Assignments

21. Give everything a final check and click **Create**.

With that, we have demonstrated how to create and upload a Win32 application to Microsoft Intune.

Automating it

Now that we know how to add an application in the GUI, we can look at automating this process using PowerShell and Graph.

This is a particularly complicated one to automate as it creates an application stub in Intune, then uploads the `intunewin` file and connects them.

Grab the script from this book's GitHub repository (`https://github.com/PacktPublishing/Microsoft-Intune-Cookbook/blob/main/Chapter-11/create-deploy-win32.ps1`). Here, we will run through what it is doing and what each function runs rather than displaying the whole script:

1. We start by setting a temporary directory that we can use to store files and scripts (we will create a sub-folder later):

   ```
   $path = "c:\temp\"
   ```

2. Specify the app name (used in the description) and the app ID (used in the group short name):

   ```
   $appname = "Remote Help"
   $appid = "RemoteHelp"
   ```

3. Now, we must specify the URL to the file we wish to package and where we wish to save it:

   ```
   $appdownloadurl = "https://aka.ms/downloadremotehelp"
   $appoutput = $apppath + "\remotehelpinstaller.exe"
   ```

4. The detection rule looks for a file, so we need to specify what we are looking for. If in doubt, install it on a temporary machine such as Windows Sandbox and install the application to check the file paths:

   ```
   $filepath = "C:\Program Files\Remote Help\RemoteHelp.exe"
   ```

5. Next, set the install and uninstall strings; these will be used on the client device:

   ```
   $installstring = "&.\remotehelpinstaller.exe /quiet
   acceptTerms=1"
   $uninstallstring = "&.\remotehelpinstaller.exe /uninstall /quiet
   acceptTerms=1"
   ```

6. Finally, we need to download the `IntuneWinAppUtil` executable:

   ```
   $intuneapputilurl = "https://github.com/microsoft/Microsoft-
   Win32-Content-Prep-Tool/raw/master/IntuneWinAppUtil.exe"
   $intuneapputiloutput = $path + "IntuneWinAppUtil.exe"
   Invoke-WebRequest -Uri $intuneapputilurl -OutFile
   $intuneapputiloutput
   ```

   Now that we have set our variables, we can run through creating, deploying, and assigning the application.

7. First, we need to create a temporary location for the files:

```
$apppath = "$path\$appid"
new-item -Path $apppath -ItemType Directory -Force
```

8. Download the installer:

```
Invoke-WebRequest -Uri $appdownloadurl -OutFile $appoutput
```

9. Create the install and uninstall groups. This involves calling a function (new-aadgroups) that populates the JSON and sends a POST request via Invoke-MgGraphRequest.

   The GroupType variable is used to distinguish the group name and description:

```
$installgroup = new-aadgroups -appid $appid -appname $appname
-grouptype "Install"
$uninstallgroup = new-aadgroups -appid $appid -appname $appname
-grouptype "Uninstall"
```

10. Next, we need to create our script to install the application. The following code creates a simple PowerShell script containing the install string we set earlier and uses the new-installscript function. Then, we must export the script's content into a PowerShell file so that we can wrap it in our IntuneWin file:

```
$installscript = new-installscript -appid $appid -appname
$appname -installstring $installstring
$installfilename = "install$appid.ps1"
$installscriptfile = $apppath + "\" + $installfilename
$installscript | Out-File $installscriptfile -Encoding utf8
```

11. We must do the same for the uninstall script:

```
$uninstallscript = new-uninstallscript -appid $appid -appname
$appname -uninstallstring $uninstallstring
$uninstallfilename = "uninstall$appid.ps1"
$uninstallscriptfile = $apppath + "\" + $uninstallfilename
$uninstallscript | Out-File $uninstallscriptfile -Encoding utf8
```

12. The final script we need is the detection script. This takes the filepath value we set earlier and uses the new-detectionscriptinstall function to run a simple Test-Path on filepath and return an exit code of 0 if the application is detected, or an exit code of 1 if the application has not been detected. Again, we output the script's content to a PowerShell script file:

```
$detectionscript = new-detectionscriptinstall -appid $appid
-appname $appname -filepath $filepath
$detectionscriptfile = $apppath + "\detection$appid.ps1"
$detectionscript | Out-File $detectionscriptfile -Encoding utf8
```

13. Now for the important part: we need to create our `IntuneWin` file using the installer and scripts we have created. For that, we will be using the `new-intunewinfile` function, which calls the executable with the parameters required, passing various details such as the filename and output location:

```
$intunewinpath = $apppath + "\install$appid.intunewin"
new-intunewinfile -appid "$appid" -appname "$appname" -apppath
"$apppath" -setupfilename "$installscriptfile"
```

As we do not want to continue until this has been completed, we need to add a pause here. The following code uses a loop that sleeps for the duration set (in seconds). As we are using a small application, 10 seconds is fine, but for larger applications, this may need to be increased:

```
$sleep = 10
foreach ($i in 0..$sleep) {
Write-Progress -Activity "Sleeping for $($sleep-$i) seconds"
-PercentComplete ($i / $sleep * 100) -SecondsRemaining ($sleep -
$i)
Start-Sleep -s 1
        }
```

14. Now for the complicated part: when a new application is created, it runs through a few stages to create an application stub, upload it to Azure storage, and then link the two together.

For this, we have a variety of nested functions.

`new-win32app` is the primary function and is where we specify the application details, install commands, uninstall commands, and detection rules:

```
$installcmd = "powershell.exe -ExecutionPolicy Bypass -File
$installfilename"
        $uninstallcmd = "powershell.exe -ExecutionPolicy Bypass
-File $uninstallfilename"
        new-win32app -appid $appid -appname $appname
-appfile $intunewinpath -installcmd $installcmd -uninstallcmd
$uninstallcmd -detectionfile $detectionscriptfile
```

First, this function calls `new-detectionrule`, which creates the appropriate JSON for the selected rule, which in this case is PowerShell. This JSON is nested in an array.

After creating the rules, it grabs the return codes using the `Get-DefaultReturnCodes` function.

The detection rule and return codes are then combined with the other information passed in the `new-win32app` command to the `Invoke-UploadWin32Lob` function.

This function tests that the source file path is valid with `Test-SourceFile`. Then, it uses `Get-IntuneWinXML` to read the `detection.xml` file that was created with `IntuneWinAppUtil`. This is used to grab the filename and `filepath`, as well as the extension.

If the extension is an MSI, it populates the JSON of the application with the details from the file using the `Get-Win32AppBody` function. If it is an executable, it simply uses the details passed to it.

Then, it adds the detection rule and return codes to the JSON containing the application details.

Next, it creates the application stub within Intune, which, if you look in the GUI, will say the application is not ready as the files are still uploading.

As the `IntuneWin` file is encrypted, the next step is to grab the encryption keys from the `detection.xml` file.

At this point, it extracts the file using this information (and the `Get-IntuneWinFile` function) to detect the file size. This information is then sent to Graph to create a new file reference for the application.

This can take a while, so the `Start-WaitForFileProcessing` function loops until the operation is complete.

Next, the file itself is uploaded to Azure using the URL given from Graph when the file is created, using the `UploadFileToAzureStorage` function.

Once uploaded, it removes the `IntuneWin` file.

Finally, the application needs to be committed after being uploaded via a Graph POST request. Again, this can take a while, so use both the `Start-WaitForFileProcessing` and `sleep` commands.

Now that our application has been created and uploaded, we simply need to assign it. For that, we can use the `grant-win32app` function, passing the application name and group details. This function simply grabs the application ID and populates the JSON for application assignment:

```
grant-win32app -appname $appname -installgroup $installgroup
-uninstallgroup $uninstallgroup
```

That is it – we have successfully packaged, uploaded, and assigned an application using only PowerShell and Graph.

Managing app supersedence and dependencies

This recipe looks at the functionality around application supersedence and application dependencies. As it involves amending existing applications we will not be looking at automating and instead why you would use these and how to implement them.

Application supersedence

When a new version of an application is released, you have a few available options:

- Replace the `IntuneWin` file with a new one and amend the detection method so that it matches the newer version

- Create a new application and swap the assignments

- Use application supersedence

Everything will work fine, but supersedence gives you the option to remove the previous version before installing, or just do a straight update. It also makes things easier to manage as you do not have to worry about duplicate assignments or monitoring multiple applications.

Dependencies

One drawback of Intune/Autopilot is their inability to sequence applications like Configuration Manager can. Therefore, traditionally, if you had an application that needed a particular application or runtime (.NET, Java, VC Libraries, and so on) to launch, you could not guarantee it would be installed in time. Before the introduction of dependencies, this meant you had to package both into one application and then install it to use the install script. This worked well, but at every application update, you had to re-package both, even if only one of the two had been updated.

This is where you use a dependency: you select the runtime or application that is required and set it as a dependency on the primary application. Intune will then check whether the application is installed; if not, it will trigger an installation of the dependency before deploying the primary application.

Getting started

To follow this recipe, you will need the following:

- Two versions of the same application for supersedence

- An application that has a dependency

How to do it...

We can now look at the steps involved in configuring these settings, starting with application supersedence.

Configuring application supersedence

For this example, we will be using 7-Zip, replacing version 19.00 with 23.00. Follow these steps to configure application supersedence within the application configuration:

1. First, click on **Apps**, then **Windows**.

2. Find your application in the list. You need the new version so that you can replace the old one – in our case, 7-Zip 23.00. Click on it.

3. Click **Properties**.

4. Scroll down to **Supersedence** and click **Edit**.

5. Click +**Add** to add the app it is replacing.

6. Find the application in the fly-out and click **Select**.

7. If your application requires a full uninstall before you can install the new version, change **Uninstall** to **Yes**. Once set as appropriate, click **Review + Save**.

8. Finally, click **Save** to confirm the changes.

This can also be configured during the initial application deployment if you are happy that the new version does not require any additional testing. Configuring it after deployment, however, allows you to test the new version for any issues before deploying it.

Now that we have covered supersedence, let us learn how to configure application dependency.

Configuring application dependency

While it is not a requirement, we will be setting the Visual C++ 2013 Redistributable package as a dependency for our new 7-Zip 23.00 version. Follow these steps to configure application dependency for our application:

1. First, click on **Apps** and then **Windows**.

2. Find your application in the list – in our case, 7-Zip 23.00 – and click on it.

3. Click **Properties**.

4. Scroll down to **Dependencies** and click **Edit**.

5. Click + **Add** to load the flyout with the application list.

6. Find and click on your application in the list and click **Select**.

7. Here, you can decide if you want the application to **Automatically Install** when the parent application is installed, or if you want to **manually deploy**. In most cases, automatic is the better option. Once everything is configured, click **Review + Save**.

8.   If you have configured any supersedence, you will be prompted to confirm them here. We already know that these are correct, so click **Review + Save** once more.

9.   Finally, confirm your application changes by clicking **Save**.

We have now learned what application supersedence and application dependencies are and how to configure them against applications in the tenant.

Deploying Office applications

The **Microsoft Office Suite of Applications** (now known as **Microsoft 365 apps**) is more than likely one of the most important applications required on your devices. For that reason, we need to be sure they are deployed correctly, reliably, and ideally forced on the **Enrollment Status Page (ESP)**.

Getting started

Within Intune, there are three different ways to deploy Microsoft 365 apps, one of which is a lot more consistent than the other. The best method is to wrap it as a Win32 application using the **Office Deployment Tool (ODT)**. We will cover this in this recipe as we can then control the deployment of it during the ESP. We also know it will be installed using the **Intune Management Extension (IME)**, which prevents applications from clashing.

Before we look at how to deploy as a Win32 application, we should look at the other options available within the portal – that is, using the **graphical user interface (GUI)** with either configuration designer selections or by entering XML:

1.   First, click on **Apps**, then **Windows**.

2.   Click **Add** and select **Microsoft 365 Apps – Windows 10 and later**, then click **Select**.

3.   Click **Next** on the initial screen to be taken to the **Configure app suite** screen.

The **Configuration designer** tool lets you quickly configure your application package without needing to amend any XML or package any applications. It is a quick way to deploy the applications, but as you have no further control, you cannot specify applications that are not to be installed, such as Skype for Business, and the control is quite limited.

Switching to **Enter XML data** lets you use custom XML created by the Office Customization Tool, which we will be using for the Win32 application. The downside of using the built-in Microsoft 365 application configuration is that it is deployed more as a policy than an application, so there is the chance it might clash with another running installation. You also lose all control over detection, custom requirements, and supersedence and dependencies (which are useful if you have applications that install Office plugins).

How to do it...

Now that we have looked at the methods we should not use, let us learn how to configure, package, and deploy an application as a Win32 application. Follow these instructions to deploy Office as a Win32 application:

1. The first thing we need to do is configure our XML file to tell the Office Deployment Tool which components to install, what languages it should use, and so on. To do that, navigate to the Office Customization Tool: `https://config.office.com/deploymentsettings`.

   Here, you can specify which Office version to install, any applications to remove, change language packs, and more.

   We will be configuring the update channel using Intune in the next recipe, so when specifying the update channel here, ideally, it should match your **Broad Ring** to save users from downgrading after installation. You can also specify which version to install should you have specific application requirements.

   - In the **Installation** options, it is advisable to set **Show installation to user** to **No** as this will be deploying in the system context anyway. Also, set **Shut down running applications** to **Yes** if you are deploying during Autopilot to avoid any timeout issues if something is already running. If you are deploying after initial configuration, it may be better to use PSADT and prompt the users to close the applications themselves as you cannot control exactly when the application will be deployed.

2. In Update and **upgrade options**, watch out for **Uninstall any MSI versions of Office, including Visio and Project** as this will remove any detected Office applications. If you are deploying the full suite, this is less likely to be an issue, but if you are deploying apps individually, such as Visio or Project, you will want to make sure this is set to **No**; otherwise, it will uninstall everything except the single app selected for installation.

3. When looking at **Licensing and activation**, first, change **Automatically accept the EULA** to **Yes** to save your end users from having to accept it themselves.

   In licensing, we have three main options:

   - **User based**: All users have a license assigned to them and can have a maximum of five installations before they are prompted to remove a licensed installation in the Office portal.

   - **Shared Computer**: This option is better for environments where staff may use a large number of different devices, such as hot-desks, or hospital environments. When a device is set in Shared Computer mode, it will not use one of the five available licenses for the users. If you wish to use this option, ensure your licenses support it.

   - **Device based**: For machines with multiple unlicensed users, the machine itself is licensed. This needs special licenses.

4. In **Application preferences**, you can configure anything that can be controlled via Group Policy or Intune Policy. For one-off configurations, this is perfectly acceptable, although using Intune policies will give you greater control and allow you to amend without having to re-package applications.

5. After configuring your settings, click **Export**.

6. Select your document format and click **OK**, then save the XML.

7. Now that we have our XML file, we need a way to use it to deploy the Office applications. For this, we will be using the Office Deployment Tool, which can be downloaded here: `https://www.microsoft.com/en-US/download/details.aspx?id=49117`.

8. Download the executable and run it to extract the files into a folder.

9. Now, we need to create our Win32 folder structure, as per *Figure 11.6*.

10. Copy the downloaded XML and `setup.exe` file from the Office Deployment Tool into the `Source` folder.

11. Also, create an `uninstall.xml` file with the following content:

```
<Configuration>
<Display Level="None" AcceptEULA="True" />
<Property Name="FORCEAPPSHUTDOWN" Value="True" />
<Remove>
<Product ID="O365ProPlusRetail">
</Product>
</Remove>
</Configuration>
```

12. Wrap it using the `IntuneWinAppUtil` tool, specify `setup.exe` as the installer, and save `intunewin` in the `Output` folder.

    Now that we have our `IntuneWin` file, we can add it to Intune.

13. Within the Intune portal, navigate to **Apps**, then **Windows**.

14. Click **Add**, select **Win32**, and click **Select**.

15. Click the folder icon, grab your `intunewin` file, and click **OK**.

16. As this is a Win32 app from an executable, we need to populate all of the details, including the icon. Once configured, click **Next**.

17. Now, we need to set our install and uninstall commands.

    For your install command, you need the following:

    ```
    setup.exe /configure Configuration.xml
    ```

    For the uninstall command, you need this:

    ```
    setup.exe /configure uninstall.xml
    ```

18. Configure any other settings and click **Next**.

19. We have set our installation to 64-bit, so set that as the requirement, along with the lowest operating system version in your estate. Then, click **Next**.

20. Detection rules can be more tricky for Office applications as they first install the Click-To-Run application, which installs the files themselves. In this case, we will check for a registry key, which will confirm that the Click-To-Run tool has finished running. Our configured registry keys are as follows:

    - **Key Path**: `HKEY_LOCAL_MACHINE\SOFTWARE\Microsoft\Office\ClickToRun\`

    - **Value**: `LastScenarioResult`

    - **Detection**: `Exists`

    As we are deploying the 32-bit version, we do not want to associate it with a 32-bit application; otherwise, it will look into `WOW6432Node` and fail the detection process. Set **Associated with a 32-bit app on 64-bit clients** to **No**.

21. Once configured, click **OK** and then **Next**.

22. We do not have any **Dependencies**, **Supersedence**, or **Scope tags** for this application as it is a core application that is required across the estate, so click **Next** on all three screens.

23. When looking at assignments, you will no doubt want this installed on all devices, so you can select **All Users**, **All Devices**, or deploy to a group. In our case, we will use the group we created in *Chapter 1* and deploy it to any users with an Office license. Once you have selected the group, click **Next**.

24. Finally, confirm that everything we have configured matches on the **Review + Create** screen and click **Create**.

That completes this recipe on Microsoft 365 application deployment. Now, let us learn how to keep the applications updated.

Updating Office applications

Now that we have deployed our Office applications, we need to make sure they remain updated. As these are core apps, it is recommended to use a similar ring approach as what we used with Windows updates, both to check for any potential issues with the line of business and also to look for any significant UI changes that may need communicating with the organization.

Getting started

Before running through the preferred approach, there are different ways to handle Office updates. We will have a look at the two main options now and then run through the configuration.

Office portal

One option is to use the Office Admin portal itself, which can be accessed at `https://config.office.com`.

Here, you can configure Office policies to set any configuration setting via **Policy Management** and also use the **Cloud Updates** menu to handle updates and version deployment.

This is a good option, but as it falls outside of the Intune portal, it is another portal to manage and also increases the risk of conflicts, with the same setting potentially being configured in two different places.

Settings catalog

By using **Settings catalog**, we can configure any ADMX-backed settings directly on the devices and use our existing update groups, or create new ones. This is what we will do in this recipe.

How to do it...

Follow these steps to configure a Settings catalog policy to handle Office updates:

1. As with all previous Settings catalog-based recipes, navigate to **Devices**, click on **Windows**, then click on **Configuration profiles**.

2. At the top, click **Create**, select **New Policy**, select **Windows 10 and later**, then select **Settings catalog** from the fly-out Window. Finally, click **Create**.

3. Give your new profile **Name** and **Description** values. For most environments, you will want at least three different profiles for the different rings, so name them accordingly. Then, click **Next**.

4. On the **Settings** page, click **Add settings** and find **Microsoft Office 2016 (Machine)** in the list. Click **Updates**. The Office 2016 policies are the most recent and are fully compatible with Microsoft 365 apps.

   Selecting the machine policies writes the keys to **HKEY Local Machine (HKLM)** and not the **HKEY Current User (HKCU)** hive, so users cannot change their update cadence.

5. For updates, we need two settings:

   - **Enable Automatic Updates**: Set to **Enabled**.
   - **Update Channel**: Set to **Enabled**. Set **Channel** according to the ring being configured.

   The available options for **Update Channel** can be found here: `https://learn.microsoft.com/en-us/deployoffice/updates/overview-update-channels`.

   You can also configure **Update Deadline** within the settings category if required.

6. Once you have selected the appropriate channel, click **Next**.

7. Click **Next** to move past the **Scope tags** page.

8. Now, assign the application in a similar manner to the Windows Updates we covered in *Chapter 4*. The user/device set may be different for Office updates, so you may wish to include some heavy Office app users in one of the earlier rings to quickly find any issues before they deploy to the larger estate. If you have users who regularly move between machines (such as IT staff), it may be worth using device groups here to stop Office versions from upgrading and downgrading as different users log in – just remember not to mix device and user groups when including and excluding groups.

9. Once you have configured your assignments, click **Next**.

10. Finally, review that everything looks correct and click **Create**.

That completes the steps for configuring Office updates in the UI.

Automating it

Of course, as this is a Settings catalog policy, we can deploy it via Graph, as covered in *Chapter 2*.

The first thing we need to consider is the update ring being deployed as the actual values differ from the display name in the portal:

- **Current**: current
- **Semi Annual**: deferred
- **Monthly**: monthlyenterprise
- **Semi Annual (Preview)**: firstreleasedeferred
- **Current Preview**: firstreleasecurrent
- **Beta**: insiderfast

Follow these steps to create a script that will automate the update profile creation process in Intune:

1. Start by setting the name, description, and URL:

    ```
    $name = "Update Ring"
    $description = "Office Updates for Monthly Enterprise"
    $url  = "https://graph.microsoft.com/beta/deviceManagement/
    configurationPolicies"
    ```

2. Now, configure the channel and group ID for assignment:

    ```
    $groupid = "xxxxxxxx-xxxx-xxxx-xxxx-xxxxxxxxxxxx"
    $channel = "monthlyenterprise"
    ```

3. When configuring the JSON, the first setting is simply to enable automatic updates. The second setting is where we set the update ring by passing the channel value directly into the JSON, which you can find here: `https://github.com/PacktPublishing/Microsoft-Intune-Cookbook/blob/main/Chapter-11/add-office-updatepolicy.ps1`.

4. Now, create the new profile and grab the ID for assignment:

    ```
    $updateprofile = Invoke-MgGraphRequest -Uri $url -Method POST
    -Body $json -ContentType "application/json" -OutputType PSObject
    $profileid = $updateprofile.id
    ```

5. Update the URL so that it includes the policy ID:

    ```
    $updateurl = "https://graph.microsoft.com/beta/deviceManagement/
    configurationPolicies/$profileid/assign"
    ```

6. Now, we need to add the group ID to the JSON and finally send the request to assign the profile to our group:

    ```
    $updatejson = @"
    {
        "assignments": [
            {
                "target": {
                    "@odata.type": "#microsoft.graph.
    groupAssignmentTarget",
                    "groupId": "$groupid"
                }
            }
        ]
    }
    "@
    Invoke-MgGraphRequest -Method POST -Uri $updateurl -ContentType
    "application/json" -Body $updatejson
    ```

With that, we have configured Office updates using Settings catalog policies, including automating their creation

Windows app protection

With more users accessing corporate data from personal devices, application protection is more important than ever.

At the time of writing, Windows **Mobile Application Management** (**MAM**) is a new addition and only supports the Microsoft Edge browser. For that reason, we are going to configure MAM in this recipe and then also add **conditional access** policies to block anything that is not Microsoft Edge for personal devices.

Getting started

The first thing to watch here is that personal devices are not allowed to enroll in Microsoft Intune; otherwise, they will bypass the conditional access rules. This will be covered in *Chapter 13, Tenant Administration*.

How to do it...

Follow these steps to configure Windows application protection:

1. The first step is to enable MAM across the tenant. This only has to be done once.
2. In **Tenant administration**, click on **Connectors and tokens** and then **Mobile Threat Defense**.
3. Add a connector for **Windows Security Center**.

> Tip
>
> Do not worry if it displays as unavailable; it will update when used.

4. Next, click on **Apps** and then click **App protection policies**.
5. Click **Create New** and select **Windows** (not **Windows Information Protection**).
6. Give your policy **Name** and **Description** values and click **Next**.
7. On the **Apps** screen, click the blue **+ Select Apps** test and select **Microsoft Edge**. Click **Select** and then click **Next**.
8. Configure your data protection settings – that is, whether you want data to be copied into or out of the application and whether to block printing. Then, click **Next**.
9. On the **Health Checks** screen, you can configure more protection around the data, including after how many days to wipe the data, and you can also add minimum application versions. Under **Device conditions**, you can specify the minimum operating system versions to block any unsupported Microsoft installations.

> Tip
>
> One health check setting worth adding here is **Disabled Account**. Set it to **Block Access** so that you can be sure any ex-employees are blocked at the personal device level.

10. Once you have configured everything, click **Next**.
11. Click **Next** on the **Scope tags** page as this is a global policy.

12. Assign as appropriate. Remember that this is happening at the user level as it is applying to devices not enrolled into Intune or Entra ID, so the group needs to contain users. There is currently no option to select all users, but you could create a dynamic group containing all members with a valid Intune license. Once configured, click **Next**.

13. Finally, check that the settings look correct and click **Create**.

14. Now that we have completed the Intune side, we need to add extra security for **conditional access**.

    Navigate to **Endpoint security** and click on **Conditional access**.

    We need to block non-corporate devices from accessing anything but the web app by requiring compliance. While you should do this for all devices, this policy is only for BYOD, so we will also use a device filter to exclude corporate-owned machines.

15. First, select **All users** (excluding your Break Glass account) and target **All cloud apps** as we do not want any data escaping unprotected.

16. As this is a Windows-only configuration, configure the device platforms to only **Windows**; we do not want this policy being applied to other platforms:

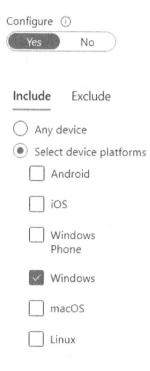

Figure 11.8 – Device platforms

17. We want to let the browser through on this one, and we will protect that on the next policy. Therefore, apply this policy to everything excluding **Browser**:

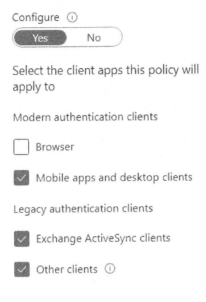

Figure 11.9 – Application clients

18. As mentioned previously, we will exclude corporate devices using the following filter as seen in the image after it:

```
device.deviceOwnership -eq "Company"
```

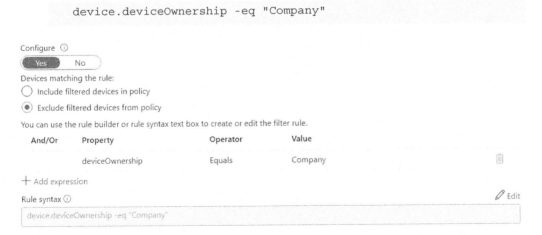

Figure 11.10 – Conditional access filter

19. Then, we need to require compliance, which will automatically block non-corporate devices. To do this, select **Require device to be marked as compliant** within **Grant access**:

Figure 11.11 – Grant access

This has locked down our non-browser access. Now, we want to lock down browser access with a second conditional access policy.

20. Again, we want to target **All users** and **All cloud apps** and also include only **Windows** devices.

21. We only want to apply this policy to **Browser**; selecting anything else will cause it to fail:

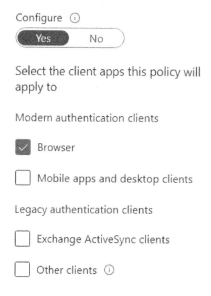

Figure 11.12 – Application client apps applicability

22. Again, ignore corporate devices with the same filter, as shown in *Figure 11.10*.

23. Most important of all, we need to **Require app protection policy** under **Grant access**:

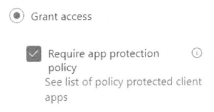

Figure 11.13 – Require app protection policy

As an extra layer of security, you can also **Block downloads (Preview)** using **Use Conditional Access App Control** in the **Session** controls:

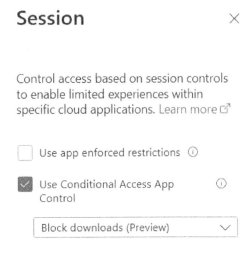

Figure 11.14 – Block downloads (Preview)

We have now secured our data within the Edge browser on personal devices and blocked access via any other methods on Windows.

Automating it

This is split into four different parts – one to enable the connector, one to add the policy, and then two conditional access policies. We will do everything with PowerShell and Microsoft Graph API. Follow these steps to create your policies:

1. Enabling the connector involves sending a simple request to set the value to `true`:

```
$url = "https://graph.microsoft.com/beta/deviceManagement/
mobileThreatDefenseConnectors"
```

```
$threatjson = @"
{
    "windowsMobileApplicationManagementEnabled": true
}
"@
Invoke-MgGraphRequest -Method POST -Uri $url -Body $threatjson
-ContentType "application/json" -OutputType PSObject
```

2. Now, we need to configure our policy. The JSON includes every available setting, even if they were not configured in the GUI, where they are simply set to `null`. The assignment is also included in this JSON rather than a separate command after creation. You can find the JSON in the script here: `https://github.com/PacktPublishing/Microsoft-Intune-Cookbook/blob/main/Chapter-11/windows-MAM.ps1`.

3. Then, we need to create our conditional access policies using the same process as in *Chapter 5*.

    First, we must configure our policy so that it requires app protection. The policy can be found here: `https://github.com/PacktPublishing/Microsoft-Intune-Cookbook/blob/main/Chapter-11/windows-mam-conditional-access.ps1`.

That completes this recipe on automating Windows MAM within the tenant using both Intune and conditional access policies.

12

PowerShell Scripting across Intune

An important and often overlooked part of Intune is its ability to run scripts on devices, whether as one-off deployments (**Platform scripts**) or more regularly via **Remediations** (previously called **Proactive Remediations**). With Windows 10 and Windows 11, PowerShell has become increasingly more powerful to the point where almost anything can be done on devices with a script.

In Intune, we can use PowerShell scripts to configure properties not yet available in the settings catalog, copy files, add registry keys, or even run a script to remove unwanted Windows bloatware for a cleaner build.

Platform scripts are run as configurations for simple configuration settings or anything required during device setup. Remediations, on the other hand, are repeatable scripts with logic that only runs when required.

Throughout this chapter, we will learn how to deploy PowerShell scripts and Remediations, but also how to write the scripts themselves and provide some example scripts to get you started. This will include not only Remediations and Platform scripts but also the usage of scripts within application deployments.

In this chapter, we will cover the following recipes:

- Deploying Platform scripts
- Configuring Remediations
- Using custom detection scripts in apps
- Using custom requirements scripts in apps

Technical requirements

For this chapter, you will need a modern web browser and a PowerShell code editor such as Visual Studio Code or PowerShell ISE.

All the scripts that are referenced in this chapter can be found here: `https://github.com/PacktPublishing/Microsoft-Intune-Cookbook`.

Deploying Platform scripts

We will start with the original option, which has been available in Intune for longer than the rest. Platform scripts run once on the device and can run in the system or user context. By default, they run in 32-bit mode, but this can be changed on deployment. This is important to note as environmental variables will differ accordingly for both system/user and 32/64-bit.

To find out more about User/System targeting, go to `https://andrewstaylor.com/2022/11/22/intune-comparing-system-vs-user-for-everything/`.

When running during Autopilot, there is no labeled step where scripts run – they run when it says **Preparing apps** in User or Device setup. If you hit a time-out issue here, it is more than likely a failed PowerShell script that has not reported a success code in time.

To troubleshoot and view the output of a script, retrieve the script ID from the address bar in the Intune portal. The output will be in the following location under a subkey with the respective ID:

```
HKLM:\Software\Microsoft\IntuneManagementExtension\Policies
```

Ideally, you should add logging in the script itself for more thorough and easily accessible output.

Getting started

In this example, we will deploy a simple script to add a registry key and remove an in-built Windows AppX application.

In your editor of choice, create a new PowerShell script and enter the following code:

```
Get-AppxPackage -allusers -Name Microsoft.BingNews| Remove-AppxPackage
-AllUsers
$Search = "HKLM:\SOFTWARE\Policies\Microsoft\Windows\Windows Search"
If (!(Test-Path $Search)) {
    New-Item $Search
}
If (Test-Path $Search) {
    Set-ItemProperty $Search AllowCortana -Value 0
}
```

This will remove Bing News and stop Cortana from appearing in the search box.

How to do it...

Now that we have written our script, follow these steps to deploy it:

1. Within the Intune portal, navigate to **Devices**, click on **Windows**, and then click **Scripts and remediations**.

2. By default, you will be taken to **Remediations**, which we will cover in the next recipe (*Configuring Remediations*). Click on the **Platform scripts** tab at the top, then click **Add**.

3. As usual, specify your script's **Name** and **Description**. Once added, you will not be able to see the script's content within the portal (there is a way to download and decode it via Graph if needed), so it is advisable to make the descriptions thorough and keep a copy of the source files. Once you have configured these, click **Next**.

4. On the script **Settings** page, select the script you added earlier. Beneath that, we have a few options:

    - **Run this script using the logged on credentials**: Setting this to **Yes** runs the scripts in the user context so that they can access the user's profile. However, unless your users have administrative rights, they cannot do anything beyond that.

    - **Enforce script signature check**: Setting this to **Yes** means the script will only run if it is signed correctly. In most cases, for homemade scripts, this needs to be set to **No**. If it is required for security purposes, make sure you sign each script before uploading them.

    - **Run script in 64 bit PowerShell host**: By default, this is set to **No**, so any registry keys you write will go to WOW6432Node and files will go to Program Files (x86). Changing this to **Yes** will write the script files and output to the primary locations.

5. In the preceding script, we need to run at the System level as we are writing to **HKEY Local Machine (HKLM)** and also need to run in the 64-bit host. Our script is unsigned, so the setting needs to be **No** for the signature check:

Figure 12.1 – Platform Script details

Once configured, click **Next**.

6. We do not require **Scope tags** for this, so again, click **Next**.

7. Now, it is a case of assigning the script. If you want it to run during the Device phase of Autopilot, deploy to a device group; for the User phase, deploy to a user group. In this case, it is a device clean script, so we will run it in the device context so that we know it has been completed before a user has logged in. Once configured, click **Next**.

8. Finally, on the **Review + Add** screen, confirm all of your settings and click **Add**.

With that, you have created, uploaded, and added a PowerShell Platform Script to Intune.

Automating it

When adding the interface, you may have noticed that there is a brief notification while the file is uploaded into Intune. Fortunately, when automating, we can convert to Base64 format within our script and remove that step.

Follow these steps to deploy our Platform Script using Graph:

1. As usual, we will start with our name, description, group ID, and URL:

    ```
    $name = "PowerShell Device Script"
    $description = "Removes Bing News AppX package and stops Cortana
    running in search box"
    $groupid = "xxxxxxxx-xxxx-xxxx-xxxx-xxxxxxxxxxxx"
    $url = "https://graph.microsoft.com/beta/deviceManagement/
    deviceManagementScripts"
    ```

2. Next, we want to add the script itself within a variable. Note that we are using a single quote around it so that it fully escapes everything in the code:

    ```
    $scriptcontent = @'
    Get-AppxPackage -allusers -Name Microsoft.BingNews| Remove-
    AppxPackage -AllUsers
    $Search = "HKLM:\SOFTWARE\Policies\Microsoft\Windows\Windows
    Search"
    If (!(Test-Path $Search)) {
        New-Item $Search
    }
    If (Test-Path $Search) {
        Set-ItemProperty $Search AllowCortana -Value 0
    }
    '@
    ```

3. Now, we need to convert the script content into Base64 format:

    ```
    $base64encoded = [System.Convert]::ToBase64String([System.Text.
    Encoding]::Unicode.GetBytes($scriptcontent))
    ```

4. Next, we must populate the JSON. This is straightforward when using standard true/false options for the 32/64-bit, User/System, and signed options. We have also added our Base64 encoded script:

```
$json = @"
{
    "description": "$name",
    "displayName": "$description",
    "enforceSignatureCheck": true,
    "fileName": "platform-script.ps1",
    "roleScopeTagIds": [
        "0"
    ],
    "runAs32Bit": false,
    "runAsAccount": "system",
    "scriptContent": "$base64encoded"
}
"@
```

5. Now, send a POST request to add the script to Intune and grab the script ID so that it can be assigned:

```
$addscript = Invoke-MgGraphRequest -Uri $url -Method Post -Body
$json -ContentType "application/json" -OutputType PSObject
$scriptid = $addscript.id
```

6. Populate the URL with the ID and assign it to our group:

```
$assignurl = "https://graph.microsoft.com/beta/deviceManagement/
deviceManagementScripts/$scriptid/assign"
$assignjson = @"
{
    "deviceManagementScriptAssignments": [
        {
            "target": {
                "@odata.type": "#microsoft.graph.
groupAssignmentTarget",
                "groupId": "$groupid"
            }
        }
    ]
}
"@
Invoke-MgGraphRequest -Uri $assignurl -Method Post -Body
$assignjson -ContentType "application/json" -OutputType PSObject
```

You have now created your first PowerShell Platform Script using PowerShell and Graph.

Configuring Remediations

While Platform scripts are excellent for run-once scenarios such as when you are provisioning a device, PowerShell is incredibly powerful and there may be situations where you want something to run more than once, or you want to view the output in the console itself.

This is where Remediations (formerly Proactive Remediations) come into play. They can be set to run on a schedule, but as they work with a detection and remediation configuration, the script itself will only run if required.

A Remediation is split into two scripts: a **Detection script** and a **Remediation script**.

The detection script is arguably the most important of the two as this decides whether the Remediation script needs to run. The key output here is the **exit code**. An exit code of 0 means the device is compliant with the check and no further action is needed. If the exit code is 1, it causes the remediation to run.

There are no restrictions on the content of the scripts, so long as the two exit codes are set. We will run through an example in this recipe, but a good repository of pre-curated scripts can be found here: `https://github.com/JayRHa/EndpointAnalyticsRemediationScripts`.

Getting started

For this recipe, we will add a Remediation that should be helpful in most environments and trigger disk cleanup if our disk space is low.

To start, we need to create two scripts (for detection and remediation). In your preferred editor, create the following PowerShell scripts:

- `Detect.ps1`:

```
$storageThreshold = 15
$utilization = (Get-PSDrive | Where {$_.name -eq "C"}).free
if(($storageThreshold *1GB) -lt $utilization){
    write-output "Storage is fine, no remediation needed"
    exit 0}
else{
    write-output "Storage is low, remediation needed"
    exit 1}
```

- Remediate.ps1:

```
$cleanupTypeSelection = 'Temporary Sync Files', 'Downloaded
Program Files', 'Memory Dump Files', 'Recycle Bin'
foreach ($keyName in $cleanupTypeSelection) {
    $newItemParams = @{
        Path        = "HKLM:\SOFTWARE\Microsoft\Windows\
CurrentVersion\Explorer\VolumeCaches\$keyName"
        Name        = <StateFlags0001>
        Value       = 1
        PropertyType = 'DWord'
        ErrorAction = <SilentlyContinue'
    }
    New-ItemProperty @newItemParams | Out-Null
}
Start-Process -FilePath CleanMgr.exe -ArgumentList '/sagerun:1'
-NoNewWindow -Wait
```

The detection script simply inspects the free space on the C drive. If it is less than 15 GB, it sends Exit code 0, which triggers the remediation to run. The other thing to consider here is the output that is sent with the exit code. You can view the detection output after running it within the Intune console, so adding write-output with something useful will help you when you are reviewing the device's status later on. We will cover this in the *There's more...* section of this recipe.

The remediation then runs the disk cleanup utility to clear out temp files, downloaded program files, memory dump files, and the recycle bin (change as appropriate for your environment). No exit code is needed for the remediation script.

How to do it...

Now that we have created our scripts, follow these steps to add them to Intune:

1. Navigate to **Devices**, click on **Windows**, and then click **Scripts and remediations**. It will default to **Remediations** at the top, so click **Create**.

2. As with the previous recipe, add **Name** and **Description** values. You can also add an author here; it will auto-populate the logged-in user, but it is a free text field. While it is good practice to add a good description, remediations can be viewed in the portal once they have been added if needed. Once configured, click **Next**.

3. On the **Settings** screen, add your **Detection** and **Remediation** scripts. You have the same options as with PowerShell scripts to set the context – that is, 32/64-bit, system, and signing. In this example, we need system context, 64-bit, and unsigned. Once configured, click **Next**:

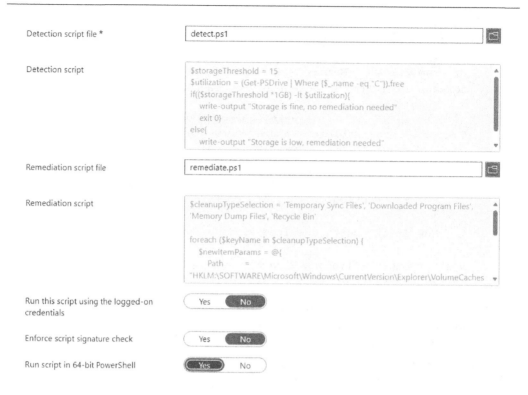

Figure 12.2 – Remediation script settings

4. We do not need **Scope tags** for a site-wide remediation such as this, so click **Next**.

5. Now, assign the Remediation as required. You will see you also have the option to add **All Devices** or **All Users**. Once you have selected your group, click the text marked **Daily**; a flyout will appear where you can select the schedule for the remediation to run. The options are **Daily** (with the ability to select how many days and at what time), **Hourly**, and **Once** (fixed date/time). You also have the option to run on-demand, which we will cover in *There's more...* section of this recipe. In this case, we are going to run it hourly as the detection script will not impact the devices significantly. Once configured, click **Next**:

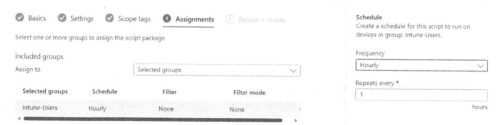

Figure 12.3 – Remediation assignments

6. Finally, ensure that everything looks correct and click **Create**. You will notice that **Version** is listed as **No Version**. This was a text field on the first screen that could not be changed. It will automatically increment as you update the scripts.

Now that we have added our remediation to the portal, we can look at automating it to quickly deploy future scripts.

Automating it

Remediations are slightly more tricky to automate as we have different options when assigning, depending on the schedule that is selected. However, we simply need to make a change in the assignment JSON. We can deal with this using an `IF` statement.

Follow these steps to automate your first remediation deployment:

1. To make things easier, we will add more variables at the start, including `Publisher`, `RunAs`, `32-bit`, `64-bit`, and the schedule itself:

```
$DisplayName = "Clean Disk Space"
$Description = "Clears if less than 15Gb free"
$Publisher = "Your Name Here"
##RunAs can be "system" or "user"
$RunAs = "system"
##True for 32-bit, false for 64-bit
$RunAs32 = "true"
##Daily or Hourly
$ScheduleType = "Daily"
##How Often
$ScheduleFrequency = "1"
##Start Time (if daily)
$StartTime = "01:00"
$groupid = "xxxxxxxx-xxxx-xxxx-xxxx-xxxxxxxxxxxx"
$url = "https://graph.microsoft.com/beta/deviceManagement/
deviceHealthScripts"
```

2. Once our variables have been set, we need to add the detection script and then convert it to Base64:

```
$detectionscriptcontent = @'
$storageThreshold = 15
$utilization = (Get-PSDrive | Where {$_.name -eq "C"}).free
if(($storageThreshold *1GB) -lt $utilization){exit 0}
else{exit 1}
'@
$detectionbase64encoded = [System.
Convert]::ToBase64String([System.Text.Encoding]::Unicode.
GetBytes($detectionscriptcontent))
```

3. We need to do the same with the remediation script, so set the script's content and encode it:

```
$remediationscriptcontent = @'
$cleanupTypeSelection = 'Temporary Sync Files', 'Downloaded
Program Files', 'Memory Dump Files', 'Recycle Bin'
foreach ($keyName in $cleanupTypeSelection) {
    $newItemParams = @{
        Path         = "HKLM:\SOFTWARE\Microsoft\Windows\
CurrentVersion\Explorer\VolumeCaches\$keyName"
        Name         = <StateFlags0001>
        Value        = 1
        PropertyType = 'DWord'
        ErrorAction  = <SilentlyContinue'
    }
    New-ItemProperty @newItemParams | Out-Null
}
Start-Process -FilePath CleanMgr.exe -ArgumentList '/sagerun:1'
-NoNewWindow -Wait
'@
$remediationbase64encoded = [System.
Convert]::ToBase64String([System.Text.Encoding]::Unicode.
GetBytes($remediationscriptcontent))
```

4. The final JSON here is very similar to a standard PowerShell script, which we covered in the previous recipe, just with extra fields available to us:

```
$json = @"
{
    "description": "$description",
    "detectionScriptContent": "$detectionbase64encoded",
    "displayName": "$displayname",
    "enforceSignatureCheck": false,
    "publisher": "$publisher",
    "remediationScriptContent": "$remediationbase64encoded",
    "roleScopeTagIds": [
        "0"
    ],
    "runAs32Bit": $runas32,
    "runAsAccount": "$runas"
}
"@
```

5. Now, we need to create our script and grab the ID for assignment:

```
$addscript = Invoke-MgGraphRequest -Uri $url -Method Post -Body
$json -ContentType "application/json" -OutputType PSObject
$scriptid = $addscript.id
```

6. Now comes the interesting part – we need to check on the schedule as `Daily` and `Hourly` using different `@odata.type` options. `Daily` also has an extra option. For that, run `IF` against `$ScheduleType`, which you set earlier, and set a variable accordingly:

```
if($ScheduleType -eq "Daily"){
    $Schedule = @"
    "runSchedule": {
        "@odata.type": "#microsoft.graph.
deviceHealthScriptDailySchedule",
        "interval": $scheduleFrequency,
        "time": "$startTime",
        "useUtc": false
    },
"@
}
else{
    $Schedule = @"
    "runSchedule": {
        "@odata.type": "#microsoft.graph.
deviceHealthScriptHourlySchedule",
        "interval": $interval
    },
"@
}
```

7. Finally, we must populate this into the `Assignment` JSON and send a `POST` request to assign the remediation:

```
$assignurl = "https://graph.microsoft.com/beta/deviceManagement/
deviceHealthScripts/$scriptid/assign"
$assignjson = @"
{
    "deviceHealthScriptAssignments": [
        {
            "runRemediationScript": true,
            $schedule
            "target": {
                "@odata.type": "#microsoft.graph.
groupAssignmentTarget",
                "groupId": "$groupid"
            }
        }
    ]
}
"@
```

```
Invoke-MgGraphRequest -Uri $assignurl -Method Post -Body
$assignjson -ContentType "application/json" -OutputType PSObject
```

We have created our first remediation using Graph.

There's more...

As mentioned earlier, remediations provide us with some additional functionality beyond scheduling that is not available with Platform scripts. Let us take a look.

Viewing output

A hidden but very useful feature is to be able to view the script's output within the console rather than having to access the device itself. To do so, follow these steps:

1. In the Intune portal, click on **Devices**, then **Windows**, then **Scripts and remediations**. In your list of scripts, click on the script in question.

2. Now, click **Device status** in the left-hand menu under **Monitor**.

    The standard status is cut down so that it fits on the screen, but click on **Columns** and you will see additional options. Tick **Pre-remediation detection output** and **Post-remediation detection output** and click **Apply**:

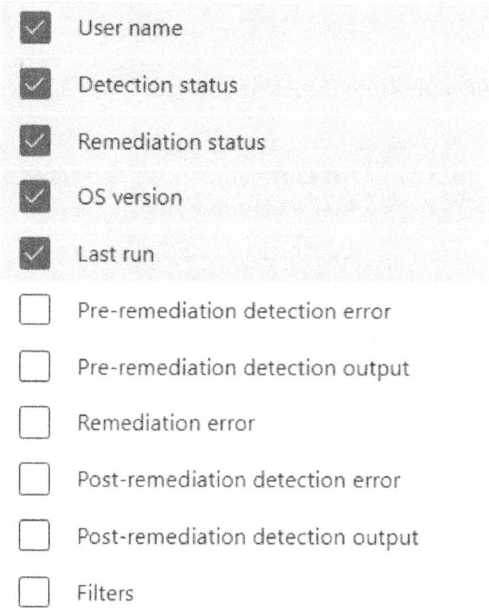

☑ User name

☑ Detection status

☑ Remediation status

☑ OS version

☑ Last run

☐ Pre-remediation detection error

☐ Pre-remediation detection output

☐ Remediation error

☐ Post-remediation detection error

☐ Post-remediation detection output

☐ Filters

Figure 12.4 – Remediation output columns

This will now show the output that is returned by the detection script before remediation and after remediation. The output here is only as good as the `write-output` that you configured in your detection script. This is worth keeping in mind when you are creating your scripts.

Now that we have learned how to view the output, we can look at running remediations on demand.

Running remediations on demand

If you need to quickly run a remediation, another useful feature is running remediations on demand. This is especially useful for any urgent security fixes or when you are troubleshooting a device. You could run a remediation with standard troubleshooting steps and then, in the detection script, output any common errors so that you know where to start. Follow these steps to run a remediation on demand against a device:

1. To run on demand, navigate to **Devices**, then click on **Windows** and click on your device in the list.

2. Now, click the three dots (**…**) and select **Run remediation**:

Figure 12.5 – Run remediation (preview)

3. You will be presented with a list of deployed remediations in the tenancy. Select the one you wish to run (you can only select one) and click **Run remediation**.

If you want to run a remediation against multiple devices at once, you can use Graph. An example script can be found here: `https://github.com/andrew-s-taylor/public/blob/main/Powershell%20Scripts/Intune/bulk-run-remediation-ondemand.ps1`.

Running remediation on demand using Graph simply requires a basic POST request, including the remediation ID to a URL and the device ID:

```
$deviceid = "DeviceID"
$remediationid = "RemediationID"
$json = @"
{
    "ScriptPolicyId": "$remediationid",
}
"@
    $url = "https://graph.microsoft.com/beta/deviceManagement/
```

```
managedDevices('$deviceID')/initiateOnDemandProactiveRemediation"
    Invoke-MgGraphRequest -uri $url -Method Post -Body $json
-ContentType "application/json"
```

Using custom detection scripts in apps

While we covered this briefly in *Chapter 11*, **detection scripts** work slightly differently from a PowerShell platform or remediation script, so this recipe will cover how they work and include some working examples.

How to do it...

The important thing to note with a custom detection script is it requires *both* an **exit code** (0) and a **standard output (STDOUT)**. Sending an exit code of 1, or not including the STDOUT, will flag the installation as failed.

Before searching the STDOUT, the script must return an output. So, the following code will suffice and mark the installation as successful:

```
Write-output "App found"
Exit 0
```

Now, we can use and deploy a custom detection script:

1. To use a custom detection script, you must add the script during packaging or after deploying. For post-deployment, click on **Apps**, then **Windows**. Find the application in question and click on it.

2. Now, click on **Properties** and click **Edit** next to **Detection rules**.

3. In the dropdown, select **Use a custom detection script** and find the detection script you created (some options will be mentioned shortly).

> **Important note**
>
> You cannot select system versus user context. One annoyance here is that custom detection scripts run exclusively in the *system* context, even if the application is at the user level. If you need to query files or registry keys in the user context, you are going to need to use your script to discover the logged-in user and add that to c:\users\ or HKCU\. There is a function in the GitHub repository for this chapter that will return the logged-on user's SID and username.

4. Set the 32/64-bit settings as appropriate. This is going to be especially important for applications as often, you will be looking for registry keys or files in the `Program Files` directory and you want to make sure the script queries the correct location.

5. Finally, enable or disable **Enforce script signature check and run script silently**. If your scripts are unsigned, set this to **No**. Do not worry about the **run script silently** part – unsigned scripts will also run in the background as they are deploying in the *system* context.

6. Once configured, click **Review + Save**.

7. Finally, confirm that everything looks correct and click **Save**.

That completes this recipe on how to use and deploy a custom detection script. Now, we can look at some real-world examples.

Examples of application detection scripts

Here are a few examples to give you an idea of how app detection scripts work. It is often easier to see a working script to fully understand the output requirements:

- This script will perform a simple registry check for 7-Zip:

```
$Path = "HKLM:\SOFTWARE\7-Zip"
$Name = "Path"
$Type = "STRING"
$Value = "C:\Program Files\7-Zip\"

Try {
    $Registry = Get-ItemProperty -Path $Path -Name $Name
-ErrorAction Stop | Select-Object -ExpandProperty $Name
    If ($Registry -eq $Value){
        Write-Output "Detected"
        Exit 0
    }
    Exit 1
}
Catch {
    Exit 1
}
```

- This script uses file detection for an application:

```
$File = "C:\windows\system32\notepad.exe"
if (Test-Path $File) {
    write-output "Notepad detected, exiting"
    exit 0
}
else {
    exit 1
}
```

> **Tip**
>
> Realistically, you would probably do these detections with the GUI tools, so we will cover some use cases that go beyond that ability.

- This example script will check that a service has been created and is running. This is useful for those apps that will not run without a running service:

```
$service = get-service -name "MozillaMaintenance"
if ($service.Status -eq "Running") {
    write-output "MozillaMaintenance detected and
running, exiting"
    exit 0
}
else {
    exit 1
}
```

- If you want to ensure the latest version has been installed but do not trust the vendor versioning within the application, you can query the last time the file was updated:

```
$filedate = (Get-Item "C:\Windows\System32\notepad.exe").
LastWriteTime
if ($filedate -gt (Get-Date).AddDays(-1)) {
    write-output "Detected"
    exit 0
}
else {
    exit 1
}
```

That completes configuring detection scripts using the UI and some examples. Now, let us look at how to automate this process.

Automating it

Follow these steps to configure a custom detection script using automation:

> **Important note**
>
> Whether you are configuring during initial deployment or afterward, the change is within the JSON that is passed when the application stub is created. The only difference is that a new application uses a POST request, whereas an update runs a PATCH request against the existing application.

1. First, similar to a Platform Script, we need to take the script's content:

```
$script = @'
$Path = "HKLM:\SOFTWARE\7-Zip"
$Name = "Path"
$Type = "STRING"
$Value = "C:\Program Files\7-Zip\"
Try {
    $Registry = Get-ItemProperty -Path $Path -Name $Name
-ErrorAction Stop | Select-Object -ExpandProperty $Name
    If ($Registry -eq $Value){
        Write-Output "Detected"
        Exit 0
    }
    Exit 1
}
Catch {
    Exit 1
}
'@
```

2. We must convert this into Base64:

```
$base64script = [Convert]::ToBase64String([System.Text.
Encoding]::Unicode.GetBytes($script))
```

3. Then, we must add it to the rules section of the JSON:

```
$json = @"
    "rules": [
        {
            "@odata.type": "#microsoft.graph.
win32LobAppPowerShellScriptRule",
            "comparisonValue": null,
            "displayName": null,
```

```
                    "enforceSignatureCheck": false,
                    "operationType": "notConfigured",
                    "operator": "notConfigured",
                    "ruleType": "detection",
                    "runAs32Bit": false,
                    "runAsAccount": null,
                    "scriptContent": "$base64script"
                }
            ],
        "@
```

Note that @odata.type changes to PowerShellScriptRule here.

You can also see that the runAsAccount option is present, but it is set to null. If you try and set this to anything else, the request will fail with the following error:

```
The RunAsAccount property may not be set for
Win32LobAppPowerShellScriptRule instances used for app detection
```

You would then populate the rest of the Win32 script and upload it accordingly.

That completes this recipe on custom application detection scripts.

Using custom requirements scripts in apps

Another PowerShell option is using custom requirements scripts. While the requirements rules are reasonably comprehensive, you may want to take these a step further – for example, only deploy an application if the device is manufactured by a particular company.

One particularly useful application for these is when you are updating *available* applications. As these are user-installed, when you deploy an update to them, the user has to manually install the latest version from the company portal (providing you have the detection rules set correctly to notice it needs re-installing). This is far from ideal, especially when you are dealing with a zero-day exploit.

In this situation, you can deploy an application *as required* to everyone and then set a requirements rule that it must detect the application is already present on the device to install.

These work differently and are closer to **compliance scripts** than remediation or detection scripts. We do not need an exit code since Intune reads the output of the script, which must match the condition that has been set within the application requirements rule.

As with the previous recipe, we will include some examples to demonstrate this further.

How to do it...

In this example, we will set a requirement that the application will only be installed if the device is manufactured by ACME (the manufacturer that was created for this example). Follow these steps to configure and deploy the requirements script:

1. The first thing we need to do is create our script. In your editor of choice, create a new PowerShell script with the following code:

    ```
    $Manufacturer = Get-WmiObject -Class Win32_ComputerSystem |
    Select-Object -ExpandProperty Manufacturer
    $Manufacturer
    ```

    This is simply grabbing the manufacturer's name from the machine's WMI and returning it.

2. Now, we need to add this to an application. Navigate to **Apps**, click on **Windows**, and find the application in question. Click on it and click **Properties**.

3. Now, click **Edit** next to **Requirements**.

4. Click + **Add** at the bottom.

5. In the flyout, under **Requirement type**, select **Script**.

6. Now, select the script we have just created, which will also auto-populate the **Name** field; you can change this if required.

7. Set the standard options for 32/64-bit, user/system context, and whether the script must be signed.

8. Now for the important part – we need to tell it what data to look for.

    You have several options here and you must select the correct one. Otherwise, your requirements script will fail, even if the device meets them:

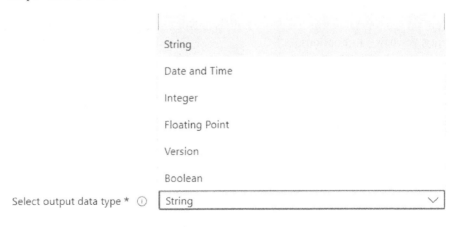

Figure 12.6 – Output data types

If you are unsure which one you need, within your script, type the variable followed by `.gettype()`.

In our case, this would look like this:

```
$manufacturer.GetType()
```

This will return the details of the output and the name you are looking for – in this case, `String`:

```
PS C:\Windows\system32> $manufacturer.GetType()

IsPublic IsSerial Name                                             BaseType
-------- -------- ----                                             --------
True     True     String                                           System.Object
```

Figure 12.7 – GetType output

To check for a numeric value, run the following code:

```
$test = 1
$Test.gettype()
```

The result will be an integer:

```
PS C:\Windows\system32> $test.GetType()

IsPublic IsSerial Name                                             BaseType
-------- -------- ----                                             --------
True     True     Int32                                            System.ValueType
```

Figure 12.8 – Integer output

9. Select the appropriate data type from the dropdown.

10. Now, set your operator, which is either **Equals** or **Not Equal to** for a string. For the other data types, you have more options.

We only want a particular result, so we are going to set this to **Equals**.

11. Finally, set the value we are looking for, which in our case is **ACME**:

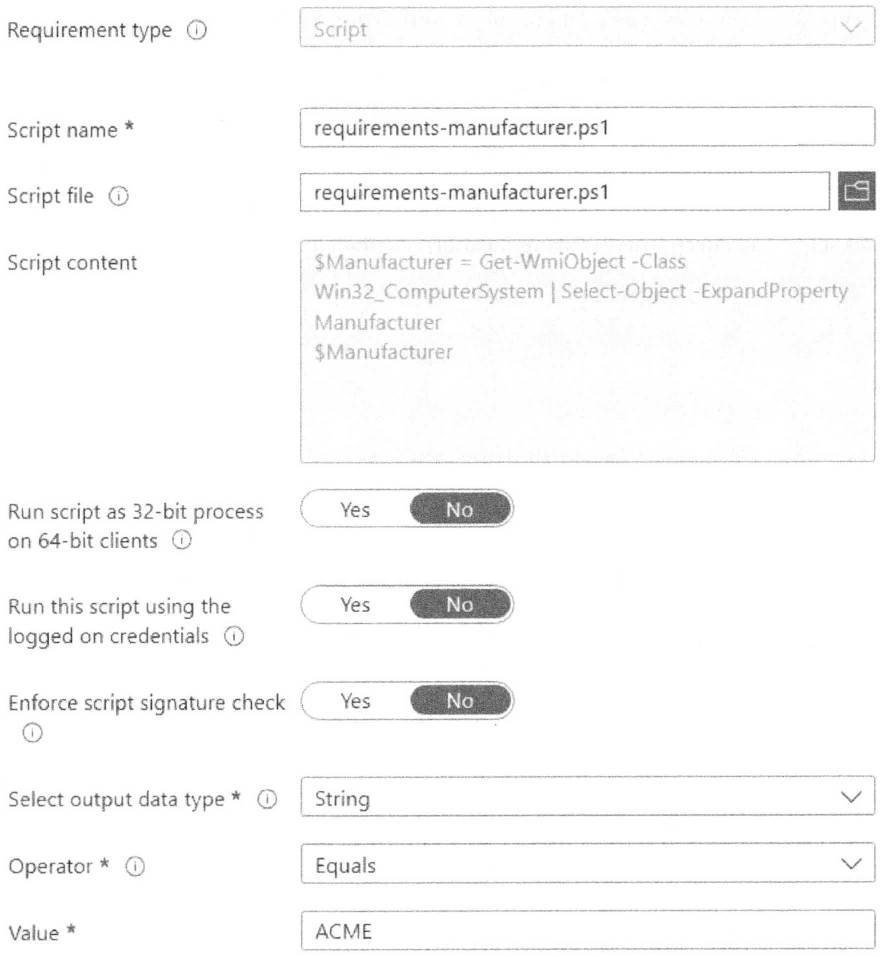

Requirement type ⓘ	Script ⌄

Script name *	requirements-manufacturer.ps1
Script file ⓘ	requirements-manufacturer.ps1

Script content

```
$Manufacturer = Get-WmiObject -Class
Win32_ComputerSystem | Select-Object -ExpandProperty
Manufacturer
$Manufacturer
```

Run script as 32-bit process on 64-bit clients ⓘ	Yes **No**
Run this script using the logged on credentials ⓘ	Yes **No**
Enforce script signature check ⓘ	Yes **No**
Select output data type * ⓘ	String ⌄
Operator * ⓘ	Equals ⌄
Value *	ACME

Figure 12.9 – Script requirements configuration

12. Now, click **OK**.

13. Back on the **Requirements** page, click **Review + Save**.

14. Confirm that everything looks okay and click **Save**.

That completes the steps to add a custom requirements script. Now, let us look at some real-world examples.

Examples of custom requirements scripts

These examples will show use cases for custom requirements scripts in application deployment:

- This script will detect and return the manufacturer:

```
$Manufacturer = Get-WmiObject -Class Win32_ComputerSystem |
Select-Object -ExpandProperty Manufacturer
$Manufacturer
```

- This script will check whether an application is installed:

```
$File = "C:\windows\system32\notepad.exe"
if (Test-Path $File) {
    write-output "Notepad detected"
}
else {
write-output "Notepad Not Detected"
}
```

In the GUI, you would be looking for a data type of **String** with an operator of **Equals** and a value of **Notepad detected** within the requirements configuration (as per *Figure 12.9*).

- This script will look for a particular hotfix on a device:

```
$hotfixid = "KB5030219"
$hotfix = Get-HotFix | where-object HotFixID -eq $hotfixid
if ($hotfix) {
    write-output "Hotfix detected"
}
else {
write-output "Hotfix Not Detected"
}
```

For this one, we need the **Hotfix detected** string.

Now that we have looked at some examples, we can learn how to automate this process.

Automating it

The automation we need to do here works the same as the custom detection scripts we covered in the previous recipe, only instead of setting the `Rules` section of the JSON, we must set the `requirementRules` section.

Follow these steps to configure our requirements script:

1. First, we need to add our script:

```
$script = @'
$Manufacturer = Get-WmiObject -Class Win32_ComputerSystem |
Select-Object -ExpandProperty Manufacturer
$Manufacturer
'@
```

2. Then, convert the script's content to Base64:

```
$base64script = [Convert]::ToBase64String([System.Text.
Encoding]::Unicode.GetBytes($script))
```

3. Then, populate the JSON with the converted script's content:

```
$json = @"
"requirementRules": [
    {
        "@odata.type": "#microsoft.graph.
win32LobAppPowerShellScriptRequirement",
        "operator": "equal",
        "detectionValue": "ACME",
        "displayName": "requirements-manufacturer.ps1",
        "enforceSignatureCheck": false,
        "runAs32Bit": false,
        "runAsAccount": "system",
        "scriptContent": "$base64script",
        "detectionType": "string"
    }
],
"@
```

Again, it uses the same @odata.type but adds our additional values, where we specify what we are looking for in the output. runAsAccount is also now open for amendment.

At this point, you would populate your Win32 JSON with the added requirements script and deploy it as required.

That completes this recipe on custom requirements scripts for Win32 applications.

13

Tenant Administration

After completing the main configuration of our new environment, we can look at its administration. The items available within **Tenant Administration** are tenant-wide and cover a variety of options, from user experience to administrative tasks for you as an admin.

This chapter will cover all of the main items and, where possible, how to access them via Graph.

It is important to understand all of the options that are available for an Intune administrator to ensure a smooth service for your end users, as well as to make your day-to-day tasks as time-efficient as possible. By following this chapter, you will be in a better position to maintain your tenant in the long run.

In this chapter, we will cover the following recipes:

- Reviewing your connectors
- Adding filters
- Configuring Intune roles
- Using scope tags
- Customizing the end user experience
- Deploying organizational messages
- Setting up terms and conditions
- Configuring multi-admin approval
- Checking your tenant version
- Using Intune's troubleshooting tools
- Enrollment notifications
- Configuring device restrictions
- Configuring Quiet time policies

Technical requirements

For this chapter, you will need a modern web browser and a PowerShell code editor such as Visual Studio Code or PowerShell ISE.

All the scripts that are referenced in this chapter can be found here: `https://github.com/PacktPublishing/Microsoft-Intune-Cookbook`.

Reviewing your connectors

We will start by looking at an important aspect you must keep an eye on – third-party connectors such as the *Apple VPP connector*, which we covered in *Chapter 6, Apple iOS Device Management*. A large selection is available, but not all of them will be used in every environment, so you need to monitor the ones that are important to you.

Getting ready

Here, we will learn about the various connectors that are available.

In the Intune portal, navigate to **Tenant administration** and select **Connectors and tokens**.

This will take you to a new section consisting of many different options. Let us take a look at what is available:

- **Windows enterprise certificate**: If you are using a code-signing certificate with MSIX packages, this is where you upload it to your tenant. After adding it, this page will show you the status of the certificate and, more importantly, its expiry date.

- **Microsoft Endpoint Configuration Manager**: If you are using Co-Management with Configuration Manager, this is where you can see the status of the Intune connector and its last successful sync.

- **Windows 365 partner connectors**: This is for estates using Windows 365 alongside either Citrix or VMWare to add the connector and then view its status. To access this screen, you will need a Windows 365 license.

- **Windows data**: There are two settings here. The first is to enable sending diagnostic data (which is a requirement for Autopatch, among other things). The other option is a license confirmation. Setting this to **Yes** tells Intune you have an Enterprise, Education, or AVD license (E3, E5, F3, F5), which unlocks SKU-specific features such as Remediations.

- **Apple VPP Tokens**: This is an important one if you are managing Apple devices as it is where you add your VPP tokens for application purchasing and management, but also where you monitor their expiry dates and renew them. If you need to quickly add a purchased application to Intune, this is also where you will find the sync button.

- **Managed Google Play**: Here, you can see the status of the Managed Google Play Connector and also optionally add a scope tag to any new applications that have been added for role-based assignment.

- **Chrome Enterprise**: This is for configuring and monitoring your ChromeOS devices that have been synchronized from your Chrome Enterprise domain.

- **Firmware over-the-air update**: At the time of writing, this option is for Zebra devices only and lets you configure a connector between Intune and Zebra Lifeguard.

- **Microsoft Defender for Endpoint**: Here, you can view the status of your MDE connector and configure tenant-wide, cross-platform settings. Remember that MDE needs appropriate licensing.

- **Mobile Threat Defense**: This option lets you add a connector for third-party antivirus products and then view their status. It is also a requirement for Windows MAM, as covered in *Chapter 11*.

- **Partner device management (JAMF)**: If you are using JAMF to manage your macOS devices and want to use JAMF compliance with Conditional access, you can use this option to set up a connector between the two.

- **Partner compliance management**: This is similar to JAMF but is for more platforms, such as MobileIron, VMware, and Blackberry, and also cross-platform options (Android, iOS, and macOS).

- **TeamViewer connector**: If you use TeamViewer for remote support, configuring the connector here adds Intune integration.

- **ServiceNow connector**: This one requires a license for Remote Help or Intune Suite. Configuring the connector adds details of ServiceNow incidents directly within the user **Troubleshooting + support** pane in Intune.

- **Certificate connectors**: This is where you can add your SCEP and NDES certificates for device-based authentication.

- **Derived Credentials**: This option is for configuring certificates so that they can be used with Smart card authentication across platforms.

Now that we know what these are all for, let us learn how to check their statuses using Graph.

How to do it...

To view the status of these connectors, simply click on them in the portal. As no real instructions are required here, we will look at the automation process instead.

Automating it

When you wish to automate connectors and tokens, fortunately, all menu options are available by using a GET request to a specific URL. This means we can build a custom menu using a PowerShell array and the out-gridview command. Follow these steps to create an automation script:

> **Important note**
>
> Some of these code blocks have been shortened. The full code can be found here: https://github.com/PacktPublishing/Microsoft-Intune-Cookbook/blob/main/Chapter-13/connectors-and-tokens.ps1.

1. The first thing we need to do is create our array:

```
$connectors = @(
    "Windows enterprise certificate",
    "Microsoft Endpoint Configuration Manager",
    "Windows 365 Partner connectors",
    "Windows data",
    "Apple VPP Tokens",
    "Managed Google Play",
    "Chrome Enterprise",
    "Firmware over-the-air (Zebra)",
    "Microsoft Defender for Endpoint",
    "Mobile Threat Defense",
    "Partner device management (JAMF)",
    "Partner compliance management",
    "TeamViewer connector",
    "ServiceNow connector",
    "Certificate connectors",
    "Derived Credentials"
)
```

2. Then, add out-gridview with the passthru command to grab the option we have selected:

```
$selectedconnector = $connectors | Out-GridView -Title "Select a
connector to check" -PassThru
```

3. We need to take this and pass it to a switch command to find the corresponding URL. This has been shortened for brevity; please see the link in the preceding *Note* box for the full code:

```
switch ($selectedconnector) {
    "Apple VPP Tokens" {
        $url = "https://graph.microsoft.com/beta/
deviceAppManagement/vppTokens"
    }
```

```
        "Managed Google Play" {
            $url = "https://graph.
microsoft.com/beta/deviceManagement/
mobileThreatDefenseConnectors?`$select=id,lastHeartbeatDateTime,
partnerState,androidEnabled,iosEnabled,
windowsEnabled,macEnabled,
androidMobileApplicationManagementEnabled,
iosMobileApplicationManagementEnabled,windowsMobileApplication
ManagementEnabled"
        }
        default {
            Write-Output "Invalid connector selected."
            Exit 1
        }
    }
}
```

4. Next, we want to run our GET request against this URL:

```
$output = Invoke-MgGraphRequest -Uri $url -Method Get
-OutputType PSObject
```

5. As the output for some arrays is inside a nested value array while some are direct, we need to add some logic to retrieve the information required from inside the array:

```
if ($output.value) {
    $output = $output.value
}
else {
    $output = $output
}
```

6. Finally, display the output in a GUI:

```
$output | Out-GridView
```

By following these steps, you have created a script to quickly check the status of any connectors.

Adding filters

As mentioned in a few of the previous chapters, **filters** are an excellent (and quicker) way to use the **All users** or **All devices** assignment but restrict who it applies to. At the time of writing, it is also the only way to add device filtering to user assignments.

At the time of writing, filters are only applicable to devices and apps (Android and iOS), while for user-based queries you need to use a Dynamic Entra Group.

To use filters during assignment, you must create them. This is what we will be covering in this recipe.

The following filter options are available:

- **Managed apps**:

  - App version

  - Device management type – unmanaged, Apple Business Manager, Kiosk, Android Enterprise, and so on

  - Device manufacturer

  - Device model

  - Operating system version

- **Managed devices**:

  - Device name

  - Manufacturer

  - Model

  - Device category

  - Operating system version

  - Is rooted (iOS, Android)

  - Device ownership – personal or corporate

  - Enrollment profile name

  - Device trust type (Windows) – hybrid or cloud-only

  - Operating system SKU (Windows)

Now that we understand what filters are for and which options are available, we can create our own.

How to do it...

Follow these steps to create your first filter:

1. Navigate to **Tenant administration** and click on **Filters**. Click **Create** and select **Managed devices** or **Managed apps**. In this example, we will be using a device filter.

2. Enter **Name** and **Description** values, select the **Platform** attribute the filter will apply to, and click **Next**.

3. On the **Rules** screen, use the rule builder to add the queries needed for your rule. In this example, we only want devices manufactured by ACME, so set **Property** to **manufacturer**, **Operator** to **Equals**, and **Value** to **ACME**. You can also manually edit the rule by clicking the **Edit** button next to **Rule syntax**:

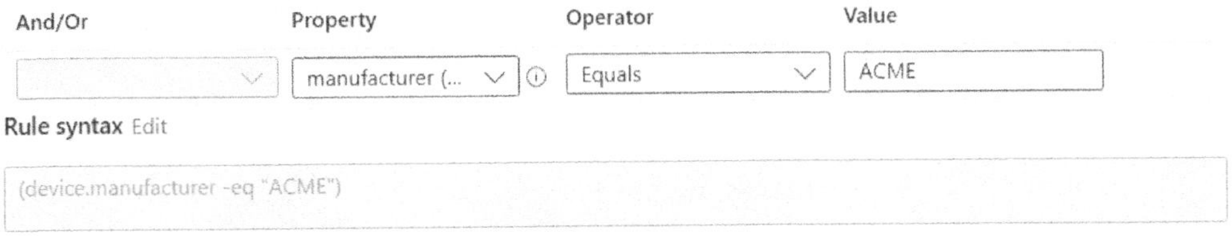

And/Or	Property	Operator	Value
⌄	manufacturer (... ⌄ ⓘ	Equals ⌄	ACME

Rule syntax Edit

(device.manufacturer -eq "ACME")

Figure 13.1 – Filters rule builder

4. Once you have set the rule, you can click **Preview** to see which devices will be detected by it. This is a good way of ensuring you have the filter configured correctly before using it during assignment.

5. Once you are happy with the rule, click **Next**.

6. We will be covering **Scope tags** later in this chapter, so click **Next** for now.

7. Finally, review that everything looks correct and click **Create**.

You have now created your first filter. Next, we will look at how to automate it.

Automating it

We have established that filters are easy to configure within the GUI, but if you want to quickly deploy many of them, Graph and PowerShell will let you accomplish this quicker, easier, and with less risk of error. Let us learn how to do so by following these steps:

1. First, we must start with the name and description:

    ```
    $name = "ACME Only"
    $description = "ACME Only Devices"
    ```

    Since all the filters post to the same location in Graph, we need to set the platform. The available options are as follows:

    *   `Windows10AndLater`

    *   `iOS` (iOS device)

    *   `Android` (Android device administrator)

- `AndroidForWork` (Android Enterprise)

- `AndroidAOSP`

- `MacOS`

- `AndroidMobileApplicationManagement`

- `iOSMobileApplicationManagement`

2. In this example, we are using Windows 10 and later:

   ```
   $platform = "Windows10AndLater"
   ```

3. Now, add the rule itself; watch the escape characters for any quotation marks:

   ```
   $rule = @"
   (device.deviceOwnership -eq \"Corporate\")
   "@
   ```

4. Add the URL to send the POST request to the following:

   ```
   $url = "https://graph.microsoft.com/beta/deviceManagement/
   assignmentFilters"
   ```

5. Populate the JSON with our settings:

   ```
   $json = @"
   {
       "description": "$description",
       "displayName": "$name",
       "platform": "$platform",
       "roleScopeTags": [
           "0"
       ],
       "rule": "$rule"
   }
   "@
   ```

6. Finally, send our POST request to create the filter:

   ```
   Invoke-MgGraphRequest -Uri $url -Method Post -body $json
   -ContentType "application/json"
   ```

That completes this recipe on filter creation, including a script to automate the creation of them.

Configuring Intune roles

While we have configured our environment using the Intune Administrator role, you may want to use different roles for different administrators within the tenant, giving admins the least privileges required for their job function. To do this, you can either use the built-in roles or create a custom role with the permissions individually selected. In this recipe, we will run through how to configure a custom role using both the GUI and PowerShell.

How to do it...

Follow these steps to configure a new Intune role.

1. Navigate to **Tenant administration** and then **Roles**.

> **Important note**
>
> Before creating a role, you can click on **My permissions** to see the current permissions you have in the tenant.
>
> Back in **All roles**, clicking on any of the built-in roles will take you to the page for that role. If you click **Properties**, you can view the permissions that have been assigned to that role. Clicking **Assignments** after will let you assign them to administrators.

2. To create a custom role, click on **All roles**, then **+ Create**, and select **Intune role**.

3. Specify your role's **Name** and **Description** and then click **Next**. In this example, we are creating a basic level role that can rotate BitLocker keys and the LAPS password, as well as both sync and reboot a machine.

4. On the **Permissions** page, select the permissions required for the role you are creating and then click **Next**.

5. For our example, the options we need are under **Remote tasks** and are labeled **Sync devices**, **Rotate BitLockerKeys**, **Reboot now**, and **Rotate Local Admin Password**. If you are unsure what a certain permission includes, click on the **i** icon to receive further details.

> **Important note**
>
> This is one time where you may wish to assign **Scope tags** should you need to delegate certain permissions to only certain devices – for example, you may want the administrator of a particular office to be able to run tasks against the machines within that office, but not across the whole tenant. We will cover scope tags in the next recipe.

6. In our example, we are creating this tenant-wide. Once configured, click **Next**.

7. Finally, review that all the settings are correct and click **Create**.

8. Now that we have created our role, we need to assign it. First, click on the newly created role and click on **Assignments**.

9. Click + **Assign**.

10. Specify your assignment's **Name** and **Description** and click **Next**.

11. Now, select an Entra group you want to assign this role to. All members of the group will then receive the role. Once selected, click **Next**.

12. If you want these admins to manage only a subset of users, you can set this on the **Scope Groups** screen. You can select **All Devices/All Users** to give them access everywhere or specify a group containing devices or users. If a group is selected, the admins will only be able to perform tasks against the members of that group. Once added, click **Next**.

13. Now, let us look at **Scope tags**. For the policy we have configured here, we are targeting device actions, so scope tags are less important than scope groups. If, however, you have a custom role with the ability to view or edit policies, you may want to lock those down so that different admins can only edit their subset of policies. In this situation, you would specify the scope tag that is used when creating the policy here.

14. Once configured, click **Next**.

15. As usual, confirm that everything looks correct and click **Create**.

You have now configured and assigned your first custom role in the UI.

Automating it

Now that we have created and assigned our role, we can see how that looks in PowerShell and Graph.

While configuring roles covers two screens within the portal, we can save effort here and run both parts in a single script. Follow these steps to create your role using PowerShell and Graph:

1. First, we need to configure the name, description, and our two group IDs for the admin group and scope group:

   ```
   $name = "ServiceDesk"
   $description = "Able to view Bitlocker Keys, Rotate LAPS
   password, Sync and Reboot"
   $admingroupid = "xxxxxxxx-xxxx-xxxx-xxxx-xxxxxxxxxxxx"
   $scopegroupid = "xxxxxxxx-xxxx-xxxx-xxxx-xxxxxxxxxxxx"
   ```

2. Next, we need the URL for the role creation itself:

   ```
   $url = "https://graph.microsoft.com/beta/deviceManagement/
   roleDefinitions"
   ```

3. That is the basic options set, but now, we need to tell it which permissions we want in there. While we could look them up and manually type them in, we can use Graph to do the hard

work for us. All permissions are listed at `https://graph.microsoft.com/beta/deviceManagement/resourceOperations`.

4. Therefore, we can run a GET request against this URL and send the output to `gridview`. We only need the ID for our policy, but we can include the name and description here to make them easier to select:

```
$allpermissions = (Invoke-MgGraphRequest -uri "https://graph.
microsoft.com/beta/deviceManagement/resourceOperations" -Method
GET -OutputType PSObject).value
$listpermissions = $allpermissions | Select-Object -Property
id,resourceName,description | Out-GridView -Title "Select
Permissions" -PassThru
```

5. This will give us an array containing our selected permissions. We need to convert it into JSON using the `convertto-json` parameter:

```
$selectedpermissions = ($listpermissions | Select-Object
-ExpandProperty id) | convertto-json
```

6. Then, add all of this to our final JSON:

```
$json = @"
{
    "description": "$description",
    "displayName": "$name",
    "id": "",
    "rolePermissions": [
        {
            "resourceActions": [
                {
                    "allowedResourceActions":
$selectedpermissions
                }
            ]
        }
    ],
    "roleScopeTagIds": [
        "0"
    ]
}
"@
```

7. Create the role and grab its ID – we will need this to assign the role:

```
$role = Invoke-MgGraphRequest -uri $url -Method Post -Body $json
-ContentType "application/json" -OutputType PSObject
$roleid = $role.id
```

8. Now, set the assignment URL and add our role and group details to the JSON:

```
$assignurl = "https://graph.microsoft.com/beta/deviceManagement/
roleAssignments"
$assignjson = @"
{
    "description": "$description",
    "displayName": "$name",
    "id": "",
    "members": [
        "$adminGroupId"
    ],
    "resourceScopes": [
        "$scopeGroupId"
    ],
    "roleDefinition@odata.bind": "https://graph.microsoft.com/
beta/deviceManagement/roleDefinitions(<$roleId>)"
}
"@
```

9. Finally, send the POST request to assign our role:

```
Invoke-MgGraphRequest -uri $assignurl -Method Post -Body
$assignjson -ContentType "application/json" -OutputType PSObject
```

That completes the steps required to create and assign a custom role.

Using scope tags

We have seen scope tags throughout this book when we created various policies or applications. Now, it is time to learn what they are used for and how to create them.

First, we will clear up the differences between **scope groups** and **scope tags**.

Scope groups are configured within an Intune role and specify which users or devices an administrator can perform actions against for roles with actions configured. They are similar to administrative units within Entra ID, where administrators can be locked out from accessing all devices and users in the tenant.

Scope tags are configured on individual items within the tenant and can be used to allow or restrict access to these items. For example, you could configure a subset of your policies with a specific scope tag and allow only certain administrators to amend this policy. For larger organizations with multiple administrative teams, this can be useful to give the local admins some freedom, but only on their own devices and policies. When looking at iOS applications, the scope tag will be inherited from the VPP token by default.

When dealing with large, distributed estates, scope tags are an essential part of your **role-based access control (RBAC)** policy of least privileged access.

They work especially well alongside group tags. If you add group tags to your machines during Autopilot enrollment, you can then create an Entra group based on that group tag and assign the group to the scope tag.

Now that we know how they work and what they are for, we can create our first scope tag.

How to do it...

Follow these steps to configure a new scope tag:

1. Navigate to **Tenant administration** and click on **Roles**.
2. From the left-hand menu, click **Scope tags** and click **+ Create**.
3. Specify your scope tag's **Name** and **Description** and click **Next**.
4. Now, simply select the groups you want this tag to be assigned to. In this case, we are using a static group containing devices from a remote office. Once configured, click **Next**.
5. Review that your scope tag has been configured correctly and click **Create**.

As you can see, scope tags are straightforward to configure in the UI, but we can also automate them to make this process even quicker.

Automating it

While in the portal, you cannot create a tag without assigning it. Within Graph, it is still a two-step process, even if the first step is just adding a name and description!

Follow these steps to create your scope tag using automation:

1. We will start with the basics, including the group for assignment, which we will need in the next step:

   ```
   $name = "Office-1"
   $description = "Devices within Office 1"
   $groupid = "xxxxxxxx-xxxx-xxxx-xxxx-xxxxxxxxxxxx"
   ```

2. Add our URL. Since scope tags live within roles in the portal, the URL also includes a role:

   ```
   $url = "https://graph.microsoft.com/beta/deviceManagement/
   roleScopeTags"
   ```

3. Now, populate the JSON, which in this case is just name and description:

```
$json = @"
{
    "description": "$description",
    "displayName": "$name"
}
"@
```

4. Create the scope tag and grab the ID:

```
$scopetag = Invoke-MgGraphRequest -Method POST -Uri $url -Body
$json -ContentType "application/json" -OutputType PSObject
$scopetagid = $scopetag.id
```

If you decide to add this scope tag to policies in the future via Graph, this is the ID you would add to the array. Here is an example:

```
"roleScopeTagIds": [
    "0",
    "2"
]
```

5. Now, add the ID to the assignment URL:

```
$assignurl = "https://graph.microsoft.com/beta/deviceManagement/
roleScopeTags/$scopetagid/assign"
```

6. Add the group ID to the JSON:

```
$assignjson = @"
{
    "assignments": [
        {
            "target": {
                "@odata.type": "#microsoft.graph.
groupAssignmentTarget",
                "groupId": "$groupid"
            }
        }
    ]
}
"@
```

7. Finally, send the POST request to assign the group to the scope tag:

```
Invoke-MgGraphRequest -Method POST -Uri $assignurl -Body
$assignjson -ContentType "application/json" -OutputType PSObject
```

That completes this recipe on scope tags.

Customizing the end user experience

We have spent all of this time and effort to make the user experience as straightforward as possible, packaged the apps for self-service installation, and configured settings for the ultimate experience. However, there is one thing we have not done – that is, making Company Portal and the general sign-in experience look better.

This recipe will concentrate primarily on the Intune side of things and configuring custom settings for Company Portal. However, in the *There's more...* section, we will run through how to customize the sign-in experience within Entra and the Microsoft 365 Admin portal.

How to do it...

Follow these steps to customize your environment for a better end user experience:

1. Navigate to **Tenant administration** and click **Customization**.

2. Here, we can either edit the default settings or, right at the bottom of the page, configure multiple policies with group assignments should different groups of users have different requirements (for example, a single tenant but with multiple sub-companies running from it). In this example, we are going to amend only the default settings, so click **Edit** next to **Settings**.

> **Tip**
> To view your changes, simply navigate to `https://portal.manage.microsoft.com/`.

There are numerous settings here, so we will go through them by section:

- **Branding**: This is all fairly straightforward – add your logos for dark and light backgrounds, set colors and organization names, and whether you wish to display just the logo or the logo and its name.

- **Support information**: This is the information that is displayed within Company Portal's help desk. The **Additional information** field is useful for providing the hours when support is available, out-of-hours contact details, or a physical location if you allow drop-ins.

- **Configuration**: This is where you can specify what can and cannot be done within Company Portal:

  - **Device enrollment**: Whether to allow the **Enroll** button itself.

  - **Privacy statement URL**: A link to your publicly available statement.

  - **Privacy message**: If you want to change the default iOS/iPadOS privacy message, you can do so here.

- **Device categories**: If you have categories configured, you can block the option for the users to select a category themselves.

- **App sources**: Additional applications to display on Company Portal. You can choose to include any Enterprise applications registered in Entra, all of the applications added to your Office portal, and any Configuration Manager applications if they are co-managed. The first two options can quickly clutter Company Portal, so be careful with these.

- **Hide features**: Select which options you do not want your users to see. On Windows and iOS/iPadOS devices, you can hide the **Remove** button to stop users from unenrolling their devices, as well as the **Reset** button, which will cause more complaints as users blindly click buttons without thinking of the consequences.

3. Once you have configured your settings as required, click **Review + Save**.

4. Check that everything looks correct and click **Save**.

Now that we have looked at the customization settings within the UI, we can learn how to automate them.

Automating it

While this is often a set-and-forget configuration, if you configure multiple tenants, you may wish to automate it. Follow these steps to configure a PowerShell script to do so:

1. When configuring via PowerShell and Graph, we must start with the text field options:

```
$companyname = "Test"
$contactTelephone = "1234"
$contactEmail = "help@help"
$contactname = "IT Helpdesk"
$contactWebsite = "https://microsoft.com"
$websitename = "Name"
$privacyUrl = "https://microsoft.com"
$additionalinfo = "More Here"
```

2. Then, we need to convert the image into Base64 format:

```
$imagepath = "PATH HERE"
$imagebase64 = [System.Convert]::ToBase64String((Get-Content $imagepath -Encoding Byte))
```

3. As this is an edit rather than us creating something, we will be sending a PATCH request, which means we need to find the ID of the current policy settings. For this, we need to send a GET request to the following URL: https://graph.microsoft.com/beta/deviceManagement/intuneBrandingProfiles.

This will return all policies that have been created. We are just editing the primary one, so we need to amend the URL to filter on only the default. Then, we need to grab the ID within the value array:

```
$customid = (Invoke-MgGraphRequest -uri "https://
graph.microsoft.com/beta/deviceManagement/
intuneBrandingProfiles?`$filter=
isDefaultProfile eq true" -method
GET -OutputType PSObject).value.id
```

4. Add the ID to the URL:

```
$url = "https://graph.microsoft.com/beta/deviceManagement/
intuneBrandingProfiles('$customid')"
```

Now, populate the JSON, which is available here: `https://github.com/PacktPublishing/Microsoft-Intune-Cookbook/blob/main/Chapter-13/customizations-intune.ps1`.

5. Finally, send the PATCH request to change the settings:

```
Invoke-MgGraphRequest -Method PATCH -Uri $url -Body $json
-ContentType "application/json" -OutputType PSObject
```

That completes the script for customizing your tenant within Intune.

There's more…

As we mentioned previously, so far, we have only configured Company Portal. For a better experience, we also want to configure the sign-in screen options in Entra and the Microsoft 365 portal. We will look at these next.

Customizations in Microsoft Entra

The first place we can add customizations is within Entra, where we can add branding to the sign-in experience. This is especially useful when using Autopilot as you will know that the correct profile has been applied when the standard Microsoft branding has been replaced with your own.

To do this, within **Entra ID**, expand **User experiences** and click on **Company branding** or go to `https://entra.microsoft.com/#view/Microsoft_AAD_UsersAndTenants/CompanyBrandingOverview.ReactView`.

Here, you can configure the branding across Entra and, most importantly, on the sign-in screen:

Sign-in form

Banner logo ⓘ	Configured
Square logo (light theme) ⓘ	Configured
Square logo (dark theme) ⓘ	Configured
Username hint text ⓘ	
Show self-service password reset ⓘ	Shown
Common URL ⓘ	
Account collection display text ⓘ	
Password collection display text ⓘ	
Sign-in page text ⓘ	Welcome to

Figure 13.2 – Entra sign-in settings

Now that we have configured Entra, let us look at the Microsoft 365 portal.

Customizing the Microsoft 365 portal

The other customization option is in **Microsoft 365 Admin Center** under **Settings | Org settings | Organization profile | Custom themes**. Alternatively, you can go to `https://admin.microsoft.com/#/Settings/OrganizationProfile/:/Settings/L1/CustomThemes`.

Clicking on **Default theme** will let you set colors and logos on the Microsoft 365 estate. You can also add additional themes for user groups should you have a multi-organization tenancy.

Deploying organizational messages

Organizational messages are a Windows-only feature (for Android and iOS, we have custom messages which will be covered in *There's more...* section of this recipe) to display important messages on end user devices.

There are three areas where these messages can appear:

- **Taskbar messages**: These appear just above the taskbar, similar to a traditional toast notification
- **Notification area messages**: These appear within the notification area, along with email alerts, Teams messages, and more
- **Get Started app messages**: These are run-once messages for post-provisioning and appear in the Get Started app

There is a licensing requirement to use **organizational messages** that you must confirm you have before continuing. You will require one of the following licenses:

- Microsoft 365 E3

- Microsoft 365 E5

- Windows 10/11 Enterprise E3 with Intune Plan 1

- Windows 10/11 Enterprise E5 with Intune Plan 1

There are a variety of message types available for these options. In this recipe, we will run through one type, but to learn about the different options, go to `https://learn.microsoft.com/en-us/mem/intune/remote-actions/organizational-messages-create?tabs=taskbar#step-1-create-a-message`.

Now that we understand organizational messages, we can configure one.

How to do it...

Follow these steps to configure an organizational message within your environment:

1. Click **Tenant administration** and then **Organizational messages**. Click **Message** at the top and then click **+ Create**.

2. In the flyout, select your **Message type** and **Message theme** and click **OK**. In this example, we will create a **Taskbar message** with an **Important action**.

The message itself is not included, so we need to include a web link to it. This could be a link to an intranet page or a news bulletin of some sor:.

1. Give your message a **Name** value, add a **Logo** value and a link, and select the **Language** value you wish to use. Then, click **Next: Schedule**.

> Important note
> For **Get Started app message**, you would need to include two messages.

2. Here, you can set a schedule for the duration of your campaign and how often you wish the message to appear. When using Get Started, the only option is **Repeat frequency**, which specifies how long the message will be displayed, but it includes the **Always On** option. Once configured, click **Next: Scope tags**.

3. If you need to delegate permissions, add **Scope tags** here; otherwise, click **Next: Assignments**.

4. On the **Assignments** page, you can *only* assign to users or user-based groups, so make sure you configure it appropriately. If you have a mixed group, it will only target the users inside it. You also have the option to deploy to **All Users** if it is an organizational-wide message.

Once configured, click **Next: Review + Create**.

That completes this recipe on how to configure an organizational message in the Intune UI.

Automating it

At the time of writing, the API is unavailable for organizational messages, with both GET and POST requests giving a forbidden error message.

There's more...

While we have looked at and configured an organizational message, they can only be applied to Windows devices. Next, we will look at custom notifications for our Android and iOS estate.

Deploying custom notifications

As mentioned previously, organizational messages are only for Windows devices. For Android and iOS devices, you can send custom notifications, which will be displayed in the **Notifications** area on the device.

Depending on your security configuration, these may display on a lock screen, so please double-check your settings before sending any confidential information via this method. Follow these brief steps to configure and deploy a custom notification:

1. Click on **Tenant administration**, then **Custom notifications**.
2. Add **Title** and **Content** values for your message, then click **Next**.
3. **Assign** as required. Again, it is *user-only*, and you cannot select **All Users** here. Once assigned, click **Next**.
4. Finally, review that everything looks correct and click **Create**.

This example can be automated. An example script is included in this book's GitHub repository: https://github.com/PacktPublishing/Microsoft-Intune-Cookbook/blob/main/Chapter-13/new-custom-notification.ps1.

Setting up terms and conditions

When enrolling a device, you want users to agree to organizational terms, especially if they are enrolling at home or using BYOD.

There are two options to do this: **Terms and conditions** within Intune and **Terms of use** within **Entra Conditional access**. Terms of use are significantly more powerful and give you more flexibility, but we will cover both options here to give you the full picture.

You can learn about the differences between the two here: `https://techcommunity.microsoft.com/t5/intune-customer-success/choosing-the-right-terms-solution-for-your-organization/ba-p/280180`.

Now that we have seen our options, let us learn how to configure them.

How to do it...

We will start with Intune's terms and conditions, which give a very simplified set of terms for the user to accept.

Setting up terms and conditions

Follow these steps to configure your Intune terms and conditions:

1. First, navigate to **Tenant administration**, then **Terms and conditions**. Click + **Create**.

2. Specify your policy's **Name** and **Description** and click **Next**.

3. Now, enter the details for the policy itself – that is, its **Title**, **Summary of terms**, and the actual **Terms and conditions**. These are plain text only; for pictures, hyperlinks, and so on, we need the terms and conditions within Entra.

4. Once you have filled in your details, click **Next**.

5. If you need to delegate permissions, add your **Scope tags**. Otherwise, simply click **Next**.

6. Now, we have to look at the term's **Assignment**. It is worth sticking to user assignments here so that you can catch as much as possible. You can assign to **All Users** as well if required. Now, click **Next**.

7. Finally, review that everything looks correct and click **Create**.

That completes the steps for Intune terms and conditions. Now, let us look at those offered in Entra.

Configuring Entra's Terms of Use

Now, we can look at the more powerful **Terms of Use** available within Entra Conditional Access. For this one, we will need a PDF containing the Terms of Use. If you want to set multiple languages, create one for each. Follow these steps to configure Terms of Use within Conditional access:

1. While these are Entra settings, we can access them within the Intune portal. Navigate to **Endpoint security** and click **Conditional Access**.

2. Click on **Terms of use** under **Manage** in the menu and click **+ New Terms**.

3. Set **Name**, **Title**, and **Language** values and add your **PDF**.

4. We have a few options available here:

    *   **Require users to expand the terms of use**: Users must expand and read the Terms of Use

    *   **Require users to consent on every device**: Users can either consent once for everything, or you can prompt per device

    *   **Expire consents**: Enforce these terms immediately and clear out any previous consent

    *   **Duration before re-acceptance required (days)**: How long before a user needs to re-accept

5. Finally, you can create a new policy to enforce these terms or select **Create conditional access policy later**, where you can add to an existing policy in the **Grant access** section. In this case, we will use an existing policy:

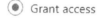

Figure 13.3 – All Users Terms of Use under Grant

6. Now, click **Create**. If you have chosen to create a new policy, you will be redirected to the familiar Conditional Access policy screen, where you can configure it accordingly.

That completes this recipe on creating our terms in the UI. Now, let us learn how to automate this process.

Automating it

Again, we will start with the terms and conditions.

Terms and conditions

Follow these steps to automate terms and conditions within Intune:

1. First, along with the usual name and description, we also need to add the details for the terms:

    ```
    $name = "Default Terms"
    $description = "Default Intune Terms and Conditions"
    $title = "Terms and Conditions"
    $summary = "Summary Here"
    $bodyText = "Policy Here"
    ```

2. We also need the group ID for assignment:

    ```
    $groupid = "xxxxxxxx-xxxx-xxxx-xxxx-xxxxxxxxxxxx"
    ```

3. Then, set the URL for the POST request:

    ```
    $url = "https://graph.microsoft.com/beta/deviceManagement/
    termsAndConditions"
    ```

4. Populate the JSON with our details:

    ```
    $json = @"
    {
        "acceptanceStatement": "$summary",
        "bodyText": "$bodyText",
        "description": "$description",
        "displayName": "$name",
        "roleScopeTagIds": [
            "0"
        ],
        "title": "$title",
        "version": 1
    }
    "@
    ```

5. Now, we need to send a POST request to create the policy and grab the ID, which we can use for assignment:

    ```
    $terms = Invoke-MgGraphRequest -Uri $url -Method Post -Body
    $json -ContentType "application/json" -OutputType PSObject
    $termsid = $terms.id
    ```

6. Populate the assignment URL with the ID:

    ```
    $assignurl = "https://graph.microsoft.com/beta/deviceManagement/
    termsAndConditions/$termsid/assignments"
    ```

7. Add the group ID to the assignment JSON and send the request to assign the policy:

    ```
    $assignjson = @"
    {
        "@odata.type": "microsoft.graph.
    termsAndConditionsAssignment",
        "target": {
            "@odata.type": "#microsoft.graph.groupAssignmentTarget",
            "groupId": "$groupid"
        }
    }
    "@

    Invoke-MgGraphRequest -Method POST -uri $assignurl -Body
    $assignjson -ContentType "application/json"
    ```

That completes the script for terms and conditions. Next, we will look at Entra's Terms of Use.

Terms of use

To automate Entra's Terms of Use, follow these steps:

1. Here, we must specify the display name, as well as the name of the file that contains the PDF:

    ```
    $displayname = "All Users Terms of Use"
    $filename = "PATH TO PDF HERE"
    ```

2. Now, we want both the Base64 content of the file and the name of the file itself. We can let PowerShell sort these for us:

    ```
    $filenamebase64 = [System.Convert]::ToBase64String([System.
    IO.File]::ReadAllBytes($filename))
    $filenameonly = [System.IO.Path]::GetFileName($filename)
    ```

3. Next, we must set the URL:

    ```
    $url = "https://graph.microsoft.com/v1.0/agreements"
    ```

4. Now, we must populate the JSON. Here, you can change your language for the PDF and also change the options for the **Yes/No** settings from before where required:

    ```
    $json = @"
    {
        "displayName": "$displayname",
    ```

```
        "file": {
            "localizations": [
                {
                    "displayName": "$displayname",
                    "fileData": {
                        "data": "$filenamebase64",
                    },
                    "fileName": "$filenameonly",
                    "isDefault": true,
                    "language": "en-GB"
                }
            ]
        },
        "isPerDeviceAcceptanceRequired": false,
        "isViewingBeforeAcceptanceRequired": false,
        "userReacceptRequiredFrequency": null
    }
    "@
```

5. Finally, send the POST request to create the Terms of Use policy:

    ```
    Invoke-MgGraphRequest -uri $url -method post -body $json
    -ContentType "application/json"
    ```

That completes this recipe on automating terms in both Intune and Entra Conditional Access.

Configuring multi-admin approvals

Multi-admin approvals is a new feature that you can implement to provide an extra layer of security when you are making changes to an environment. At the time of writing, if configured, any scripts or applications that are deployed will need to be approved by a second administrator before they can go live. Anything other than scripts and applications is currently unsupported.

How to do it...

Follow these steps to set up multi-admin approvals in your tenant.

1. Navigate to **Tenant administration** and click on **Multi Admin Approval**.

    Here, you can see any current requests (**All requests**), any requests you have submitted (**My requests**), and the policies that have been configured (**Access policies**).

2. Click on **Access policies** and click **+ Create**.

3. Specify your policy's **Name** and **Description** and select if it is for **App** or **Script**. Then, click **Next**.

4. On the **Approvers** screen, you need to select a group that contains administrators who can approve requests. Once added, click **Next**.

5. Finally, check that everything looks correct and click **Create**.

6. Now, we will look at the process of using them. When adding a new application or script, you will be prompted to provide a business justification. Instead of there being a **Create** button, we have a **Submit for approval** button.

7. We can then see the request in **Multi-Admin Approval**:

Requested on ↓	Resource type ↑↓	Operation ↑↓	Business justification ↑↓	Requested by ↑↓	Status ↑↓
04/12/2023, 14:14:58	Powershell script	Create	New script		⚠ Needs approval

Figure 13.4 – Viewing approvals

8. Logging on with an approver and clicking on **Business justification** will load the details of the request in a flyout, including details of the script's content and why it was submitted.

9. At the bottom of the flyout, enter some notes and then either **Approve request** or **Reject request**.

10. The originator then has to **Complete** the request in the **Multi-Admin Approval** portal, which will then add the application or script so that it is ready to be assigned. When you click the **Create** button, it grabs the details from the **payload** in the request and submits that back into Graph.

That completes this recipe on both configuring and using multi-admin approvals within Intune.

Automating it

Multi-admin approvals are very straightforward to automate so that you can create policies, as well as approve them.

Automating the policy creation process

Follow these steps to automate the multi-admin approval policy:

1. To create the policy, we need its name, description, and group ID:

    ```
    $name = "Script Approvals"
    $description = "Require Approvals for Scripts"
    $groupid = "xxxxxxxx-xxxx-xxxx-xxxx-xxxxxxxxxxxx"
    ```

2. Then, we need to set the policy type, which can be either "apps" or "scripts":

    ```
    $policytype = "scripts"
    ```

3. Configure the URL for our POST request:

```
$url = "https://graph.microsoft.com/beta/deviceManagement/
operationApprovalPolicies"
```

4. Populate the JSON with our configured variables:

```
$json = @"
{
    "approverGroupIds": [
        "$groupid"
    ],
    "description": "$description",
    "displayName": "$name",
    "policyType": "$policytype"
}
"@
```

5. Then, send the POST request to create the policy. We do not need to do anything further, so we do not need to grab the output of the request:

```
Invoke-MgGraphRequest -uri $url -Method Post -Body $json
-ContentType "application/json"
```

That completes the script for creating the policy. Now, we can learn how to approve the request programmatically.

Automating the request approval process

Follow these steps to approve a request within PowerShell:

1. For approval, we need to find the ID of the request itself. We can do this by sending a GET request to the following URL and grabbing the value. As the number of requests could grow in a large environment, we will use the getallpagination function to retrieve everything:

```
$requests = getallpagination -url "https://graph.microsoft.com/
beta/deviceManagement/operationApprovalRequests"
```

2. Now, we only want those not completed, so we are going to use where-object on the *Status* column and then output to out-gridview with the passthru parameter:

```
$selecectedrequest = $requests | where-object status -ne
"completed" | Out-GridView -PassThru
```

3. Next, we need the ID of the request we are approving/rejecting:

```
$requestid = $selecectedrequest.id
```

4.   Populate the request ID you retrieved in the URL:

```
$url = "https://graph.microsoft.com/beta/deviceManagement/
operationApprovalRequests('$requestid')/approve"
```

5.   Set the approval or rejection, which can be `Approved` or `Denied`:

```
$approval = "Approved"
```

6.   Now, add the JSON and send the `POST` request to reply to the request:

```
$json = @"
{
    "justification": "$approval"
}
"@
Invoke-MgGraphRequest -uri $url -Method Post -Body $json
-ContentType "application/json"
```

With that, we have learned how to approve or deny admin approvals using PowerShell and Graph.

Checking your tenant version

Intune has regular updates with monthly major service updates. At the time of writing, these are in *YYMM* format – for example, September 2023 would be 2309.

You can follow all of the new features here: `https://learn.microsoft.com/en-us/mem/intune/fundamentals/whats-new`.

As Intune is globally distributed across multiple data centers worldwide, when a new version is released, it may not necessarily update your tenant straight away. For that, we can check out the tenant version.

How to do it...

Follow these brief steps to check the tenant version in your environment:

1.   Navigate to **Tenant administration** and click on **Tenant status**.

2.   In the first tab, you can view your tenant details, including the tenant version and location:

Tenant details   Connector status   Service health and message center

Tenant name	MDM authority Microsoft Intune	Service release 2311
Tenant location Europe 0601	Account status Active	Total enrolled devices
Total licensed users		
Total Intune licenses		

Figure 13.5 – Tenant details

3. The **Connector status** tab will show a quick overview of the connectors that have been configured. If you see any issues here, you can follow the recipe from earlier to diagnose further (*Reviewing your connectors*).

4. Finally, the **Service health and message center** area will show any central issues with Microsoft, any active incidents in your tenant that you need to take action on, and any messages, which are usually around new changes, functionality, and so on.

With that, we have learned how to check the service release and other key details about our tenant.

Using Intune's troubleshooting tools

We have created our tenant using best practices, carefully packaged our applications, and tested everything to ensure it is working. However, we all know that users are users and things will go wrong. For that, we need to be able to troubleshoot issues. Fortunately, Intune has excellent troubleshooting tools where we can quickly review what issues a user may be having.

How to do it...

Follow these steps to troubleshoot your devices:

1. Click on **Troubleshooting + support**. Then, from the menu, click **Troubleshoot**.

2. Select a user from the list; all their information will be grabbed automatically.

   The first thing we must do is look under **User status** to rule out anything basic, such as a disabled or unlicensed user.

The **Summary** screen gives an overview of everything for the user across devices, policies, compliance, applications, and more.

The following tabs are available:

- **Devices**: All devices for the user, including Intune compliance, Entra compliance, and app life cycle status (failed app installs).

- **Groups**: Entra groups the user is a member of.

- **Policy**: The policies that have been applied to the user.

- **Applications**: Cross-platform applications that have been assigned to the user and the number of devices applicable for each.

- **App protection policy**: The policies that have been assigned to the user and the status of them.

- **Updates**: The update policies that have been applied to the user's devices.

- **Enrollment restrictions**: The platform restrictions and limits that apply to this user. Comparing this to the **Devices** tab will show us if the user has hit the limit and cannot enroll any further devices.

- **Diagnostics**: The output of any diagnostics requested.

3. To request diagnostics, navigate to the device in question and press the **Collect Diagnostics** button. After a while, a ZIP file will be exported containing all key diagnostics for the machine.

   A full list of what is collected can be found here: `https://learn.microsoft.com/en-us/mem/intune/remote-actions/collect-diagnostics#data-collected`.

With that, we have learned how to troubleshoot our user and device configurations.

Enrollment notifications

Introduced in release 2301 (January 2023), enrollment notifications alert a user when a new device has been added to Intune from their account. At the time of writing, it only alerts the user and there is no way of alerting admins without exchanging mail forwarding rules.

How to do it...

Follow these steps to configure enrollment notifications for your users:

1. First, click on **Devices**, then click on **Enrollment**. Select the tab for the platform you wish to set the notifications for. You will need one policy per platform.

2. Click on **Enrollment notifications** and click **+ Create notification**.

3. Specify your notification's **Name** and **Description** and click **Next**.

4. On the **Notification Settings** screen, you can select which type of notification to send – that is, **Push notification** or **Email notification** (or both).

For a push notification, you simply need the title and text to include:

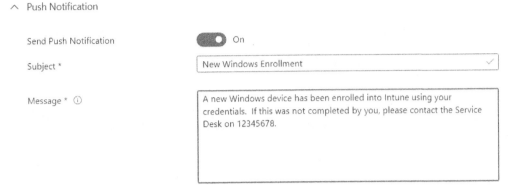

∧ Push Notification

Send Push Notification   ⬤ On

Subject *   New Windows Enrollment   ✓

Message * ⓘ   A new Windows device has been enrolled into Intune using your
                                credentials. If this was not completed by you, please contact the Service
                                Desk on 12345678.

Figure 13.6 – Enrollment notifications

For an email notification, you have more options available:

- You can set the email's **Subject** and **Message** (with the ability to include HTML by switching on the raw HTML editor).

- You can include a header using the image we set when we customized the tenant in an earlier recipe (*Customizing the end user experience*).

- You can also include the company name, contact information, and a link to Company Portal where a user can see their enrolled devices. These details are all retrieved from the customization settings within Tenant Administration. A very useful option is the ability to include the device details in the footer so that the user can check which device was enrolled and if there are queries that supply the information when reporting it.

5. Once configured, click **Next**.

6. If you want to delegate access to the notifications, add a **Scope tag** value. If not, click **Next**.

7. **Assignment** has to be at the user level as the device will not exist until after enrollment. Therefore, either select a user-based group or deploy to **All Users**. Then, click **Next**.

8. Finally, review that everything looks correct and click **Create**.

This completes the instructions for configuring enrollment notifications in the UI.

Automating it

In terms of automating this process, there are two separate Graph POST requests we can use – one for push notifications and one for email notifications after creating the policy itself. Follow these steps to automate your enrollment notifications:

1. First, we need to set the name and description of the policy:

    ```
    $policyname = "Windows Enrollment"
    $policydescription = "Windows Enrollment Policy"
    ```

2. Then, we need the subject title and content for the notifications themselves:

    ```
    $emailsubject = "New Windows Device Enrolled"
    $pushsubject = "New Windows Enrollment"
    $emailcontent = "A new Windows device has been enrolled using
    your credentials. (see device details)\r\nIf this was not
    completed by you, please contact us on the details below.\r\n\r\
    nTo view a list of your devices, click on the link to Company
    Portal."
    $pushcontent = "A new Windows device has been enrolled into
    Intune using your credentials. If this was not completed by you,
    please contact the ServiceDesk"
    ```

3. Now, we must create the policy itself. So, add the URL:

    ```
    $notificationurl = "https://graph.microsoft.com/beta/
    deviceManagement/deviceEnrollmentConfigurations"
    ```

4. Populate the JSON. You will see the platform type as well as the on/off options for the email template here. These can be amended as required:

    ```
    $notificationurl = "https://graph.microsoft.com/beta/
    deviceManagement/deviceEnrollmentConfigurations"
    $notificationjson = @"
    {
        "@odata.type": "#microsoft.graph.
    deviceEnrollmentNotificationConfiguration",
        "brandingOptions":
    "includeCompanyLogo,includeCompanyName,includeCompanyPortalLink,
    includeContactInformation,includeDeviceDetails",
        "defaultLocale": "en-US",
        "description": "$policydescription",
        "displayName": "$policyname",
        "notificationTemplates": [
            "email_00000000-0000-0000-0000-000000000000",
            "push_00000000-0000-0000-0000-000000000000"
        ],
    ```

```
            "platformType": "windows",
            "roleScopeTagIds": [
                "0"
            ]
        }
    "@
```

5. Now, create the policy with a POST request. We need the output of this to find the message templates that will be used:

```
$notificationpolicy = Invoke-MgGraphRequest -Uri
$notificationurl -Method Post -Body $notificationjson
-OutputType PSObject -ContentType "application/json"
```

Each enrollment notification creates new templates containing the notification data itself. These are stored in the same location in Graph as the custom compliance notifications we covered in *Chapter 8*: https://graph.microsoft.com/beta/deviceManagement/notificationMessageTemplates.

Fortunately, these template IDs are stored in an array within our policy output and the ID starts with the notification type (Email_PolicyID or Push_PolicyID).

We can use PowerShell to retrieve these for us from the policy output:

```
$emailtemplateid = ($notificationpolicy.notificationtemplates |
Where-Object { $_ -like "Email*" }).split("_")[1]
$pushtemplateid = ($notificationpolicy.notificationtemplates |
Where-Object { $_ -like "Push*" }).split("_")[1]
```

For each one, we are finding the appropriate template, splitting on "_", and grabbing the second value, which is the ID. When working with arrays, the first value is [0], so the second value will be [1].

6. Finally, we must populate these into the URLs, populate the JSON, and send a POST request with the content for each of them.

Now that we have created the policy, we must create the email templates themselves.

Email templates

For email templates, we are using the following URL and JSON to create the template:

```
$emailurl = "https://graph.microsoft.com/beta/
deviceManagement/notificationMessageTemplates/$emailtemplateid/
localizedNotificationMessages"
$emailjson = @"
{
    "isDefault": true,
    "locale": "en-US",
```

```
        "messageTemplate": "$emailcontent",
        "subject": "$emailsubject"
    }
"@
Invoke-MgGraphRequest -Uri $emailurl -Method Post -Body $emailjson
-OutputType PSObject -ContentType "application/json"
```

We will move on to push templates now.

Push templates

Alternatively, for push templates, we need the following URL and JSON:

```
$pushurl = "https://graph.microsoft.com/beta/deviceManagement/
notificationMessageTemplates/$pushtemplateid/
localizedNotificationMessages"
$pushjson = @"
{
        "isDefault": true,
        "locale": "en-US",
        "messageTemplate": "$pushcontent",
        "subject": "$pushsubject"
}
"@
Invoke-MgGraphRequest -Uri $pushurl -Method Post -Body $pushjson
-OutputType PSObject -ContentType "application/json"
```

That completes this recipe on configuring enrollment notifications both in the UI and using automation.

Configuring device restrictions

Device restrictions are an often overlooked yet critical part of managing your Intune environment. With the inclusion of MAM across platforms, the first step is to block the enrollment of personal devices, which can only be performed within Intune.

You can also specify device limits, as well as operating system versions and even manufacturers and models of devices!

How to do it...

There are two different settings to configure here: device limit restrictions and device platform restrictions. We will look at device limit restrictions first.

Device limit restrictions

To set up device limit restrictions, follow these steps:

1.   Click on **Devices**, then **Enrollment**.

2.   Select any platform and click **Device limit restriction**.

     Here, you can create new restrictions or edit the default restriction, which applies to all. The restrictions are queried in numerical order, with the highest number being queried first. When it finds the restriction that applies to the user, it stops reviewing any further policies.

     If you need different groups of users to have different restrictions, create additional policies. If, however, you want a blanket approach, simply edit the default policy.

     In this example, we are going to add a new policy to allow more granular control.

3.   Click + **Create restriction**.

4.   Specify the policy's **Name** and **Description**.

5.   Under **Device limit**, select a limit. This can be between 1 and 15 devices.

Important note

Keep your device clean-up rules in mind here. If you set the device limit to 1 and a user replaces their machine, you will need to manually remove the old one before they will be able to enroll a new device. If you have personal devices disabled, there should not be any risk from having this as a higher number as the devices will all be corporate-owned anyway.

---

6.   Once configured, click **Next**.

7.   If you wish to delegate this policy, add a **Scope tag** value here. If not, click **Next**.

8.   On the **Assignments** screen, assign the policy as required. You cannot select **All Users** as that is the assignment for the default policy, so you will need to select a user group here. Once selected, click **Next**.

9.   Finally, review that your restriction limit and assignment look correct and click **Create**.

This completes setting device limit restrictions. Now, let us look at device platform restrictions.

Device platform restrictions

When we look at our platform restrictions, things are more granular. You can either edit the default policy, which is applied to all platforms, or create individual policies for each platform.

As we want to block BYOD enrollment across platforms, in this example, we are going to edit the default policy.

Follow these steps to configure device platform restrictions:

1. Click on **Devices**, then **Enrollment**.

2. Select any platform and click **Device platform restriction**.

3. Now, click the blue text labeled **All Users**.

4. Click **Properties** and then click the **Edit** text next to **Platform settings**.

   Here, you can set which platforms you want to allow entirely, minimum and maximum operating system versions, personal devices, and manufacturers (Android only).

   If you decide to block at the version level, make sure you continuously review the settings as new versions are released and older ones are put out of support; otherwise, you may find yourself either blocking new devices or allowing anything.

   As **Android device administrator** is reaching its end of support, we are going to block that, as well as block all personally owned devices:

Figure 13.7 – Enrollment restrictions

5. Once configured, click **Review + Save**.

   There are no assignment or scope tags here as this is the default policy at the tenant level. If you need to have different settings for different groups or wish to delegate access, create individual policies to layer on top of the default.

6. Finally, review that everything looks correct and click **Save**.

With that, we have configured enrollment restrictions in the UI.

Automating it

As with the interactive configuration, we will split this into two parts, starting with automating the device limit restrictions.

Device limit restrictions

Creating a device limit restrictions policy is one of the more straightforward options in PowerShell and Graph as it is cross-platform and the only field is numerical. Follow these steps to configure it in your tenant using PowerShell:

1. First, set the name and description:

```
$name = "New device restriction limit"
$description = "Set to 10 devices"
```

2. Next, set the device limit:

```
$limit = 10
```

3. Add the group ID for the assignment:

```
$groupid = "xxxxxxxx-xxxx-xxxx-xxxx-xxxxxxxxxxxx"
```

4. Set the URL to send the POST request to:

```
$url = "https://graph.microsoft.com/beta/deviceManagement/
deviceEnrollmentConfigurations"
```

5. Populate the JSON with the details:

```
$json = @"
{
    "@odata.type": "#microsoft.graph.
deviceEnrollmentLimitConfiguration",
    "description": "$description",
    "displayName": "$name",
    "limit": $limit,
    "roleScopeTagIds": [
        "0"
    ]
}
"@
```

6. Send the request to create the policy and then retrieve the ID:

```
$restrictionpolicy = Invoke-MgGraphRequest -uri $url -Method
POST -Body $json -ContentType "application/json" -OutputType
PSObject
$policyid = $restrictionpolicy.id
```

7. Add the ID to the assignment URL:

```
$assignurl = "https://graph.microsoft.com/beta/deviceManagement/
deviceEnrollmentConfigurations/$policyid/assign"
```

8. Add the group ID to the JSON and send the POST request to assign the new policy:

```
$assignjson = @"
{
    "enrollmentConfigurationAssignments": [
        {
            "target": {
                "@odata.type": "#microsoft.graph.
groupAssignmentTarget",
                "groupId": "$groupid"
            }
        }
    ]
}
"@
Invoke-MgGraphRequest -uri $assignurl -Method
POST -Body $assignjson -ContentType
"application/json" -OutputType PSObject
```

This completes the script for device enrollment limits. Now, we can look at platform restrictions.

Device platform restrictions

As we are amending the default settings, the first step is to grab the ID of the policy so that we can send a PATCH request to it. Follow these steps to configure it accordingly:

1. We know that the priority is going to be 0, so the first thing we can do is filter the URL on that: https://graph.microsoft.com/beta/deviceManagement/deviceEnrollmentConfigurations?$filter=priority eq 0.

2. This will return the device limit restrictions, the platform restrictions, and the **Windows Hello for Business (WHfB)** settings, so we need to query @odata.type to return only the correct policy. Within that, we only want the ID:

```
$policyid = (((Invoke-MgGraphRequest -Method
GET -Uri "https://graph.microsoft.com/beta/deviceManagement/
deviceEnrollmentConfigurations?`$filter
=priority eq 0" -OutputType PSObject).value) | where-object '@
odata.type'
-eq "#microsoft.graph.deviceEnrollmentPlatformRestrictions
Configuration").id
```

Note the backtick (`) to pass through $filter in the URL by escaping the special character.

3. Now, we must add the policy ID to the URL:

    ```
    $url = "https://graph.microsoft.com/beta/deviceManagement/
    deviceEnrollmentConfigurations/$policyid"
    ```

    Add our JSON with the restrictions added, which are all Boolean values. The JSON can be found here: https://github.com/PacktPublishing/Microsoft-Intune-Cookbook/blob/main/Chapter-13/update-deviceplatformrestrictions.ps1.

4. Then, send a PATCH request to update the policy with these new values:

    ```
    Invoke-MgGraphRequest -Uri $url -Method
    PATCH -Body $json -ContentType "application/json"
    ```

That completes this recipe on device platform restrictions.

Configuring Quiet time policies

Introduced in the 2305 release of Intune (May 2023), Quiet time policies give admins a way to mute Outlook and Teams notifications on devices centrally, either by day of the week or for specific date ranges on Android and iOS devices (only).

This can be used to stop notifications out of hours, such as on weekends, for a standard Monday-Friday user. The date-specific option is useful should you want to add public holidays in addition to the standard weekly quiet times.

How to do it...

Follow these steps to configure your Quiet time policies:

1. To configure Quiet Time policies, click on **Apps**, then **Quiet time**.

2. Click the **Policies** tab and then click **+ Create Policy**.

3. In the flyout, select the **Policy type** value you wish to set and click **Create**.

4. Specify your policy's **Name** and **Description** and click **Next**.

5. The first option you have here is giving the user the ability to change the settings. Unless you have strict requirements, leave this set to **Yes**.

6. In the **Certain Hours** section, you can set notifications to be muted at certain times of the day. Set these around your expected staff working hours; remember, they can always change this. If you plan on blocking notifications on a weekend, untick **Saturday** and **Sunday** from this section as we will configure that shortly.

7. Now, in the **Allday** section, select **Saturday** and **Sunday**, or whatever your days off are (it should auto-select those when set to **Require** and **Configured**).

8. Once configured, click **Next**.

9. If you want to delegate access, add a **Scope tag** value here. If not, click **Next**.

10. When considering your **Assignments**, look at the organization as a whole. If you have staff who work on-call (IT staff, for example), make sure you exclude them from the policy. You may also find that some executive staff work longer hours and do not want to have to manually change the settings so often that they may be worth excluding.

    If you run shift work, consider creating multiple policies to reflect the different shift times, although you would probably need some HR system integration to manage the group memberships for each user's shift patterns.

    Once you have configured your assignments, click **Next**.

11. Finally, review that everything looks correct and click **Create**.

12. If you are configuring a **Date Range** policy, the basic settings are all the same, but **Configuration settings** is a simple date range selection.

With that, we have learned how to configure Quiet time policies in the UI. Now, let us learn how to automate them.

Automating it

Quiet Time policies run on the *Unified Settings catalog*, as covered in *Chapter 2*. This helps to standardize policy settings across the platform but makes the PowerShell script significantly more complicated. Follow these steps to configure Quiet time policies using PowerShell and Graph.

1. First, we start with our usual name, description, and group ID:

```
$name = "Quiet Time - Evenings Weekends"
$description = "Turn off notifications evenings and weekends"
$groupid = "xxxxxxxx-xxxx-xxxx-xxxx-xxxxxxxxxxxx"
```

2. Then, add the URL:

```
$url = "https://graph.microsoft.com/beta/deviceManagement/
configurationPolicies"
```

3. In the JSON, we start with the basic details, including the platform:

```
$json = @"
{
    "description": "$description",
    "name": "$name",
    "platforms": "android,iOS",
    "roleScopeTagIds": [
        "0"
    ],
```

4. Now, we move on to the settings themselves, which are split into different sections:

```
"settings": [
```

5. First, we must set the all-day quiet time for Saturday and Sunday (days 6 and 0).

The all-day setting uses the following template ID:

```
c19aaaf1-afe1-4c49-a6b1-80b51ccdf5ec
```

The individual days are under the following ID:

```
4f48386d-2faa-4f1b-bd23-a75b0f513e42
```

We will now be referencing code blocks within the script listed on GitHub at `https://github.com/PacktPublishing/Microsoft-Intune-Cookbook/blob/main/Chapter-13/new-quiettime-policy.ps1`.

6. Combining these gives us this section of the settings (*lines 18-53* in the script):

```
    ],
    "settings": [
        {
            "@odata.type": "#microsoft.graph.
deviceManagementConfigurationSetting",
            "settingInstance": {
                "@odata.type": "#microsoft.graph.
deviceManagementConfigurationChoiceSettingInstance",
                "choiceSettingValue": {
                    "@odata.type": "#microsoft.graph.
deviceManagementConfigurationChoiceSettingValue",
                    "children": [
                        {
                            "@odata.type": "#microsoft.graph.
deviceManagementConfigurationChoiceSettingCollectionInstance",
                            "choiceSettingCollectionValue": [
                                {
                                    "@odata.type": "#microsoft.
graph.deviceManagementConfigurationChoiceSettingValue",
                                    "children": [],
                                    "value": "device_vendor_
msft_policy_config_quiettime_mutenotificationsallday_
daysoftheweek_0"
                                },
                                {
                                    "@odata.type": "#microsoft.
graph.deviceManagementConfigurationChoiceSettingValue",
                                    "children": [],
                                    "value": "device_vendor_
msft_policy_config_quiettime_mutenotificationsallday_
```

```
                        daysoftheweek_6"
                                             }
                                    ],
                                    "settingDefinitionId": "device_
vendor_msft_policy_config_quiettime_mutenotificationsallday_
daysoftheweek"
                            }
                    ],
                    "settingValueTemplateReference": {
                            "settingValueTemplateId": "4f48386d-
2faa-4f1b-bd23-a75b0f513e42"
                    },
                    "value": "device_vendor_msft_policy_config_
quiettime_mutenotificationsallday_1"
                },
                "settingDefinitionId": "device_vendor_msft_
policy_config_quiettime_mutenotificationsallday",
                "settingInstanceTemplateReference": {
                        "settingInstanceTemplateId": "c19aaaf1-afe1-
4c49-a6b1-80b51ccdf5ec"
                }
            }
        },
```

7. Next, we must set the out-of-hours quiet times to days 1 to 5 (lines 54-59):

```
        {
                "@odata.type": "#microsoft.graph.
deviceManagementConfigurationSetting",
                "settingInstance": {
                    "@odata.type": "#microsoft.graph.
deviceManagementConfigurationChoiceSettingInstance",
                    "choiceSettingValue": {
                        "@odata.type": "#microsoft.graph.
deviceManagementConfigurationChoiceSettingValue",
                        "children": [
```

8. We start with the start time (lines 61-68):

```
                    {
                        "@odata.type": "#microsoft.graph.
deviceManagementConfigurationSimpleSettingInstance",
                        "settingDefinitionId": "device_
vendor_msft_policy_config_quiettime_mutenotificationsdaily_
starttime",
                        "simpleSettingValue": {
                            "@odata.type": "#microsoft.
graph.deviceManagementConfigurationStringSettingValue",
```

```
                                "value": "18:00:00"
                        }
                },
```

9. Then, we add the days individually (lines 69-99).

10. Then, we must specify the end time (lines 100-106):

```
                {
                        "@odata.type": "#microsoft.graph.
deviceManagementConfigurationSimpleSettingInstance",
                        "settingDefinitionId": "device_
vendor_msft_policy_config_quiettime_mutenotificationsdaily_
endtime",
                        "simpleSettingValue": {
                                "@odata.type": "#microsoft.
graph.deviceManagementConfigurationStringSettingValue",
                                "value": "07:00:00"
                        }
                }
```

Now, we must close off these settings with the template details (lines 108-119):

```
                ],
                "settingValueTemplateReference": {
                        "settingValueTemplateId": "ce97e111-
08b3-4fa2-bf1e-837771a6aa61"
                },
                "value": "device_vendor_msft_policy_config_
quiettime_mutenotificationsdaily_1"
        },
        "settingDefinitionId": "device_vendor_msft_
policy_config_quiettime_mutenotificationsdaily",
        "settingInstanceTemplateReference": {
                "settingInstanceTemplateId": "a9c35a12-ed79-
40f9-89bb-7b5bc3718d9b"
        }
    }
},
```

11. At this point, we must allow users to change the setting and close off the device management part of the settings array (lines 120-137):

```
        {
                "@odata.type": "#microsoft.graph.
deviceManagementConfigurationSetting",
                "settingInstance": {
                        "@odata.type": "#microsoft.graph.
deviceManagementConfigurationChoiceSettingInstance",
```

```
                      "choiceSettingValue": {
                          "@odata.type": "#microsoft.graph.
deviceManagementConfigurationChoiceSettingValue",
                          "children": [],
                          "settingValueTemplateReference": {
                              "settingValueTemplateId": "c018501f-
5efb-49ee-8da0-b472c212d9f4"
                          },
                          "value": "device_vendor_msft_policy_config_
quiettime_allowusertochangesetting_1"
                      },
                      "settingDefinitionId": "device_vendor_msft_
policy_config_quiettime_allowusertochangesetting",
                      "settingInstanceTemplateReference": {
                          "settingInstanceTemplateId": "3c68cbb1-bf32-
405b-92d8-65070f55b8c5"
                      }
                  }
              }
          ],
```

12. Finally, we must add the template to `ExchangeOnline` (lines 139-145):

```
    "technologies": "exchangeOnline",
    "templateReference": {
        "templateDisplayName": "Days of the week",
        "templateId": "2479e1bb-612c-4b98-96b0-157f334143dd_1"
    }
}
"@
```

13. Now that we have our JSON, we can send a `POST` request to create the policy and grab the ID for assignment:

```
$quiettime = Invoke-MgGraphRequest -Method POST -Uri $url -Body
$json -ContentType "application/json" -OutputType PSObject
$quiettimeid = $quiettime.id
```

14. Populate the assignment URL:

```
$assignurl = "https://graph.microsoft.com/beta/deviceManagement/
configurationPolicies('$quiettimeid')/assign"
```

15. Add the group ID to the JSON and assign it with another POST request:

```
$assignjson = @"
{
    "assignments": [
        {
            "target": {
                "@odata.type": "#microsoft.graph.
groupAssignmentTarget",
                "groupId": "$groupid"
            }
        }
    ]
}
"@
Invoke-MgGraphRequest -Method POST -Uri $assignurl -Body
$assignjson -ContentType "application/json" -OutputType PSObject
```

That completes this recipe on configuring a Quiet time policy.

14

Looking at Intune Suite

Intune Suite is a set of paid add-ons grouped together into one single monthly license. In this chapter, we will learn about the currently available features of Intune Suite, how to deploy them, how to use them, and, more importantly, how to automate them.

In this chapter, we will cover the following recipes:

- Deploying and using Remote help
- Learning about Microsoft Tunnel for Mobile Application Management
- Reviewing device anomalies
- Configuring Endpoint Privilege Management
- Future developments

Technical requirements

For this chapter, you will need a modern web browser and a PowerShell code editor such as Visual Studio Code or PowerShell ISE.

All the scripts referenced can be found here:

```
https://github.com/PacktPublishing/Microsoft-Intune-Cookbook/tree/
main/Chapter-14
```

Chapter materials

At the time of writing, Intune Suite costs $10 per user per month (or the equivalent in local currency) and includes the following:

- **Advanced endpoint analytics**: This uses machine learning to improve the Endpoint Analytics offering and look for themes and trends across the estate by detecting anomalies for proactive monitoring. It also includes advanced scope tags and an improved device timeline.

- **Endpoint Privilege Management**: Also available as a stand-alone add-on, this is used to elevate specified applications without users needing administrative rights.
- **Microsoft Tunnel for Mobile Application Management**: Also included in Intune Plan 2, this is a VPN tunnel for mobile applications on iOS and Android.
- **Remote help**: This is a remote assistance tool for Windows, macOS, and Android and is also available as a stand-alone add-on.
- **Specialized devices management**: This allows for the management of devices such as HoloLens and Surface Hub and is also included in Intune Plan 2.

Also in development for addition to Intune Suite are the following:

- **Enterprise Application Management**: This includes pre-packaged applications for easier deployment and updating
- **Microsoft Cloud PKI**: This gives you the ability to manage and deploy certificates directly from Intune

You can find out more about the Intune Roadmap here:

```
https://www.microsoft.com/en-gb/microsoft-365/
roadmap?rtc=3&filters=Microsoft%20Intune#owRoadmapMainContent
```

There is a lot of work going into Intune Suite, so it is definitely worth considering if any of the current or planned features are useful.

Intune Suite can be purchased as a trial by going to **Tenant administration** and clicking **Intune add-ons**. One thing worth noting is that each item can have different licensing requirements, so look into that before purchasing.

You can learn more about the licensing requirements here: `https://www.microsoft.com/en-us/security/business/microsoft-intune-pricing`

Deploying and using Remote help

Remote help is a remote assistance tool available for Windows, macOS, and Android. It allows for connections to unenrolled devices and can be fully managed with granular **role-based access control (RBAC)** and custom Intune roles.

Getting started

There are multiple parts required for using Remote Help. This recipe will cover configuring the policies and RBAC, but you also need to have the applications deployed to your devices.

For Windows devices, the installer can be found here and packaged following the instructions in *Chapter 11, Packaging Your Windows Applications*:

```
https://aka.ms/downloadremotehelp
```

For Android, the application can be found here and deployed using the Managed Google Play Store, as covered in *Chapter 5, Android Device Management*:

```
https://play.google.com/store/apps/details?id=com.microsoft.intune.remotehelp
```

The macOS version runs entirely in the web browser, so there is no requirement for application deployment.

How to do it...

We will now run through enabling Remote Help in the tenant and configuring an RBAC role to allow selected admins to use it:

1. To enable Remote Help, navigate to **Tenant administration** and click **Remote help**.

2. Click **Settings** and then **Configure**.

3. In the fly-out, change **Enable Remote Help** to **Enabled**. Here, you can also allow or block chat, as well as enable Remote Help for unenrolled devices.

4. Once configured for your needs, click **Save**.

5. Now we can configure our new role:

    I.   Click on **Tenant administration** and then click **Roles**.

    II.   Click **Create** and select **Intune role**.

6. Set your **Name** and **Description** and click **Next**.

7. In the roles, scroll down to **Remote Help app** and select your access for the role. You can select from the following:

    • **View screen**: Simple view-only access

    • **Elevation**: Allows the admin to UAC elevate on the machine

    • **Unattended control**: This does not require the end user to grant access

    • **Take full control**: Allows the admin to control the machine rather than just viewing it

    You may want to create different roles for different admin levels.

    Once configured, click **Next**.

8. If you wish to set the roles to a particular business unit, you can add your scope tags on the next screen. Once completed, click **Next**.

9. Finally, check that everything looks correct and click **Create**.

In this recipe, we have enabled Remote Help and configured a custom role to allow admins to use it. We will now look at how we can complete this using PowerShell and Graph.

Automating it

When scripting the steps of this recipe, we can combine both into one PowerShell script to speed up deployment further:

1. The first step is to set a name and description to use when creating the role:

    ```
    $rolename = "Remote Help Admins"
    $roledescription = "Access to Remote Help"
    ```

2. We then want to start by enabling Remote Help in the tenant, so we want to configure the URL to send our POST request:

    ```
    $enableuri = "https://graph.microsoft.com/beta/deviceManagement/
    remoteAssistanceSettings"
    ```

3. When setting the JSON, look for any double negatives as one of the settings is an enable whilst the other is a block so pay close attention to the setting name when configuring the value:

    ```
    $json = @"
    {
        "allowSessionsToUnrolledDevices": true,
        "blockChat": false,
        "remoteAssistanceState": "enabled"
    }
    "@
    ```

4. There is no assignment required for this as it is at the tenant level, so we are sending a basic POST request without needing to retrieve the output of the request:

    ```
    Invoke-MgGraphRequest -Method PATCH -Uri $enableuri -Body $json
    ```

5. After enabling Remote Help, we want to configure our role and, again, we start with the URL:

    ```
    $roleurl = "https://graph.microsoft.com/beta/deviceManagement/
    roleDefinitions"
    ```

6. The JSON for the role is similar to that in *Chapter 13, Tenant Administration*. The settings do not have a value; any enabled roles are added to the `"allowedResourceActions"` list:

    ```
    $rolejson = @"
    {
        "description": "$roledescription",
    ```

```
        "displayName": "$rolename",
        "id": "",
        "rolePermissions": [
            {
                "resourceActions": [
                    {
                        "allowedResourceActions": [
                            "Microsoft.Intune_RemoteAssistanceApp_
ViewScreen",
                            "Microsoft.Intune_RemoteAssistanceApp_
Elevation",
                            "Microsoft.Intune_RemoteAssistanceApp_
Unattended",
                            "Microsoft.Intune_RemoteAssistanceApp_
TakeFullControl"
                        ]
                    }
                ]
            }
        ],
        "roleScopeTagIds": [
            "0"
        ]
    }
    "@
```

7. Again, there is no assignment required here, so we also need to send a POST request with our JSON without needing to retrieve the output:

```
Invoke-MgGraphRequest -Method POST -Uri $roleurl -Body $rolejson
-ContentType "application/json"
```

We have now configured Remote Help and assigned it to a custom role using PowerShell.

Learning about Microsoft Tunnel for Mobile Application Management

Microsoft Tunnel for **Mobile Application Management (MAM)** is a way to require applications to connect to an on-prem VPN solution on an unmanaged device running Android or iOS.

Getting started

Microsoft Tunnel for MAM extends the existing Tunnel VPN functionality. Therefore a pre-requisite is for the Microsoft Tunnel connection to be active and connected to your on-premises environment.

More information about setting up Microsoft Tunnel can be found here:

`https://learn.microsoft.com/en-us/mem/intune/protect/microsoft-tunnel-configure`

For devices running Android, both the Company Portal and Microsoft Defender for Endpoint apps need to be deployed to them. There are no app requirements for iOS.

How to do it...

Microsoft Tunnel for MAM is configured within app protection policies. We covered the creation of these in *Chapter 5, Android Device Management* and *Chapter 6, Apple iOS Device Management*. Follow these steps to configure Microsoft Tunnel for your mobile apps:

1. Navigate to **Apps** and select **App protection policies**.

2. Either create a new policy or amend a policy we created earlier.

3. On the **Data Protection** screen, scroll to the bottom and set **Start Microsoft Tunnel connection on app-launch** to **True**.

4. Finally, click **Save** or **Create** for the policy depending on whether you have edited a previous policy or created a new one.

This completes the recipe to configure Microsoft Tunnel for MAM.

Reviewing device anomalies

Advanced Endpoint Analytics is another feature of Intune Suite, and it is split into three components:

- **Device anomaly detection**: This uses machine learning to look for trends across your estate and alert you of any potential issues. This is what we will be covering in this recipe.

- **Custom device scopes**: This allows you to add scope tags to the Endpoint Analytics Reports to give different permissions to different groups of administrators. For example, you could provide a business unit access to only review reports for their particular devices. You can find out more about this at `https://learn.microsoft.com/en-us/mem/analytics/device-scopes`.

- **Enhanced device timeline**: This expands the history of events for any particular device to give a more thorough view of what has been happening. You can learn more about this feature at `https://learn.microsoft.com/en-us/mem/analytics/enhanced-device-timeline`.

You can then leverage anomaly detection with Azure Automation to trigger automated alerts via email or Teams when issues are detected.

Now we understand the components, we can learn how to review our device anomalies.

How to do it...

We can now look at how to review device anomalies within Intune:

1. To start, click on **Reports** and then click **Endpoint analytics**.

2. On the overview screen, click on **Anomalies** at the top.

3. Here, you can see all of the anomalies detected on your devices. By default, they are sorted by severity, but you can sort on any of the columns.

4. Clicking on a title will drill down into further details, including the affected devices and any similarities between the devices and the detected anomaly (**device correlation groups**).

Device anomaly detection is an incredibly useful tool for being proactive in your device support and can also add extra weight to any issues that need to be escalated to a hardware supplier.

Now we have looked at how to review our anomalies in the UI, we can cover how to retrieve them using Graph and PowerShell.

Automating it

In this section, we will look at using PowerShell and Graph to grab these details automatically. This uses the same functionality as we looked at in *Chapter 10, Looking at Reporting*:

1. Start by setting a path should we wish to export the data:

    ```
    $exportpath = "c:\temp\anomalies.csv"
    ```

2. Then, as this uses a simple Graph GET request, we can use the pagination function, so we need to add that early in the script:

    ```
    function getallpagination () {
    [cmdletbinding()]
    param
    (
        $url
    )
        $response = (Invoke-MgGraphRequest -uri $url -Method Get
    -OutputType PSObject)
        $alloutput = $response.value
        $alloutputNextLink = $response."@odata.nextLink"
        while ($null -ne $alloutputNextLink) {
            $alloutputResponse = (Invoke-MGGraphRequest -Uri
    $alloutputNextLink -Method Get -outputType PSObject)
            $alloutputNextLink = $alloutputResponse."@odata.
    nextLink"
            $alloutput += $alloutputResponse.value
    ```

```
}
return $alloutput
}
```

3. The function requires a URL to be passed, so we now need to set that. We will add a parameter to sort by severity to match that in the UI, but this is not required. Note the backtick escape character as well to pass $ directly:

```
$url = "https://graph.microsoft.com/beta/deviceManagement/
userExperienceAnalyticsAnomaly?=&`$orderBy=severity asc"
```

4. Now we grab all of the output, ready to work with it further:

```
$fulloutput = getallpagination -url $url
$selectedoutput = $fulloutput | Select-Object *
```

5. We then pop-up a window with options to decide whether to export the data or view it in a UI using a Windows form:

```
Add-Type -AssemblyName System.Windows.Forms
$form = New-Object System.Windows.Forms.Form
$form.Text = "Export or View"
$form.Width = 300
$form.Height = 150
$form.StartPosition = "CenterScreen"
$label = New-Object System.Windows.Forms.Label
$label.Text = "Select an option:"
$label.Location = New-Object System.Drawing.Point(10, 20)
$label.AutoSize = $true
$form.Controls.Add($label)
$exportButton = New-Object System.Windows.Forms.Button
$exportButton.Text = "Export"
$exportButton.Location = New-Object System.Drawing.Point(100,
60)
$exportButton.DialogResult = [System.Windows.Forms.
DialogResult]::OK
$form.AcceptButton = $exportButton
$form.Controls.Add($exportButton)
$viewButton = New-Object System.Windows.Forms.Button
$viewButton.Text = "View"
$viewButton.Location = New-Object System.Drawing.Point(180, 60)
$viewButton.DialogResult = [System.Windows.Forms.
DialogResult]::Cancel
$form.CancelButton = $viewButton
$form.Controls.Add($viewButton)
$result = $form.ShowDialog()
```

6. Now run an `IF` query to check what was selected. If we selected **Export**, simply send the data to `export-csv`. As the report can potentially be empty, we will do a check first for data and report back if there is none because if we do not, the script will just exit:

```
if ($result -eq [System.Windows.Forms.DialogResult]::OK) {
    # Export code here
    if ($null -eq $selectedoutput) {
        write-host "Nothing to display"
    }
    else {
        $selectedoutput | export-csv $exportpath
    }
}
```

7. If **View** is selected in the popup, after looking for an empty dataset, we display the output in a `GridView`, but here, we add the `Passthru` parameter so we can drill down further:

```
elseif ($result -eq [System.Windows.Forms.DialogResult]::Cancel)
{
    # View code here
    if ($null -eq $selectedoutput) {
        write-host "Nothing to display"
    }
    else {
    $allanomalies = $selectedoutput | Out-GridView -PassThru
```

The `passthru` populates our `$allanomalies` variable with the details of the anomaly selected.

8. We need the ID of that anomaly to grab further details:

```
$anomalyid = $allanomalies.id
```

9. Add the ID to the URL. Run another GET request against this URL, send the details to the UI via `Out-GridView`, and close the loops:

```
$anomalydetailsurl = "https://graph.microsoft.com/beta/
deviceManagement/userExperienceAnalyticsAnomaly/$anomalyid"
    $anomalydetails = Invoke-MgGraphRequest -Uri
$anomalydetailsurl -Method Get -OutputType PSObject
    $anomalydetails | Out-GridView
    }
}
```

We have now learned how to retrieve and manipulate anomalies using Graph and PowerShell.

Configuring Endpoint Privilege Management

Endpoint Privilege Management (**EPM**) is a mechanism for elevating particular applications for end users without granting them administrative rights across the device. This could be for a particular line-of-business application that requires elevation or for your helpdesk to be able to run particular tools on devices. We can configure rules for EPM to allow automatic elevation or have it require approval first.

This recipe will demonstrate how to configure EPM and then add a file rule to allow a particular application to run elevated.

How to do it...

First, we will run through how to configure EPM in the UI:

1. Navigate to **Endpoint security** and click on **Endpoint Privilege Management**.

2. We need to start with a settings policy, so click **Create** and then, in the fly-out, select **Windows 10 and later** and **Elevation settings policy**. Then, click the **Create** button.

3. Give your policy a **Name** and **Description** and click **Next**.

4. On this screen, the first thing we need to do is enable EPM. We can then specify the diagnostics data to report on (**Diagnostic data only**, **Diagnostic data and all endpoint elevations**, or **Diagnostic data and managed endpoint elevations only**). You can also set a **Default elevation response** (**Not configured**, **Deny all requests**, or **Require user confirmation**).

5. Once configured for your requirements, click **Next**:

Figure 14.1 – EPM tenant settings

6. If you need to delegate permissions to a particular group of administrators, add your scope tags on the next screen. If not, simply click **Next**.

7. Assign the policy as required. If you are not using scope tags, this is a tenant-wide setting, so applying to **All users** or **All devices** would be a sensible choice. Once assigned, click **Next**.

8. Finally, check that everything looks correct and click **Create**.

Now we have EPM configured at the tenant level, we can add our first rule to allow an application to be elevate:

1. Within the same **Endpoint security** > **Endpoint Privilege Management** menu blade, click **Create Policy**, and, in the fly-out panel, select **Windows 10 and later** and then **Elevation rules policy**. Then click **Create**.

2. Give your policy a **Name** and **Description**. Remember that you may end up with multiple multiple policies for your different EPM rules, so a good naming convention will be useful here. Then click **Next**.

3. On the **Configuration settings** screen, you can add multiple different applications by clicking the **Add** button. You will notice there is already an item in there so click **+ Edit instance** to edit this one:

+ Add 🗑 Delete Elevation Rule Name		
☐ Elevation type	Rule name	Configure settings
☐ User confirmed		+ Edit instance

Figure 14.2 – EPM file settings

4. In the fly-out, enter a **Rule name** and **Description**.

5. In **Elevation conditions**, you can select whether this application will automatically approve or if it requires the user to confirm with a selected reason (**Business justification**) or with credentials (**Windows authentication**). These are useful for auditing, so they are worth considering.

6. You can also select the action for child processes. You can either allow them automatically, deny them automatically, or have them require their own rule. For example, if you elevate the Command Prompt application and the user tries to launch Notepad, you can specify in which context Notepad will be launched.

7. Next, we move on to the file information, which Intune and Windows use to decide if the application can be elevated. You have two options for configuring the application here. You can use `filehash`, which can be retrieved by running the following PowerShell command:

```
Get-filehash -path "path to executable"
```

Alternatively, you can upload a certificate for the file to use instead.

A certificate can be exported using the following PowerShell command:

```
Get-AuthenticodeSignature -FilePath "path to executable"
```

If you have multiple applications from the same publisher, you can reuse the same certificate using the **Reusable settings** option.

You must also enter a **File name** value here. You can also optionally add **File path**, **Minimum version**, **File description**, **Product name**, and **Internal name values**.

8. Once configured, click **Save** and then **Next**.

9. On the **Scope tags** screen, if you need to delegate, do so here, then click **Next**.

10. Assign as required. Work according to the least privilege model here, so keep the assignments to a minimum, especially if allowing child processes. Once configured, click **Next**.

11. Finally, check that everything looks correct and click **Create**.

That completes the configuration and deployment of our first EPM policy within the Intune UI.

Automating it

After learning how to configure in the UI, we can now learn how to set up EPM using PowerShell to automate further. While we could combine both policies into one script because one is a one-off tenant-level configuration and the other could be used multiple times, in this case, we will split them into two. The second script, however, will automate a lot of the previous manual steps for us.

Both of these use the unified settings catalog underneath, so the code will look familiar to that covered in *Chapter 2, Configuring Your New Tenant for Windows Devices*:

1. Starting with the tenant-wide policy, we start with our name, description, and URL:

    ```
    $name = "Elevation Settings Policy"
    $description = "Elevation Settings Policy"
    $policyuri = "https://graph.microsoft.com/beta/deviceManagement/
    configurationPolicies"
    ```

    When looking at the policy JSON, the drop-down options from the UI are set in the value code block with a numerical value after the name rather than an enabled/disabled setting, as this allows for more options, for example: device_vendor_msft_policy_elevationclientsettings_ reportingscope_2.

2. We need to populate the JSON with our preceding variables, and this example uses the same settings we configured in the UI (*Figure 14.2*):

    ```
    $policyjson = @"
    {
        "description": "$description",
        "name": "$name",
        "platforms": "windows10",
        "roleScopeTagIds": [
            "0"
    ```

```
        ],
    "settings": [
        {
            "@odata.type": "#microsoft.graph.
deviceManagementConfigurationSetting",
            "settingInstance": {
                "@odata.type": "#microsoft.graph.
deviceManagementConfigurationChoiceSettingInstance",
                "choiceSettingValue": {
                    "@odata.type": "#microsoft.graph.
deviceManagementConfigurationChoiceSettingValue",
                    "children": [
                        {
                            "@odata.type": "#microsoft.graph.
deviceManagementConfigurationChoiceSettingInstance",
                            "choiceSettingValue": {
                                "@odata.type": "#microsoft.
graph.deviceManagementConfigurationChoiceSettingValue",
                                "children": [
                                    {
                                        "@
odata.type": "#microsoft.graph.
deviceManagementConfigurationChoiceSettingInstance",
                                        "choiceSettingValue": {
                                            "@
odata.type": "#microsoft.graph.
deviceManagementConfigurationChoiceSettingValue",
                                            "children": [],
                                            "value": "device_
vendor_msft_policy_elevationclientsettings_reportingscope_2"
                                        },
                                        "settingDefinitionId":
"device_vendor_msft_policy_elevationclientsettings_
reportingscope"
                                    }
                                ],
                                "value": "device_vendor_msft_
policy_elevationclientsettings_senddata_1"
                            },
                            "settingDefinitionId": "device_
vendor_msft_policy_elevationclientsettings_senddata"
                        }
                    ],
                    "settingValueTemplateReference": {
                        "settingValueTemplateId": "a13cc55c-
307a-4962-aaec-20b832bf75c7"
                    },
```

```
                              "value": "device_vendor_msft_policy_
elevationclientsettings_enablepm_1"
                        },
                        "settingDefinitionId": "device_vendor_msft_
policy_elevationclientsettings_enablepm",
                        "settingInstanceTemplateReference": {
                            "settingInstanceTemplateId": "58a79a4b-ba9b-
4923-a7a5-6dc1a9f638a4"
                        }
                    }
                }
            ],
            "technologies": "mdm,endpointPrivilegeManagement",
            "templateReference": {
                "templateId": "e7dcaba4-959b-46ed-88f0-16ba39b14fd8_1"
            }
        }
"@
```

3. Then, send a POST request to create the policy, grab the ID, and use it to populate the assignment URL:

```
$addpolicy = Invoke-MgGraphRequest -method POST -Uri $policyuri
-Body $policyjson -ContentType "application/json" -OutputType
PSObject
$policyid = $addpolicy.id
$policyassignuri = "https://graph.microsoft.com/beta/
deviceManagement/configurationPolicies/$policyid/assign"
```

4. We are assigning this to all users, so there is no group ID to populate here. Simply send a POST request with the JSON:

```
$policyassignjson = @"
{
    "assignments": [
        {
            "target": {
                "@odata.type": "#microsoft.graph.
allLicensedUsersAssignmentTarget"
            }
        }
    ]
}
"@
Invoke-MgGraphRequest -Method POST -Uri $policyassignuri -Body
$policyassignjson -ContentType "application/json"
```

When moving on to the settings rule, the JSON is complex, so we will run through the key aspects here, which you can run through with the code from the GitHub repository (https://github.com/PacktPublishing/Microsoft-Intune-Cookbook/blob/main/Chapter-14/create-epm-rule.ps1). We are going to combine both policy configurations into one script and let PowerShell do the work, whether for a file hash or certificate.

5. The first thing to set is the elevation type, which can be User, where the user must request elevation, or Auto, where the application will elevate itself automatically. The setting here will change the JSON passed to the request. We also want a description and, of course, the group ID for the assignment:

```
$elevationtype = "Auto"
$typedescription = "Automatically approved"
$groupid = "xxxxx-xxxxx-xxxxx-xxxx"
```

6. Now we need to decide whether to use the file hash or certificate method by setting $authtype to either hash or cert. Of course, we also need the path to the executable, which needs to be available on the machine we are running the script from:

```
$authtype = "hash"
$filepath = "C:\windows\System32\cmd.exe"
```

7. From the file path, we want to grab the name and path so we can populate the JSON with them:

```
$filename = $filepath | Split-Path -Leaf
$pathonly = ($filepath | Split-Path) -replace '\\','\\'
```

Now we want to query whether it is a file hash or certificate and take appropriate action. We do this with an If statement.

For a file hash, we simply use the get-filehash command and grab the output:

```
if ($authtype -eq "hash") {
$hash = Get-FileHash -Path $filepath
$hash = $hash.Hash
}
```

For a certificate, we have to upload the contents of the .cer file in Base64 content, so for this, we need to export it, grab the details, and delete it:

```
if ($authtype -eq "cert") {
    $cerpath = "$env:temp\$filename.cer"
    Get-AuthenticodeSignature -FilePath $filepath | Select-
Object -ExpandProperty SignerCertificate | Export-Certificate
-Type CERT -FilePath $cerpath
    ##Convert to $cerpath to base64
    $bytes = Get-Content -Path $cerpath -Encoding Byte
$base64 = [System.Convert]::ToBase64String($bytes)
##Delete cert
```

```
remove-item $cerpath
}
```

8. Before setting the JSON, we also need the URL for our request:

```
$addurl = "https://graph.microsoft.com/beta/deviceManagement/
configurationPolicies"
```

9. Next, we split the JSON into multiple sections so we can select whichever is appropriate for our earlier selections.

10. After adding the JSON, we run further queries to populate a variable with the appropriate selections:

```
if ($authtype -eq "hash") {
    $json1 = $jsonhash
}
else {
    $json1 = $jsoncert
}
if ($elevationtype -eq "Auto") {
    $finaljson = $json + $json1 + $json2auto + $json3
}
else {
    $finaljson = $json + $json1 + $json2user + $json3
}
```

11. Finally, we send our POST request with this final JSON:

```
$addpolicy = Invoke-MgGraphRequest -method POST -Uri $addurl
-Body $finaljson -ContentType "application/json"
```

12. As usual, we need the policy ID to populate the assignment URL:

```
$policyid = $addpolicy.id
$assignurl = "https://graph.microsoft.com/beta/deviceManagement/
configurationPolicies('$policyid')/assign"
```

13. Finally, add the group ID to the assignment JSON and submit our final POST request:

```
$jsonassign = @"
{
    "assignments": [
        {
            "target": {
                "@odata.type": "#microsoft.graph.
groupAssignmentTarget",
                "groupId": "$groupid"
            }
```

```
        }
    ]
}
"@
Invoke-MgGraphRequest -method POST -Uri $assignurl -Body
$jsonassign -ContentType "application/json"
```

You have now configured your first EPM rules policy using PowerShell and Graph.

Future developments

As mentioned at the start of the chapter, Intune Suite is still being heavily developed, and at the time of writing, there have been two future features that have been announced but not yet released. In this section, we will look at these features based on the information currently available.

Advanced Application Management

The first addition is Advanced Application Management. As you know from *Chapter 11, Packaging Your Windows Applications*, packaging your applications is relatively time-consuming, and you also have to keep them updated, which can involve regularly checking the vendor's website, packaging, testing, and deploying.

To make this process simpler, Microsoft is looking to add a curated selection of pre-packaged applications that can be deployed through a simple UI in the portal. These applications will also be kept updated and allow for a simple method of updating pre-deployed applications.

Hopefully, this will also include an API into Microsoft Graph to ease the automation and deployment of applications.

Microsoft Cloud PKI

Certificate management is often required in larger organizations for authentication, which currently requires on-premises infrastructure, a certificate authority, **Simple Certificate Enrollment Protocol (SCEP)**, and **Network Device Enrollment Service (NDES)**, which have to be accessible by the devices.

These can be tricky to configure, as you can see in the official guidance here: https://learn.microsoft.com/en-us/mem/intune/protect/certificates-scep-configure

The idea behind Cloud PKI is that your certificate authority will live within Intune and you can use that to deploy your certificates. This would eradicate the need for the current on-premises infrastructure and massively reduce the complexity of certificate authentication.

If you are using or considering MSIX packaging, it will also allow for the cheaper and easier deployment of code-signing certificates for your applications.

Index

C

D

M

Packtpub.com

Subscribe to our online digital library for full access to over 7,000 books and videos, as well as industry leading tools to help you plan your personal development and advance your career. For more information, please visit our website.

Why subscribe?

- Spend less time learning and more time coding with practical eBooks and Videos from over 4,000 industry professionals

- Improve your learning with Skill Plans built especially for you

- Get a free eBook or video every month

- Fully searchable for easy access to vital information

- Copy and paste, print, and bookmark content

Did you know that Packt offers eBook versions of every book published, with PDF and ePub files available? You can upgrade to the eBook version at packtpub.com and as a print book customer, you are entitled to a discount on the eBook copy. Get in touch with us at customercare@packtpub.com for more details.

At www.packtpub.com, you can also read a collection of free technical articles, sign up for a range of free newsletters, and receive exclusive discounts and offers on Packt books and eBooks.

Other Books You May Enjoy

If you enjoyed this book, you may be interested in these other books by Packt:

Cloud Penetration Testing for Red Teamers

Kim Crawley

ISBN: 978-1-80324-848-6

- Familiarize yourself with the evolution of cloud networks
- Navigate and secure complex environments that use more than one cloud service
- Conduct vulnerability assessments to identify weak points in cloud configurations
- Secure your cloud infrastructure by learning about common cyber attack techniques
- Explore various strategies to successfully counter complex cloud attacks
- Delve into the most common AWS, Azure, and GCP services and their applications for businesses
- Understand the collaboration between red teamers, cloud administrators, and other stakeholders for cloud pentesting

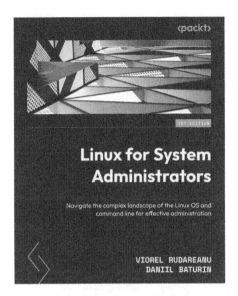

Linux for System Administrators

Viorel Rudareanu, Daniil Baturin

ISBN: 978-1-80324-794-6

- Master the use of the command line and adeptly manage software packages
- Manage users and groups locally or by using centralized authentication
- Set up, diagnose, and troubleshoot Linux networks
- Understand how to choose and manage storage devices and filesystems
- Implement enterprise features such as high availability and automation tools
- Pick up the skills to keep your Linux system secure

Packt is searching for authors like you

If you're interested in becoming an author for Packt, please visit `authors.packtpub.com` and apply today. We have worked with thousands of developers and tech professionals, just like you, to help them share their insight with the global tech community. You can make a general application, apply for a specific hot topic that we are recruiting an author for, or submit your own idea.

Share Your Thoughts

Now you've finished *Microsoft Intune Cookbook*, we'd love to hear your thoughts! Scan the QR code below to go straight to the Amazon review page for this book and share your feedback or leave a review on the site that you purchased it from.

`https://packt.link/r/1805126547`

Your review is important to us and the tech community and will help us make sure we're delivering excellent quality content.

Download a free PDF copy of this book

Thanks for purchasing this book!

Do you like to read on the go but are unable to carry your print books everywhere?

Is your eBook purchase not compatible with the device of your choice?

Don't worry, now with every Packt book you get a DRM-free PDF version of that book at no cost.

Read anywhere, any place, on any device. Search, copy, and paste code from your favorite technical books directly into your application.

The perks don't stop there, you can get exclusive access to discounts, newsletters, and great free content in your inbox daily

Follow these simple steps to get the benefits:

1. Scan the QR code or visit the link below

https://packt.link/free-ebook/9781805126546

2. Submit your proof of purchase
3. That's it! We'll send your free PDF and other benefits to your email directly

Made in United States
North Haven, CT
18 January 2025

64635501R00313